The International Series in

GUIDANCE AND COUNSELING

Consulting Editor

R. WRAY STROWIG

University of Wisconsin

READINGS IN
GROUP COUNSELING

READINGS IN
GROUP COUNSELING

Edited by

JAMES J. MURO   **STANLEY L. FREEMAN**

Department of Counselor Education
University of Maine

INTERNATIONAL TEXTBOOK COMPANY
Scranton, Pennsylvania

Second Printing, June 1969

CONTENTS

INTRODUCTION *1*

Chapter I A RATIONALE FOR GROUP COUNSELING *5*
1 *Multiple Counseling: Why? When? How?* E. Wayne Wright *13*
2 *Achieving Change in People: Some Applications of Group Dynamics Theory*
   Dorwin Cartwright *23*
3 *Theory and Principles of Group Counseling in the Elementary School*
   Don C. Dinkmeyer. *36*

Chapter II THE DIMENSIONS OF GROUP COUNSELING . . *41*
4 *Psychodrama and Creative Counseling in the Elementary School*
   Cecilia G. Wells *59*

Chapter III CAN COUNSELING BE A GROUP FUNCTION? . *67*
5 *Must Counseling Be Individual?* Clifford Froehlich *69*
6 *Small-Group Discussion As An Aid In Counseling* Helen Irene Driver *77*
7 *Group and Individual Counseling in Modifying Behavior* Donald H. Ford . . . *84*
8 *Group Counseling, Individual Counseling and a College Class in Vocations*
   Vivian H. Hewer. *90*
9 *Multiple Counseling: A Catalyst for Individual Counseling* Angelo V. Boy,
   Henry L. Isaksen and Gerald J. Pine *98*
10 *Group Counseling: More Than A Catalyst*
   John Gawrys and O. Bruce Brown *103*
11 *A Comparison of Individual and Multiple Counseling for Test Interpretation Interviews* E. Wayne Wright. *112*

Chapter IV GROUP COUNSELING IN ACTION *125*
12 *Mechanisms and Practical Techniques In Group Counseling In the Elementary School*
   Manford A. Sonstegard *127*
13 *Group Counseling As a Method of Modifying Attitudes in Slow Learners*
   Francis J. Lodato, Martin A. Sokoloff and Lester J. Schwartz *137*
14 *Group Counseling for Slow Learners* Francis J. Lodato and
   Martin A. Sokoloff. *141*
15 *An Experiment with Underachievers* Pearl Harris and Frank Trotta *144*
16 *A School Report on Group Counseling* Benjamin Cohn and A. Mead Sniffen . *148*
17 *A Project In Group Counseling In a Junior High School* S. Theodore Woal . . . *156*
18 *The Effect of Group Counseling on Junior High School Boys' Concepts of Themselves
   in School* Stanley W. Caplan *160*

19 *Multiple Counseling With Underachieving Junior High School Pupils of Bright—*
Normal and Higher—Ability Oscar G. Mink. *167*

20 *The Effects of Group Counseling on Gifted Underachieving Adolescents*
John Broedel, Merle Ohlsen, Fred Proff and Charles Southard *174*

21 *Themes in Group Counseling With Adolescents* Marilyn Bates *186*

22 *A Project in Group Counseling With High School Underachievers*
John A. Schulz. *198*

23 *Group Counseling at the Eleventh-Grade Level* Harold H. Metcalf *203*

24 *A Comparison of Three Methods of Assisting Underachieving High School Students*
Feriha B. Baymur and C. H. Patterson *209*

25 *Group Counseling With Students Unable to Speak in Class*
Stephen J. Golburgh and Edward C. Glanz. *219*

26 *Group Counseling and The Academic Performance of Anxious College Freshman*
Charles D. Spielberger, Henry Weitz, J. Peter Denny *223*

27 *A Program of Group Counseling* Theodore Volsky and Vivian H. Hewer. . . *237*

Chapter V *RESEARCHING GROUP COUNSELING.* *243*

28 *A Developmental Model for Counseling Groups* Walter J. Foley and
Warren C. Bonney. *250*

29 *Behaviors in Group Guidance (Socio-Process) and Group Counseling (Psyche Process)*
C. Gratton Kemp *257*

30 *Problems Discussed by Underachievers in Different Treatment Groups*
Betty J. Bosdell and John Teigland *264*

31 *To What Extent is Affect a Function of Topic and Referent in Group Counseling?*
W. W. Wigell and M. M. Ohlsen *271*

32 *Evaluation of a Group Counseling Procedure* William Ofman *280*

33 *Effects of Group Counseling on Dimensions of Self Acceptance, Dogmatism, and*
Preference for Complexity with Teacher-Education Students James J. Muro and
Fred W. Ohnmacht *292*

34 *Group Counseling with Parents of Underachieving Sixth Grade Children*
Robert S. Southworth *297*

35 *Effects of Group Counseling on Role Behavior of Counselors in Training*
George M. Gazda and Warren C. Bonney *304*

Chapter VI *GROUP COUNSELING OPERATIONALIZED:*
SOME QUESTIONS AND ANSWERS *313*

36 *Homogeneous Versus Heterogeneous Groups* William Furst. *325*

37 *Effects of Group Size* Edwin J. Thomas and Clinton F. Fink *328*

38 *Some Principles and Procedures for Group Psychotherapy* Walther Joel and
David Shapiro *346*

39 *A Beginning Counselor's Experience With Group Counseling*
Wallace K. Harris. *357*

40 *Counseling Within a Group Setting* Merle M. Ohlsen. *362*

41 *Group Counseling: Applying the Technique* Charles F. Combs,
Benjamin Cohn, Edward J. Gibian, A. Mead Sniffen. *369*

42 *The Transition Stage in Group Counseling in Terms of Congruence Theory*
Warren C. Bonney and Walter J. Foley. *378*

43   *So You Want to Try Groups*   David W. Catron *383*

   Chapter VII   *GROUP COUNSELING: SOME SPECIAL*
                   CONSIDERATION. *389*

   INDEX *401*

INTRODUCTION

Although numerous texts have been written about the nature of group work in guidance, comparatively few articles, and only two books, have been devoted wholly to the topic of group counseling. Recent works by Glanz [2][1], Lifton [4], and Kemp [3] have been primarily concerned with such topics as group procedures in guidance, group process, group dynamics, and the role of the counselor in working with groups. Only texts by Driver [1] and Mahler and Caldwell [5] are primarily concerned with group counseling, while books by Ohlsen [6], Warters [8] and Shertzer and Stone [7], have each included a chapter on counseling the individual within a group setting. Perhaps a major reason for the paucity of texts in group counseling stems from the fact that a group approach to counseling is a fairly recent addition to the field and does not have the historical roots of individual counseling.

Most secondary schools in America and a large portion of elementary schools and colleges perform a segment of their guidance function through the utilization of group procedures. Counselors frequently dispense educational and occupational information in groups, teach classes in group guidance, and conduct group interpretations of standardized test results. Group counseling, however, has not kept pace with other group procedures in guidance largely because of the traditional emphasis of counseling as a one-to-one process. In addition, relatively few school counselors receive in their training more than a superficial grounding in group theory, fewer still have had didactic instruction in group counseling, and practicum experience for group counselors is indeed rare. Thus, an area of guidance that provides promise is underutilized. Growing interest in group counseling, however, is evidenced by the amount of space devoted to the topic in professional journals. Group counseling, then, which was once considered a contradiction in terms by many counselors, has now moved into an era of new respectability. No longer considered as a starter and rapport builder for individual counseling, group counseling is emerging as a special part of the guidance program with merits of its own.

In recognition of this new stature of group counseling, this book has been organized to give further support to the trend toward effective and

[1]Bracketed numbers refer to references at the end of each particular chapter or article.

appropriate use of the group as a tool in counseling. The book reproduces a number of significant articles which have appeared in scattered locations in the literature, making them more easily available to the scholars and practitioners who will build on these beginnings a finer art and science of group counseling.

The selections in this text were identified through an extensive review of bibliographies in guidance textbooks, professional journals, and listings in *Education Index* having to do with group counseling. An effort has been made to include only those articles which deal specifically with group counseling although the confusion of terminology in the literature and the lack of a definitive practice of "group counseling" have led the editors to include material which, in their opinion, moves away from group counseling into other aspects of group work. The reader is invited, throughout this text, to seek a concept of group counseling which enables him to establish meaningful boundaries for the term, whether or not he accepts the definition suggested by the editors.

In Chapter I the editors have taken the opportunity and the responsibility to state a position with reference to group counseling. Readers are invited to use the materials of this book and their own experiences further to define a rationale for group counseling in order that this tool may come to be used for the right purposes and for the right reasons.

In the final chapter, the editors have again offered their own thoughts and suggestions for the practice of group counseling. The material in Chapter VII is not presented as a last word. Rather the several topics of this chapter are indications of the urgent need for further research and experience to be reported out of which more trustworthy guidelines for the practice of group counseling may be drawn in the future.

The middle sections of the book, Chapters II through VI, provide a survey of the literature on group counseling. Chapter II reviews the terminology related to group counseling as it appears in guidance literature. Chapter III reproduces articles which bear on the question of whether counseling can be a group function. Chapter IV presents articles which illustrate group counseling in action. Chapters V and VI include articles emphasizing current research and practice in group counseling.

REFERENCES

1. Driver, Helen I. *Counseling and Learning Through Small Group Discussion* (Madison, Wisconsin: Monona Publication, 1958).

2. Glanz, Edward C. *Groups in Guidance* (Boston: Allyn and Bacon, 1962).

3. Kemp, C. Gratton. *Perspectives on the Group Process* (Boston: Houghton Mifflin, 1964).

4. Lifton, Walter M. *Working with Groups: Group Process and Individual Growth* (New York: John Wiley and Sons, 1966).

5. Mahler, Clarence A. and Caldwell, Edson. *Group Counseling in Secondary Schools* (Chicago: Science Research Associates, 1961).

6. Ohlsen, Merle M. *Guidance Services in the Modern School* (New York: Harcourt, Brace and World, 1964).

7. Shertzer, Bruce and Stone, Shelley C. *Fundamentals of Guidance* (Boston: Houghton Mifflin, 1966).

8. Warters, Jane. *Group Guidance: Principles and Practices* (New York: McGraw-Hill Inc., 1960).

Chapter **I**

A RATIONALE FOR GROUP COUNSELING

The use of groups as a tool in guidance is by no means a new phenomenon. Instructional groups with guidance objectives appeared in the early history of the guidance movement. In reaction to some of the failures and disappointments of these early efforts, "group guidance" fell into disuse. As small group research has generated new insights into group processes, however, "groupwork has become a major tool in the kit of the guidance worker" [6, p. 16]. If group counseling has a legitimate place in the tool kit, it must be that it has a unique contribution to make to the objectives of guidance. It is the purpose of this chapter to consider the goals which have been held in guidance and to determine what, if any, particular value may lie in group counseling to help achieve these goals.

GOALS OF GUIDANCE AND COUNSELING

In its earlier days, guidance held several worthy and uncomplicated objectives. Among these was the aim of helping young people become knowledgeable about and oriented to the world of work, eventually to achieve a desirable degree of "fit" between the individual and the occupational structure. Another focus of early guidance activities is found in the character guidance emphasis exemplified by the Inor Guidance Series of Richard Allen [1]. Social adjustment and mental health were other goals of guidance. All of these goals of guidance gradually came under attack as emphasizing conformity at the expense of individuality. "Life adjustment" was viewed as an anti-intellectual goal by critics of education in general as well as guidance in particular. Adjustment of either social or vocational nature was found to be too static a goal in a world of increasing change while new insights in psychology suggested that human goals transcend a state of adjustment and move beyond homeostasis into the stimulation of man becoming.

Thus the goals of guidance have shifted to dynamic process goals. Guidance now aims to support the individual in his search for self-understanding and the power to make decisions in the context of a continually changing and increasingly complex environment. The goal is not a once-and-for-all announcement of one's identity, but a combination of ego strength and openness to the world which will support a continuous processing of new experience and the production of higher levels of integration. The person to whom guidance counselors would point with pride as a successful product "might be described as an *integrating* person who can appropriate the values of each new experience and come to terms with inner and outer changes without a disintegrating loss of equilibrium" [3, p. 4].

Such goals for education, including guidance, have received increasing attention from persons interested in curriculum reform. Teaching the process skills of inquiry and problem-solving has become more important than the communication of data and conclusions. Such new procedures are based in part on the realities of the knowledge explosion which threatens the early obsolescence of almost every fact which can be taught today. Another basis upon which to urge a greater emphasis on processes of discovery in formal learning situations is the existence of "the need to know for its own sake, for the sheer delight and primitive satisfaction of knowledge and understanding *per se*" [9, p. 60]. Maslow posits growth needs which are the basic impulses to normal development, impulses which spur the person on rather than turn him off when they are satisfied. "The appetite for growth is whetted rather than allayed by gratification. Growth is, *in itself*, a rewarding and exciting process . . ." [9, p. 28]. Gardner Murphy, like Maslow, has studied healthy personalities and has uncovered a human nature "whose essence is the quest for understanding" [10, p. 197]. Thus, there is testimony to support the notion that guidance, as part of education, should be designed to enhance innate tendencies to gain new experience and insights.

Learning is often defined as an activity of the organism which results in a change in behavior. While there is much value in such a definition for the operationalist interested in evaluating teaching and learning, one might assume that behind a change of behavior there may exist a change of meaning. It may be that understanding, or misunderstanding, is the determinant of the behavior displayed and that the basic objective of the school should be to change the understandings which students hold. Frankl finds that "striving to find a meaning in one's life is the primary motivational force in man" [5, p. 99]. Not, however, a meaning that is given ready-made by society or circumstances, nor a meaning that emerges from existence, but one that is created by each individual for himself. "This meaning is unique and specific in that it must and can be fulfilled by him alone; only then does it achieve a significance which will satisfy his own *will* to meaning" [5, p. 99]. To earlier generations, the meaning, or at least the appearance of meaning for one's life was given by instinctive patterns and tradition. As Riesman [13] has shown, we now are endangered by a culture in which direction and meaning for life is given to us by others without the stability of traditional values. The challenge for each person now is to increase his autonomy, to construct meanings and values with which he may deliberately choose his behaviors. "To be sure, man's search for meaning and values may arouse inner tension rather than inner equilibrium. However, precisely such tension is an indispensable prerequisite of mental health" [5, p. 105]. In his search for meaning the individual may well encounter conflicts between values, but such conflicts become the occasion for inquiry rather than regression. Cognitive dissonance may be resolved by action rather than inaction.

The goals of guidance, then, include the provision of conditions in which a search for meaning and values may go on. If the academic cafeteria serves up predigested facts, if the peer group serves up ready-made, albeit, transient, values, if life itself serves up a kaleidoscope of changing experience, guidance can provide a time and place for meditation and integration of all the relevant variables into a deliberately chosen, responsible commitment to living.

> The fulfillment of human potentialities lies not in separating the man more cleanly from his world and enriching his implicit nature by a finer inner differentiation. Rather, it consists in making that implicit nature come to life through its necessary reciprocity with that which is coming to life as it makes contact with man [10, p. 323].

GROUPS AND GOALS

While the foregoing has remarked upon guidance goals in general, we are here concerned with those goals which may be especially well served by use of groups. Frequently the use of groups is advocated on grounds of economy and efficiency. "School counselors have become increasingly interested in group counseling, partly because of the serious shortage of qualified counselors. . . . Appropriate use of group counseling . . . makes more efficient use of the counselor's time" [11, p. 147]. "The economy of assisting a small or a class-sized group, or even a larger group in some instances, with a common guidance problem, rather than dealing with all phases of the problem in separate individual interviews, would seem to need no proof or arguments . . ." [3, p. 161].

A more important decision in favor of using a group approach is one based on the goals and objectives for which groups provide an especially effective contribution. Glanz has identified three purposes or functions for which groups exist: "(1) to accomplish a task, (2) to develop or change the participants, or (3) to provide a structured learning situation" [6, p. 10]. Task-centered groups are those which yield a performance or product through collaborative effort of the members without any deliberate intent to change the members as persons. Committees, industrial work groups, community pressure groups, and the task force in government are examples of task-centered groups.

Growth-centered groups, on the other hand, are those which accomplish some deliberate modifications in the members without any deliberate effort to generate a tangible product of group effort. They "are concerned primarily with aiding members to gain skills, to develop insights, to socialize, or even to change their personalities or achieve a therapeutic experience" [6, p. 10]. Groups may have dual or even triple functions, of course. The classroom group provides a structured learning situation within which individual growth is expected and at times a task, such as a class newspaper, may be accomplished. Insofar as the goals of guidance are concerned, however, growth-centered groups are undoubtedly the most significant. Structured learning groups may continue to have a place, for example, in the dissemination of occupational and educational information until computer-assisted instruction is widely available, but those group situations which provide opportunity for personal growth in discovery of meaning appear to be increasingly important.

Groups for growth purposes have been identified by several names depending on the dimensions of growth to be emphasized. Study groups such as the Great Books program have aimed primarily at cognitive growth through group discussion and analysis of meanings partially embedded in a common intellectual experience. "T Groups" have been developed as tools with special growth purposes by the staff of the National Training Laboratories.

> A T Group is a relatively unstructured group in which individuals participate as learners. The data for learning are not outside these individuals or remote from their immediate experience . . . The data are the transactions among members, their own behavior in the groups, as they struggle to create a productive and viable organization, a miniature society . . . [4, p. 1].

These groups aim to assist members to grow in sensitivity in human relationships and to increased control of their own human relations skills. Therapy groups exist to provide help for persons classified as patients. The goals for therapy groups listed by Johnson are "(1) to improve their reality testing, (2) to aid in their socialization, (3) to foster the development of psychological aptitude . . . (4) to provide motivation for continued improvement in function through additional therapy . . ." [7, p. 2]. Group therapy may deal with both conscious and unconscious conflicts, and is always concerned with group members whose personal and social functioning is inadequate in general society.

In terms of facilitating growth, each of the groups identified above has a contribution to make, one which overlaps with the others on a continuum of emphasis. If self-understanding is the general objective of all growth groups, we may place groups on a continuum representing self-understanding with certain special targets delineated as shown in the accompanying diagram:

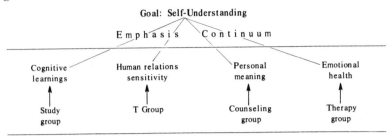

Supporting Group Activity

The diagram is used to suggest that there is a region of personal growth for which an activity known as "group counseling" has a particular contribution to make, one that is related to other growth group functions and having especially close relationships with T Groups and Group Therapy.

A RATIONALE FOR GROUP COUNSELING

"The term *group counseling* has become very popular, and practices under this name have been introduced rather widely in school systems. One might almost call it an epidemic" [3, p. 136]. Yet the confusion of meanings and references in the literature about group procedures in guidance led Wright to characterize the field as the Tower of Babel [14]. By 1966 Kagan had decided, in reviewing the literature, to avoid the use of the terms *group counseling* and *group guidance* altogether [8]. Nevertheless, the confusion will not be eliminated by coining other terms, but rather by making more precise the meanings of those already employed. Glanz offered the following definition of group counseling:

> The establishment of a group of persons for the purposes of individual growth and development in the area of personal and emotional problem solving . . . normally employed with nonneurotic and nonpsychotic persons within a developmental or growth climate [6, p. 326].

Ohlsen and Proff adopted the same term "to indicate that they were working with normal youth in a nonmedical setting" [12, p. 150].

With this foundation, it is proposed that group counseling be retained in the literature as a term to refer to a form of small group activity in which the participants are psychologically healthy and engaging in mutually supportive and stimulating inquiry into the values and meanings which are becoming attached to their lives in the larger world outside the group. Such a definition is intended to distinguish group counseling from T Groups, on the one hand, in which "healthy" members seek heightened self-understanding exclusively from analysis of the "here-and-now" dynamics of the small group. It is also to distinguish group counseling from group therapy in which "unhealthy" members seek to reduce anxiety and ineffective behavior through analysis of conscious and unconscious conflicts which exist in their lives outside the group. The definition is intended to show, however, that there are common elements with T Groups and with therapy groups. Some of the activity in group counseling deals with here-and-now relationships in the group including the reactions of group members to each other as representatives of a wider society beyond the group. Another activity in group counseling deals with supportive explorations of individual conflicts whose origins are in life outside the group and whose manifestations may be within the "normal" range of emotional distress.

Yet the core of group counseling is the effort, through group interaction, to help each individual gain different perspectives on the many experiences he has in coping with a world of change and to find through these new perspectives a personal meaning and set of values which will guide his decision-making and his problem-solving outside the group. Among the new perspectives to be nurtured by group counseling is that from inside the individual, tuning in on the creative, subjective processing of experience which may be hidden under a too exclusively abstract, verbal, and bookish experience in formal education.

There are several aspects to group counseling which mark it as a useful tool for the objectives indicated. To begin with, the group counseling situation offers the quality of relationship which has been well documented as the secret ingredient of individual counseling. "Acceptance is a necessary condition for honest communication, and teachers who establish such relationships create a climate which helps students develop insights into themselves in process. . . .When a group feels relatively secure and friendly there is much its members can learn from each other" [2, p. 242]. Acceptance by one other person encourages growth. Acceptance by a group multiplies the growth potential.

Acceptance in turn provides support of peers. The discovery by anxious young people that among their friends are others fretting about the same problems of growing, about the absence of certainty in life, is a discovery which contributes immeasurably to reduced tension and increased freedom to pursue a rational line of inquiry and problem solving.

A group counseling experience provides the opportunity for each person to offer help to others thus contributing directly to the definition of meaning in individual existence. One of the key elements of group counseling is the opportunity for members to observe a model of helping displayed by the counselor and to acquire some of the helping behaviors themselves. Thus each member of the group is engaging both directly and empathically in the search for meaning.

The unstructured nature of group counseling allows members to identify and work on problems or concerns that arise within the group, although the origins may be outside the group. This is in contrast to the structured study group in which some content or data is the starting point for learning. In group counseling, members have the opportunity to discover problems as well as solutions, thus again gaining skill in a process of inquiry which must be used over and over to establish meaningful relationships with the world.

As a group member engages in his own inquiry process, sharing it through discussion with his peers, he will receive immediately the feedback which reinforces or extinguishes the tentative idea, meaning, or value he is exploring. The group becomes a miniature society in which to test out meanings before one approaches the world at large with them. The question of standards against which the group will measure individual meanings is important. Groups may, in fact, reinforce false or wrong values and meanings. Thus it becomes a major task of the group counselor to set a climate in which suspended judgment and openness to ambiguity are high. Given the climate of acceptance and safety in the group, the rush to judgment may be slowed and when thoughtful analysis of a proposal is completed, the commitment to the decision will be strong. The group counseling experience can be expected to add weight of peer group approval to decisions taken by individuals thus promising more lasting changes in behaviors and meanings as they transfer from group to daily life.

SUMMARY

Group counseling has been viewed as a special form of growth group with clear relationships to T Groups on the one hand and group therapy on the other. Yet group counseling has a somewhat specific target, helping individuals to support and stimulate each other in the process of searching for and establishing meaning and values in a world of constant change and contradiction. The group counseling structure capitalizes on the supportive, reinforcing, and interactive elements of the small group to do its work.

In the selections which follow, other points of view on a rationale for group counseling are presented. The reader is invited to watch for conflicts among authors and to develop his own position in defense of group counseling.

REFERENCES

1. Allen, Richard D. *The Inor Group Guidance Series* (New York: Inor Publishing Company, 1952).

2. Association for Supervision and Curriculum Development. *Perceiving, Behaving, Becoming* (Washington, D.C.: The Association, 1962).

3. Bennett, Margaret E. *Guidance and Counseling in Groups*, 2d ed. (New York: McGraw-Hill Book Company, 1963).

4. Bradford, Leland P., *et al* (Eds.). *T-Group Theory and Laboratory Method* (New York: John Wiley and Sons, 1964).

5. Frankl, Viktor E. *Man's Search for Meaning* (Boston: Beacon Press, 1962).

6. Glanz, Edward C. *Groups in Guidance* (Boston: Allyn and Bacon, Inc., 1962).

7. Johnson, James A. Jr. *Group Therapy* (New York: McGraw-Hill Book Company, 1963).

8. Kagan, Norman. "Group Procedures," Chapter VI in *Review of Educational Research*, Vol. 36, No. 2 (April 1966).

9. Maslow, Abraham H. *Toward A Psychology of Being* (Princeton, New Jersey: D. Van Nostrand Company, 1962).

10. Murphy, Gardner. *Human Potentialities* (New York: Basic Books, 1958).

11. Ohlsen, Merle M. *Guidance Services in the Modern School* (New York: Harcourt, Brace and World, 1964).

12. Ohlsen, Merle M. and Proff, Fred C. *The Extent to Which Group Counseling Improves the Academic and Personal Adjustment of Underachieving Gifted Adolescents*. Cooperative Research Project No. 623. (Urbana: University of Illinois, 1960).

13. Riesman, David, *et al. The Lonely Crowd* (New Haven: Yale University Press, 1950).

14. Wright, E. Wayne. "Group Procedures," Chapter VIII in *Review of Educational Research*, Vol. 33, No. 2 (April 1963).

1

*Multiple Counseling: WHY? WHEN? HOW?**

E. Wayne Wright

Current literature indicates that present-day concepts of counseling have evolved from a "coming together" of several major theories, disciplines, and fields of professional specialization. This merging of different streams of development and the resultant evolution of counseling theories and practices have been referred to by Super [28] as a "transition: from vocational guidance to counseling psychology." As might be expected during periods of transition or flux, the development of counseling concepts has not been without considerable controversy among writers concerning the definitive nature of the process itself or the specific goals that this process, if effective, should achieve. Indeed, many differences of opinion still exist among writers in this field, and, ironical as it may be, the reader is often confused as he attempts to improve or clarify his understanding of counseling through keeping abreast of all the publications by all the "authorities."

One issue that has persisted throughout the transition in counseling theory is inherent in the concept still held by many that counseling, by definition, is, and must be, a one-to-one relationship. It is with this concept of counseling that the present paper takes issue as the writer discusses a process of "multiple counseling" and attempts to show some of the benefits to be derived from counseling with groups.

It goes almost without saying at this point that those who ascribe to the one-to-one concept of counseling have difficulty accepting the idea of group counseling because of the obvious inconsistency in using the term *group* with the *individual* connotation of counseling as defined. These unbelievers in group counseling circumvent the problem of semantics by referring to counselor-individual relationships as "counseling" and to counselor-group relationships as "group guidance," "study groups," "group procedure in counseling," or the like. A problem with defining counseling this way is that such a definition becomes meaningless when one considers the variety of

*Reprinted by permission of the author and publisher from the *Personnel and Guidance Journal*, 37 (1959), 551–557.

situations in which a counselor may have "individual" contacts that are not counseling and "group" contacts that are not group guidance. On the other hand, if a counselor is able to establish an effective counseling relationship and achieve some of the goals of counseling even when working with several counselees simultaneously, is he not actually counseling? Many would concede that he is doing more than just group guidance, broadly conceived. It would seem that modifiers such as "individual" and "group" could be reserved to designate conditions under which counseling takes place and not be used to define the term itself.

MULTIPLE COUNSELING—WHAT IS IT?

In recent years, the concept that counseling must be a one-to-one relationship has been challenged. One who has led in this respect is Froehlich [10] who asserts that as long as the process has the same objectives of individual counseling and attempts to achieve these objectives it can be called counseling.

The objectives of counseling, whether individual or group, Froehlich sees as being essentially to assist the individual in the following: (1) evaluation of himself, or gaining knowledge necessary for wise choices—*i.e.*, *learning;* (2) decision making and self-direction—or *growth* in the ability to make decisions and be responsible; and (3) carrying through of learning to action—*ie., changed behavior.* With these objectives for counseling in mind, Froehlich originated the term "multiple counseling" [10] to describe a situation in which the counselor counsels with more than one individual at a time, but each on a coordinate basis. In other words, multiple counseling, thus conceived, is concerned with helping each counselee make individual decisions within a group situation.

The term "multiple counseling" fulfills several needs for counselors who believe that effective counseling can and does take place in group settings. (1) It provides for a broader concept of the conditions under which counseling principles are operative. (2) It avoids, to some degree, the semantics problem felt by those who cannot accept the term "group counseling." (3) It makes for a clearer distinction of the multiple counseling process from the already-confusing terms "group guidance," "group procedures in counseling," "group therapy," etc.

While the process of multiple counseling as described by Caplan [6, p. 5] "differs somewhat from teaching and group guidance (with their emphasis on the imparting of facts) and from group psychotherapy (with its emphasis on treatment), the multiple counselor may at times 'teach' (impart facts), and he may at times aid the individual to understand and objectify his emotions (do therapy)."

The unique characteristics of multiple counseling as expressed by

Froehlich [10] and reported by Bennett [2] are summarized as follows:

1. *All members of the group have a common problem.* The common element may be the need for making an occupational choice; it may be that all are low scholarship students; all may have an interest in the results of tests they have taken; they may all be having difficulty resolving the same personal problem; or some other common element may exist which helps them identify with the group. This common element for the group does not mean homogeneity in the strictest sense. Instead the common element may exist more in terms of a situation problem than as a psychological dynamic. For example, the common problem may be that all members of the group are on academic probation. However, one student may be failing because of low ability, another may lack interest or motivation for school, while a third may be failing deliberately as a means of expressing hostility toward his parents.

2. *All of the members identify with this common element which has real meaning for them.* The effectiveness of the counseling function is dependent upon the ability of each individual to identify with and participate in the thinking of the group. His ability to do so depends upon the importance of the common element to him.

3. *The counselor functions as the leader of the group but does so from within the group.* In this role, the counselor at times serves "as a resource person, providing needed information," at other times as a "stimulator of discussion," and sometimes as merely a "listener" [10]. The skillful counselor will attempt as much as possible to keep the locus of responsibility for the discussion centered within the group members. At the same time, however, he must be alert to the dynamics of the group and be ready to counteract or redirect undesirable elements without destroying the permissiveness of the situation. He is also trying to identify those who might profit from additional help through individual counseling.

4. *A permissive atmosphere favors free expression.* This characteristic is an axiom for any kind of counseling. For effective interaction, the relationship among all of the group members must be permissive, free, and safe.

5. *Interactions and mutual help among members is essential, and members have the opportunity to evaluate pressures created by the group situation.* After the counselor has been able to establish rapport and structure the permissiveness of the situation, he can point out the common element that he feels exists in the group and give each individual an opportunity to identify with the common element. This can be done by letting each individual express his own reactions about the problem or his suggestions for handling it. By this sort of interaction, group members help each other to express feelings and to gain insights concerning the problem as it affects each individual. In a sense, the group members serve as "multiple

counselors" for each other in that they assist each other in expression of emotions, they interpret meanings, they clarify feelings, they give support, they exert some influence on behavior, etc.

6. Finally, if the multiple counseling is effective, *the participants are stimulated by group standards to accomplish the goals of counseling suggested earlier, i.e., evaluation of self and opportunities, making wise choices, accepting responsibility, and initiating courses of action.*

WHY USE MULTIPLE COUNSELING?

Some of the benefits of multiple counseling which are not obtained by the exclusive use of the traditionally accepted individual approach to counseling have their basis in principles of group dynamics. Therefore, the use of multiple counseling can be supported in terms of previous research with similar group processes. A review of the literature dealing with theories of group dynamics and with the recent wide-spread growth of group work follows.

In discussing the influence of interpersonal relations on everyday psychological processes, Katz and Lazarsfeld [16] give persuasive evidence to support the thesis that groups influence individual opinions, attitudes, and actions. Theory and research reported by these writers indicate the following as social factors which influence individuals' opinions and actions: (1) benefits which befall the individual who conforms to group norms. These benefits are experienced in terms of satisfaction which comes with acceptance by the group and achievement of desired status; (2) the individual's dependence on others about him for the definition of "social reality." "What exists as 'reality' for the individual is to a high degree determined by what is socially accepted as reality;" (3) interaction among individuals operates to produce shared standards of judgment, opinions, and ways of behaving. Friendship groups adopt shared ways of thinking, and private opinions and attitudes are developed through association with others of similar opinions and attitudes; and (4) groups of people demand conformity of individual members to maintain the status of the group. Katz and Lazarsfeld conclude that (1) individuals in primary group interaction develop norms governing their interactions, (2) even an individual's personal opinions and attitudes may be by-products of interpersonal relations, and (3) any attempts to change an individual's opinion or attitude will fail if his opinion is one which he shares with others to whom he is attached and if the others do not concur in the change. Katz and Lazarsfeld, therefore, suggest *group change* as the "target" for initiating individual attitude and behavior changes.

GROWTH OF GROUP WORK

Recent years have seen a considerable increase of research in the field of group dynamics. Crutchfield [7, pp. 171, 182] feels that this evidenced growth in group research demonstrates quite convincingly "how crucial psychological variables can be dealt with experimentally in genuine group settings." According to Crutchfield, the size of the group can be reduced to as few as three members without loss of effective group pressure.

With the growth of group dynamics research has come an increased acceptance and use of group approaches in many psychological and guidance processes. This diversified application of group procedures is evidenced by studies reporting the use of groups in the treatment of psychotics [23], as a training device for doctors, nurses, and patients in a private clinic.[22], as seminars with executives in business [18], in industry [4], in counseling with families in a casework agency [13], in penal institutions [21], with alcoholics [19], for marriage counseling [12], as a preventive approach in promoting mental hygiene [17], as orientation for counseling [25], in education [15], and for multiple counseling [8, 10]. In addition, a review of group psychotherapy bibliographies by Locke [20] shows the use of therapy in many new areas.

A number of writers [5, 14, 24, 28] have concluded that counseling and psychotherapy have much in common relative to their process and goals. As stated by Wrenn [29], "the differences between counseling and psychotherapy appear to be differences in *degree*, not in kind, as existing on a continuum rather than being of a dichotomous nature." Therefore, in light of the growth of group therapy and the status *that* process has achieved, it follows that if one accepts a similarity of process and goals between counseling and therapy, he lends support to the process of multiple counseling.

It is recognized that the group approach to counseling is not without limitations. However, in the opinion of this writer, the limitations of the multiple process do not obviate the values that can obtain from *judicious* use of this process. Some of the limitations in multiple counseling consist of: (1) the inability of some students to relate to the common element or problem, thus never really feeling a part of the group; (2) the need that some individuals have to identify more directly and more closely with one person (presumably the counselor) before being able to relate to or interact comfortably with a *group* of persons; (3) the probability that there is less warmth or closeness of relationship between the counselor and individual group members; and (4) a danger that the relative safety or anonymity of the group, and the expressions of other group members, may lead some individuals to experience catharsis or disturbing insights too much or too rapidly to be adequately dealt with during the particular session. In the latter instance, it is possible that the counselor may not even recognize the individuals in the group who may be experiencing this kind of upset.

On the other hand, the *values* of multiple counseling that do not seem to be experienced in individual counseling can be restated in terms of (1) the life-like setting for making decisions and choices, thus helping individuals to discover new ways of relating to others, (2) the influences of peers through group interaction and group norms, (3) the opportunity for free expression of opinions and emotions with less personal reference, and (4) the opportunity to give and receive support as a group member. Other advantages of the multiple process from the viewpoint of the counselor's needs include the following: (1) it permits the counselor to meet more students with common problems and to disseminate information of general interest or value in solving these problems; (2) it provides opportunity to identify students who need individual help while also making more time available to see individuals with specific problems; and (3) it advertises the availability of the counseling services, stimulates demand for individual counseling, and prepares students for individual counseling.

RESEARCH WITH MULTIPLE COUNSELING

Since the tenability of any premise must be determined by empirical evidence, it is appropriate at this point to review the research studies which have investigated the effectiveness of multiple counseling.

Driver [8, 9] used small discussion groups to test the usefulness of such groups in aiding so-called students to gain self-understanding, understanding of others, and interpersonal skills. The study involved eight separate experimental groups, each consisting of eight to ten persons, with each group holding six sessions over a period of three weeks. Several months after the conclusion of the study, retention and carryover of learning were measured by followup questionnaires. The returns indicated that the students learned new facts, appreciations, and/or skill in interpersonal relations. Driver concluded that "small group discussions carried on in a permissive atmosphere are an excellent learning medium for personality growth of high school, college, and adult students."

Froehlich [11] and Bailey [1], working independently with different high school populations, but both using the same criterion of improvement in accuracy of self-knowledge, found no difference in the effectiveness of individual and multiple counseling. In both of these studies, self-knowledge was measured by agreement between self-ratings and test scores before and after counseling.

Caplan [6] tested multiple counseling in terms of its effectiveness in changing the self-concepts and improving the school achievement of a group of high school "problem" boys. Significant differences between the experimental and control groups at the conclusion of the study were in favor of the multiple-counseled. Caplan concluded that multiple counseling is a useful technique for school counselors.

In the writer's doctoral dissertation [30], the relative effectiveness of individual and multiple counseling for disseminating and interpreting test data to students was compared. Both counseled groups were also compared with a non-counseled control group. Comparisons were made in terms of pre- and post-counseling measures on four criteria: accuracy of self-concept, acquisition of information about tests, feasibility of vocational choice, and counselee satisfaction. The results showed that both counseled groups made significant gains on post-counseling criteria measures over precounseling measures, and that these gains, through counseling, represented a significant improvement over the non-counseled group. However, no differences of any significance were found between the individual-counseled and the multiple-counseled groups.

Although relatively few in number, the findings of the foregoing studies give credence to the belief that multiple counseling holds promise as an efficient and effective counseling technique.

WHEN TO USE MULTIPLE COUNSELING?

When should multiple counseling be used? Generally speaking, multiple counseling seems indicated whenever one wants to achieve the unique advantages of the group setting suggested earlier, or when the objectives of individual counseling can be achieved more efficiently and/or more effectively by the group process than by individual counseling alone. Greater efficiency in counseling might connote either a conservation of time and effort in seeing the same number of students or in being able to provide counseling for more students in the same period. Efficiency in this sense, of course, assumes that the quality of the counseling does not diminish. The effectiveness of the counseling will be measured largely in terms of the degree to which one is able to achieve the counseling goals he has considered important.

The few research data already mentioned support the value of multiple counseling for achieving most or all of the generally-accepted goals of individual counseling. Indications have also been presented that multiple counseling can often be more efficient than individual counseling and at least comparable in effectiveness. It is suggested, therefore, that the use of multiple counseling be considered whenever staff skills and physical facilities permit and when a common problem among groups of students is identifiable. In each case, however, the particular purposes for counseling and the amount of opportunity to evaluate the process employed and the outcomes achieved should ultimately determine the advisability of the procedure selected.

HOW TO DO MULTIPLE COUNSELING?

This is probably the most difficult aspect of the present paper to treat briefly. The problem in trying to present specifics about methods in counseling is that those techniques which are successful for one way may not be successful at all for another. It is therefore unwise for any counselor merely to accept at face value techniques suggested by someone else and to attempt to counsel by employing such techniques if the procedures suggested are not really genuine or comfortable for him. The experience that each counselor has with different techniques will indicate the procedures that are best for him. However, this need not prevent a brief consideration at this point of the skills necessary for effective multiple counseling.

Many may concur with the point of view that multiple counseling utilizes to some extent the same principles applicable in individual counseling. Similarities between individual counseling and counseling with groups have been shown to exist not only in similar objectives, but also in skills and techniques [2, 12, 26, 27]. Therefore, the counselor contemplating the use of multiple counseling should first identify those procedures which he has found successful in dealing with individuals and then utilize these procedures in a manner appropriate to the demands of each particular group setting.

But the mere application of individual procedures is not enough if multiple counseling is to be most effective. The counselor who would work with groups must not only be cognizant of the uniqueness of the multiple counseling situation, but he must also be skilled in principles of good leadership and be able to guide interactions on the basis of a solid understanding of group dynamics. In brief, acting as a leader from within the group, the counselor must provide a warm, permissive atmosphere in which interpersonal relationships and group interaction may develop by each individual identifying with, and contributing to, a discussion of a problem which has relevance for him and some measure of commonality to the group as a whole.

A NEED FOR MULTIPLE COUNSELING

A last word in favor of continued research with multiple counseling can be stated in terms of a growing concern among school personnel. Since currently increasing enrollments at most educational institutions are already placing considerable stress on counselors' time, and since predicted expansions see the situation as becoming even more critical, it seems desirable to look ahead to the ultimate value of group procedures in counseling. Research to date supports a belief in the potential of multiple counseling. Continued evaluation of this process in various settings may well indicate a need to reorient thinking relative to the practice of complete reliance on individual counseling.

REFERENCES

1. Bailey, Bruce. "A Comparison of Multiple and Individual Counseling in Terms of Self-knowledge." Unpublished manuscript, University of California, 1955.

2. Bennett, Margaret E. *Guidance in Groups* (New York: McGraw-Hill, 1955).

3. Berdie, Ralph F. "Counseling, An Educational Technique," *Educ. Psychol. Measmt.* (1949), 9, 89–94.

4. Blum, Milton L. "Group Dynamics in Industry," *Int. J. Group Psychother.* (1954), 4, 172–176.

5. Bordin, Edward S. *Psychological Counseling* (New York: Appleton-Century-Crofts, 1955).

6. Caplan, Stanley William. "The Effect of Group Counseling on Junior High School Boys' Concepts of Themselves in School," *J. Counsel. Psych.* (1957), 4, 124–128.

7. Crutchfield, Richard S. "Social Psychology and Group Processes," *Annual Rev. Psychol.* (1954), 5, 171–202.

8. Driver, Helen I. *Multiple Counseling: A Small Group Discussion Method for Personal Growth* (Madison: Monona Publications, 1954).

9. Driver, Helen, I. "Small Group Discussion," *Personnel Guid. J.* (1952), 30, 173–175.

10. Froehlich, Clifford P. *Multiple Counseling: A Research Proposal.* Unpublished manuscript, University of California, Berkeley.

11. Froehlich, Clifford P. *Must Counseling Be Individual.* Unpublished monograph, University of California, Berkeley. In press for *Educ. Psychol. Measmt.*

12. Gaskill, Evelyn R., & Mudd, Emile Hartshorne. "A Decade of Group Counseling," *Soc. Casewk.* (1950), 31, 194–201.

13. Grunwald, Hanna. "Group Counseling in a Case Work Agency," *Int. J. Group Psychother.* (1954), 4, 183–192.

14. Gustad, John W. "The Definition of Counseling," in Berdie, R. F., "Roles and Relationships in Counseling," *Minnesota Studies in Student Personnel Work No. 3* (Minneapolis: University of Minnesota Press, 1953).

15. Herrold, Kenneth F. "Applications of Group Principles to Education," *Int. J Group Psychother.* (1954), 4, 177–182.

16. Katz, Elihu, & Lazarsfeld, Paul F. *Personal Influence* (Glencoe, Illinois: The Free Press, 1955).

17. Klems, Marvin A., & Kallejian, Vern J. "The Group Psychotherapist in Industry: A Preventive Approach," *Int. J. Group Psychother.* (1955), 5, 91–98.

18. Laughlin, Henry P. "A Group Approach to Management Improvement," *Int. J. Group Psychother.* (1954), 4, 165–171.

19. Lerner, Arthur. "Self Evaluation in Group Counseling With Male Alcoholic Inmates," *Int. J. Group Psychother.* (1954), 5, 286–298.

20. Locke, Norman. "Trends in the Literature on Group Psychotherapy," *Int. J. Group Psychother.* (1955), 5, 181–184.

21. McCorkle, Lloyd W. "Guided Group Interaction in a Correctional Setting," *Int. J. Group Psychother.* (1954), 4, 199–203.

22. Patton, John D. "The Group As a Training Device and Treatment Method in a Private Psychiatric Hospital," *Int. J. Group Psychother.* (1954), 4, 419–428.

23. Preston, Burman H. "The Class Method in the Treatment of Psychotic Patients," *Int. J. Group Psychother.* (1954), *4*, 321–330.

24. Rogers, Carl R. *Client-centered Therapy* (New York: Houghton Mifflin, 1951).

25. Shostrom, Everett L., & Brammer, Lawrence M. *The Dynamics of the Counseling Process* (New York: McGraw-Hill, 1952).

26. Slavson, S. R. "A Contribution To a Systematic Theory of Group Psychotherapy," *Int. J. Group Psychother.* (1954), *4*, 3–30.

27. Super, Donald E. "Group Techniques in the Guidance Program," *Educ. Psychol. Measmt.* (1949), *9*, 495–510.

28. Super, Donald E. "Transition: from Vocational Guidance to Counseling Psychology," *J. Counsel. Psychol.* (1955), *2*, 3–9.

29. Wrenn, C. Gilbert. "Counseling Theory." In press for *Encyclopedia of Educ. Resch.* Third edition, anticipated date 1960.

30. Wright, E. Wayne. *A Comparison of Individual and Multiple Counseling in the Dissemination and Interpretation of Test Data.* Unpublished doctoral dissertation, University of California, 1957.

2

*Achieving Change in People: Some Applications of Group Dynamics Theory**

Dorwin Cartwright

I

We hear all around us today the assertion that the problems of the twentieth century are problems of human relations. The survival of civilization, it is said, will depend upon man's ability to create social inventions capable of harnessing, for society's constructive use, the vast physical energies now at man's disposal. Or, to put the matter more simply, we must learn how to change the way in which people behave toward one another. In broad outline, the specifications for a good society are clear, but a serious technical problem remains: How can we change people so that they neither restrict the freedom nor limit the potentialities for growth of others; so that they accept and respect people of different religion, nationality, color, or political opinion; so that nations can exist in a world without war, and so that the fruits of our technological advances can bring economic well-being and freedom from disease to all the people of the world? Although few people would disagree with these objectives when stated abstractly, when we become more specific, differences of opinion quickly arise. How is change to be produced? Who is to do it? Who is to be changed? These questions permit no ready answers.

Before we consider in detail these questions of social technology, let us clear away some semantic obstacles. The word "change" produces emotional reactions. It is not a neutral word. To many people it is threatening. It conjures up visions of a revolutionary, a dissatisfied idealist, a troublemaker, a malcontent. Nicer words referring to the process of changing people are education, training, orientation, guidance, indoctrination, therapy. We are more ready to have others "educate" us than to have them "change" us. We, ourselves, feel less guilty in "training" others than in

*This paper is based on a lecture delivered at Wayne University, Detroit, in the Leo M. Franklin Lecture Series, 1950–51. Reprinted by permission of the author and publisher from *Human Relations*, 4 (1951), 381–392.

"changing" them. Why this emotional response? What makes the two kinds of words have such different meanings? I believe that a large part of the difference lies in the fact that the safer words (like education or therapy) carry the implicit assurance that the only changes produced will be good ones, acceptable within a currently held value system. The cold, unmodified word "change", on the contrary, promises no respect for values; it might even tamper with values themselves. Perhaps for this very reason it will foster straight thinking if we use the word "change" and thus force ourselves to struggle directly and self-consciously with the problems of value that are involved. Words like education, training, or therapy, by the very fact that they are not so disturbing, may close our eyes to the fact that they too inevitably involve values.

Another advantage of using the word "change" rather than other related words is that it does not restrict our thinking to a limited set of aspects of people that are legitimate targets of change. Anyone familiar with the history of education knows that there has been endless controversy over what it is about people that "education" properly attempts to modify. Some educators have viewed education simply as imparting knowledge, others mainly as providing skills for doing things, still others as producing healthy "attitudes," and some have aspired to instil a way of life. Or if we choose to use a word like "therapy," we can hardly claim that we refer to a more clearly defined realm of change. Furthermore, one can become inextricably entangled in distinctions and vested interests by attempting to distinguish sharply between, let us say, the domain of education and that of therapy. If we are to try to take a broader view and to develop some basic principles that promise to apply to all types of modifications in people, we had better use a word like "change" to keep our thinking general enough.

The proposal that social technology may be employed to solve the problems of society suggests that social science may be applied in ways not different from those used in the physical sciences. Does social science, in fact, have any practically useful knowledge which may be brought to bear significantly on society's most urgent problems? What scientifically based principles are there for guiding programs of social change: In this paper we shall restrict our considerations to certain parts of a relatively new branch of social science known as "group dynamics". We shall examine some of the implications for social action which stem from research in this field of scientific investigation.

What is "group dynamics"? Perhaps it will be most useful to start by looking at the derivation of the word "dynamics." It comes from a Greek word meaning force. In careful usage of the phrase, "group dynamics" refers to the forces operating in groups. The investigation of group dynamics, then, consists of a study of these forces: what gives rise to them, what conditions modify them, what consequences they have, etc. The practical application of group dynamics (or the technology of group dynamics) consists of the utilization of knowledge about these forces for the achievement of some purpose. In keeping with this definition, then, it is clear that group dynamics, as a realm of investigation, is not particularly novel, nor is it the exclusive property of any person or institution. It goes back at least to the outstanding work of men like Simmel, Freud, and Cooley.

Although interest in groups has a long and respectable history, the past fifteen years have witnessed a new flowering of activity in this field. Today, research centers in several countries are carrying out substantial programs of research designed to reveal the nature of groups and of their functioning. The phase "group dynamics" has come into common usage during this time and intense efforts have been devoted to the development of the field, both as a branch of social science and as a form of social technology.

In this development the name of Kurt Lewin has been outstanding. As a consequence of his work in the field of individual psychology and from his analysis of the nature of the pressing problems of the contemporary world, Lewin became convinced of society's urgent need for a *scientific approach* to the understanding of the dynamics of groups. In 1945 he established the Research Center for Group Dynamics to meet this need. Since that date the Center has been devoting its efforts to improving our scientific understanding of groups through laboratory experimentation, field studies, and the use of techniques of action research. It has also attempted in various ways to help get the findings of social science more widely used by social management. Much of what I have to say in this paper is drawn from the experiences of this Center in its brief existence of a little more than five years [2].

II

For various reasons we have found that much of our work has been devoted to an attempt to gain a better understanding of the ways in which people change their behavior or resist efforts by others to have them do so. Whether we set for ourselves the practical goal of improving behavior or whether we take on the intellectual task of understanding why people do what they do, we have to investigate processes of communication, influence, social pressure—in short, problems of change.

In this work we have encountered great frustration. The problems have been most difficult to solve. Looking back over our experience, I have become convinced that no small part of the trouble has resulted from an irresistible tendency to conceive of our problems in terms of the individual. We live in an individualistic culture. We value the individual highly, and rightly so. But I am inclined to believe that our political and social concern for the individual has narrowed our thinking as social scientists so much that we have not been able to state our research problems properly. Perhaps we have taken the individual as the unit of observation and study when some larger unit would have been more appropriate. Let us look at a few examples.

Consider first some matters having to do with the mental health of an individual. We can all agree, I believe, that an important mark of a healthy personality is that the individual's self-esteem has not been undermined. But on what does self-esteem depend? From research on this problem we have discovered that, among other things, repeated experiences of failure or traumatic failures on matters of central importance serve to undermine one's self-esteem. We also know that whether a person experiences success or failure as a result of some undertaking depends upon the level of aspiration which he has set for himself. Now, if we try to discover how the level of aspiration gets set, we are immediately involved in the person's relationships to groups. The groups to which he belongs set standards for his behavior which he must accept if he is to remain in the group. If his capacities do not allow him to reach these standards, he experiences failure, he withdraws or is rejected by the group and his self-esteem suffers a shock.

Suppose, then, that we accept a task of therapy, of rebuilding his self-esteem. It would appear plausible from our analysis of the problem that we should attempt to work with variables of the same sort that produced the difficulty, that is to work with him either in the groups to which he now belongs or to introduce him into new groups which are selected for the purpose and to work upon his relationships to groups as such. From the point of view of preventive mental health, we might even attempt to train the groups in our communities—classes in schools, work groups in business, families, unions, religious and cultural groups—to make use of practices better designed to protect the self-esteem of their members.

Consider a second example. A teacher finds that in her class she has a number of trouble-makers, full of aggression. She wants to know why these children are so aggressive and what can be done about it. A foreman in a factory has the same kind of problem with some of his workers. He wants the same kind of help. The solution most tempting to both the teacher and the foreman often is to transfer the worst trouble-makers to someone else, or if facilities are available, to refer them for counselling. But is the problem really of such a nature that it can be solved by removing the trouble-maker from the situation or by working on his individual motivations and emotional life? What leads does research give us? The evidence indicates, of course, that there are many causes of aggressiveness in people, but one aspect of the problem has become increasingly clear in recent years. If we observe carefully the amount of aggressive behavior and the number of trouble-makers to be found in a large collection of groups, we find that these characteristics can vary tremendously from group to group even when the different groups are composed essentially of the same kinds of people. In the now classic experiments of Lewin, Lippitt, and White [7] on the effects of different styles of leadership, it was found that the same group of children displayed markedly different levels of aggressive behavior when under different styles of leadership. Moreover, when individual children were transferred from one group to another, their levels of aggressiveness shifted to conform to the atmosphere of the new group. Efforts to account for one child's aggressiveness under one style of leadership merely in terms of his personality traits could hardly succeed under these conditions. This is not to say that a person's behavior is entirely to be accounted for by the atmosphere and structure of the immediate group, but it is remarkable to what an extent a strong, cohesive group can control aspects of a member's behavior traditionally thought to be expressive of enduring personality traits. Recognition of this fact rephrases the problem of how to change such behavior. It directs us to a study of the sources of the influence of the group on its members.

Let us take an example from a different field. What can we learn from efforts to change people by mass media and mass persuasion? In those rare instances when educators, propagandists, advertisers, and others who want to influence large numbers of people, have bothered to make an objective evaluation of the enduring changes produced by their efforts, they have been able to demonstrate only the most negligible effects [1]. The inefficiency of attempts to influence the public by mass media would be scandalous if there were agreement that it was important or even desirable to have such influences strongly exerted. In fact, it is no exaggeration to say that all of the research and experience of generations has not improved the efficiency of lectures or other means of mass influence to any noticeable degree. Something must be wrong with our theories of learning, motivation, and social psychology.

Within very recent years some research data have been accumulating which may give us a clue to the solution of our problem. In one series of experiments directed by Lewin, it was found that a method of group decision, in which the group as a whole made a decision to have its members change their behavior, was from two to ten times as effective in producing actual change as was a lecture presenting exhortation to change [6]. We have yet to learn precisely what produces these differences of effectiveness, but it is clear that by introducing group forces into the situation a whole new level of influence has been achieved.

The experience has been essentially the same when people have attempted to increase the productivity of individuals in work settings. Traditional conceptions of how to increase the output of workers have stressed the individual: select the right man for the job; simplify the job for him; train him in the skills required; motivate him by economic incentives; make it clear to whom he reports; keep the lines of authority and responsibility simple and straight. But even when all these conditions are fully met we are finding that productivity is far below full potential. There is even good reason to conclude that this individualistic conception of the determinants of productivity actually fosters negative consequences. The individual, now isolated and subjected to the demands of the organization through the commands of his boss, finds that he must create with his fellow employees informal groups, not shown on any table of organization, in order to protect himself from arbitrary control of his life, from the boredom produced by the endless repetition of mechanically sanitary and routine operations, and from the impoverishment of his emotional and social life brought about by the frustration of his basic needs for social interaction, participation, and acceptance in a stable group. Recent experiments have demonstrated clearly that the productivity of work groups can be greatly increased by methods of work organization and supervision which give more responsibility to work groups, which allow for fuller participation in important decisions, and which make stable groups the firm basis for support of the individual's social needs [3]. I am convinced that future research will also demonstrate that people working under such conditions become more mature and creative individuals in their homes, in community life, and as citizens.

As a final example, let us examine the experience of efforts to train people in workshops, institutes, and special training courses. Such efforts are common in various areas of social welfare, intergroup relations, political affairs, industry, and adult education generally. It is an unfortunate fact that objective evaluation of the effects of such training efforts has only rarely been undertaken, but there is evidence for those who will look that the actual change in behavior produced is most disappointing. A workshop not infrequently develops keen interest among the participants, high morale and enthusiasm, and a firm resolve on the part of many to apply all the wonderful insights back home. But what happens back home? The trainee discovers that his colleagues don't share his enthusiasm. He learns that the task of changing others' expectations and ways of doing things is discouragingly difficult. He senses, perhaps not very clearly, that it would make all the difference in the world if only there were a few other people sharing his enthusiasm and insights with whom he could plan activities, evaluate consequences of efforts, and from whom he could gain emotional and motivational support. The approach to training which conceives of its task as being merely that of changing the individual probably produces frustration, demoralization, and disillusionment in as large a measure as it accomplishes more positive results.

A few years ago the Research Center for Group Dynamics undertook to shed light on this problem by investigating the operation of a workshop for training leaders in intercultural relations [8]. In a project, directed by

Lippitt, we set out to compare systematically the different effects of the workshop upon trainees who came as isolated individuals in contrast to those who came as teams. Since one of the problems in the field of inter-cultural relations is that of getting people of good will to be more active in community efforts to improve intergroup relations, one goal of the training workshop was to increase the activity of the trainees in such community affairs. We found that before the workshop there was no difference in the activity level of the people who were to be trained as isolates and of those who were to be trained as teams. Six months after the workshop, however, those who had been trained as isolates were only slightly more active than before the workshop whereas those who had been members of strong train-ing teams were now much more active. We do not have clear evidence on the point, but we would be quite certain that the maintenance of height-ened activity over a long period of time would also be much better for members of teams. For the isolates the effect of the workshop had the characteristic of a "shot in the arm" while for the team member it produced a more enduring change because the team provided continuous support and reinforcement for its members.

<h2 style="text-align:center">III</h2>

What conclusions may we draw from these examples? What principles of achieving change in people can we see emerging? To begin with the most general proposition, we may state that the behavior, attitudes, beliefs, and values of the individual are all firmly grounded in the groups to which he belongs. How aggressive or cooperative a person is, how much self-respect and self-confidence he has, how energetic and productive his work is, what he aspires to, what he believes to be true and good, whom he loves or hates, and what beliefs and prejudices he holds—all these character-istics are highly determined by the individual's group memberships. In a real sense, they are properties of groups and of the relationships between people. Whether they change or resist change will, therefore, be greatly in-fluenced by the nature of these groups. Attempts to change them must be concerned with the dynamics of groups.

In examining more specifically how groups enter into the process of change, we find it useful to view groups in at least three different ways. In the first view, the group is seen as a source of influence over its members. Efforts to change behavior can be supported or blocked by pressures on members stemming from the group. To make constructive use of these pres-sures the group must be used *as a medium of change*. In the second view, the group itself becomes the *target of change*. To change the behavior of individuals it may be necessary to change the standards of the group, its style of leadership, its emotional atmosphere, or its stratification into cliques and hierarchies. Even though the goal may be to change the behavior of *individuals*, the target of change becomes the group. In the third view, it is recognized that many changes of behavior can be brought about only by the organized efforts of groups *as agents of change*. A committee to combat intolerance, a labor union, an employers association, a citizens group to in-crease the pay of teachers—any action group will be more or less effective depending upon the way it is organized, the satisfactions it provides to its members, the degree to which its goals are clear, and a host of other proper-ties of the group.

An adequate social technology of change, then, requires at the very least a scientific understanding of groups viewed in each of these ways. We shall consider here only the first two aspects of the problem: the group as a medium of change and as a target of change.

THE GROUP AS A MEDIUM OF CHANGE

Principle No. 1. If the group is to be used effectively as a medium of change, those people who are to be changed and those who are to exert in-fluence for change must have a strong sense of belonging to the same group.

Kurt Lewin described this principle well: "The normal gap between teacher and student, doctor and patient, social worker and public, can . . . be a real obstacle to acceptance of the advocated conduct." In other words, in spite of whatever status differences there might be between them, the teacher and the student have to feel as members of one group in matters involving their sense of values. The chances for re-education seem to be in-creased whenever a strong we-feeling is created [5]. Recent experiments by Preston and Heintz have demonstrated greater changes of opinions among members of discussion groups operating with participatory leadership than among those with supervisory leadership [12]. The implications of this prin-ciple for classroom teaching are far-reaching. The same may be said of su-pervision in the factory, army, or hospital.

Principle No. 2. The more attractive the group is to its members the greater is the influence that the group can exert on its members.

This principle has been extensively documented by Festinger and his co-workers [4]. They have been able to show in a variety of settings that in more cohesive groups there is a greater readiness of members to attempt to influence others, a greater readiness to be influenced by others, and stronger pressures toward conformity when conformity is a relevant mat-ter for the group. Important for the practitioner wanting to make use of this principle is, of course, the question of how to increase the attractiveness of groups. This is a question with many answers. Suffice it to say that a group is more attractive the more it satisfies the needs of its members. We have been able to demonstrate experimentally an increase in group cohesiveness by increasing the liking of members for each other as persons, by increasing the perceived importance of the group goal, and by increasing the prestige of the group among other groups. Experienced group workers could add many other ways to this list.

Principle No. 3. In attempts to change attitudes, values, or behavior, the more relevant they are to the basis of attraction to the group, the greater will be the influence that the group can exert upon them.

I believe this principle gives a clue to some otherwise puzzling phenomena. How does it happen that a group, like a labor union, seems to be able to exert such strong discipline over its members in some matters (let us say in dealings with management), while it seems unable to exert nearly the same influence in other matters (let us say in political action)? If we examine why it is that members are attracted to the group, I believe we will find that a particular reason for belonging seems more related to some of the group's activities than to others. If a man joins a union mainly to keep his job and to improve his working conditions, he may be largely uninfluenced by the union's attempt to modify his attitudes toward national and international affairs. Groups differ tremendously in the range of matters that are relevant to them and hence over which they have influence. Much of the inefficiency of adult education could be reduced if more attention were paid to the need that influence attempts be appropriate to the groups in which they are made. (*sic*)

Principle No. 4. The greater the prestige of a group member in the eyes of the other members, the greater the influence he can exert.

Polansky, Lippitt, and Redl [11] have demonstrated this principle with great care and methodological ingenuity in a series of studies in children's summer camps. From a practical point of view it must be emphasized that the things giving prestige to a member may not be those characteristics most prized by the official management of the group. The most prestige-carrying member of a Sunday School class may not possess the characteristics most similar to the minister of the church. The teacher's pet may be a poor source of influence within a class. This principle is the basis for the common observation that the official leader and the actual leader of a group are often not the same individual.

Principle No. 5. Efforts to change individuals or subparts of a group which, if successful, would have the result of making them deviate from the norms of the group will encounter strong resistance.

During the past few years a great deal of evidence has been accumulated showing the tremendous pressures which groups can exert upon members to conform to the group's norms. The price of deviation in most groups is rejection or even expulsion. If the member really wants to belong and be accepted, he cannot withstand this type of pressure. It is for this reason that efforts to change people by taking them from the group and giving them special training so often have disappointing results. This principle also accounts for the finding that people thus trained sometimes display in-creased tension, aggressiveness toward the group, or a tendency to form cults or cliques with others who have shared their training.

These five principles concerning the group as a medium of change would appear to have readiest application to groups created for the purpose of producing changes in people. They provide certain specifications for building effective training or therapy groups. They also point, however, to a difficulty in producing change in people in that they show how resistant an individual is to changing in any way contrary to group pressures and expectations. In order to achieve many kinds of changes in people, there-fore, it is necessary to deal with the group as a target of change.

THE GROUP AS A TARGET OF CHANGE

Principle No. 6. Strong pressure for changes in the group can be established by creating a shared perception by members of the need for change, thus making the source of pressure for change lie within the group.

Marrow and French [9] report a dramatic case-study which illustrates this principle quite well. A manufacturing concern had a policy against hiring women over thirty because it was believed that they were slower, more difficult to train, and more likely to be absent. The staff psychologist was able to present to management evidence that this belief was clearly un-warranted at least within their own company. The psychologist's facts, however, were rejected and ignored as a basis for action because they vio-lated accepted beliefs. It was claimed that they went against the direct ex-perience of the foremen. Then the psychologist hit upon a plan for achiev-ing change which differed drastically from the usual one of argument, persuasion, and pressure. He proposed that mangement conduct its own analysis of the situation. With his help management collected all the facts which they believed were relevant to the problem. When the results were in they were now their own facts rather than those of some "outside" expert. Policy was immediately changed without further resistance. The important point here is that facts are not enough. The facts must be the accepted property of the group if they are to become an effective basis for change. There seems to be all the difference in the world in changes actually carried out between those cases in which a consulting firm is hired to do a study and present a report and those in which technical experts are asked to collabo-rate with the group in doing its own study.

Principle No. 7. Information relating to the need for change, plans for change, and consequences of change must be shared by all relevant people in the group.

Another way of stating this principle is to say that change of a group ordinarily requires the opening of communication channels. Newcomb [10] has shown how one of the first consequences of mistrust and hostility is the avoidance of communicating openly and freely about the things producing the tension. If you look closely at a pathological group (that is, one that has trouble making decisions or effecting coordinated efforts of its members), you will certainly find strong restraints in that group against communicating vital information among its members. Until these restraints are removed there can be little hope for any real and lasting changes in the group's functioning. In passing it should be pointed out that the removal of barriers to communication will ordinarily be accompanied by a sudden increase in the communication of hostility. The group may appear to be falling apart, and it will certainly be a painful experience to many of the members. This pain and the fear that things are getting out of hand often stop the process of change once begun.

Principle No. 8. Changes in one part of a group produce strain in other related parts which can be reduced only by eliminating the change or by bringing about readjustments in the related parts.

It is a common practice to undertake improvements in group functioning by providing training programs for certain classes of people in the organization. A training program for foremen, for nurses, for teachers, or for group workers is established. If the content of the training is relevant for organizational change, it must of necessity deal with the relationships these people have with other subgroups. If nurses in a hospital change their behavior significantly, it will affect their relations both with the patients and with the doctors. It is unrealistic to assume that both these groups will remain indifferent to any significant changes in this respect. In hierarchical structures this process is most clear. Lippitt has proposed on the basis of research and experience that in such organizations attempts at change should always involve three levels, one being the major target of change and the other two being the one above and the one below.

IV

These eight principles represent a few of the basic propositions emerging from research in group dynamics. Since research is constantly going on and since it is the very nature of research to revise and reformulate our conceptions, we may be sure that these principles will have to be modified and improved as time goes by. In the meantime they may serve as guides in our endeavors to develop a scientifically based technology of social management.

In social technology, just as in physical technology, invention plays a crucial role. In both fields progress consists of the creation of new mechanisms for the accomplishment of certain goals. In both fields inventions arise in response to practical needs and are to be evaluated by how effectively they satisfy these needs. The relation of invention to scientific development is indirect but important. Inventions cannot proceed too far ahead of basic scientific development, nor should they be allowed to fall too far behind. They will be more effective the more they make good use of known principles of science, and they often make new developments in science possible. On the other hand, they are in no sense logical derivations from scientific principles.

I have taken this brief excursion into the theory of invention in order to make a final point. To many people "group dynamics" is known only for the social inventions which have developed in recent years in work with groups. Group dynamics is often thought of as certain techniques to be used with groups. Role playing, buzz groups, process observers, post-meeting reaction sheets, and feedback of group observations are devices popularly associated with the phrase "group dynamics." I trust that I have been able to show that group dynamics is more than a collection of gadgets. It certainly aspires to be a science as well as a technology.

This is not to underplay the importance of these inventions nor of the function of inventing. As inventions they are all mechanisms designed to help accomplish important goals. How effective they are will depend upon how skilfully they are used and how appropriate they are to the purposes to which they are put. Careful evaluative research must be the ultimate judge of their usefulness in comparison with alternative inventions. I believe that the principles enumerated in this paper indicate some of the specifications that social inventions in this field must meet.

REFERENCES

1. Cartwright, D. "Some Principles of Mass Persuasion: Selected Findings of Research on the Sale of United States War Bonds," *Human Relations* (1949), Vol. II, No. 3, 253–267.

2. Cartwright, D. *The Research Center for Group Dynamics: A Report of Five Years' Activities and a View of Future Needs* (Ann Arbor: Institute for Social Research, 1950).

3. Coch, L., and French, J. R. P., Jr. "Overcoming Resistance to Change," *Human Relations* (1948), Vol. I, No. 4, 512–532.

4. Festinger, L., *et al. Theory and Experiment in Social Communication: Collected papers* (Ann Arbor: Institute for Social Research, 1950).

5. Lewin, K. *Resolving Social Conflicts* 67 (New York: Harper and Brothers, 1948).

6. Lewin, K. *Field Theory in Social Science* (New York: Harper and Brothers, 1951), 229–236.

7. Lewin, K., Lippitt, R., and White, R. K. "Patterns of Aggressive Behavior in Experimentally Created 'Social Climates'," *Journal of Social Psychology* (1939), *10*, 271–299.

8. Lippitt, R. *Training in Community Relations* (New York: Harper and Brothers, 1949).

9. Marrow, A. J., and French, J. R. P., Jr. "Changing a Stereotype in Industry," *Journal of Social Issues* (1945), *1*, 3, 33–37.

10. Newcomb, T. M. "Autistic Hostility and Social Reality," *Human Relations* (1947), Vol. I, No. 1, 69–86.

11. Polansky, N., Lippitt, R., and Redl, F. "An Investigation of Behavioral Contagion in Groups," *Human Relations* (1950), Vol. III, No. 4, 319–348.

12. Preston, M. G., and Heintz, R. K. "Effects of Participatory vs. Supervisory Leadership on Group Judgment," *Journal of Abnormal and Social Psychology* (1949), *44*, 345–355.

3

Theory and Principles of Group Counseling in the Elementary School*

Don C. Dinkmeyer

Group counseling is an interpersonal process through which individuals work within a peer group and with a counselor to explore problems, feelings, attitudes, and values, in an attempt to modify attitudes and perceptions so that they are better able to deal with developmental problems.

The group counseling process recognizes that most problems are primarily social and interpersonal, and the child must learn to interact effectively within his group. A child's character is expressed through his social movement and interaction, and group counseling provides an opportunity to reveal convictions and develop self-understanding. The process also provides the opportunity to see the nature of the child's interaction and have him benefit from the corrective influences and encouragement of the group.

In the group, members can identify with others and understand their own problems by observing the behavior of others. The process helps the child become aware of and consider the alternatives. The group, then, can become a value-forming element. It provides the opportunity to explore problems, opinions, feelings, assumptions, and convictions, in an attempt to modify attitudes and the perceptual field.

The counseling proceeds from the assumption that man is an indivisible, social, decision-making being whose actions have a social purpose.[1]

Group counseling is based on certain conceptual foundations:

1) *All behavior has social meaning.* Man is primarily a social being and behavior must be understood in terms of its social context. It is only within the group that man can function and fulfill himself; he is actually dependent upon group membership for his development. The significance of behavior lies in its social consequences.

2) *Belonging is a basic need.* A child has the need to identify and be-

---

°Reprinted with the permission of the author.

[1]Rudolf Dreikurs and Manford Sonstegard, "Rationale of Group Counseling in the Elementary Schools," *Readings in Guidance in the Elementary School* by Don Dinkmeyer (1965).

long. Man is not self-actualized unless he belongs. The capacity to give and take in the framework of interpersonal relationships is an important component of normality.

3) *Behavior is best understood on a holistic basis, in terms of its unity and pattern.* The emphasis is placed on focusing on the total pattern and the psychological movement.

4) *The individual must be understood in terms of his phenomenological field.* The child is understood in terms of his subjective point of view, how he perceives life, and the meaning that a specific event possesses for him. We must come to comprehend how his anticipation of lack of success or acceptance actually provokes responses from others which reinforce his interpretation of his place in life.

5) *Each individual has the creative power to make biased interpretations.* The child does more than receive stimuli, he has the creative power to interpret and assign personalized meanings. To quote Adler, "A perception is never to be compared with a photographic image, because something of the peculiar and individual quality of the person who perceives it is inextricably bound up within it."[2]

Behavior, thus, is not only reactive but it is creative, and necessitates more than a stimulus response conception of behavior. This model would consider the stimulus, the individual's capacity to interpret and perceive his experiences, and his response. It suggests we predict better when we understand the individual's style of life, but that we also need to allow for his capacity to give a personalized interpretation to all events.

6) *Motivation can be understood in terms of the striving for significance, the movement to enhance the self-esteem.* Psychological movement is seen as a pull toward the goal, not a push by the drive. As we understand the master motive, how the child strives to be significant or accepted, we understand the force that is directing his behavior.

7) *Behavior is goal-directed and purposive.* All psychological movement has a purpose. The counselor focuses on the goal as a final cause, or explanation. The goal is subjective, creative, and frequently unconscious. Goals become the psychic stimuli that motivate the individual's behavior. Behavior and misbehavior can make sense in terms of the individual's convictions, attitudes, and purposes. The goal-directed nature of behavior is perhaps best understood in terms of the goals of misbehavior. These goals have been referred to by Dreikurs as attention-getting, the struggle for power, the desire to retaliate or get even, and the display of inadequacy or assumed disability.[3]

[2]Alfred Adler, *Understanding Human Nature* (New York: Fawcett Publications, Inc., 1957), p. 49.

[3]Rudolf Dreikurs, *Psychology in the Classroom* (New York: Harper and Brothers, 1957).

This approach is in alignment with Allport when he concludes "goal striving is the essence of personality."[4]

8) *It is more important to understand the psychology of use than the psychology of possession.* We need to determine what conclusions the child has drawn from his experiences. Any individual at any moment does that which accomplishes his purposes.

9) *Social interest is a key concept in the understanding of behavior.* Social interest is more than a feeling of belonging. It reflects our attitudes toward our fellow man. The individual with adequate social interest accepts responsibility and desires to cooperate. He has a concern for others, and he is willing to participate in the give and take of life. "The social interest has no fixed objective. Much more truly it can be said to create an attitude to life, a desire to cooperate with others in some way and to master the situations of life. Social interest is the expression of our capacity for give and take."[5]

These conceptual foundations are fundamental to the principles utilized in the group counseling process. Recognition that the problems of all children are basically social gives group counseling special significance, both for the diagnosis and solution of the child's problems.[6]

Since human beings are social beings they will express their social goals in the interaction of the group process. Group counseling permits the trained counselor to observe how the child finds his place in the group. It enables him to identify the way in which the child perceives self and others. The way that the child finds his place, interprets, and makes his decisions always reveals his self-concept and his convictions and assumptions about life. This enables the counselor to use the most powerful influence of all, the peers, to influence the child. The group can be most effective in encouraging and serving as a corrective influence. Group counseling teaches each member to deal with each other as an equal and it becomes a social force in the peer culture.

Group counseling recognizes that the child has become "dysfunctioning" or "maladjusted," as a result of faulty assumptions and mistaken approaches about the most effective way to find his place in the group. This hypothesizes that the problems of children are essentially interpersonal, social-interaction problems. The study of the social interaction helps us become aware of the way in which the individual expresses his social orientation and intentions.

A group, then, has common purposes, values, established norms, roles,

[4]Gordon Allport, *The Nature of Personality* (Reading, Mass.: Addison-Wesley Press, 1950), p. 169.

[5]Rudolf Dreikurs, *Fundamentals of Adlerian Psychology* (Jamaica, B. W. I. : Knox Publications, 1958), p. 9.

[6]Rudolf Dreikurs and Manford Sonstegard, "Rationale of Group Counseling in the Elementary Schools."

and rules. The interaction which develops in the group provides the opportunity to develop a feeling of belonging. The group setting increases the child's receptiveness to ideas and concepts which come from the peers. Most important of all, it provides the child with the opportunity to have a place not based on competition but cooperation, not based on self-elevation but based on the opportunity to offer help because of his social interest. For both the child and the counselor it provides an opportunity to experiment in a real social situation.

Group counseling operates as a learning process, and the counselor looks for the development of new convictions about self and others and new perceptions of ways to relate to others. It provides the opportunity for the child to receive feedback from the members of the group, and perhaps disclosure from the group leader. It provides the setting in which there is an opportunity to examine feelings and convictions, question ideas, confront each other, and benefit from mutual encouragement and a feeling of belonging and identification. It is important to recognize that children are more often encouraged by their peers than by their teachers or counselors.

The group provides the opportunity for mutual help, to give of oneself, to provide acceptance and love. Thus, an opportunity to give love is provided which is as important as the need to receive love and be accepted. The group assists in the dissolving of social isolation while at the same time providing the aggressive child with the opportunity to benefit from the natural and logical consequences of group interaction.

While group counseling at times may appear to operate at random, it is important to be aware of the structure. The group counseling process consists of (1) the establishment and maintenance of proper relationships; (2) an examination of the purpose of each group member's action or behavior; (3) revealing to each student the goals he is pursuing, called psychological disclosure; and (4) a reorientation and a redirection."[7]

In group counseling one will observe certain fundamental principles: 1) the effective counseling relationship is based upon mutual respect and mutual goal alignment; 2) the child's psychological movement and purposes become more obvious in interaction with group members; 3) disclosure and confrontation can be used preferably on a tentative hypothesis basis in a statement such as: "Could it be—," or "Is it possible—" and then alluding to the purpose; and 4) group counseling utilizes the mirror effect not only of the counselor but of the peers. The child frequently may perceive or even state, "I recall I used to think that way or do that." The child is made aware of his faulty assumptions and erroneous concepts which may make a change in his whole pattern of interpersonal living and approach of life.

[7]Rudolf Dreikurs and Manford Sonstegard, "Rationale of Group Counseling in the Elementary Schools."

Group counseling, then, provides the elementary counselor with a unique opportunity to utilize a dynamic interpersonal process for the modification of attitudes, the changing of behavior, and the development of a problem-solving approach to a variety of developmental problems.

Chapter II

THE DIMENSIONS OF
GROUP COUNSELING

DEFINITION OF TERMS

A major problem that seems to confront the neophyte in the field of guidance is the oft-times confusing technical jargon that appears in guidance and counseling texts and periodicals. Beginning graduate students in guidance often use the terms guidance and counseling synonymously, administrators often refer to counselors as "guidance teachers" and parents speak of guidance personnel as "vocational counselors."

The terminology used in group work in guidance is also somewhat confusing. A counselor who is asked if he performs group counseling may reply in the affirmative although his conception of group counseling may range from a large class in educational and vocational guidance to small group work with a few individuals. In addition, such terms as group dynamics, group process, multiple counseling, and group guidance are often used interchangeably by counselors to describe quite different functions.

Since the meanings of various terms in group work in guidance may be unclear in the minds of some readers, a review of the way such terms have been defined by various authors may be beneficial. A complete review of all terms related to group guidance and group counseling is beyond the scope of this book; however, some of the terminology that seems to be most confusing is presented here to provide the reader with a minimal understanding of basic terms.

GROUP

Obviously, any group work done in guidance depends upon the formation of a group. Some counselors see groups merely as a collection of individuals but most writers would agree that a group has additional attributes. Gulley points out that a dozen people sitting at a railroad station waiting room *do not* constitute a group. They may *become* a group, however, under certain conditions—a common goal, interaction, and oral communication [10].

Cattell has defined a group as "a collection of organisms in which the existence of all (in their given relationships) is necessary to the satisfaction of certain individual needs in each" [6, p. 169]. Homans defines a group as "a number of persons who communicate with one another over a span of time, and who are few enough so that each person is able to communicate with all others, not at second hand, through other people, but face to face" [13, p. 1].

A similar definition to those presented by Gulley, Cattell, and Homans is given by Warters [27] although she indicates that a collection of individuals does constitute a group whether there is interaction of the members or not. Without such interaction, however, the group is merely an aggregation. For guidance and counseling purposes, Warters is not concerned with aggregations but with *functional groups*. Her definition of a functional group includes group purposes, satisfactions, needs, interaction, and interdependence:

> In short, common purposes, satisfaction of individual needs, interaction,
> and interdependence of members are conditions essential to the existence
> of a functional group [27, p. 9].

Glanz [9] defines a group as simply a collection of persons operating together to achieve a mutually related purpose or function, and Kemp [14] points out that any definition of the group must include at least the size, quality of interaction, and the potential for change.

It is now possible to draw together several themes into a definition of a group. A group then is a collection of individuals who:

(1) have a common goal

(2) interact

(3) are interdependent

(4) have similar or common needs

(5) stay together for a period of time

GROUP DYNAMICS

The term *group dynamics* is commonly found in the literature on group guidance and group counseling. In some cases, group dynamics is erroneously used as a synonym for group counseling and group guidance. In a recent counseling class taught by one of the editors thirty students were asked to write a definition of group counseling and group dynamics. Although there was wide variation in the individual definitions, 23 of the 30 students indicated that they thought the two terms were essentially the same. Since there are probably others who hold similar opinions, several definitions of the term group dynamics are presented here to show that group counseling and group dynamics are not synonomous.

Shertzer and Stone present a brief, but clear definition of group dynamics:

> Group dynamics is a term which refers to the interacting forces within
> groups as they organize and operate to achieve their objectives [24, p. 169].

Bonner defines group dynamics as formation and change in the functions and structures of psychological grouping:

> We can now define group dynamics as that division of social psychology which investigates the formation and change in the structure and functions of the psychological and grouping of people into self directing wholes [4, p. 5].

Cartwright and Zander give a comprehensive definition of group dynamics:

> In summary then, we have proposed that group dynamics should be defined as a field of inquiry dedicated to advancing knowledge about the nature of groups, the laws of their development, and their interrelations with individuals, other groups, and larger institutions. It may be identified by four distinguishing characteristics: (a) an emphasis on the theoretically significant research, (b) an interest in dynamics and the interdependence among phenomena, (c) a broad relevance to all the social sciences, and (d) the potential applicability of its findings in efforts to improve the functioning of groups and their consequences on individuals and society [5, p. 9].

Broadly speaking then, the term group dynamics refers to the "why" of group functioning. As a field of inquiry group dynamics asks—Why do groups form? Why do changes take place in groups? Why are some groups more cohesive than others? Why do pressures arise in groups? Why are some groups able to communicate more effectively than others?

It should be noted at this point, however, that concern for group dynamics alone will not lead to adequate understanding in a counseling group. Luchins in his text on group therapy points out that a focus on group dynamics by the therapist tends to cause him to neglect the individual and focus on theoretical constructs rather than on the actual behavior of the individual on a phenomenal level. He acknowledges that both psychodynamics and group dynamics provide clues to the understanding of therapy but warns against the use of either as a "sole" approach:

> Each may be regarded as a different approach to understanding and explaining what takes place in group therapy. But it seems inappropriate to regard group therapy as "nothing but" a certain kind of psychodynamics or "nothing but" group dynamics, or "nothing but" a certain phenomenally oriented description [17, p. 91].

Although Luchins is directing his views to group therapists, the essence of his message would also seem to apply to group counselors.

GROUP GUIDANCE

Although some authors distinguish between the terms group guidance and group counseling, the differences are not always sharply defined. In fact some authors have indicated that the terms are essentially similar. For example, Glanz feels that newer skills and programming can bring group guidance and group counseling closer together:

> Group guidance techniques have been concerned with occupational data collection, educational collection, test interpretation, case study discussion, mental health and human relations. Certainly these are also counseling issues. Newer skills and program designs can bring counseling and group guidance closer together [9, p. 16].

Bennett defines group guidance in rather broad terms although her definition of the term is somewhat similar to that of Glanz:

> . . . .group guidance refers to any phase of a guidance program carried on with groups of individuals rather than between counselor and counselee, or clinician and client in the face-to-face situation [2, p. 2].

Lifton defines group guidance in an educational setting by contrasting it to group therapy. The difference is one of emphasis in which the group guidance function is concerned with the imparting of information while group therapy focuses on the exploration of feelings and attitudes:

> . . . .group therapy in an educational setting is here considered to be operating in any group where the *emphasis* is upon providing group members with opportunities to explore their own feelings and attitudes rather than upon imparting information [16, p. 14].

The common thread running through these definitions seems to be that group guidance may be any procedure that involves a group of students working toward a guidance objective. All aspects of the guidance program that are content centered and involve such counselor activities as dispensing occupational and educational information, planning and conducting orientation programs, group follow-up meetings, and group testing may be considered to be group guidance activities.

The following transcript is part of a group guidance session with college-bound seniors in a New Jersey High School:

Counselor: A number of you have been posing questions to me lately with regard to college admissions. Since many of you seem to be interested in getting answers to the same questions, I thought we might do this in a group. I'll try to answer any questions that you may have and perhaps other members of the group here will have some answers to things that I don't know about. I know that several of you have recently visited some schools and perhaps you'll be willing to share some of this information. Now, who wants to start?

John: I know this isn't interesting to the girls here, but what about R.O.T.C.? Do I have to enroll in that when I get in school?

Counselor: No, you won't *have* to enroll in R.O.T.C. This is just a program that many colleges offer for those students who want to become officers after they graduate. You know, of course, that you do have a military obligation when you reach the age of 18 but there are other ways to fulfill this obligation without joining a R.O.T.C. unit.

Mike: Some colleges have different ones—ah—you know Army, Navy, and Coast Guard, don't they?

Counselor: Well, generally speaking, that's true, except for the Coast Guard. They get most of their officers from the Coast Guard Academy in New London, Connecticut. That's a special type of program that you must make special preparation for. I have the information in my office if you want it. On the other point though, remember that all colleges don't have R.O.T.C. programs and all colleges don't have programs in all branches of the services.

Sue: I'm wondering about my College Board Tests. Patty took them last spring and she said that the English (verbal) section was really tough. Do you absolutely need them to get into college?

Counselor: Well, not absolutely, but most colleges today require either the SAT's or the tests of the American College Testing Program. There are, however, some schools that do not require either of these tests. If you have particular schools in mind you should carefully check their catalogues to determine exactly what you need to do in order to apply.

Carol: I understand that we're allowed to visit colleges during the school year. How do we go about that?

Counselor: First of all you should write to the director of admissions of the particular school that you want to visit and make a definite appointment. The school board will allow you to be absent from school for two days of your junior and senior year to visit colleges providing you are not failing any subjects. If you want to do this you should get permission slips from my secretary, complete them, and have your parents sign them. They must be in my office at least two weeks prior to the time you plan to make a visit.

Harry: We're being hit with the importance of grades in almost every class we go into. Are they that important? I mean how will the college decide whether to let me in or not? Will my grades be the most important or will my college boards (SAT's) count most?

Counselor: Most schools use a combination of things to rule on your admission. They'll look at your rank in class, the results of your tests and your recommendations. Some schools seem to put more weight on grades than others, and some look for good test scores. Where you live may also have something to do with your admission also—for example, some schools in the South may want a certain amount of students from the North and vice versa. A large number of New Jersey students attend college in other states.

Carol: I know that's true. My sister had only about a C+ average, but she had a 700 on her English (verbal) and I think she had a 500 on her math. They took her at _____ which is a good school!

John: Yes, but she's also a good musician. That school likes to get people good in music or at least that's what I heard.

Nancy: What about scholarships, Mr. _____ ? I think I'm going to need help.

This discussion continued with this give and take approach for the remainder of the period. The reader will note that the discussion is content oriented and concerned primarily with student requests for information about college admission.

GROUP COUNSELING

Group counseling is most commonly defined as a group procedure where the emphasis is on personal exploration rather than on the provision and discussion of guidance material. This contrast is evident in the definitions presented in some of the more recent texts that deal with group guidance and counseling.

An early definition of the term group counseling appeared in Helen Driver's 1958 edition of *Counseling and Learning Through Small Group Discussion.* She preferred to use the term "multiple counseling" rather than group counseling and emphasized that group methods should be used in conjunction with individual counseling:

> The multiple counseling method described in this book uses small group discussion activity as the learning medium for personal growth participants in conjunction with individual counseling by the group leader [7, p. 19].

Later definitions of group counseling did not specify that group methods should be used in conjunction with individual methods. The emphasis of group counseling in definitions presented by Warters and Mahler and Caldwell is one that focuses on the problems of youth:

> Group counseling is not individual counseling applied to groups although it is a group method designed to help individuals with problems—the normal emotional problems of everyday living, as well as severe or serious problems [27, p. 170].

> Group counseling is a social process that deals with the developmental problems and attitudes of youth in a secure setting. The counseling content covers the common needs and interests of a great majority of the students. Examples are such topics as boy-girl relationships or how to get along with parents [18, p. 24].

The primary focus in the counseling group would be on students' personal *reactions* to test scores, occupational information, and life experiences. For example, the counselor who explains the admission requirements of colleges may be considered to be performing a group guidance function. The same counselor who works with a group of students in an attempt to attach personal meaning to college exploration is performing a group counseling function. Obviously, a given group session may initiate as group guidance and develop into group counseling if the counselor and the members of the group move from a content-centered discussion to a more affective one. Since group counseling requires the establishment of a high degree of rapport and interaction within the group, the life of a counseling group will be somewhat extended.

In order to provide the reader with the flavor of a group counseling session, a portion of a group meeting is presented in the following transcript. In this instance the counselor is working with a group of college freshmen. About fifteen minutes of group time have elapsed.

Joel: And yesterday I wore bermudas. Maybe it was because I seemed to enjoy it. I love it with shorts on when the sun is shining. It's fun to be a nonconformist.

Carol: It is?

Pat: Yeh, but when you're like the rest of us that isn't being a nonconformist.

Joel: Well, I guess I really didn't mean to be different yesterday. I just had a touch of spring fever and the sun was shining. But I want to be myself—I want to express my personality if I can.

Pat: I guess I know what you mean. You know we can't always express our real personalities on the outside. (She means outside the group.)

Sue: You mean you're not really expressing your personality on the outside?

Nick: I disagree—everything you do is your personality.

Pat: Yeh, but I mean you go up to someone on the outside and say "Hi" or somethin'. You deal with just surface things. In here we can sort of express our more inner feelings that we don't express to other people.

Counselor: (to group) Do you understand what she's saying?

Kip: I think so. In here we are expressing a part of our personality, a different part than we usually express.

Bob: There's a lot of difference between theory and practice. We come in here and say we're one thing and go outside and do the exact opposite.

Counselor: You seem to be saying that we're quite different people when we're not in this group.

Pat: Like I said—we deal with surface things on the outside, in here we don't. Well, for example, we've talked about sex. You just don't go up to someone and say—what do you think about sex!

(group laughter)

Kim: Yeh, but you're always who you are. You can't be anyone other than yourself.

Counselor: So you think you can't be any different than who you are. You're about the same in here as you always are. I think Nick has a different view of that.

Nick: I guess so. This group—well it gives me a way to get things off my chest. I'm different on the outside not because I want to be but because—

Sue: You can't be or you're afraid to be.

Nick: Well, I got in a fight last week because of Italian jokes, something about Italians not having freckles because they slide off their face.

Joel: Well, I think you're oversensitive because you're Italian, but I know what you mean. I have to take a lot of Jewish jokes in stride. There are some guys that I don't like and after a while it gets on my nerves. Well, I know the guy in the section (dorm) that Jimmy was talking about. (Jimmy is a Negro boy.) He put on that deep Southern accent and got on his nerves after a while. But on the outside I don't say much because people start thinking "That guy's awful sensitive about that" and they'll avoid you and won't say anything to you.

Jim: Well, if anybody ever told me a Negro joke, I couldn't take it. It's the one thing I can't stand, that Southern drawl—I just can't take it.

Sue: Why does it get you so bad Jimmy? Can you figure it out?

Jim: No—I'm trying to figure it out—

Counselor: Three of you—Nick, Joel, and Jim have expressed some concerns about this topic. Perhaps the group can help. You seem to have some thoughts on it, Sue—

The group continued on this topic for the rest of the session with Nick, Joel, and Jim examining their feelings within the context of the perceptions of group members. At other group meetings personal concerns of other members were examined with Nick, Joel, and Jim functioning quite differently than they were in this session.

GROUP THERAPY

The counselor who has satisfied himself with adequate definitions of group guidance and group counseling must also determine how his work in group counseling differs from that of the group therapists.This may not be an easy task since the term group therapy is not easily defined. The reasons for the confusion that surrounds the term are pointed out by Luchins:

> Some of the confusion surrounding the term may be attributed to the diversity of its connotations. The term refers simultaneously (a) to methods and processes carried out by others in order to induce certain changes in

the patient or in the group; (b) to processes going on within the patient himself; and (c) to the resultants or outcomes of such processes [17, p. 12].

While the definitions of group therapy may be confusing because of the reasons that Luchins presents, attempts have been made to define the process. Hinckley and Hermann define group therapy along four dimensions:

(1) the therapeutic aim of the unit with lack of group goal; (2) the alleviation of emotional tensions by sharing experiences, a process involving catharsis, partial reliving of old experiences and increasing self-awareness, (3) the permissive and supportive role of the therapist, and (4) the direct interest and attack on personal problems in order to foster attitudinal modification [12, pp. 19–21].

Mahler and Caldwell define group therapy in terms of the seriousness of the disturbances of group members:

Group therapy operates in an educational setting when the basis for the organization of a student group is emotional disturbance so severe that it seriously impedes educational progress. Such a situation demands a therapy relationship designed to help the students understand how the emotional life, feelings, habits are interfering with school progress [18, p. 26].

A similar view is presented by Warters:

Group therapy rather than group counseling is needed when the clients are seriously disturbed or maladjusted and when the worker should be competent to function as a clinical psychologist or psychiatrist [27, p. 172].

While the term group therapy may be somewhat elusive of concrete definition, the definitions presented here may well lead one to the conclusion that the distinctions between group counseling and group therapy are fairly obvious.

First of all, the group leader is called a "counselor" not a clinical psychologist or psychiatrist. Secondly, the counselor works with "normal" individuals who are generally referred to as clients, counselees or students while the therapist works with "seriously" disturbed individuals called patients. In addition, the counselor is generally located in an educational setting while the therapist works in private practice or in an institution. The goal of the group counselor is to aid his counselees in the development of personal meaning and values which will guide their decision making and in group therapy the desired goal is an improvement of personal and social functioning through an emotional reeducational and relearning experience.

A sample of group therapy is illustrated in the following transcript.[1] In this instance the therapist is working with patients in a state hospital in Maine. All patients are male veterans with a primary or secondary diagnosis of alcoholism. All patients in this group have met for at least four

[1] Certain "earthy" words have been omitted from this transcript.

months twice a week. The therapist for this group, Dr. M., is working primarily to strengthen the egos of the members of the group and to help them gain insight into the underlying emotional problems which the use of alcohol tends to defend or cover up.

John: You ain't afraid after you're half drunk.

Harold: That's for sure.

Dr. M: I think what John was trying to say before was that he wants to test himself out. I don't think he wants to test himself out as far as drinking goes—he wants to test his own courage, really.

John: That's right. I want to see what I can do well.

Dr. M: What I think Cookie was wondering, is it worth proving that or can you prove something else? Is proving you can't drink much a great goal or can you prove something else? You're proving you can't drink or you're proving that you won't. Can you go out and try to prove that you will do something? It's a difference between a negative and a positive goal.

John: I drank heavy one winter. Real heavy. Then I got so sick I couldn't drink. A guy offered me a job in the summer building houses. You know, just like plumbers. (Looks at Robert) Putting shingles up, picking up around, sawing, you know, and things like that. Every afternoon at 2:00, he'd say, "Oh,"—we were only about from here across the hall from the store—"let's go get a couple of king size beers." I could do it and I could drink the one can of beer. It was hot, you know. But I didn't seem to crave it. But when I'm laying around and go to a local joint for a king size beer, I'm there for the rest of the time.

Dr. M.: That's what we were wondering about. If you're sitting around doing nothing, worrying if you're going to a beer joint or not, this is torture.

John: I'd go home at night. Even at night I'm feeling great and I'd drink a can of beer while eating supper. Other times, I can't wait to get done so I can go on a drunk. I had money all saved up and had to get rid of it. Especially when things begin to slacken off and they begin laying off. Instead of using my head and saving that money and keeping on looking. I looked all right. I went to a different bar every day. The bartender ain't going to get me a job as long as I'm sitting there spending my money. If I'd had the gumption to go out and look around a little bit, I might have found something. So everybody's different.

Dr. M.: Or basically the same?

Cookie: Yes, basically the same.

Dr. M.: It boils down to a lot of the same.

Cookie: The job like Paul and I had for instance. Trying to get by with drinking and working at the same time. If you're working for somebody else, you can't do that. You can get away with it for a while working for yourself but eventually, you can't get away with that either.

John: I worked all last summer drunk every day but it got the best of me in the end.

Cookie: It isn't only your boss that notices it—it's the customer. And it's you yourself that notices it.

John: Even my broom is looking at me.

Dr. M.: Your broom?

John: Yeh, sweeping the streets. (John was a street sweeper.) I always made sure I swept past the liquor store at 9:30. I'd look up and down the street and park my broom in the alley.

Dr. M.: And then buy a pint.

John: Yes, of wine. Then later I'd see another good alley way and do the same. I got away with it for quite awhile and then they started noticing it. "Gee, you're flushed this morning." I'd had a hard night but I couldn't wait to get to work. Then in the end it got so I couldn't work.

Dr. M.: Well, it caught up with you. At first, what were you trying to do?

John: At first?

Dr. M.: Yes. In the end, it caught up with you and you had to quit but at first, what were you trying to do?

John: I thought I could do it.

Dr. M.: Yes, but you were having fun with this. This was a game.

John: But I didn't get rum sick. I didn't give myself a chance to get rum sick.

Dr. M.: You were working it off, too. But it was like a game, wasn't it.?

John: Well, there was a store down by the bridge and I knew the woman there. So I'd say, Rosie it's time for a break, ain't it? I'd get a can of beer and go in the back room and set my broom outside. In case the boss happened to ride by, I'd have a bottle of Pepsi open. Of course, he knew it all the time but he couldn't catch me. He didn't care so long as I kept the street clean.

Dr. M.: That's right. You lost your job after you couldn't keep the street clean.

John: I didn't lose my job. I just went in to collect my money, went on a drunk and just didn't go back.

Dr. M.: You mean you resigned before you got fired. Really, you couldn't do the work any more.

John: That'a right. I couldn't do it any more so I packed some clothes in a suitcase and went to ———.

Dr. M.: Then what?

John: Then the men in a white coat came after me. (And brought him to the ——— State Hospital)

Dr. M.: When you started out this street sweeping job, what were you thinking?

John: $65 a week and don't do nothing.

Dr. M.: Well, you *had* to sweep the street.

John: Well, I had a cart and I would bring it to the manhole and push most of it (the dirt) into the manhole. So.

Dr. M.: So the whole thing was a good deal for you.

John: Yes, until the time came to clean the manhole.

Dr. M.: Isn't it something like pushing responsibility in the manhole until it catches up with you.

(There follows several moments of silence followed by general discussion of job possibilities in the Augusta area. The group, practically speaking, is in "recess" without adjournment. Apparently Robert's request to be excused to go to the toilet precipitated this situation. Herb brings in his prospective summer job and I remind him that he has to begin to plan for next winter even now, if possible, unless he is honestly planning to come back here which he says he doesn't want to do. He is encouraged to feel that he can do better than simply sitting out the winter at ——————. Herb discusses a program on how he could have his pay spread throughout the year rather than in lump sum for the summer and have enough to live on during the winter. Cookie suggests that he get a job in a hotel that has a Florida branch and avoid the winter unemployment. Herb, obviously, not wanting to work all year around, brings in age as an excuse. Cookie retorts that for the kinds of jobs that he does, hotels don't worry too much about the employee's age. Robert reenters and when he is seated, interrupts the ongoing conversation.)

GROUP PROCESS

A term often appearing in the literature in guidance and counseling is *group process*. In many instances the term is used interchangeably with *group dynamics* and *group counseling* and is not clearly defined.

Strang defines group process along the dimensions of group interaction and the role of the individual in the group. To her group process:

> . . . .implies a free interaction in which each member stimulates others to use their special abilities—also involved is a study of the role of the individual in the group—how he is influenced and how he influences others [26, p. 7].

The manual of the National Training Laboratories speaks of group process as a function of the focus of the observer of group interaction:

> When we observe what a group is talking about, we focus on the content.
> When we try to observe how the group is handling its communication, we are focusing on group process [21, p. 20].

Shertzer and Stone define process as continuous, dynamic, and directional in movement. Their definition of group process is somewhat similar to those of Strang and the National Training Laboratories:

> Group process refers to the interactions used by a group to maintain its
> identity as a group and its effects upon individuals who compose a group
> [24, p. 170].

In a broad sense group process refers to the "what" of group
behavior. It answers such questions as: What is happening in the group?
Who is interacting with whom? What effect are individuals having on each
other? What emotions and tasks are being discussed? What problems are
brought up for discussion and what decisions are being made?

PSYCHODRAMA—SOCIODRAMA

Psychodrama in essence is a technique in which the focus of activity
is upon an individual rather than the group although an audience group is
essential. Other essential elements for a psychodramatic production include
a stage, director, and auxiliary egos. The person who is the focal point of
the production may be enacting problems, events, and scenes from his
past or present or projecting himself into the future. The director serves
as coordinator of the production, and may call for responses from the
audience. Auxiliary egos may function as counselors and play "significant
other" roles in the process of the psychodrama. Through group discussion
following the enactment of a personal experience, participants gain new
insights into their own behavior and that of others.

The essential difference between psychodrama and sociodrama is one of
focus. In psychodrama the focus is upon a given individual and his particular problems while in sociodrama the main point of concern is with problems
of a group nature. For example a sociodrama may be conducted for a group
of teachers who are faced with problems of integrating Negroes into an
all-white school. The problem is one which concerns the school as a whole—
not just one staff member. Obviously the two are related and elements of
psychodrama spill over into sociodrama and vice versa.

Since psychodramatic and sociodramatic techniques can be employed
in group counseling, it would be beneficial for the reader to consult the
works of J. L. Moreno. Two excellent sources are *Group Psychotherapy—A
Symposium* [19] and *Psychodrama* [20] plus the prolific efforts of Moreno
and his associates in the journal *Group Psychotherapy*. A close study of
Cecilia Wells' article will illustrate the use of psychodrama in an educational setting.

GROUP STRUCTURE

As a group develops, membership roles become differentiated, status
positions emerge, and sub-groups begin to form providing the group with
an identifiable structure. The group will tend to place individuals in

various roles and individuals will begin to do the things they feel they can do in an efficient manner. The group "clown" may attempt to constantly punctuate the discussion with laughs, the chronic complainer may insist on viciously attacking the school, his classes or others in the group. Structure is also influenced by the status the member enjoys in social circles outside the group. Certain members of the group may direct their comments to individuals of high status and ignore those who do not occupy such positions.

Definitions of group structure seem to vary. Bennett defines group structure as all interrelated group behaviors:

> "Group structure" refers to all the behavior relationships within the group such as the status gradients depending upon the varying roles of individual members, clique relationships which involve the whole field of sociometry, and the nature of leadership [2, pp. 88–89].

Bonner writes of the psychological structure of the group and shows how group structure contributes to new learnings:

> Within this substructure of existing standards new regulations and norms emerge, roles are assumed by or ascribed to the members, hierarchial relations involving some differentiation of status arise and members begin to perceive themselves in relation to others and to their own common problem. Each person brings to the collective situation not only his own psychological being, but his society as a structure of norms and standards. When he enters into reciprocal relationship with others, he does not completely unlearn what he has already acquired, but modifies it in accordance with the expectations that arise in a new situation [4, p. 64].

Cartwright and Zander [5] indicate that structure has been achieved in a group when a group acquires some stability in the arrangement of relationship among its members. Glanz [9] emphasizes that group structure will determine the patterns of operation and action in a group. For example, free expression may be inhibited by a structure of superiority—inferiority relationships.

GROUP COHESIVENESS

Many investigations have been conducted to study such factors as the consensus in groups, the relative solidarity or lack of it in group functioning and the *espirit de corps* of groups. Many of these studies have attempted to determine what differences exist between groups characterized as cohesive and those which are not. Other research has attempted to analyze forces that tend to disrupt group functioning. In general researchers who have studied such problems are investigating certain aspects of *group cohesiveness* or those elements that bind groups together. Since group counseling is frequently concerned with some change in behavior of the group members, the concept of group cohesiveness is important in that the influence a group has in any behavior change of members is correlated with the attractiveness of the group for its members.

Group cohesiveness has been broadly defined by various authors and researchers. Glanz writes of group cohesiveness along the dimensions of attention, loyalty, and participation of members. To him cohesiveness is:

> . . . .the ability of the group to hold the attention, loyalty, and participation of its members. Cohesiveness is thought to be compounded out of group attractiveness, peer pressures, and personal motivations [9, p. 325].

Warters states that the cohesive group is characterized by high morale, teamwork and trust. Factors affecting cohesiveness are group goals, activities, size, organization, status and the ability to satisfy individual needs:

> Solidarity or cohesiveness is the overall attractiveness of a group for its members and its power to influence members and hold them in the group. The cohesive group is characterized by high morale, smooth teamwork, and mutual trust. In general its members are friendly together, understand and accept the groups' goals, feel strongly loyal to the group, like to brag about it, and are willing to work and even to sacrifice for it [27, p. 18].

Group cohesiveness, or lack of it, is of obvious concern to the group counselor. Students who are not used to counseling either as an individual process or in groups are not likely to be attracted to group counseling sessions unless the group is made attractive to them, and they can envision the counseling group as meeting certain individual needs. Counseling groups which do not develop into cohesive units are likely to be unproductive, and the counselees will tend to miss meetings, refuse to participate, or terminate counseling. The counselor cannot assume that placing students in a group will automatically generate cohesiveness.

GROUP NORMS

A group norm or group standard is simply a code of behavior that is accepted by the members of a group. As such it is a factor in group development that is related to group structure, cohesiveness, and other psychological phenomena of groups.

As a counseling group develops, a set of norms or standards for behavior tends to emerge. The way a group attacks a problem, the methods and procedures used to deal with topics and issues, and the patterns of communication evolve in ways that are approved by the group. The individual who joins a counseling group either knows or soon learns that his individual actions must generally be acceptable to the group as a whole. He does not talk when he pleases, and he may have to delay gratification of his own needs when the group is functioning on a topic that is not of direct concern to him. Acceptance in the group carries with it obligations to abide by the norms of the group. Too rigid enforcement of a norm by the group may serve to hinder group interaction and cause premature termination of a discussion or of counseling itself. At least one group therapist, Luchins, [17] feels that since norms are inevitable in groups, they should be formalized so that they are readily recognized and openly discussed. In contrast Slavson [25], among others, feels that group therapy is hindered by norms and goals.

NONVERBAL COMMUNICATION

In counseling groups as well as other situations where interpersonal relations are involved, the major form of communication is speech. In other words people talk to each other, listen to each other, and form attitudes, make decisions, and react to each other largely through use of the printed or spoken word. The whole nature of counseling, for example, is based on the concept of individuals verbally interacting and it is through such interaction that benefits occur.

On the other hand, most writers in the fields of counseling and therapy recognize the universality of nonverbal communication. Berger defines nonverbal communication as all of those messages other than verbal which reach ourselves and others about ourselves in the time-space continuum of our world.

> All those manifest and latent messages, other than verbal which reach ourselves and others about ourselves and the time-space continuum of the world we live in. These messages may be perceived through any of our body senses such as seeing, hearing, smelling, tasting, touching, and through thinking, feeling, dreaming, intuiting as well as extrasensory and other ways still unknown but in process [3, p. 161].

For Allport, nonverbal communication is a form of expression. It

> . . . .has a more limited meaning when it refers to such bodily changes as blushing, laughing, dilation of the pupil, quaking of the knees [1, p. 161].

Fromm seems to be speaking directly to both the individual and the counselor in discussing the importance of nonverbal communication:

> We express our moods by our facial expression and our attitudes and feelings by movements and gestures so precise that others recognize them more accurately from our gestures than our words [8, p. 17].

Lawson [15] points out that certain gestures and body movements play an important part in the lives of most individuals. Head movements for "yes" and "no" and hand and body movements are frequently used to communicate certain meanings. In the military services, especially in the infantry, soldiers are required to recognize and react to the nonverbal commands of the platoon leader.

We do not know enough at this point to attach specific meanings to each movement or facial expression of a student; nor may we ever be able to be completely certain of just what is meant by all gestures and body movements. The interpretation of nonverbal behavior in counseling is based on a consensus among writers and researchers [11].

REFERENCES

1. Allport, G. W. *Pattern and Growth in Personality* (New York: Holt, Rinehart and Winston, 1961).

2. Bennett, Margaret E. *Guidance in Groups* (New York: McGraw-Hill, 1955).

3. Berger, M. M. "Non-verbal Communication in Group Psychotherapy," *International Journal of Group Psychotherapy* (1954), 8, p. 161.

4. Bonner, Hubert. *Group Dynamics: Principles and Applications* (New York: The Ronald Press, 1959).

5. Cartwright, Dorwin and Zander, Alvin, (Eds). *Group Dynamics: Research and Theory* (New York: Harper and Row, 1960).

6. Cattell, Raymond B. "New Concepts for Measuring Leadership in Terms of Group Syntality," *Human Relations* (1951), 4, pp. 161–184.

7. Driver, Helen I. and others. *Counseling and Learning Through Small Group Discussion* (Madison, Wisconsin: Monona Publications, 1962).

8. Fromm, Erich. *The Forgotten Language* (New York: Rinehart, 1951).

9. Glanz, Edward C. *Groups in Guidance* (Boston: Allyn and Bacon, 1962).

10. Gulley, Halbert E. *Discussion, Conference and Group Process* (New York: Henry Holt, 1960).

11. Hahn, M. E. and MacLean, M. S. *Counseling Psychology* (New York: McGraw-Hill, 1955).

12. Hinkley, Robert G. and Hermann, Lydia. *Group Treatment in Psychotherapy* (Minneapolis: University of Minnesota Press, 1951).

13. Homans, George C. *The Human Group* (New York: Harcourt, Brace, 1950).

14. Kemp, C. Gratton. *Perspectives on the Group Process* (Boston: Houghton Mifflin Company, 1964).

15. Lawson, Joan. *European Folk Dance* (London: Pitman Co., 1953).

16. Lifton, Walter M. *Working with Groups: Group Process and Individual Growth* (New York: John Wiley and Sons, 1966).

17. Luchins, Abraham S. *Group Therapy: A Guide* (New York: Random House, 1964).

18. Mahler, Clarence A. and Caldwell, Edson. *Group Counseling In Secondary Schools* (Chicago: Science Research Associates, 1961).

19. Moreno, J. L. *Group Psychotherapy* (New York: Beacon Press, 1945).

20. Moreno, J. L. *Psychodrama* (New York: Beacon Press, 1946).

21. National Training Laboratories. *Reading Book, Seventeenth Annual Laboratories in Human Relations Training* (Washington, D.C.: National Education Association, 1963).

22. Patterson, C. H. *Counseling and Psychotherapy* (New York: Harper and Brothers, 1959).

23. Rogers, C. R. *On Becoming a Person* (Boston: Houghton Mifflin, 1961).

24. Shertzer, Bruce and Stone, Shelley C. *Fundamentals of Guidance* (Boston: Houghton Mifflin Company, 1966).

25. Slavson, S. R. "Group Psychotherapies" in J. L. McCary (Ed) *Six Approaches to Psychotherapy* (New York: Holt, Rinehart and Winston, 1955).

26. Strang, Ruth. *Group Work in Education* (New York: Harper and Brothers, 1958).

27. Warters, Jane. *Group Guidance, Principles and Practices* (New York: McGraw-Hill, 1960).

4

Psychodrama and Creative Counseling in the Elementary School*

Cecilia G. Wells

Detroit elementary schools have no sepcially designated counselors, that role being given to teachers, assistant principals and principals. Several years' experience with sociometric devices[1] as sociograms, role playing, sociodrama and some psychodrama have given the writer a background and feeling for the uses and values of these techniques in her counseling, one of several administrative responsibilities. In using these techniques the author was ever mindful of her role of assistant principal, and not that of therapist. With such an orientation, psychodramatic techniques were used as often as possible. Administrative limitations made it necessary to vary to some degree the traditional procedures of role playing, sociodrama and psychodrama. For us there could be no stage and seldom even a classroom. A crowded office, the hallway, the clinic, and even the stairway have been the loci of our role playing counseling. Such limitations, far from proving a handicap, served to stimulate more creative effort on the part of the counselor.

The problems of normal children included: quarrels over possessions, rivalry for position in a game or line, tripping or hitting each other—especially on the playground, interference with each other's classroom activities, classroom behavior unacceptable for the learning situation, and academic inadequacies. There was considerable range in degree of severity among these children from the first through eighth grade. There were occasions when role playing had to be postponed for another hour, or even days later, partly due to time and situation necessities, and sometimes because the writer was unaware of the psychodramatic possibilities until later.

Varying aspects of the psychodramatic process appeared, or were deliberately planned for use to tease out behavioral responses. The warm-up

°Presented at the Annual Meeting of the American Society of Group Psychotherapy and Psychodrama, April 25, 1959, in New York City. From *Group Psychotherapy*, 15 (1962), J. L. Moreno, M.D. Ed., Beacon House, Inc. publisher.

[1]Special thanks are herewith extended to Dr. Robert S. Drews, President of the Michigan Institute of Group Psychotherapy and Psychodrama. His inspiring guidance has made this work possible for the writer.

was included in the act which had caused the child to seek help, or to be brought to my attention. The warm-up continued in the re-playing of their own roles for clarification of the director and themselves. This preliminary action was also a readiness for the assumption of roles of others, or for new roles for themselves.

One noted how frequently the child mirrored the behavior of another. Occasionally the director was the "mirror," the scene sometimes ending in chuckles and giggles at the unprecedented behavior of the assistant principal exaggerating or even assuming the normal role of a child.

It was decidedly useful, and often fun, to be able to create an imaginary "Agg" or "Doe" for the occasion when it might have proved embarrassing or difficult to have the real child present. Not even the auxiliary chair is needed as such, although it was used when the situation might be improved by its use. Young children love to pretend and even twelve and thirteen year olds are not averse to use of the imaginary figures to address, or on which to vent anger.

Role reversal, double ego, soliloquy and conscience—all have been used, as well as a form of ego-building technique (although every form of role playing or sociodrama can contribute to ego-building).

The children and the writer have served in a variety of roles: directors, auxiliary egos, double egos, and protagonists interchangeably. The children are usually unaware of the designation and may be unaware that they are role playing.

The examples which follow represent only a single contact and in no respect indicate the follow-up which was in many instances a necessary part of the counseling at a later date.

PSYCHODRAMA IN SITU

For the child whose role has been constantly that of attention-getting in the classroom in undesirable ways, it may be ego-building to place him in a new role, one in which he is sent to the office for commendable reasons. Michael's story is of interest here. He is a seven year old boy in the second grade, whose frequent rule infractions had nearly depleted the stock of "better behavior tricks." One afternoon, in front of his class and teacher, the director asked that Michael be sent to the office every day—but for a new reason—that he was to bring one piece of acceptable quality work, or because he had been observed in one thoughtful act. He grinned at the assignment, his teacher cooperated beautifully, and Michael has brought at least fair work daily, except once; this he explained, was because his regular teacher being absent, there had been no written work to show. "But I did open the door for you, didn't I?" Last week he brought a treasured photograph of himself to show. Yesterday, though, he was guilty of very rough playground behavior and consequently must stay off the playground for a while. Perhaps the noon hour can be used for a different form of role playing, to help him in this other area.

For the boy or girl whose too rough playground behavior causes physical hurt to another, the role of attendant and nurse's aide helps toward a realization of the consequences of the act, and substitutes a role of service for an act of harm.

The untidy child at the table may one day be placed in the role of a "Service" boy or girl, helping to prepare the tables for the next group of children to use. Once or twice in that role is usually sufficient, although I have occasionally discovered a child intentionally being untidy, so as to be given that special attention that a lonely child may seek from an adult. One must be careful that the fun of role playing problems does not become so attractive as to cause the children to remain indoors seeking the company of adults instead of the company of their peers.

The younger ones frequently seek the director in the hall at noon, complaining of one kind of mistreatment or another on the playground, and expecting me to "settle" the argument or quarrel, and punish the other child. "Show me what *you* did" often forces him into quick recognition of his own shortcomings, and with a slight grin of embarrassment, he may make a hasty exit.

"*Show me how*" are magic words, unlocking many a situation, and dispensing with the need for adult pronouncements and punitive measures because of the added dimension of insight resulting from psychodramatic devices.

PSYCHODRAMA "ON THE SPOT"

As the director entered her office at noontime, she saw a mother and two six year old boys waiting on an office bench. Tommy and his mother had come because Ray had been involved *again* in a "fight" with her son. Mrs. M. disgustedly held up a pair of torn and very muddy trousers. "The third time this week," she explained. She added that she knew her son was no angel, "but. . . ." The boys were almost too ready to tell what happened, each talking so rapidly, and interrupting each other so constantly that the tale was incoherent. "Show me what happened, boys." They didn't understand, and began to talk again. "*Show me* just what each of you did." A few more efforts, and they began to act out the drama, without words. But the action was incomplete, and still a mystery to the mother and director. They were asked to reverse roles, and the director noted a little more of the story. Then the counseler assumed the role of Ray. He was asked to assume the role of the assistant principal trying to decide what to do about this situation. The director's role as Ray was one of pretended aggressiveness, even to seeming to push Tommy down. Surprisingly enough, it was not Ray who protested, but Tommy, who called out, "But he didn't push me down, Mrs. W. We were playing mud boats and we both fell in the mud, and I tore my pants on a tree stump." Tommy's mother was a silent but intrigued witness to this drama. At the conclusion of her son's statement, she nodded understandingly and said, "I'm satisfied. I don't feel so badly now. The trousers can be repaired and washed." For the director there was no need for the usual assignment of blame or punishment. The children were still friends, and the mother pleased at her son's role of truth teller.

More obvious sessions of role playing have been utilized by the writer for other counseling purposes: seeing individuals in their relationships within the group; facilitating deeper understanding of the dynamics of individual and group behavior; freeing a group or individuals from tensions; assessing the spontaneity-creativity potential.

PSYCHODRAMATIC FUTURE ENACTMENT

A class of thirty-five sixth grade boys and girls—eleven year olds—recently was introduced to role playing as such for the first time, and with delightful results. The children were asked to imagine themselves acting in a career role they might be assuming some twenty years hence. They were instructed to show only bodily action, exclusive of speech, unless imagining a partner or auxiliary ego to whom they wished to talk. One by one they enthusiastically came forward.

Rex set a fine example, eagerly and unmistakably becoming an auto mechanic, entering so completely into the spirit of the occasion that he lay on his back on the floor, repairing the car suspended above him. His spontaneity made it easier for others to participate freely.

Sandra, without hesitation, let us know of her love for horses, and proceeded to use the mare as guide for training the young colt in its routine.

Carol had a similar interest, but wanted to raise horses, not train them. She gave the colts tender care, patting them freely as she fed them, and showing her pleasure at the act.

Serious Sammy, with more restricted, tense body, conducted an orchestra at rehearsal, mimicing a "No" to an erring group of violinists. One wondered at his satisfactions.

In the role of artist, pale Lorraine came alive. She seemed happy and relaxed as she examined her oil painting and found it to her satisfaction.

We were a little less sure of Pat's role—perhaps because she was unsure. Was she a mother wheeling a baby carriage, as many thought? Urging her to enlarge on her action, we learned that she wanted to be a nurse, and watched her get mixed up in her handling of the instruments to the doctor. Pat then volunteered, "My mother always wanted to be a nurse, and I guess that's why I want to be." What a responsive note that struck with the director, who had become a teacher for a similar reason, and was able to empathize with the child.

Nancy also wanted to be a nurse, explaining her desire as an outgrowth of an experience caring for an older sister during an acute illness. We did not feel enthusiasm in her role.

What dreams Sue has of being a pianist! This tense little girl pretended to play, quite aloof form the group—her customary relationship. Her fingers stiffly manipulated the keys. Perhaps this revelation of herself could be of some importance in understanding and working with this tired-looking child.

As another Michael competently moved at his workbench with test tubes and chemicals, one felt sure of him—that he would be capable in whatever career he chose, whether developing new chemical formulae for a space age, or medicines for a hospital—as he indicated.

Perhaps the action of Dennis was most enjoyed and most revealing in this group. He almost literally threw himself into the role of baseball batter. Surely he had made a home run after that resounding whack at the ball. This was not pretend! Here was a boy who had difficulty selecting from among three sports to demonstrate, and hoped to be a baseball player and football team member so as to be employed all year round in sports." Frankie does that," he indicated forcefully. Here was a boy constantly in trouble for shoving and pushing and knocking down other children at noon. What tremendous energy, and definiteness of purpose, needing to be channeled. He gave significant clues for his guidance.

PSYCHODRAMA IN THE "HERE AND NOW"

As the class was leaving, two boys began to pummel each other quite angrily. In raising their hands to answer a question, they had bumped arms, and became angry over the supposed intent to hurt on the part of each. They remained in the room while a new class came in. The boys were asked to re-play the situation, for each blamed the other for striking first. How quickly this had happened! How ready they were to fight. Each was then asked to take the role of the other. This they did less well. On being asked how they felt, Marshall said, "Sad." "Worried," Bob answered. They really were worried, lest in the role of assistant principal the director punish them for fighting, by calling their parents. This was not the first time these two had clashed. Bob was asked to be the assistant principal—to the accompaniment of much giggling by the new pupils now in the room. The director took Bob's role, and soliloquized the worries over the form of punishment, hoping that the assistant would let them make up and be friends instead of calling in their parents to help. Marshall uneasily joined the director in conversation—and understandingly so. The boys, in their own roles again, were able to shake hands, weakly at first, then more vigorously. They seemed to have patched up their differences, the original incident and anger dispelled by the novelty of a new way of settling a fight.

For the director, there were special insights from this occurrence. The boys saw the assistant only as one who punishes, and who calls their parents. How often had the mother and father been placed in a threat role, unintentionally! In her future dealings with children there will be more careful evaluation of the role into which parents are cast.

The twisted face of Marshall in anger will not easily be forgotten. Much more counseling is going to be needed by that boy.

This had been a revealing and worthwhile forty minutes, to the director and to the pupils. The class was unified by their interest in performing, and in seeing the the performances of their classmates. When could they finish, and do this again? The director was aware of their personalities, not only through their role playing, but through the observations some had made of the action, noting smiles and other facial expressions, as well as bodily postures of the performers. The director felt the contagious quality of both the sure, competent acting person, as well as the negative quality of the unsure child. The tone of this group seemed of a positive nature, judging from the spontaneity exhibited.

The eight-year-old children had watched the role playing of the two angry boys with fascination. Their music teacher had not arrived, so the activity could be continued with them. Here was a perfect opportunity to share with them a new kind of experience.

PSYCHODRAMATIC ROLE PERCEPTION AND ENACTMENT

This time four children from a row were asked to show some actions of a policeman. The audience was to watch for the actions that told them the performers were really in role. Each of the four responded with different degrees of enthusiasm and accuracy. One gave a motorist a ticket and a stern lecture, another blew his whistle vigorously to stop traffic, and signalled with his arms for the traffic to cross in the other direction. One waited and watched, as a policeman might, while the fourth imitated another. Grant gave the most convincing performance, putting himself happily and energetically into role. The director noted with care the child who imitated.

A second group of four were clowns. Such spotaneity in this group! Russell's performance gave most evidence of pleasure as he tumbled, turned somersaults, pretended to trip, and gave himself completely to the act. Here was Russell in as happy a mood as the director had ever seen—a little boy whose home conditions were certainly conducive to strain and tension.

The two little girls were true to themselves, as they tried at first to take part, and gradually stood by to watch. After all, this was not for girls—this tumbling about on the floor with pretty dresses.

Individuals were then called upon, to enact any role they chose. We learned that Jimmy would love to be a fireman, and his face was smiling as he slid down the pole at the engine house.

Ellen seriously tap danced for us, displaying the carefully measured actions of the professional dancing school. The director hoped for an opportunity to see her improving. She didn't seem at all happy in her chosen role.

Peter chose to be a rifleman, getting more and more vigorous as he managed his machine gun, and obvious pleasure in "mowing 'em down."

Debbie was the last to show herself in role. She too is from a "broken" family, a noisy, aggressive, very talkative child—frequently the despair of her teachers. The director was stunned by her portrayal. She quietly pretended to lift a baby from its bed, lovingly and tenderly rocked it, eyes closed, head bowed, and humming a soft tune. She wanted to be a mother! This was complete role reversal for Debbie. Could this be the expression of her own great need to be tenderly cuddled and mothered? At lunch time she explained that it was hard for her to do what she did, but as she spoke, her eyes were shining! Her action had seemed so relaxed and spontaneous, that it was difficult to believe the action had not been easy. Her teachers are going to learn about the Debbie the director saw and began at that moment to love.

What magic keys these children had given, today and previously—keys for unlocking doors to their own futures, if need be. One must guard against reading into the actions one sees, however. Keys were best used by the counseler to *open* doors, not close them.

For the children role playing creates a new means for dealing with some of their day-to-day and face-to-face situation. Insight seems to follow action and feeling. For the writer, the abovementioned psychodramatic techniques have facilitated the counseling process. They have caused her to invent new words, places and ways to meet unexpected situations. Her own role of an administrator has changed from one of decision-making for the children to one of guidance in formulating their own decisions, making their own choices and taking greater responsibility for their own actions than heretofore.

The writer is aware of her own growth in ability to understand and use these psychodramatic tools creatively. Earliest experiences were all of the more obvious nature, with emphasis on the dramatic, role acting, as a device to help one teach less routinely. As understanding develops through practice and interpretation the subtleties and nuances of the method become apparent, particularly in a sensing of the personal roles that we are constantly assuming. One learns to utilize knowledge of these roles for more effective personal relationships without a stage or even role casting as such. "Among the things in his own world which man creates is his self—his personality."[2]

The word creative as used by this writer is synonymous with spontaneity, as she understands the terms. Even though a child's responses to a situation may seem stilted, cliched, and of the conforming variety, there is in every action something of the unique quality of that individual which can be noted and utilized; something new and unrehearsed which can lead to self-acceptance and self-fulfillment.

Listening is creative when there is reached a point of awareness of the time to interpose a question, to repeat a word or phrase, or to continue listening. No less artistry is required for role playing than is required in combining pigments for a special color on the palette, or the precise numbers and colors of strands for the beautifully woven fabric.

Continued use of psychodramatic techniques gives to this counseler a heightened awareness of human roles and their significance for education. She has learned to sense and utilize to greater degree the possibilities of these tools. She has learned to use clues arising from the spontaneous and creative behavior of the children to help them grow in power to give point and direction to their own lives, improving the quality of their inter-personal relationships, and enriching their moments with more creative experiences.

[2]Robert B. Haas, *Psychodrama and Sociodrama in American Education* (New York: Beacon House, 1949).

Chapter III

CAN COUNSELING BE A GROUP FUNCTION?

The traditional definitions of counseling have almost always implied that successful counseling was an individual relationship in which effective growth was the result of a specialized relationship between two individuals. As a result, group counseling has failed to experience the rapid growth that has characterized individual counseling.

Opponents of counseling in groups have pointed out that such matters as confidentiality are hard to control, that the individual receives only partial help from the counselor, and that students are reluctant to discuss personal problems in the presence of peers. While counselors have long used groups to teach occupation classes and dispense career material, many have been reluctant to initiate group sessions where the emphasis is on the personal concerns of the student. Some have contended that counseling as it is generally defined is impossible in group situations.

Opponents of group counseling, however, have failed to recognize the importance of groups to the individual. Wrenn[1] states that it is the rare counselor indeed who can enter into the world of the adolescent since most youth consider the adult too far removed from what they consider to be important. Thus many seek the help of their peers for answers to important questions in their lives. Other writers, among them Ohlsen, indicate that group counseling is particularly appropriate for adolescents since a client who participates in a group can discover:

> (1) that his peers have problems too, (2) that in spite of his faults which his peers want him to correct they can accept him, (3) that at least one adult, the counselor, can accept and understand him, (4) that he is capable of understanding, accepting, and helping his peers, (5) that he can trust others, and (6) that expressing his own real fears about himself and others, and about what he believes helps him understand and accept himself [3, p. 148].

If we can accept such reasoning, it would seem that group counseling is not only possible, but in some instances to be preferred to individual counseling.

---

[1] Personal communication.

Individual growth is possible within the group setting since complete development of the individual is contingent upon interaction with his peers. The child who participates in a counseling group learns to face his problems, analyze them in the light of the perceptions of others, and discover ways to solve some of his problems. We have also long known that children need approval from others, and more than anything else desire such approval from peers. Group interaction provides the client with a psychological climate that can be stimulating rather than competitive, a condition that is often lacking in the academic aspects of school life.

Bradford and Lippitt [1] in attempting to show that the individual can gain from group participation point out that among other gains the individual (1) becomes sensitive to the needs of individual members, (2) shares in the setting of group goals, and (3) is encouraged to feel independent, and to grow and improve. The counselor who is working with groups must remember that the growth of the individual is his foremost concern, but that the use of groups to promote individual growth has definite advantages.

The articles in this section have been selected primarily to allow the reader to become acquainted with some of the writings of those who have been concerned with the question of counseling as an individual or a group function. Must counseling be individual? Does group counseling merely serve as a catalytic agent for individual counseling, or is it effective in its own right? Is group counseling as effective as individual counseling in modifying behavior, and can group counseling be used in test interpretation? What available evidence do we have to show that group counseling is more or less effective than individual counseling in helping the student select a vocation? The following selections may provide some answers to these questions.

REFERENCES

1. Bradford, L. P. and Lippett, L. "The Individual Counts—In Effective Group Relations," *Group Development*, National Training Laboratories (Washington, D.C.: National Education Association, 1961).

2. Hinkley, R. G. and Hermon, Lydia. *Group Treatment In Psychotherapy* (Minneapolis: University of Minnesota Press, 1951).

3. Ohlsen, Merle M. *Guidance Services In The Modern School* (New York: Harcourt, Brace and World, 1965).

5

Must Counseling Be Individual?*

Clifford P. Froehlich

Traditionally, definitions of counseling have stated or implied that the individual interview was THE *modus operandi* of counseling. This position has been challenged by the writer and others who, from their own experience, have felt that the group approach was a potentially effective avenue to counseling objectives. The writer coined the term "multiple counseling" to designate a procedure in which a counselor works simultaneously with several counselees manifesting symptoms of at least one problem in common. The details of the multiple counseling approach have been reported elsewhere [4, 5]. To date, the relative effectiveness of multiple and individual counseling has been largely a matter of conjecture. Bilovsky [1] reported a comparison of individual and group counseling, but the data were not reported in a manner which yielded clearcut evidence of counseling effectiveness. Driver [3] and Peres [7] also presented research on the effectiveness of multiple counseling, but they did not compare it with individual counseling. It is the purpose of this study[1] to do so.

The most difficult task confronting the person who wishes to evaluate counseling is the selection of a criterion, because there is none about which it is feasible to collect data and which has been widely accepted by counselors. The major criterion in this study, therefore, was not selected because of its general acceptance; rather, it was chosen because, from the writer's orientation, it reflects a logical outcome of counseling, and because it is being used in a series of studies of which this is one.

The criterion was agreement between self-rating and test scores. Both pre-counseling and post-counseling ratings are compared with test scores. Application of the criterion assumes that a person should learn about himself during counseling. If he does, presumably his self ratings should be in closer agreement with his tested abilities after counseling than before.

The students used as subjects in this study were seniors in a large California high school. The problem they had in common was an indicated

*Reprinted by permission of the publisher and with the consent of Mrs. Edna P. Froehlich from *Educational and Psychological Measurement*, 18 (1958), 681–689.
[1]The writer is indebted to Mr. Shepard Insel, Director, Student Personnel Services and Research, Sequoia Senior High School District, California, for his assistance in gathering data for this study.

desire for more information about themselves in order to make post-high-school plans. The students participated in the testing and counseling program voluntarily; part of the testing was done outside of school hours. The decision regarding which students were provided with individual counseling and which had multiple counseling was made arbitrarily and was influenced primarily by practical consideration of scheduling. Seventeen students were counseled individually, and 25 were counseled in small groups of four to six students.

In this study, self-ratings were obtained by asking students to rate themselves before counseling and again after counseling. Each subject rated himself on a five point scale in each of the areas measured by the *Differential Aptitude Tests*; these areas are listed in Table 2. In order to facilitate statistical treatment of the data, each step on the rating scale was assigned a numerical value from one through five; the highest rating was assigned five, the next highest, four; and so on. Because the extreme steps contained so few cases, they were combined with adjacent steps when the data were processed. That is, ratings of one were combined with ratings of two, and ratings of five were combined with ratings of four. Hence, for each subject there were eight pre-counseling ratings and eight post-counseling ratings distributed on a three-step scale: the first step which was given a value of two included ratings of one and two, the next step with a value of three contained only ratings of three, and the last step with a value of four included ratings of four and five.

In addition to rating himself before and after counseling each student completed the *Differential Aptitude Test* battery. The scores on this test were converted to centile ranks and were then assigned numerical values of two, three, or four in a manner similar to the assignment of numerical values to the rating scale steps. Centile ranks of 76 or above were assigned a value of four, ranks from 25 through 75 were given the value of three, and ranks below 25 were classified as two. As a result, each student had a rated-test-score value of two, three, or four for each of the eight areas of the *Differential Aptitude Test*. Throughout the remainder of this report, the phrase "test score" is used to refer to rated-test-score value obtained in the manner just described.

THE FINDINGS

The data in Table 1 summarize the agreement between ratings and test scores for all eight areas taken together. The first category indicates the total number of ratings that were the same as the corresponding test score both before and after counseling. In other words, the rating was correct before counseling. Hence, no change in rating was required to bring it into the agreement with the corresponding test score. The post-counseling rating

Table 1

Agreement of Ratings and Test Scores before and after
Counseling by Two Methods of Counseling

Categories of Agreement	Individual counseling	Multiple counseling	Total by category
Pre- and post-counseling ratings both agree with test score (no change, none required)	48	78	126
Pre-counseling rating not in agreement with test, but post-counseling rating agreed (correct change)	27	38	65
Pre- and post-counseling ratings agree with each other, but not with test score (no change, one required)	29	51	80
Pre- and post-counseling do not agree with each other; the post-counseling rating does not agree with test score (incorrect change)	32	33	65
Total ratings (8 times number of subjects)	136	200	xxx

was the same as the pre-counseling rating; therefore, it also agreed with the test score. Of the 336 ratings available, 126, or 38 per cent required no change. The counseling objective in this case was merely one of confirming the counselee's original rating.

The second category of Table 1 contains those pre-counseling ratings which were not in agreement with test scores before counseling but the corresponding post-counseling ratings were in agreement. Such a change in ratings reflects a desired outcome of counseling if it is assumed that correctness of ratings is related in a meaningful way to self-concept and this in turn to choices which might be made by the counselee. Sixty-five, or 19 per cent of all ratings were of this type.

In the third classification are those post-counseling ratings which were the same as corresponding pre-counseling ratings neither of which agreed with its test-score counterpart. These were 80 such ratings, 24 per cent of the total. Essentially, counseling in this instance was ineffective.

The final category contains cases in which the first rating was not the same as the second rating and neither the first nor second rating agreed with the rated test score. Persons whose ratings fell into this category may be considered counseling failures according to the criterion applied in this study. There were 65 ratings of this type, 19 per cent of the total.

The distributions of agreement of ratings and test scores by categories for individual and multiple counseling reported in Table 1 were tested by chi-square to see if the hypothesis that they came from the same population was tenable. It must be remembered that for chi-square to be an appropriate test in this instance the independence of the entries in the cells of Table 1 had to be assumed [6, 8]. On this assumption chi-square was found to be 3.032, which is not statistically significant. Hence, it was concluded that no difference in the effectiveness of counseling methods are judged by the agreement criterion used in this study was revealed by the data in Table 1. This finding is negative in the sense that the superiority of either individual or multiple counseling is not demonstrated. Because it was believed that the assumption or method of treating the data may have not revealed differences further analyses were made.

The criterion was applied to the data in another manner. This was done by comparing the number of ratings which agreed with test scores before counseling with the number which agreed after counseling. The results of this comparison are reported in percentage form in Table 2. The first row

Table 2

Percentage of Ratings in Agreement with Test Score

D.A.T. Area	Individual Counseling		Multiple Counseling	
	Pre-counseling rating	Post-counseling rating	Pre-counseling rating	Post-counseling rating
Verbal reasoning	59	71	64	68
Numerical reasoning	53	53	48	76
Abstract reasoning	59	76	60	56
Space relations	47	59	36	52
Mechanical reasoning	59	35	48	72
Clerical speed and accuracy	47	47	44	48
Spelling	41	47	60	76
Sentences	35	65	52	60

of this table indicates that 59 per cent of the pre-counseling ratings of verbal reasoning agreed with test scores and 71 per cent of the post-counseling ratings agreed. Comparable figures for multiple counseling are 64 and 68, respectively. Succeeding rows in this table, with few exceptions, reveal substantially the same picture a slightly higher percentage of agreement for post-counseling ratings than for pre-counseling ratings. Albeit, when a test of significance was applied, none of the differences between the pre- and post-counseling percentage of agreement was statistically significant.

The number of agreements upon which the percentage in Table 2 are based, were summed for all areas of the test. The resulting totals and corresponding percentages are presented in Table 3.

Table 3

Agreement between Test Scores and All Ratings
for Individual and Multiple Counseled Group

	Individual		Multiple	
	Number	Per cent [a]	Number	Per cent [b]
Pre-counseling rating	68	50	103	52
Post-counseling rating	77	57	127	64

[a] Based on N = 136 ratings, 8 for each of 17 individuals before and after counseling.
[b] Based on N = 200 ratings, 8 for each of 25 individuals before and after counseling.

The significance of the difference between the percentage of ratings in agreement with tests before individual counseling and the percentage after counseling was found to be at .10 level. In contrast, the comparable difference for the multiple counseled group was significant at the .008 level. After multiple counseling the subjects in this study apparently brought their ratings into closer agreement with their scores than before counseling. Individual counseling appears not to have influenced self rating in a significant way.

Another approach to evaluation of the data was made through the use of an index number which reflected relative agreement between an individual's test score and his rating. Preliminary to computing this index, a numerical value was assigned to each rating and test score in the manner previously described. The pre-counseling-agreement index was computed by subtracting the test-score value from the pre-counseling rating value and adding a constant of five to eliminate negative numbers and summing these figures for the eight areas for each individual. The process is illustrated by the following data concerning one student:.

	D.A.T. Areas							
	1	2	3	4	5	6	7	8
Pre-counseling-rating value	3	4	2	3	4	3	4	2
Test-score value	2	3	3	3	4	3	2	2
Rating value less score value plus constant of five	6	6	4	5	5	5	7	5

In the first column the result of the subtraction of the test-score value from the pre-counseling-rating value and the addition of a constant of five was six, shown in the last row. When all of the eight figures in the last row were added, the total was found to be 43, his pre-counseling-agreement index. The post-counseling agreement index was computed in a similar manner except that post-counseling ratings were used. The mean and standard deviation for pre-counseling and for post-counseling indices for the individual counseled group and for the multiple counseled group were computed, the resulting statistics are reported in Table 4. When the significance of the differences between the means in Table 4 was evaluated by the t-ratio,

Table 4

Means, Standard Deviations, and t-Ratios between
Means of Total Agreement Indices

	Individual Counseled		Multiple Counseled		t between means in same row
	Mean	Standard Deviation	Mean	Standard Deviation	
Pre-counseling index	39.8	3.18	41.2	2.72	1.44
Post-counseling index	40.7	3.84	41.0	2.79	.27
Between means in same column	1.10		.29		

none was found to be significant. The conclusions based on this method of analysis must be stated in negative terms: neither individual nor multiple counseling appeared to affect the means of the agreement indices. Likewise, the means of the individual and multiple groups are essentially the same.

The agreement index has a definite shortcoming in that the effect of ratings which were too high in terms of corresponding test score could be cancelled out by low ratings. The net result is an obliteration of the individual's variability of agreement between his ratings and score. Cronbach and Gleser [2] have discussed a method of profile analysis which overcomes this limitation. The method defines similarity between profiles in terms of the linear distance between the respective points on the profiles being compared. The eight pre-counseling ratings were treated as one profile, the post-counseling ratings as another, and the test scores as the third. A pre-counseling-profile-agreement score was computed by the formula (rating value—score value)^2 The method of computation is illustrated by the data for the student who was used to illustrate the computation of the agreement index.

	D.A.T. Areas							
	1	2	3	4	5	6	7	8
Pre-counseling rating value	3	4	2	3	4	3	4	2
Test-score value	2	3	3	3	4	3	2	2
Rating value minus score value	1	1	-1	0	0	0	2	0
(Rating value minus score value)^2	1	1	1	0	0	0	4	0

In the first column, the test-score value has been subtracted from the pre-counseling-rating value, the difference was one, the square of this was one, as shown in the third and fourth rows, respectively. The figures in the last row were added, their total, seven, is the pre-counseling-profile-agreement score. In a like manner, the post-counseling-profile-agreement scores were computed. The mean and standard deviation of the pre- and post-counseling-profile-agreement scores for the individual counseled group and for the multiple counseled group were obtained and are shown in Table 5. The difference between the mean of the pre-counseling-profile-agreement

Table 5

Means, Standard Deviations, and t-ratios
between Means of Profile-Agreement Scores

	Individual Counseled (N = 17)		Multiple Counseled (N = 25)		t-ratio between means in same row
	Mean	S.D.	Mean	S.D.	
Pre-counseling-profile score...........	2.176	.859	2.284	.514	.452
Post-counseling-profile score..........	2.146	.992	1.992	.338	.592
t-ratio between means in same column....	.136		2.584		

scores and the mean of the post-counseling-profile-agreement scores for the multiple counseled group is significant at the .05 level, no other difference between the means in Table 5 is significant. This analysis of the data appears to favor the conclusion that multiple counseling is more effective in terms of the criterion than is individual counseling. These data also point out that the individual and multiple counseled were very similar both before and after counseling.

In addition to the criterion described, a supplementary criterion based on counselee rating of counselor helpfulness was also used. Counselees rated on a five-point scale the amount of help they thought they had received from the counselor. This criterion was used to determine if the counselees would be more favorably impressed by an individual interview than by the group situation. Some counselors believe that because a counselee gets individual attention in a private interview a situation is created in which he feels comfortable and is helped thereby to move toward counseling objectives. On the other hand, these counselors view the group situation as threatening and productive of negative attitudes toward the process. After the ratings were converted to numerical values in the manner previously described, the mean of the individual counseled group was found to be 4.06 and the standard deviation equaled .56. The multiple counseled group was found to have a mean of 3.94, the standard deviation was .68. A t-test of the difference between means revealed that it was not statistically significant. The subjects in both groups were apparently not different in their evaluation of their counselor's helpfulness.

DISCUSSION

Of course, like other studies of counseling effectiveness the criteria used in this study may be questioned because they do not indicate what actions the counselee took as a result of counseling. But if self-knowledge is a necessary prelude to intelligent planning and doing, then the self-rating criterion has the endorsement of a logical approach.

The writer recognizes the limitations imposed upon the conclusions by the smallness of the sample, the use of a single test, and similar shortcomings. Nevertheless, the data presented in this report point to one major conclusion: Insofar as the criteria used in this study reflect desirable counseling outcomes, the findings do not support the claim that counseling must be individual.

REFERENCES

1. Bilovsky, David and others. "Individual and Group Counseling," *Personnel and Guidance Journal*, XXXI (1953), 363–365.

2. Cronbach, Lee J. and Gleser, Goldine C. "Assessing Similarity between Profiles," *Psychological Bulletin*, L (1953), 456–473.

3. Driver, H. I. "Small Group Discussion," *Personnel and Guidance Journal,* XXXI (1952), 173–175.

4. Froehlich, C. P. *Multiple Counseling*—A Research Proposal (Berkeley: School of Education, University of California (no date), p. 7) mimeo.

5. Hoppock, Robert. *Group Guidance: Principles, Techniques, and Evaluation* (New York: McGraw-Hill, 1950).

6. Lewis, Don and Burke, C. J. "The Use and Misuse of the Chi-square Test," *Psychological Bulletin*, XLVI (1949), 433–489.

7. Peres, H. "An Investigation of Nondirective Group Therapy," *Journal of Consulting Psychology*, XI (1947), 159–172.

8. Peters, Charles C. "The Misuse of Chi-square—A Reply to Lewis and Burke," *Psychological Bulletin*, XLVII (1950), 331–337.

6

Small-Group Discussion as an Aid in Counseling*

Helen Irene Driver

Can sociodrama and small-group discussion be used in the counseling program of a high school? Do they have value as learning media? Does their use help the student gain in self-understanding and in understanding and tolerance of others? Do they increase his skill in interpersonal relations? These were some of the questions investigated by the writer in a recent study.

Many psychiatrists and guidance experts emphasize the value of group activity as an adjunct to the counseling process. There is a definite need for multiple counseling in school guidance programs. In multiple counseling small-group discussion activity, in which the counselor is a nondirective leader and participant, is combined with individual counseling interviews, where a counselee privately discusses personal problems with which he became concerned through the group activity.

The writer believed that small-group discussion might prove to be as significant for the personality growth of so-called "normal" individuals as it has been found to be in the reintegration and rehabilitation of the maladjusted. The effort to test that belief consisted in an exploratory investigation of multiple counseling using small-group discussion on three maturity levels: high-school, university undergraduate, and adult. This article is a report on the high-school project.

Professor Ruth Strang recently presented a strong case for group activity as a learning medium in in personality development. She criticized the narrow concept of vocational guidance in schools because social aspects, such as interpersonal skills and the welfare of society, are neglected. She says: "Guidance *to what* and guidance *for what* have been neglected. . . . There is little evidence that either counselors or students are actually concerned with the social aspects of their life adjustment."[1]

°Reprinted from *School Review*, LIX (1951), pp. 525–530, by Helen Irene Driver by perr ..on of The University of Chicago Press. Copyright 1951 by The University of Chicago.

[1]Ruth Strang, "Social Aspects of Vocational Guidance," *School Review*, LVII (September 1950), 327.

Neglect of human relations areas in the family, community, and on the job would seem to be inexcusable when we know that lack of skill in understanding and getting along with others is the basic cause of failures rather than the lack of technical skills.

PROCEDURES OF THE PROJECT

The writer organized the high-school multiple counseling project as an activity club called Personology Club. It was publicized through the Senior home rooms with the following announcement:

> This club is open to a limited number of Seniors who are interested in learning more about their own personalities and skills in getting along with other people. The club will meet for group discussions at the regular activity hour, Monday and Thursday, from 1:40 to 2:30. Individual vocational-aptitude and personality tests will be given to all group members.

Three boys and seven girls elected the club for the first semester. In the second semester five boys and five girls were selected for club membership from the fifteen who signed up for it. Selection was made to provide heterogeneity of race, religion, and socioeconomic background. The group was limited to ten members so that all could participate in free discussions, which consumed approximately thirty minutes of each activity period. Seventeen discussion mettings were held each semester, and additional periods were used for group tests and written evaluations. The writer served as group leader and counselor. She administered an individual projective test and held two counseling interviews with each student during the project.

The discussion topics focused on self-understanding, individual differences, and interpersonal relations. Sociodramas and introductory talks provided the springboard for the free discussions. Questions thrown out to the group were similar to those raised in books for teen-agers, such as *Understanding Ourselves*[2] and *Discovering Myself*.[3]

The writer worked on the assumption that understanding and accepting one's self is essential to understanding and accepting others. However, social problems, such as racial and religious prejudices and ways to develop tolerance for others, were also important discussion topics. As a learning medium, the free discussions were used to analyze the personal experiences, viewpoints, and prejudices of group members and to develop principles of human behavior for self-adjustment and for social adjustment of everyday living.

The two groups (those in the first semester and those in the second se-

[2]Helen Schacter, *Understanding Ourselves* (Bloomington, Illinois: McKnight & McKnight, 1945).

[3]Bernice L. Neugarten, *Discovering Myself* (Chicago: National Forum, Inc. 1946).

mester) of high-school students were very different in membership and re-acted in contrasting fashion to the discussions. Group I, made up of three boys and seven girls, consisted of a majority of poorly adjusted students, unhappy in school or home relationships. The five boys and five girls in Group II were well-adjusted students, several of whom were school leaders. While Group I was vitally interested in discussions pertaining to "why we like or dislike people" (teachers, parents, siblings, "dates," etc.), Group II was bored with such topics and preferred to concentrate on vocational goals, development of inter-personal skills, and social adjustability.

The characteristics of the groups varied greatly. Group I members were emotional, aggressive, and uninhibited. At the beginning of the semester, the girls disliked the boys, and there was much controversy between the two sexes. This slowly dissolved as the members became better acquainted. After seventeen meetings the majority of the students agreed that they had gained understanding, respect, and liking for one another. Group II members were restrained, tactful, and unemotional. Only one member was uninhibited and able to speak freely of her personal feelings and problems. The discussions were on an intellectual level, and the writer was treated as a teacher or faculty adviser rather than as a fellow-participant (as in the Group I discussions).

Both groups enjoyed the sociodramas, and all students showed talent in spontaneous role-taking of unrehearsed dramatizations. The topics included racial and religious discrimination, right and wrong ways to apply for a job, individual differences in emotional reactions, motivational patterns, life-adjustment goals, and defensive behavior. Sociodrama was especially valuable for shy students and for students who were not able to express their feelings in words. They were able to perform creditably even though they appeared tongue-tied in the general discussions.

In addition to the discussion meetings, students wrote self-appraisals, sociograms, and autobiographies. They were given the Minnesota Multiphasic Personality Inventory, the Strong Vocational Interest Blank, and the Make-a-Picture-Story projective personality test.

The first counseling interview with each student was held during the last week of the group meetings. Its purpose was to give the student a picture of himself as shown by the inventories, sociograms, behavior observations, and comments of his fellow-discussants. The discussion which followed compared the student's self-concept with the concept of him held by others. Directive counseling for self-adjustment and social adjustment climaxed the interview hour. The student and the counselor worked out together constructive activities which the student could use to correct personal weaknesses and to improve his skill in interpersonal relationships. A follow-up interview was held with each student one to two months later to evaluate his progress and to discuss any new problems or needs.

Because of the excellent rapport which had been established through co-participation of counselor and students in the discussion activity of the group meetings, all students appeared to welcome the opportunity to talk confidentially and to ask assistance in the first counseling interview.

OUTCOMES OF THE PROJECT

The twenty students in the high-school project could be classified according to their felt needs, which were stated or implied aims in electing Personology Club: (1) well-adjusted students who enjoyed group discussion as an activity; (2) well-adjusted students who wished to learn more about personality and interpersonal skills; (3) shy or nonverbal students, dissatisfied with their participation in group discussion activity and with their verbal ability, who wished to improve their social skills; (4) students who were dissatisfied with vocational plans or choices and wished to get help through vocational guidance; and (5) poorly adjusted students who were dissatisfied with their self-adjustment and social adjustment and wished to get help in these areas.

The case-study method was used in evaluating the learning gained through the project experience. The kind of learning gained by a student depended on his interest and need. However, he was exposed to fundamental principles of self-adjustment and social adjustment, to the "whys" of tolerance and respect for viewpoints of others. The social-learning core of the project was the essential difference between an individual counseling process and a multiple-counseling process based on small-group discussion. Herein lies the significance of outcomes which are socially based rather than individualistic.

If we use a definition of "personality" as the social stimulus value of a person, then personality growth must be associated with group or social interaction. Thus, small-group discussion focused on daily-life experiences of its members should be an effective learning medium for individual and social competence. Outcomes for the twenty students in this investigation agreed with this assumption. Changes in self-understanding, in understanding and acceptance of others, improvement in self-adjustment and in social adjustment are illustrated by statements made by individual students at the end of the project or in the following counseling interview. Samples of these statements follow.

CONCERNING SELF

Knowledge (Insight)

I could see how my opinion and others could both be right.

It irritated me when kids are rebellious to other people's views, yet I know I am that way too.

Comparision of myself with the others helped to give me a clearer picture of myself.

I am more moody and self-centered than is good.

I learned that I shouldn't make snap judgments of people.

Attitudes and Appreciations

I should accept different points of view more than I've done in the past.

I should be more friendly to others, try to get along better with others.

Arguing and talking was fun.

You had a chance to explain yourself; it makes you feel better and clears up one's ideas.

I could feel just like the ones in the sociodramas, could see both points of view.

The club gave me a feeling of being worth something as an individual; we don't get this in classes.

Skills (Behavior)

Before this I couldn't stand up in English class and give a book report; now I can and have given two in succession.

The test results helped settle my mind, made me feel I was going in the right direction.

I've learned to make conversation a little better lately.

I've been doing things in groups more and find I enjoy it.

I'm working on my weaknesses and have made some improvement.

CONCERNING OTHERS

Knowledges

I understand why [member of family, teacher, boy friend] acts the way he does.

I think I have improved in tolerance toward other people and groups; understanding them better makes for more tolerance.

I learned how some people can be hurt by the actions of others.

I found that other members of the group have similar problems to mine.

Attitudes and Appreciations

I am more curious about reasons why people act the way they do.

Now I have a different way of looking at people; I don't just react emotionally to them without thinking.

I shouldn't be so backward about taking leadership in a group.

Perhaps I'm not quite as shy in groups as I was; after I got to know the others it wasn't so bad.

One should be able to forgive people for some of the ways they act.

Skills (Behavior)

I have learned to be more tolerant in racial, religious, or political areas .

I've improved in expressing my ideas before a group, have more self confidence.

I think I am making better decisions as to boy friends, etc., not acting so foolish because I think before I act.

I try to see the other person's point of view, try to put myself in his place.

SUMMARY OF RESULTS

Eight general results in terms of learning gained by the majority of the students in both groups are as follows:

1. *Enjoyment and satisfaction from project participation.*—All twenty students said they were sorry when the meetings ended. All attended club meetings regularly and met all appointments for tests and counseling interviews.

2. *Positive changes in attitudes or skill in interpersonal relationships.*— All twenty students believed they had learned facts, attitudes, and skills pertaining to self-understanding and social competence. The majority of them were able to give evidence of meaningful learning through improved self-adjustment and social adjustment in daily living.

3. *Improved understanding of vocational interests and aptitudes.*—The majority of students believed they had been helped through the vocational-guidance aspects of the project. In some cases, this consisted in reassurance of chosen vocational goals. In other cases, information and test results made the students aware of new possibilities which should be considered.

4. *Facilitation of the counseling process.*—Rapport between the counselor and all students was firmly established through the group activity before the first counseling interview. All students were eager to talk confidentially concerning personal anxieties or adjustment problems in the first counseling interview.

5. *Experience in sociodrama was satisfying and helpful.*—The majority of students gained in spontaneity and empathy through role-taking or audience participation. They voted for sociodrama as a much better springboard for free discussion than introductory talks.

6. *The camaraderie in the group was a positive force for tolerance of others.*—The great majority of students gained respect for viewpoints and personality differences of fellow-members. Many were able to carry over feelings of tolerance into other life-situations.

7. *Poorly adjusted and shy students gained social skills.*—The majority of the poorly adjusted and shy students improved their attitudes toward participation in social groups and gained in self-confidence and in determination to be more outgoing.

8. *Well-adjusted students gained in appreciation of the importance of interpersonal skills and tolerance toward others.*—The majority of the well-adjusted students were motivated toward improvement of their own interpersonal relationships and development of leadership skills.

Meaningful learning in self-adjustment and social-adjustment areas results from a multiple-counseling program which includes small-group discussions for students who elect the activity because of interest or felt need. This conclusion refers to the twelfth-grade students described here, although the same conclusion was also found for two other maturity levels, namely, university undergraduates and adult students in university graduate study. Judging from the generally recognized need for guidance programs and from the success achieved in this study through use of multiple counseling, it would seem worth while for more schools to experiment with this guidance method.

7

Group and Individual Counseling
in Modifying Behavior*

Donald H. Ford

This paper will briefly describe a way of looking at behavior, apply that general scheme to characterize the counseling situation, point out the implications of the scheme for group counseling procedures, describe a group counseling program which follows from the scheme, and finally mention some of the practical values which have accrued as a result.

A CONCEPTUAL SCHEME

Behavior refers to a stream of events occurring constantly from birth to death. Within that stream there are different *kinds* of behavior such as thoughts, feelings, and acts. Any attempt to modify behavior, then, must recognize that a *variety* of behaviors is *always* occurring, that the particular kind of behavior to be modified is associated with other kinds of behavior, that modification may be temporary or permanent, and that one may be modifying a response other than that which he intends to modify, since many kinds of responses are occurring at once.

Another stream runs parallel to the behavior stream. We might call it the environmental stream. As is true of behavior, environmental events are continually occurring, and are continually influencing the behavior stream, just as the banks of a river influence its depth, direction, and so forth. Only under very artificial conditions is it possible to deprive behavior of all environmental stimulation. Research on behavior under such conditions (sometimes called stimulus deprivation) suggests that the occurrence of behavior is *dependent upon* stimulation and that without environmental events, behavior gradually declines and conceivably could eventually disappear.

When one wishes to change behavior it is typically done by manipulating events so that some responses are modified in some way. We cannot forget that there are *always* other behaviors occurring besides the ones we seek to modify. These may help or hinder our efforts. There are also other

*Reprinted by permission of the author and publisher from the *Personnel and Guidance Journal*, XL (1962), 770–773.

environmental events occurring which may be influential besides those we are manipulating. The implications of these general notions have not been fully worked through here. We have pursued them far enough for our present purpose, however.

If we apply these ideas to the counseling situation, we might describe it diagrammatically as follows:

$$\rightarrow S \rightarrow r \rightarrow R \rightarrow S \rightarrow$$

The capital S represents environmental events such as sounds, objects, and the behaviors of others. The little r represents behaviors which cannot be directly observed by others, such as thoughts, feelings, and physical sensations. The big R refers to behaviors which others can observe, such as walking, talking, and blushing. The arrow preceding the first S indicates that the stream of environmental and behavioral events has been occurring prior to the situation about which we are concerned, and the arrow following the last S indicates that the stream continues. However, that segment of the stream represented in the diagram we may consider to be the counseling situation.

Environmental events may function in two ways. First, they may *elicit* behavior, and in our diagram this is represented by the first S. For example, asking the client a question typically will elicit an answer. Asking a client to describe emotions which occur when someone is criticizing him will elicit thoughts on the client's part (r) and verbal statements (R) which follow from those thoughts. The verbal statements may or may not accurately reflect the thoughts, *i.e.*, clients sometimes lie or do not accurately report upon their thoughts. The last S represents a behavior modifier. When environmental events are manipulated in an attempt to bring about a relatively permanent change in both observable (R) and mediating (r) behavior and to cause that change to occur in a variety of situations outside the counseling setting, we think of it as a modifier. Interpretation, information giving, suggestions, and instructions are examples of counselor responses intended as modifiers. Modifiers may have a cumulative effect such as that found in reinforcement procedures, and reflection of feeling exemplifies a counselor response which sometimes functions as a cumulative modifier. Unfortunately, we too frequently assume that modifying overtly observable behavior, such as talking, is the same thing as modifying the mediating responses, such as thoughts, which preceded it. This is not true, of course, although it is only through the observable responses that we can seek to modify the mediating ones.

In summary, then, the counselor's problem is to elicit the particular behaviors he wishes to modify and apply behavior modifiers to those behaviors when they occur. This process repeats itself over and over in every counseling situation. It may differ in terms of the *kinds* of behavior one attempts to modify and the *events manipulated* to do so. In the vocational counseling situation, we are seeking to modify thoughts, feelings, and actions relevant to self-appraisal, vocational choice, and job or educational performance.

AS APPLIED TO COUNSELING

Returning to the diagram, let us examine how it suggests some ideas concerning group counseling. For any client in a group, the counselor and all other members of the group may apply behavior elicitors and modifiers. Thus, the number, type, and rate of elicitors or modifiers applied are only partially under the control of the counselor. Under such circumstances, the client may be confused by too many elicitors or may have so many competing responses elicited that it becomes more difficult to apply effective modifiers. What is a behavior elicitor for one client may have exactly the opposite effect for another. A behavior modifier effective for one client may be quite ineffective for another. Thus, group counseling is difficult because the counselor has so many more events to observe, so many more contingencies affecting his inferences, and so many more conditions influencing the effectiveness of the behavior modifiers applied.

However, if we look at our diagram again, we may ask, "Within this stream, is it really necessary that the *same counselor* who applies the behavior elicitors must also apply the behavior modifiers, and is it necessary that the elicitors and modifiers be applied in the *same situation?* If we answer that question in the negative, a new possibility suggests itself. We can divide our diagram into two halves:

$$\rightarrow S \rightarrow r \rightarrow r \qquad \text{and} \qquad r \rightarrow R \rightarrow S \rightarrow$$

In the first half we have the behavior elicitors and the mediating r's. In the second half we have the observable behaviors and the behavior modifiers. If we can apply *group* procedures to the first and *individual* procedures to the second, we will have avoided the difficulty of trying to modify a variety of behaviors simultaneously in a variety of people with a variety of modifiers.

The utility of this point of view may be exemplified by describing a counseling program at The Pennsylvania State University. One phase of our program involves providing intensive vocational and educational counseling to all of our entering freshmen and their parents. Last summer, we counseled over 4,500 families. Obviously we needed some mass procedures. The entire program cannot be described here, but one of the meetings will illustrate our use of group procedures within the rationale previously described. Each day we see 60 to 80 families. Prior to the counseling day, we have obtained extensive information about each student through tests, high school records, and personal information blanks. We want to tell the students about their test results in such a fashion that the test indices of students' behavior will be used by the students in wise and effective planning. The purpose of two meetings is primarily to elicit behavior, while the purpose of the third is primarily behavior modification.

In the first meeting 60 to 80 students meet with one counselor. The counselor describes the manner in which test results can be useful in the context of the students planning their university and life careers. Each student is given his or her test reports. Then the manner in which each test should be interpreted is discussed gradually, factually, and in lay language by the counselor. The formats of the test reports are designed to facilitate this discussion. We have paid a great deal of attention to developing a presentation which is simple but clear, and always use one of our most competent staff members for this purpose. The test reports themselves and the counselor's statements elicit mediating behaviors in the students. We are quite aware that many thoughts are started, and some emotional responses of varing intensity occur. Naturally, it is very important that *some* of the thoughts and emotions elicited be modified, but no behavior modifiers specific to a particular student are applied at that point.

The students move from that meeting to a second meeting in which each spends time reading a folder of occupational information prepared for him by his counselor. Two counselors circulate among the group, answering questions, making suggestions, and obtaining additional information from the files, when requested by the students. Our primary purpose in this meeting is to elicit thoughts about a variety of occupational and educational possibilities, many of which the student has not yet considered.

The third meeting is an individual interview in which the primary purpose is to modify behavior. First the counselor applies elicitors to get the client to reveal the mediating responses which have been occurring as a result of the previous meetings. For example, he may ask, "How did the test results strike you?" or "Were you surprised at your interest scores?" or "How do you think your parents will feel about it?" or "You're pretty disappointed about the results, aren't you?" Such elicitors will produce discussion of thoughts, feelings, and evaluations. As the client responds in the interview, the counselor begins to apply behavior modifiers. For example, he may say, "That's exactly what it means" or "You decide what you think is right and we will help your parents understand" or "I can understand how you might feel frightened and worried, but we will always be here to talk with you, if you need us."

When we first started our program, we did not use the group lecture. Each student was seen in an individual interview. We retained the individual interview because we believe, for our purposes in this particular program, the application of idiosyncratic behavior modifiers is necessary. However, the length of each individual interview is now typically no more than 40 minutes, while previously the interviews used to run 60 to 75 minutes. Thus, we are saving a minimum of 20 minutes per student. With a minimum of 60 students a day, this is 20 man hours of work per day, which has been replaced by one hour of group work. This saving of time is financially significant.

Another consequence is even more important. We are convinced we have improved the *quality* of our work. In the first place, we can use our best personnel to do the test interpretations. Second, this *standardization* of the interpretation means that *variations* in students' responses to elicitors are entirely a product of their own test reports and their own responses to the interpretation, rather than partly a result of different interpretations given to students. Thus, since the counselor conducting the individual interview knows that the test interpretation is the same for all students, he can more readily discover the distortions of the facts that each student may give him. Sometimes the test interpretation is so upsetting to students they don't hear half of what is said. Since time elapses between the test interpretation and our attempt to modify the responses which result, the student has had a chance to get his emotions under control, and we have a second chance both to modify the emotions and get across a clear understanding of the test results. When the interpretation and modification are attempted in the same interview, private emotional responses which the client may not share with the counselor may interfere so drastically as to ruin the effectiveness of the whole procedure.

Finally, our counselors do a better job and enjoy their work more. Under our old procedure each counselor saw four students a day. To each student the counselor had to explain each test and how it could be interpreted. Since the tests were identical from student to student, even though the students' scores differed, the counselor spent a good bit of time from interview to interview saying the same things. For example, to each student he had to describe the Strong Vocational Interest Blank and its significance before moving to a description of the student's individual scores on the test. Naturally, such repetition day after day with four clients a day was boring, monotonous, and tiring to the counselor. By using the group procedure we have removed this monotonous part of the interview, and all of our counselors report that it made a real difference for them. They can now focus upon the students' *responses* to the test data and the other significant information given them and plan the modification of those responses. Of course, the counselors still face the problem of exploring important factors, such as family influence and personality difficulties which were not covered in the group sessions.

We have applied the same conception to our work with parents, and Dr. Harvey Wall has described that meeting in another paper [1].

The task of counseling is behavior change. A way of conceptualizing behavior and clear specification of the behaviors to be changed are essential in making decisions about the most effective procedures for producing the change.

REFERENCE

1. Wall, Harvey. "A Counseling Program for Parents of College Freshmen." Staff Paper, the Division of Counseling, The Pennsylvania State University.

8

Group Counseling, Individual Counseling, and a College Class in Vocations*

Vivian H. Hewer

Because counseling is such a new profession, the future, responsibility, and status of the occupation as a service to college students is increasingly confusing. Even in vocational counseling, the area of particular concern in this paper, there are many uncertainties about who should receive counseling and what the process of vocational choice is.

Psychologists [1, 5] have suggested that counseling should be a part of every college student's education. Most psychologists would agree with them, but with college enrollments in some colleges reaching the 20,000 mark and with professional counseling staffs of these colleges approximating 15 to 20, the majority of college students are not going to get much individual counseling. Maybe most of them do not need vocational counseling, since most people choose their careers without the help of a professional counselor. But if they do, budgetary restrictions and lack of trained personnel suggest that the goal of individual vocational counseling for all students will not be met for many years. Those who will continue to receive counseling in our colleges are those who seek it out.

The following research is concerned with a class in the choice of a vocation. This group method of assisting students in the choice of their vocations is worthy of investigation, for if it is effective, more students could be assisted by a single counselor than in individual counseling.

A course designed to assist students in the choice of a vocation has been offered since 1948 in the College of Science, Literature and the Arts (SLA) at the University of Minnesota by the writer. It emphasizes two major areas, differential psychology and its implications for the student who is seeking a vocational choice, and occupational information. Following Stone's [6] research, the present instructor always has supplemented the class meetings with counseling for each student. Within the last few years, group counseling techniques have been used increasingly, and

*Reprinted by permission of the author and publisher from *The Personnel and Guidance Journal* XXXVII (1959), 660–665.

currently they are used for the class as a whole to the exclusion of individaul counseling.

This research was originally concerned primarily with an evaluation of the comparative effectiveness of the two methods, group and individual counseling, but as it progressed, questions arose about the over-all effectiveness of the class as a technique for assisting students in choosing a vocation. Both evaluations are reported.

Only a few research studies are directed at an exploration of these problems. Stone's research has been mentioned. Bilovsky, *et al.* [3] concluded in a study concerned with the counseling of high school students that there were no significant statistical differences in the realism of vocational goals of those students counseled individually and of those counseled in groups. There was no indication that this counseling supplemented a class in vocations.

Of immediate implication to this research is that of Hoyt [4], since it was patterned after it. It differs from Hoyt's in that the students in his study were not members of a class, the group methods differed, and no control or no "no treatment" group was used in this study. Hoyt's findings indicated no differences in effectiveness between the group and individual methods of counseling.

METHOD

SAMPLE

The sample was composed of students taking the course in Choosing Your Vocation during spring and fall quarters, 1955, and winter quarter, 1956. The class enrollment was restricted to 35 persons each quarter, and the total sample was 93. After the first class meeting each quarter, 16 members of the class were randomly chosen for group counseling, and the remainder were assigned for individual counseling, or, in the total sample, 48 received group and 45 individual counseling. The sample was preponderantly male. Descriptive characteristics of the sample studied included: mean high school rank (HSR); mean scores on the American Council on Education Psychological Examination, 1952 College Edition, (ACE '52) and Cooperative English Test, Lower Level, Form Z (Coop Eng Z); and mean honor point ratio (HPR). The mean honor point ratio for the samples was lower than that for all SLA men. On the other three measures, HSR, ACE, and Coop Eng, the members of the class had significantly lower scores (significant at 1 per cent level) than did SLA freshmen as a whole. These results raise the question of whether those college students with lower college ability have more vocational problems than do those with better ability or whether motivations for taking the course were other than vocational.

PROCEDURES IN CLASS AND COUNSELING

During the first meeting of the class, each student completed a form stating as specifically as possible what his vocational choice was at that time and checked on an 11-point scale degree of satisfaction and certainty with the choice [4]. This choice was known as the pre-course choice. The post-course choice was given the last day of the class on a similar form.

All students in the class had a basic test battery, including the Strong Vocational Interest Blank, the Minnesota Multiphasic Personality Inventory, the Cooperative English Test, the American Council on Education Psychological Examination, the Ohio State Psychological Examination, and a personal history form.

Students who were to be counseled individually were given appointments with counselors in the Student Counseling Bureau and treated as the usual student there. Of the remaining members of the class, two groups of eight students were formed, with the instructor and one of the counselors,[1] from the Bureau serving as leaders. By the time the groups met, the meaning and measurement of vocational interest, scholastic aptitude, special aptitudes, and personal values had been discussed in the class.

The case conference or case study approach was used in the group, and each student was the object of a case study during one 50-minute session. The student who was to be discussed in the group knew the day on which he would be discussed and that he would remain anonymous to the other members. During the group meeting, the leader supplied information as the group requested it about the individual discussed, his interests, aptitudes, family history, and vocational choices. The group experience became in effect a kind of laboratory experience in which the materials discussed in the lecture could be applied, although the instructor saw vocational decision or the application of the method of reaching such a decision as the primary goal of the group work.

EVALUATION

OBJECTIVES, CRITERIA, MEASUREMENT

The objectives of the class and the supplementary counseling were three of those used by Hoyt [4]: (1) satisfaction with vocational choice, (2) certainty of vocational choice, and (3) realism of vocational choice. Certainty of and satisfaction with pre-course and post-course choices were measured on an 11-point scale filled out on the first and last day of class. Realism of vocational choice was determined by expert opinion based on judgements

[1]Appreciation is due Dr. Theodore Volsky for serving as a group leader and for valuable suggestions on group procedure.

of four counselors.[2] Again following Hoyt [4], judges were asked to evaluate realism on the basis of whether a student could complete training for the job, whether there was sufficient opportunity for employment, and whether the student would succeed and remain in the job over a long period of time. In judging the realism of the two vocational choices, the judges were unable to determine which was pre-course or post-course or whether the student was group or individually counseled. Data on the students that were available to the judges included all test data, grades, and a personal history form.

In a preliminary evaluation of the results of the first quarter, it was found that there was no difference in the effect that group counseling produces on certainty of and satisfaction with vocational choice among students, as compared to that of individual counseling. In the evaluation on the basis of the third criterion, realism of vocational choice, as determined by expert opinion, it was found there was not a high level of agreement among the judges. There was, however, no difference in realism of vocational choices of the students counseled individually and of those counseled in a group.

As a result of this preliminary study, realism of vocational choice for the total sample was analyzed. The results on satisfaction and certainty for the first quarter were similar to Hoyt's [4]; students who were counseled by the group method reported that they were equally certain of and satisfied with their vocational choices when compared to reports of students counseled individually. Consequently, the total sample for the three quarters was not analyzed on this basis. The analysis of the results from all three quarters reported in the following section will be concerned with the reliability of the judges' ratings, the over-all effectiveness of the class, and the comparative effectiveness of the two methods of counseling.

RESULTS

RELIABILITY OF THE CRITERION OF REALISM

Two methods were used to determine the extent to which the four judges agreed in their rating of vocational choices as realistic or unrealistic. The first was to determine the extent to which the judges agreed with one another in rating the pre-course and post-course choices separately as realistic or unrealistic. Chi-square analyses indicated that ratings of pre- or post-course choice by each rater were related to the respective rating of pre- or post-course choice by every other rater. The average percentage agreement among the judges, each judge compared with every other,

[2]Appreciation is due to Dr. Theda Hagenah, Dr. Wilbur Layton, Dr. Cornelia McCune, and Dr. Mabel Powers for their assistance as judges.

was 75.3 per cent on the ratings of the pre-course choices and 71.8 per cent on the ratings of the post-course choices.

The second method of checking the extent to which the judges agreed was to check their agreement on the ratings of patterns of pre-course and post-course choices for any given student. In other words, the agreement had to be on four patterns of ratings of realism of pre-course and post-course choices respectively; realistic to realistic, unrealistic to realistic, realistic to unrealistic, and unrealistic to unrealistic. In the analysis the pattern of choices was designated by a code. If both pre- and post-course choices were rated as realistic by a judge, the pattern was designated 3; if pre-course was unrealistic and post-course realistic, 2; if pre-course was realistic and post-course unrealistic 1; and if both choices unrealistic, 0.

The average percentage agreement in judging patterns was 59.6 per cent, compared to the agreement of 75.3 per cent when pre-course choice was judged separately and 71.8 per cent when post-course choice was judged separately. An even more marked difference will be noted if reliability of the judges on evaluating change is noted. They agreed 48.1 per cent of the time that pattern 2 had occurred, 33.3 per cent of the time on 1, or 44.6 per cent of the time if 2 and 1 are considered together. So low a percentage of agreement indicates that the criterion adopted for judging the comparative effectiveness of the counseling methods or of the course has such low reliability as to require that any conclusions based on these judgments be tentative.

EVALUATION OF THE COURSE

The change occurring in the realism of the vocational choice of the student when the pre-course choice was compared to the post-course choice could be used as an index of the effectiveness of the course. The pattern of realistic to realistic is difficult to evaluate for a student may not have changed his choice or he may have substituted one realistic choice for another. An increase in degree of satisfaction and certainty with vocational choice would have reflected a beneficial effect of the course. Changes from unrealistic to realistic are positive or reflect a beneficial effect from the course, but there is little that is salutary in a vocational course that causes a student's vocational choice to change from realistic to unrealistic. An analysis of the change occurring would require a comparison of these latter two patterns, 2 and 1. The last group, pattern 0, were those who started with unrealistic choices and ended with unrealistic choices. In terms of the criterion, they are no better off than when they started the course. To gain agreement among the raters on the patterns, a rating was assigned which was believed to represent best the judgment of the raters, whether in pairs, threes, or fours, on the realism or lack of it for the choices, pre-course and post-course, separately.

To evaluate the course in terms of change, the data were analyzed by chi-square to determine whether there was a relation between the ratings given to the pre-course choice and those given to the post-course choice. In every instance, pre-course rating was positively related to post-course rating, or, in other words, the rating, realistic or unrealistic, that the judges gave to the vocational choice made by the students at the end of the course was frequently the same as the rating given to the choice at the beginning of the course.

To analyze the effectiveness of the course still further, an analysis was made of the type of changes occurring, that is, whether the proportion of unrealistic choices changing to realistic was significantly different and larger than the proportion of realistic responses changing to unrealistic. Chi-square analyses were used to determine whether a greater proportion of initially rated unrealistic choices changed to realistic post-choices than initially rated realistic pre-choices changed to unrealistic post-choices. These results are presented in Table 1. If a probability of less than 0.05 is employed, the proportion of unrealistic responses changing to realistic

Table 1

Chi-square Tests of Independence of Classification Involving Change from Unrealistic to Realistic and Realistic to Unrealistic N = 93.

Judges	X^2	Probability		
1	13.682*		0.001	
2	5.081*	0.02	P	0.05
3	4.162*	0.02	P	0.05
4	0.566	0.30	P	0.50
1 & 2	1.555	0.20	P	0.30
1 & 3	1.473	0.20	P	0.30
1 & 4	0.025	0.80	P	0.90
2 & 3	1.473	0.20	P	0.30
2 & 4	0.232	0.50	P	0.70
3 & 4	0.010	0.90	P	0.95
1, 2, 3	4.721*	0.02	P	0.05
1, 2, 4	2.529	0.10	P	0.20
1, 3, 4	4.169*	0.02	P	0.05
2, 3, 4	0.312	0.50	P	0.70
Three judges of 4	0.983	0.30	P	0.50

DF — 1
2 X 2 table

responses is significantly larger than the proportion of realistic responses changing to unrealistic responses for three of four judges taken individually, for none of the six pair-wise combinations of judges, and for two of the four triplet combinations of judges.

These results again reflect the low level of inter-rater agreement, particularly for the pairs of raters. In general, these results indicate the difficulty of determining the extent to which changes occur in realism of vocational choices during the period when counseling was conducted. The course and counseling procedures may be producing desirable results, but they cannot be evaluated since the reliability of judgments is so low.

EVALUATION OF METHOD OF COUNSELING

After the evaluation was done of the over all effectiveness of the total class and counseling experience, whether group or individual, the effectiveness of the two methods of counseling was compared. Judges' ratings from only those five instances in which significant differences were found in the above analysis were used. In other words, chi-square tests were run to determine whether there is an independence of classification for change (UR–R) and no change (UR–UR) of initially rated unrealistic pre-choices and counseling classification, individual and group. In no case was a significant difference obtained between the two methods.

DISCUSSION

The lack of agreement among the judges on realism of vocational choices made by members of the class requires that all conclusions drawn from this study be tentative. The criterion of change in realism of vocational choice was accepted for evaluation of the course. Distributions of pre-course ratings in terms of post-course ratings, three of four judges agreeing, indicated that about half of the class completed the course with realistic choices and about half with unrealistic. Thirty-one or about 33 per cent were in category 3, realistic to realistic; 38 or slightly over 41 per cent were in 0, unrealistic to unrealistic; 16 or about 16 per cent in 2, or unrealistic to realistic; and 8 or about 8 per cent in 1, or realistic to unrealistic. Whether these are beneficial results or not depends on the expectations one sets for counseling.

The lack of agreement among the judges may have been due in part to characteristics of the group. The students in the study were significantly below average in ability and achievement in high school and possibly college when compared to the rest of their class. Since they came to college, it seems most likely that they have chosen vocations that require college training. Since many of the students indicated occupational choices requiring college training and since many have below average or marginal college ability, the judges were faced with the problem of trying to predict whether these students could complete college. This prediction is easier for the extremes of the distribution, and it is possible that for this experimental group, which was marginal in ability, prediction of success in college was almost on a chance basis.

The low academic capacity of the experimental group in relation to their vocational choices may have been the reason why a large number of their choices were judged to be unrealistic. If this is true, changes in the course should be considered, such as giving more emphasis to occupations below the professional level. Other criteria for evaluation should be considered, of which follow-up of each student is one. Questions could also be raised as to what other gains might be made by students who had this class. If the choice of a vocation is a developmental process, will the student eventually reach an optimal vocational adjustment that will have been accelerated by the course in spite of poor initial choices, bad attempts, or wrong starts along the way?

With respect to the major problem of the study, the evaluation of group and individual methods of counseling, there is no evidence that one method is superior to another. Again, however, because of the lack of agreement of the judges, this is only a tentative finding.

CONCLUSIONS

In view of the lack of consistent inter-rater agreement, it cannot be determined if real changes occured in realism of vocational choices during the period in which the class and counseling were conducted. Because of this, no definite conclusion can be drawn concerning the effectiveness of either counseling approach, group or individual. Should further experimentation contrasting these two vocational counseling approaches be undertaken, a control group should be used, drawn from the same population as that from which the class comes. Appropriate criteria should be explored as well as adaptation of class technique and content of membership. Continued exploration and evaluation of group techniques, both with and without a class background, appears necessary if any methods are to be found to meet the increasing need and demand for counseling.

REFERENCES

1. Berdie, R. F. "Counseling—An Educational Technique," *Educ. Psychol. Measmt.* (1949), 9, 89–94.

2. Berdie, R. F. Unpublished survey of counseling centers.

3. Bilovsky, D., McMasters, W., Shorr, J. E., & Singer, S. L. "Individual and Group Counseling," *Personnel Guid. J.* (1953), 31, 363–365.

4. Hoyt, D. P. "An Evaluation of Group and Individual Programs in Vocational Guidance," *J. Appl. Psychol.* (1955), 39, 26–30.

5. Shoben, E. J., Jr. "The College, Psychological Clinics, and Psychological Knowledge," *J. Counsel. Psychol.* (1956), 3, 200–205.

6. Stone, C. H. "Are Vocational Orientation Courses Worth Their Salt?" *Educ. Psychol. Measmt.* (1958), 8, 161–181.

7. Super, D. E. "A Theory of Vocational Development," *Amer. Psychologist* (1953), 8, 185–190.

9

*Multiple Counseling: A Catalyst for Individual Counseling**

Angelo V. Boy

Henry L. Isaksen

Gerald J. Pine

The counselor with adequate background in personality theory can use multiple counseling to make the process of working with individuals more effective.

Multiple counseling is a process in which one counselor is involved in a relationship with a number of clients at the same time. Froelich suggests that *multiple counseling* is a term which describes a specific counseling situation involving more than one counselee [2]. Slavson indicates that in effect multiple counseling is a special application of the principles of individual counseling to two or more persons simultaneously [6].

The number of clients may vary. From her work with maladjusted students, Driver recommends six as the optimum number of individuals in a group [l]. As the result of experimentation in this area, Froelich recommends four to eight members as a possible optimum number [2].

Multiple counseling is psychologically a deep relationship between the counselor and the group to the end that group members have the opportunity to explore the causal factors that have influenced the growth of their particular problems. Because of the depth of the relationship, the process demands that the counselor be well versed in the dynamics of behavior. The beginner who engages in multiple counseling without due recognition of his limitations may expose his subjects to unwarranted danger.

Group members exist in a free atmosphere in which they are able to express their emotions and sift over the circumstances of life that have caused them concern. The counselor enables group members to involve themselves in the process of self-discovery essentially through an empathic attitude which encourages group members to untangle the reasons why they are what they are. Group members proceed with ease since they have

*Reprinted by permission of the authors and publishers from the *School Counselor*, 11 (1963), 8–11.

a positive reaction to the acceptant and understanding atmosphere which characterizes the counseling relationship [3].

FORMING A GROUP

In an effort to provide group members with a maximal growth situation, there are certain principles that should govern the formation of a group for multiple counseling.

The group members should be somewhat alike in their problem area. For example, all may have difficulty relating to parents, all may be overly tense in normal testing situations or all may have personality conflicts with one or more teachers [2].

The group members should be voluntarily involved in the process of counseling. A student's membership in a group should not come because of any coercion. The student should be involved in the counseling relationship because he has a desire for counseling assistance rather than because it is merely the parent's, principal's, teacher's or counselor's desire [3, 5]. Each of the group members should have the freedom to drop out at any time. In other words, the probability is little that a client will make any sort of progress if he is compelled to continue against his wishes. [5].

THE COUNSELOR

The creation of a growth-producing atmosphere depends largely upon the counselor's ability to communicate empathically with members of the group. Since a deep relationship is more dependent upon the counselor's genuineness in the association, this relationship cannot be accomplished merely by the use of certain techniques. Such an approach to counseling usually results in a superficial relationship between client and counselor rather than the meaningful relationship achieved only by the embodiment of a wholesome attitudinal structure that is a genuine and integral part of the counselor's person.

If we can accept counseling as a depth relationship between client and counselor, it would seem that the law of diminishing returns would set in when we attempt to relate to a group of individuals. A sensitive counselor finds it difficult to relate deeply to even one individual, and when he attempts to relate to a group, it becomes even more difficult to involve himself deeply with any one member of the group. Multiple counseling cannot provide for each pupil the full attention of the counselor that individual counseling can give [5].

The larger the counseled group, the more difficult it becomes to relate to each individual within the group. As the counselor attempts to establish a significant relationship with client A, client B expresses himself and the counselor must switch his involvement to client B. If he has been deeply entwined with client A, however, his involvement with client B cannot be quite as meaningful.

When clients C, D, E and F become involved in the process, the counselor is constantly pulled away from a significant relationship with one, toward a more superficial relationship with all.

If the counselor were going to maintain a significant relationship with client A, this could be accomplished only by sacrificing, to some degree, relationships with clients B, C, D, E and F. A truly professional counselor, deeply interested in the effectiveness of his work, will want ultimately to dissolve his relationship with the group and work with each member of the group on an individual basis.

For the competent counselor it is often easy to establish a deep and meaningful counseling relationship with an individual client. A skilled counselor can give his full self to this one client in an attempt to bring about a relationship which will result in the client becoming an independent, freely functioning individual who can handle his own life.

But when the counselor attempts to "give of himself" to many, he finds that although each may have a part of his involvement, his involvement is not as complete with any one as it should be, since he cannot become fully and effectively involved with more than one at a given time.

The counselor cannot relate deeply to any one member of the group since the other members are seeking "pieces" of his involvement. The group members, although able to function with comfort and ease, still verbalize at a somewhat superficial level because they do not perceive the counselor as relating to them individually and deeply.

They also do not have as much time to talk about their problems in the multiple counseling session as they would in an individual session [5].

The deep and innermost feelings of individual members of the group are seldom brought out since the individual has to deal not only with his own feelings but with the reactions of the group members. They cannot always move with safety in the revelation of certain feelings. These feelings are acceptable to the counselor but perhaps not to other members of the group. For some students multiple counseling is inappropriate because of the disturbing effect these students may have upon the group, or because of the disturbing effect the group may have upon them [5].

Even though the group affords a form of safety and protection in the opportunity for the client to conceal his feelings, the group member is not apt to explore himself thoroughly in depth. As someone else speaks, he can only be fractionally involved with his own feelings and growth.

VALUE

On the other hand, multiple counseling should be an important aspect of a school's counseling program. Although multiple counseling presents communicative limits for the empathic school counselor, the relationship does provide the hesitant client with a beginning point. It should not serve, though, as a replacement for the one-to-one relationship between client and counselor.

Some believe that the principal value of multiple counseling is that it enables the counselor to help more pupils each day and, therefore, results in more economical use of the counselor's time.

However, Ohlsen warns that multiple counseling is not a substitute for individual counseling:

"This (group counseling) should not lead to the elimination of individual counseling; educators must be more concerned with the best service for each individual than with cost. The eventual cost to society of a permanently maladjusted person far exceeds any saving which could come from eliminating individual counseling in the school" [5].

Some contend that the results of multiple counseling by itself approximate those of individual counseling. Wolberg questions the validity of this notion, contending that multiple counseling is a valuable *adjunct* to individual counseling [8]. Driver looks upon multiple counseling as an enrichment of individual counseling and not a substitute for it [1]. Super feels group work can accomplish much if it is preventive in nature, but it is not a replacement for individual counseling [7].

The primary value of multiple counseling lies in the opportunity it affords the counselor to establish contact with individuals who may need a different kind of help from that of an individual counseling relationship.

There is the strong possibility that some students will find it easier to relate to a group of their peers in the presence of a counselor than to establish a one-to-one relationship directly with the counselor. There is some supportive value to a client in an experience that causes him to realize that he is not alone in his feelings.

As indicated earlier, there is a certain degree of safety and protection in a group. A given member of the group may be more inclined to recognize and express his feelings toward teachers or parents, or his inadequacy to cope with the demands of the school atmosphere.

He may also be encouraged by the experience of having other students accept his feelings without criticism. Finally, he may find it easier to arrange an appointment with the counselor when he discovers that other members of his group are doing so.

Multiple counseling should serve as a basis for establishing a good individual counseling relationship with students who have need of it.

A group can be formed for multiple counseling with a stated time limit of, say, six one-hour counseling sessions. During these six sessions the counselor proceeds to penetrate the feelings of members of the group as deeply as possible and creates, to the best of his ability, a growth-producing atmosphere. Members of the group understand the structure before they begin and accept the limit of six sessions.

Near the end of the series, group members are invited to meet with the counselor on an individual basis. Those members of the group who are not in need of, or who are not yet ready for, the individual counseling will undoubtedly profit from the experience of participating in the six group counseling sessions. On the other hand, those who are more deeply troubled will want to continue the relationship. They will have had the opportunity to begin the process of self-exploration and they will desire an opportunity to go even further.

Multiple counseling can serve as a meaningful beginning point in establishing an effective counseling relationship with individual students. Viewed in this perspective, multiple counseling can serve as a process of readiness for individual counseling but never as a substitute for an effective one-to-one relationship between client and counselor [4].

REFERENCES

1. Driver, Helen Irene. *Multiple Counseling: A Small Group Discussion Method for Personal Growth* (Madison, Wisconsin: Monona Publications, 1954).

2. Froelich, Clifford P. *Multiple Counseling—a Research Proposal.* Berkeley, California: University of California (mimeographed).

3. Hobbs, Nicholas. "Group-Centered Psychotherapy" in Carl R. Rogers, *Client-Centered Therapy* (Boston: Houghton Mifflin, 1951), 278–319.

4. McDaniel, Henry B. *Guidance in the Modern School* (New York: The Dryden Press, 1956), 380.

5. Ohlsen, Merle M. *Guidance: An Introduction* (New York: Harcourt, Brace, 1955), 294–325.

6. Slavson, S. R. Ed. *The Practice of Group Therapy* (New York: International Universities Press, 1947), 9.

7. Super, D. E. "Group Techniques in the Guidance Program," *Educational and Psychological Measurement* (1949) 9, 496–510.

8. Wolberg, Irving. *The Technique of Psychotherapy* (New York: Grune and Stratton, 1954), 569.

10

Group Counseling: More Than a Catalyst*

John Gawrys, Jr.

O. Bruce Brown

Guidance programs today are imbued with the concept that the primary role of the counselor is counseling [8]. All too often, however, this refers to the individual encounter, with those attempting group counseling being divided in opinion as to its chief value. Some see the group process as supplementing or complementing the individual relationship; others as an efficient and expedient method for dealing with larger numbers of students; and still others as a catalyst for the individual counseling relationship. And curiously enough, research has not resolved the dilemma.

The authors would like to suggest that group counseling is another valid method for assisting persons in need—with legitimate potential in its own right for helping individuals become better-functioning and more self-reliant social persons. A closer look will be taken at this group process, the controversy which exists regarding its nature, and some of the underlying counselor attitudes which must exist in order for the effective group counseling relationship to occur.

DEFINITION

Group counseling is a relatively new approach for many counselors, requiring a sound understanding of counseling and group dynamics. It is an approach which has basically the same objectives as individual counseling but calls for a wealth of new and broader understandings. It is not individual counseling in a group, but it does call for the establishment of a climate characterized by warmth and acceptance which allows each individual to examine himself and his choice of action. Primary objective is establishment of intra-member-counselor relationships to help members function better outside the group.

No distinction is made here between multiple counseling and group counseling. While the latter term is perhaps more recognizable, much semantic confusion exists. For purposes of clarification, however, both terms,

*Reprinted by permission of the authors and publisher from the *School Counselor*, 12 (1965), 206–213.

multiple and group counseling, will be used synonymously as recognized by some of the researchers in the field [13].

Multiple counseling is a process in a group setting designed to assist individuals with normal, developmental concerns. It is not individual counseling applied to a group but rather an experience in "living" with others and developing the kinds of multiple relationships which are related to the numerous social groups in one's life. It is unique insofar as a "safe" environment is created which permits each individual to take a more inward look in the presence of others while allowing him also to see and share another's life. It is a process in which attitudes, emotions, self-and-other-concepts are the foci with ultimate responsibility for change, direction, and movement resting squarely on the shoulders of the members of the group.

Originally, multiple counseling received its impetus as a result of World War II when it was perceived by many to be an expedient method of dealing with large numbers of troubled individuals. However, with the increasing utilitization of this approach, workers have found values to be inherent in the group approach itself. Group counseling was found to be more than a matter of economy but rather a process with values not always attainable through individual counseling.

Clifford P. Froehlich, in an article by Wright [14], is generally credited with coining the term "multiple counseling." To him this term had the same connotation (and objectives) as individual counseling. Caplan [3], viewing multiple counseling similarly, differentiates it from teaching and group guidance. Traditional group guidance and teaching emphasize an imparting of facts or the giving of information. Counseling is a relationship through which the counselor aids the individual to understand and objectify his emotions. It is also a relationship in which the counselor may provide information.

Goldman [6] in like manner defines multiple counseling as a meeting of a counselor with a group whose members exhibit various anxieties, concerns, and/or needs. It is distinguished from teaching by the fact that the latter usually deals with academic content which comes from outside the group and which is presented by a person, usually the teacher, to the group. It is further distinguished from group guidance in that the latter deals with information on an intellectual plane. The group counseling process may vary, but it usually is a collaborative one dealing with various attitudes, opinions, and concerns, school-related and otherwise, which originate from within the group.

VALUES AND OBJECTIVES

The objectives of group counseling are similar to those of individual counseling, i.e., to assist individuals in coming to a fuller realization and acceptance of self and others. While this goal is not achieved by all members who participate in such a group experience, many may gain, according to Warters [12]. ". . . an increase in self-confidence, an improvement in social skills, and a reduction in tensions."

The group situation provides the individual the opportunity to re-define certain perceptions of self in relation to others. Thus the group serves as a potent therapeutic tool. While each man is an island unto himself in his phenomenological world, he cannot avoid interacting with other individuals. The group provides the opportunity for the individual to realize the worth of human relations while assisting him in appraising his values. It is protective for those who may be reticent to verbalize or who may wish to withdraw when the content becomes painful or threatening. It can provide a certain element of security, especially to one who might otherwise experience anxiety in a one-to-one relationship. Such an individual feels safer within the group and thus less threatened by the presence of the counselor.

Since the group is collectively more powerful than the counselor and its members relatively less helpless in their relationship to him, they are apt to be less fearful and less defensive. It must be recognized that communication barriers can and do exist between client and counselor in a one-to-one relationship. The group situation can lower such barriers. Rossberg [11] cites an example, a person who had been a participant in a number of group discussions. When queried as to why he enjoyed the group experience and why he felt greater freedom to discuss things which ordinarily he would have avoided, the patient replied, "We outnumber you."

The group experience may be valuable in aiding individuals to realize that their concerns are not idiosyncratic, thus reducing their guilt feelings. Corsini [4] refers to this quality of the group situation as universalization. Often group members are amazed as they discover that others have experienced many of the same fears, feelings of inadequacy, hatreds, doubts, and rejections as they. With this realization members are less apt to see themselves as unique or different from others. No longer is there any need for the individual to isolate himself with the conviction that he is different from others, an oddball. Such a realization of "likeness" allows an individual to become more comfortable with himself and thus more acceptant and understanding of others.

The group situation provides an opportunity for reality-testing and the experience of dealing with other individuals. Since the group collectively is more apt to represent society's mores than is the individual, members' reactions are likely to be perceived as less threatening than if the counselor were to attempt to justify existing standards. The group permits the individual to experiment with new behaviors and ways of dealing with life in a protected environment which provides acceptance and understanding. In such a group, the individual cannot fail. Thus he can regain his self-confidence and experience that "new birth of freedom."

WHAT IS THE DIFFERENCE?

The essential difference between group counseling and individual counseling is that several persons interact during the therapeutic process. The group process provides a qualitative difference in experience with unique therapeutic potentialities [5]. While it is recognized that the creation of an individual growth-facilitating relationship poses a demand upon the person of the counselor in his attempts to be genuine, warm, acceptant, permissive, and empathically understanding, the fact that more than one client is involved with a counselor in many ways increases the difficulties in creating a safe and growth-facilitative relationship. It is one thing to be assured that the counselor possesses attitudes of confidence and respect; it is quite another to be assured that the members of the group will likewise be acceptant, genuine, warm, and understanding. On the other hand, if the counselor can provide and subsequently nurture such feelings and attitudes within the members of the group, the result is likely to have greater significance than in the individual counseling relationship. *To be accepted and understood by the counselor is a satisfying experience; to be accepted and understood by a number of individuals who are also giving of themselves is profound.* This appears to be the ingredient or quality which is unique to the group experience. The individual becomes both a giver and receiver of help. The group members, by providing a diversity of value patterns, offer each individual the opportunity to make a final choice by himself. As individuals begin to share more and more of themselves with each other, a cohesivesness or syntality becomes evident. Such a unity is not unlike that which exists in the effective individual counseling relationship.

NATURE OF THE RELATIONSHIP

There appears to be a diversity of opinion among writers in the field of group or multiple counseling and/or therapy about the nature of the multiple counseling relationship. Solvy, Moreno, Hobbs, and Schauer have recognized the therapeutic potential of the group as a result of the interactions among members [7]. Hobbs suggests that the most challenging new element for the counselor in the group situation is the possibility of releasing the therapeutic potential of the group itself [5]. It would appear that these writers are referring to "counseling through the group" in which the primary focus is not upon the counselor but upon member-member interactions. The designated leader does not submerge himself; he avoids assuming the central role. Each member has the opportunity to act as counselor (used synonymously with "helping person"). Emphasis is placed upon the help which is potentially forthcoming from the members of the group. Thus focal or leader positions switch and the multiple relationship is characterized by free movement. There is an implicit freedom with more concern with the group process and the role which each individual plays within the group. The counselor or leader acts as facilitator and plays a more ambiguous role, with structure and content coming from the group itself. In such a relationship the group's focus is not upon the solution of specific problems of individuals but rather upon the development of social awareness and the mutual sharing and resolution of common problems of concern to the group members. The interaction process may be depicted by the following illustration:

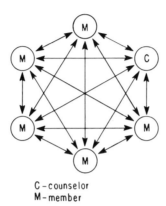

C – counselor
M – member

Lowrey [4], taking an opposing point of view, states emphatically that the lines of relationship are between each member and the therapist. He denies therapy by or through the group and adds that gains are made by each member independently by virtue of his relationship with the therapist. A similar position appears to be taken by Boy, Isaksen and Pine [2] when they suggest that the law of diminishing returns sets in when the counselor attempts to relate to a group of individuals. They go on to suggest that when the counselor is involved with Client A, an involvement less than meaningful results when Client B expresses himself. When the other members of the group become involved, the counselor is forced into superficial relationships rather than significant ones. Thus, it would appear that these authors are referring to "counseling in a group" in which the counselor assumes and maintains the central position, bringing about what is, in reality, individual counseling in a group setting. The primary bonds of relationship would appear to be between the counselor and each individual, and movement, if it exists at all, usually would be around the counselor. This would appear to be more a leader-centered rather than a group-centered experience, with the counselor and his relationship with each group member being the sole ingredients for growth to occur. The group as a therapeutic potential takes on less importance and the emphasis appears to be on what the individual gets out of his experience with the counselor in the presence of others. Such a relationship may be character-ized by the following illustration:

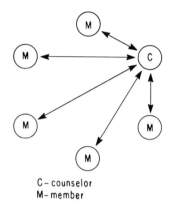

C – counselor
M – member

It would appear that the counselor who functions in such a manner could not easily avoid being perceived as the center of attraction or the nucleus of control. The phenomena of centeredness and member percep-tions of the counselor or group leader as authority are well demonstrated by Bach [1] as he cites the work of Alexander Bavelas (1948) on communication research at the Massachusetts Institute of Technology. Through this re-search Bavelas and his co-researchers found that leadership authority is assigned by group members to the individual holding the central position in a pattern of communication. If the intention of multiple counseling is to provide a group experience, then it necessarily follows that communica-tion must be between and among members of the group rather than re-volving about the counselor.

Corsini [4], in commenting on the phenomenon of counseling or therapy "in a group" or "through the group" feels that it is incorrect to dis-regard the relationships between members of a group. He adds that while the group leader (counselor or therapist) may be of greater value because of his special skills to facilitate group interaction and movement, he is not the sole ingredient, and to consider him as such is an error.

COUNSELING—ATTITUDE, NOT TECHNIQUE

It is a relatively simple task to point up differences of opinion regard-ing the nature and operation of groups and to recognize and expound upon variant philosophies dealing with the counseling process. It becomes far more difficult but no less essential for the counselor to recognize and as-sume responsibility for his own values and biases and the way these operate to influence the relationship between himself and another individual or group of individuals. What one does and how one operates are real indicators of what one believes. One's actions are his philosophy.

To this extent, one cannot conceive of counseling as a series of techniques to be imposed upon individuals for the attainment of certain *desired* goals. Desirability is a relative matter, and if one is to be a proponent of the individuality and independence of man, or any other belief, one cannot be anything else but what one is. Respect for and acceptance of others are not conditions which can be turned whimsically off and on. Faith in the innate ability of man to be self-directing and self-actualizing cannot be merely ingredients existent during a particular kind of encounter. They must be lived; they must be expressed; they must be real and genuine. Only then can they be communicated.

Counseling, therefore, becomes an attitude, not a technique, a way of looking at and living with people rather than a method for manipulating them; a way of life rather than a performance. The attitudes of the counselor influence the nature of the counseling process, whether individual or group, and affect the outcomes of the encounter. Techniques are secondary to this.

The counseling relationship, whether individual or group, is essentially a human relationship; an interaction between and among people; a helping relationship. It is characterized by warmth, acceptance, permissiveness, and empathy. It is genuineness and human confrontation at a most fundamental level. It is love.

Counseling, as an attitude, is nonpossessive love for another individual. Rogers has referred to this quality as an "unconditional positive regard" for another [10]. The helping relationship is one in which the counselor has as his primary goal the promotion of a richer and fuller self-awareness and self-realization of the other person, the client.

While techniques may be considered to be effective implementors of existing attitudes within the person of the counselor, they become but mere hollow physical attempts when what is said or done by the counselor is not congruent with his inner beliefs, his inner feelings, his inner person. In other words, if the counselor is simply applying techniques that are not in accord with his underlying attitudes toward the client or the group, then he is being incongruent and will probably be perceived as such. The counselor as a person must be genuine in his relationship with a client in order to provide the kind of helping relationship of which we speak. Genuineness on the part of the counselor, indeed on the part of any individual, requires a tremendous amount of courage—courage to be what one is—to be willing to express the feelings and attitudes which are existent within one.

Counselors are, after all, merely human beings with all the inadequacies and strengths of human beings. It becomes essential, therefore, that the counselor be able to recognize not only his positive attitudes but also his negative attitudes and be able to live with them comfortably. He must accept these attitudes within himself before he can even hope to accept them within others, either individually or collectively.

Preference for individual counseling or group counseling as well as the nature of the interaction process, i.e., movement around the counselor or among the members of the group, is a function of a counselor's bias and thus indicative of his underlying attitudes. Belief in man's innate capacity to self-actualize and to grow cannot be conditional. Much of the literature in the area of groups says that it does not necessarily follow that an effective individual counselor will be an effective group counselor. We raise the question, "Why must this be so?" If the counselor possesses the attitudes necessary for growth in individuals, then the apparent dichotomy of individual and group counseling disappears as it relates to counselor philosophy. If the counselor communicates an attitude of regard for a client in the one-to-one relationship, why must he be less effective in communicating such an attitude in a group relationship and trusting that the members have the potential for incorporating and subsequently communicating similar attitudes? While it is recognized that the group counselor must possess certain skills and have an understanding of group dynamics, the apparent inability to function in a group setting, it would seem, is a function of his personal biases and needs rather than merely a manifestation of an accepted principle.

It has been suggested that the kind of helping relationship characterized in the counseling relationship is nonpossessive love. By this is meant far more than a mere physical attraction for another person, but rather a warm acceptance and liking for the other person as an individual regardless of the feelings which he may possess as an individual, and an unbending trust that he has the capacity more than anyone else to determine his own destiny.

A study by Quinn [9] which has significant implications for all counselors showed that the creation of a helping relationship is facilitated by the counselor's desire to understand the communication and feelings and attitudes of the client. Passive acceptance would not appear to be a sufficient condition for a helping relationship to exist. It would appear that it is the sharing with another person—another person who is willing to listen and to understand and to accept—which is the essential quality present in a helping relationship. Only as the other person can accept me for what I am do I dare to really look into myself to see all the hidden pockets of self-discontent which I have kept from awareness for such a long period of time.

Perhaps each counselor needs to ask himself how willing he is to listen, to understand, to accept; to allow others to understand the communication and feelings and attitudes of their peers; to allow others to give as well as to receive help; to permit others not to need him and thus be more self-reliant;

how willing he is to be a member, not a leader of a group, giving of himself with no demands for reciprocity. If counselors can truly be helping persons, is not the group a ready medium for such an experience and not just a catalyst for individual counseling?

REFERENCES

1. Bach, George R. *Intensive Group Psychotherapy* (New York: The Ronald Press Company, 1954).

2. Boy, Angelo V., et al. "Multiple Counseling: A Catalyst for Individual Counseling," *The School Counselor*, published by The American School Counselor Association, 11 (October 1963), 8–11.

3. Caplan, Stanley Williams. "The Effect of Group Counseling on Junior High School Boys' Concepts of Themselves in School," *Journal of Counseling Psychology* (1957), 4, 124–128.

4. Corsini, Raymond J. *Methods of Group Psychotherapy* (New York: Mc-Graw-Hill Book Company, Inc., 1957).

5. Hobbs, Nicholas. "Group-Centered Psychotherapy," in Carl R. Rogers, *Client-Centered Therapy* (Boston: Houghton Mifflin Company, 1951).

6. Goldman, Leo. "Group Guidance: Content and Process," *Personnel and Guidance Journal*, 40 (1962), 518–522.

7. Gorlow, Leon, et al. *The Nature of Non-directive Group Psychotherapy* (New York: Teachers College Bureau of Publications, 1952).

8. *Proposed Statement of Policy for Secondary School Counselors and Proposed Guidelines for Implementation of the ASCA Statement of Policy for Secondary School Counselors* (Washington, D. C.: American School Counselor Association, 1964).

9. Quinn, R. D. *Psychotherapists' Expressions as an Index to the Quality of Early Therapeutic Relationships.* Unpublished doctoral dissertation University of Chicago, 1950.

10. Rogers, Carl R. *On Becoming a Person* (Boston: Houghton Mifflin Co., 1961).

11. Rossberg, Robert and Jacques, Marceline. "The Role of the Group in Patient Evaluation Counseling and Management," *Personnel and Guidance Journal* (October 1961), pp. 135–142.

12. Warters, Jane. *Group Guidance* (New York: McGraw-Hill Book Company, Inc., 1960).

13. Wright, E. Wayne. "Group Procedures," *Review of Educational Research*, American Educational Research Association, 33 (April 1963), 206.

14. Wright, E. Wayne. "Multiple Counseling—Why? When? How?," *Personnel and Guidance Journal*, 57 (1959), 551–557.

ADDITIONAL REFERENCES

Glanz, Edward C. *Groups in Guidance* (Boston: Allyn and Bacon, Inc., 1962).

Kennedy, Eugene C. *Characteristics of the Counselor.* Unpublished manuscript at Maryknoll Seminary, Glen Ellyn, Ill. & Loyola University, Chicago.

Lewin, Kurt. *Resolving Social Conflicts* (Harper and Brothers, c1948).

Lifton, Walter M. *Working with Groups* (New York: J. Wiley and Sons, Inc., 1962).

11

A Comparison of Individual and Multiple
Counseling for Test Interpretation
Interviews*

E. Wayne Wright

The relative effectiveness of individual and multiple (group) counseling in test interpretation interviews was evaluated in terms of pre- and post-counseling measures on four criteria: (a) accuracy of self ratings; (b) acquisition of information about tests; (c) feasibility of vocational choice; and (d) counselee satisfaction. The two experimental groups were also compared with a noncounseled control group, each group comprising a random sample of 100 university freshmen. Although no differences existed among the study groups at the outset of the study, postcounseling criteria measures showed significant gains by both experimental groups over the control. Relatively few postcounseling differences of any significance, however, were observed between the individual and multiple-counseled. The results of the study supported the use of multiple counseling as an effective approach for disseminating and interpreting test information.

Group procedures in counseling and guidance have long been considered (and used) by counselors as an expedient for accomodating increasing counselee loads [11,14,21,24]. However, research in group dynamics during the past decade suggests that the use of groups for various guidance and psychological functions might often provide advantages, other than just expediency, that are not attainable in individualized processes alone 6,8,19 . There seems a need, therefore, for counselors to determine the unique contributions to be made by group, as well as individual procedures in counseling, and to identify guidance and counseling tasks for which each process may be best indicated.

One group procedure that has received increased attention, recently, in educational settings is multiple (or group) counseling [4,5,10,25]. However, any distinctive merits of multiple counseling are still inconclusive in comparison with the more-generally-accepted individual approach. Relatively few experimental studies have reported this comparison as their purpose [1,2,3,15,16]. Hoyt [17] and Hoyt and Moore [18] support a belief

*Reprinted by permission of the author and publisher from *Journal of Counseling Psychology*, 10 (1963), 126–135.

in the potential of multiple counseling, but indicate the need for further comparisons of the group process with individual counseling in different settings and for various purposes. Wrenn [26] suggests the desirability of identifying the distinctive values of each process, and Hewer [16] points up the importance of including a comparable control group in the experimental design.

PURPOSE OF THE STUDY AND HYPOTHESES

The purpose of the present study was to investigate the relative effectiveness of individual and multiple counseling procedures for disseminating and interpreting test data to students. Comparisons among the study groups were made in terms of pre- and postcounseling measures on four criteria: (1) accuracy of self-ratings; (2) acquisition of information about tests; (3) feasibility of vocational choice; and (4) counselee satisfaction.

In brief, it was hypothesized that (1) both experimental groups (individual and multiple counseled) would show significant improvement through counseling, (2) both experimental groups would improve significantly more than the control group (not counseled), and (3) there would be no significant postcounseling differences between the two experimental groups.

DESIGN AND METHOD

SUBJECTS

A random sample[1] of 750 freshmen at Brigham Young University were stratified by age and sex and were divided into three groups of 250 students each. From this universe a final sample of 300 subjects (100 from each of the three stratified groups) was selected by a table of random numbers to comprise two experimental groups and a control of 100 students each.

Groups I and II were invited by letter to make a counseling appointment to review the results of their freshman guidance tests. Students of Group I who responded were seen in individual interviews only. Group II respondents were scheduled in groups of five to ten students each. Since Group III was to serve as a control, students of this group were not invited to receive counseling. Students of Group III who requested counseling on their own

[1]The study universe represented approximately one-fourth of the freshman class and consisted of the total number of students assigned to the two counselors who participated in the study. The assignment of all entering freshmen to a counselor was accomplished by distributing orientation schedule cards, each bearing a counselor's name, to the entire freshman class assembled at the orientation meeting. By "stacking the cards" so that the name of each of the eight university counselors appeared alternately, every eighth card, it was assumed that the sample assigned to any one counselor would be representative of the total group. Chi-square tests of equivalency between the universe of 750 students and the remainder of the freshman class confirmed the assumed randomness in the factors of age, sex, scholastic aptitude, and high school grade point average.

initiative were scheduled for appointments after the conclusion of the study. Although some students of Groups I and II requested counseling appointments after the conclusion of the experimental period, only those who received a counseling appointment during the period of the study and who completed the postcounseling measures were retained in the study sample. The resultant groups numbered as follows: Group I, 24 males and 32 females; Group II, 30 males and 34 females; Group III, 28 males and 37 females. Chi-square tests of equivalency showed the resultant three groups to be comparable to each other, as well as to the original universe, in factors of age, sex, intelligence, and high school grade point average. Precounseling measures on the study criteria, also, indicated no differences in these characteristics among the study groups at the outset of the experimentation.

CRITERIA

1. Using the technique reported by Cronbach and Gleser [7] for assessing similarities between profiles, the accuracy of self-ratings criterion was evaluated in terms of the degree to which a student's self-ratings (on a five-point scale) of his performance on standardized tests approached congruence with the quintile equivalents of his actual scores on the tests. Two types of comparisons were made with this criterion: (a) t tests between the *mean* self-rating accuracy of subjects on each of the tests, and (b) chi-square tests between the incidence of self-ratings which were "correct" (coincident with test score) and "incorrect" (not coincident with test score).

Three standardized tests were used for evaluating self-rating accuracy. These were the American Council on Education Psychological Examination, 1949 College Edition, the Kuder Preference Record, Vocational Form CM, and the Cooperative General Culture Test, Form YY. All of these tests had been previously administered to the subjects of the study at the time of freshman orientation. Test results were reported in quintile scores.

2. The acquisition of information criterion was based on the assumption that one must have a knowledge about tests in order to interpret their results properly. The amount of test knowledge held by the subjects of the study was measured by a quiz covering four areas deemed important for valid test interpretation: (a) differentiation between types of tests, (b) values and limitations of tests, (c) normative data, and (d) kinds of interpretative scores. The test items were refined by a group of counselors and students and were tested for reliability prior to use in the study.

3. Feasibility of vocational choice was judged by three counselors, each of whom was asked to make an independent evaluation of each student's vocational goal and to judge whether the stated goal of the student seemed to be at all feasible in light of the student's measured ability, interests, and achievements or not. Agreement in rating by at least two of the

three counselors was required for a goal to be rated "feasible" or "not feasible." Cases lacking concurrence by two or more judges were rated "uncertain."

4. The measure of counselee satisfaction was obtained by means of a follow-up questionnaire designed to sample counselee feelings on four dimensions: (a) warmth of the relationship, (b) coverage of the test information, (c) clarity of the test interpretation, and (d) value of the test interpretation for educationl and vocational planning. The subjects were requested to rate each area on a five-point scale, with item descriptions ranging from negative (low satisfaction) to positive (high satisfaction) feelings.

METHOD

Prior to the scheduling of appointments, subjects of both experimental groups were assigned, by means of a table of random numbers, to one of two participating counselors. Thus, both counselors saw approximately the same number of counselees, and both conducted multiple as well as individual counseling sessions.

Precounseling measures of the test of information and the self-rating scale were obtained for students of both experimental groups at the time each student arrived for his appointment and immediately preceding introduction to his counselor. The counseling sessions were then conducted in accord with the needs of each individual or group, but semistructured regarding the method of test interpretation and the coverage of general information. All interviews were scheduled for fifty-minute periods.

During the interview, each student was given the quintile values of his test scores and was asked to mark these on the self-rating profile sheet he had completed prior to the interview. Following the counselor's explanation of the various tests and of the meaning of scores, each student was encouraged to observe the differences between his self-ratings and actual scores and to raise questions relevant to needed clarification of the test interpretation. Hypothetical cases, as well as the subject's own scores, were discussed to illustrate the relationship of test scores to success in various educational courses and subsequent vocational goals.

While all students were encouraged to return for further appointments whenever they desired, those seen in group sessions were particularly urged to request a subsequent appointment individually if they felt upset by the test interpretation or if they had any questions that were not answered in the group.

Immediately following the interview, all counseled students were asked to complete the satisfaction questionnaire. A second measure of satisfaction feelings, as well as the postcounseling measures for each of the other criteria, were obtained by mail approximately three months after counseling for both of the experimental groups. At the same time, the control group was also reached by mail and asked to complete the same measures. Tests of significance, utilizing either the *t* ratio or chi-square method, were made of the changes that occurred (a) *within* each experimental group, (b) *between* the two experimental groups, and (c) between each of the experimental groups and the control group.

RESULTS

WITHIN-GROUP COMPARISONS (COUNSELED)

With few exceptions, both counseled groups showed significant gains after counseling, with the greatest amount of improvement in both groups being evidenced in the accuracy of self-ratings.

1. Table 1 shows that while both groups made significant improvement in self-rating accuracy of *aptitude* and *achievement* profiles, only Group I (individually-counseled) improved significantly in *interest* self-ratings. However, the net improvement in self-ratings with all three tests combined was equally significant for both groups.

Table 1

Within-group Changes in Self-Rating Accuracy

Test	Group [a]	N	Mean Self-Rating Accuracy		Diff. Means	r_{ab} [c]	S.E. Diff.	t
			Pre-couns.	Post-couns.				
ACE	I	56	1.853	1.229	.624	.394	.142	4.394**
	II	62	1.626	1.156	.470	.452	.128	3.672**
Kuder	I	55	4.026	3.481	.545	.449	.140	3.893**
	II	63	4.089	3.856	.233	.320	.141	1.652
Coop. General	I	53	2.794	2.009	.785	.141	.178	4.410**
Culture	II	62	2.752	1.820	.932	.452	.128	7.281**
Total [b]	I	164	2.886	2.236	.650	.646	.144	4.514**
	II	187	2.829	2.286	.543	.542	.148	3.669**

[a] I Individual Counseled.
II Multiple Counseled.

[b] Mean self-rating accuracy determined for the profile of all three tests combined.
[c] Correlation between precounseling (a) and postcounseling (b) measures.
**Significant at the .01 level of confidence.

In addition to showing postcounseling gains in *mean* self-rating accuracy, both groups also improved in predicting some of their highest scores, but the latter gains were not uniform for all tests. By weighting predictions according to correctness of rank order (i.e. whether the score was correctly predicted as highest, second highest, or third highest) the differences between pre- and postcounseling predictions of high *interests* produced *t* ratios of 3.378°° and 1.422 for Group I and Group II, respectively. In other words, Group I improved in predicting their three highest interest

°° Significant at the .01 level of confidence.

scores, but Group II did not. Both groups improved, however, in predicting high *achievement* scores (*t* ratio of 3.677°° for Group I and 3.943°° for Group II). Neither group improved significantly in predicting highest *aptitude* (Q or L), but analysis of precounseling predictions of aptitudes revealed little chance for improvement on this test, since most students predicted their high aptitude score correctly in the beginning.

Another analysis of self-ratings, using a chi-square test, showed that a significantly greater number of self-ratings on each test had changed from "incorrect" (disagreed with test score) before counseling to "correct" (agreed with test score) after counseling than had changed from correct to incorrect. For Group I these changes were significant at the .01 level on all three tests. Group II gains were significant at the .02, .05, and .01 levels for the ACE, Kuder, and Cooperative General Culture Tests, respectively.

2. Group II, the multiple-counseled group, showed significant improvement on the postcounseling test of information scores while Group I, the individually-counseled group, did not.

3. Neither group showed change in purported vocational goals during the time period of this study.

BETWEEN-GROUP COMPARISONS (COUNSELED AND NONCOUNSELED)

In general, few significant differences were observed between the two counseled groups; however, *both* experimental groups showed significant improvement over the noncounseled group. These findings are reported in Tables 2 and 3.

Table 2

Between-group Comparisons of Self-Rating Accuracy

Test	Group [a]	N	Mean Self-Rating Accuracy Pre-couns.	Post-couns.	Group Comparison	Precounseling Diff. Mean	S.E. Diff.	t	Postcounseling Diff. Mean	S.E. Diff.	t
ACE	I	56	1.853	1.229	I-II	.227	.177	1.282	.073	.178	.410
	II	62	1.626	1.156	I-III	.031	.175	.177	.655	.177	3.701**
	III	64		1.884	II-III	.258	.172	1.500	.728	.170	4.282**
Kuder	I	55	4.026	3.481	I-II	.063	.172	.366	.375	.188	1.995*
	II	63	4.089	3.856	I-III	.184	.193	.953	.729	.199	3.663**
	III	64		4.210	II-III	.121	.183	.661	.354	.191	1.853
Coop.	I	53	2.794	2.009	I-II	.042	.187	.225	.189	.203	.931
General	II	62	2.752	1.820	I-III	.132	.188	.702	.917	.189	4.852**
Culture	III	62		2.926	II-III	.174	.185	.941	1.106	.200	5.530**
Total	I	164	2.886	2.236	I-II	.057	.145	.393	.050	.157	.318
	II	187	2.829	2.286	I-III	.122	.145	.841	.772	.149	5.181**
	III	190		3.008	II-III	.179	.145	1.234	.722	.154	4.688**

[a] I Individual Counseled.
II Multiple Counseled.
III Not Counseled.

* Significant at the .05 level of confidence.
** Significant at the .01 level of confidence.

Table 3

Within-group and Between-group Comparisons on the Test of Information

Group[a]	N	Mean Score Pre-couns.	Post-couns.	r_{ab}[b]	Group Comparison	Precounseling Diff. Means	S.E. Diff.	t	Postcounseling Diff. Means	S.E. Diff.	t
I	51	16.196	17.539	.375	I_a-I_b				1.343	.697	1.927
					I-II	1.474	.762	1.934	.159	.836	.190
II	63	14.722	17.698	.500	II_a-II_b				2.976	.506	5.881**
					II-III	.278	.686	.405	2.698	.776	3.477**
III	65		15.000		I-III	1.196	.806	1.484	2.539	.816	3.112**

[a] I Individual Counseled.
II Multiple Counseled.
III Not Counseled.
[b] Correlation between precounseling (a) and postcounseling (b) measures.
**Significant at the .01 level of confidence.

1. The greatest differences between the experimental and control groups were evidenced on the self-rating criterion. It can be seen in Table 2 that, with only one exception, students of both counseled groups improved significantly over noncounseled students in the accuracy of their self-ratings. The exception, as noted above in the comparisons *within* the two counseled groups, was on the Kuder profile. The Kuder was the only test area in which there was no difference between multiple-counseled and noncounseled students and in which there *was* a difference between individually-counseled and multiple-counseled students, the difference being in favor of the individually-counseled.

Counseled students also predicted their three highest interest and achievement scores more accurately than noncounseled students, with weighted predictions producing differences between both experimental groups and the control group significant at the .01 level on both test areas. There was no difference on this particular analysis between the two counseled groups.

As indicated above, a significant number of students were able to predict their highest score on the ACE both before and after counseling, hence, no differences were observed among the groups in their postcounseling predictions of highest aptitude score.

2. Differences observed on the test of information criterion are found in Table 3. Even though Group II made a greater change than Group I on this criterion, the postcounseling difference *between* the two groups was not beyond the chance level. Significant differences on the test of information were found, however, between both experimental groups and the control group.

A final analysis of the improvement shown by each of the counseled groups on the criteria of self-ratings and acquisition of information, was made by tabulating the number of students in each group who "improved," "got worse," or "did not change." Tabulations were made separately for improvement shown on the test of information and for accuracy of self-ratings on each of the ACE, Kuder and Coop. General Cultural tests. Chi-square tests between the two groups showed a significant difference (chi square of 5.440°) only on the test of information, with Group II having a greater number of students than Group I who improved on this criterion. Other than this, both groups had about the same number of students who "improved," "got worse," or "did not change." A similar analysis between the counselees of the two participating counselors showed that improvement was not unique to the subjects of either counselor, since both produced essentially the same number of counselees who improved, got worse, or did not change.

3. The vocational choice criterion showed no differences among any of the groups in the number of "feasible" and "not feasible" postcounseling goals. A majority of student goals in all three groups were judged "feasible" even before counseling, and the same held true after counseling.

4. The two counseled groups differed in several instances in the comparisons of their immediate and delayed responses to the satisfaction questionnaire. Although both groups reported a predominance of favorable responses, Group I students, the individually-counseled, responded with a greater number of highly-positive ratings ("very effective," "very complete," "could not be better") than did Group II students, the latter group tending more toward moderately-positive and neutral feelings (i.e. "Adequate," "only a few questions not answered," "of some value"). The differences in ratings between the two groups were greater, however, on the responses immediately following counseling than on the delayed measures of satisfaction. After the "cooling off" period of three months, both groups reduced their ratings toward more neutral feelings, with Group I ratings making the greater change and becoming more similar to the ratings of Group II. On the immediate questionnaire, all of the differences in ratings between the two groups were significant at the .01 level of confidence, but this reduced in each case to the .05 level on the delayed responses.

5. Although opportunity was provided students of both experimental groups to request second or third interviews following the initial test interpretation session, there was no significant difference in the number of either group who did so. Relatively few students requested repeat interviews during the time of the study and these were divided about equally between the two experimental groups.

DISCUSSION

That test interpretation interviews contribute to a student's better understanding of himself, seems a justifiable conclusion on the basis of the present study. Equally tenable is the hypothesis that multiple counseling

° .05 level of confidence.

might serve some functions of counseling as well as the traditional one-to-one approach.

It should be clarified at this point that those who have supported the use of multiple counseling [9,13,20,27] have not intended for the group process to replace individual contacts. On the contrary, previous research has shown that multiple counseling not only motivates more students to take advantage of the counseling service, but also serves to prepare them better for the individual interview [22,23]. It has, therefore, been contended by exponents of this group process that multiple counseling can and should supplement individual counseling by (1) providing some kinds of counseling experiences more effectively through the unique advantages of group interaction, and (2) accomplishing certain types of routine guidance tasks more economically than seems possible by the exclusive use of individual interviewing. The economic factor of multiple counseling should not be construed only as a time saver, however, but as a means by which counselors would have increased opportunity for a thorough follow-up of a greater number of students who need and might benefit from more extensive help.

The multiple counseling sessions of the present study were not only more *economical* than the individual interviews (in terms of the number of counselees seen per counselor-hour), but equally as *effective* in contributing to improved counselee learning about self. In fact, on the test of information criterion, students of the group sessions apparently retained even more knowledge than students seen individually (however, it is not suggested that this was due especially to group interaction, since the kind of interview described in this study was primarily informational). An attempt to explain this difference between the two groups raises a question: "Might a counselor (consciously or unconsciously) give more time and thoroughness in presenting and clarifying information when he knows that one presentation, to a group of students, will replace the need for monotonous repetition of the same information to a number of counselees separately?" One may also wonder if a counselor feels a greater urgency to be more thorough in providing test information in group sessions than in individual interviews because of the implication that multiple-counseled students may receive less individual counselor attention and must, therefore, carry more responsibility for interpreting their own scores. While it is no doubt desirable to present information clearly and to involve the client in the interpretation of the information, it is also true that in his desire for thoroughness the counselor might talk *too* much. This suggests the need for research evaluating the amount of counselor-client talk and the division of responsibility in multiple counseling as compared with the individual counseling.

The only other difference between individual- and multiple-counseled students in terms of the learning that occurred in the present study was found in self-ratings on the Kuder profile. Individually-counseled students were able to rate their interest scales more accurately after counseling than multiple-counseled students. Not only is it probable that the accurate retention of interpreted scores decreases as the number of test scales increases, but it may also be that counselors and students attach less importance to *interest* measures than to *aptitudes* and *achievements* and thus "gloss over," somewhat more, the interpretation of interest profiles. This particular finding regarding the differences between Groups I and II in Kuder ratings might also be viewed in terms of Festinger's [12] theory of cognitive dissonance (the application of which to self-rating studies in counseling seems an interesting direction for additional research). Inasmuch as students seen individually no doubt had more opportunity than those counseled in groups to discuss each separate scale on their test profiles, it seems likely that the individually-counseled students may have been made more aware of subtle, as well as sharp, differences between their perceived and measured interests. Conversely, multiple-counseled students, when asked to view their own test profiles in light of the general *group* discussion, may have overlooked less marked discrepancies between ratings and test scores (particularly on those scales less important to their self concepts) if their first, or over-all impression regarding their *major* areas of interest confirmed their general expectations. This would produce little or no feelings of dissonance (or felt need for change) in their perceived interests.

The lack of movement on the vocational choice criterion of this study raises several questions, for this writer, which would seem to bear further investigation: (1) does the fact that the majority of students in this study already had "feasible" vocational goals even *before* counseling suggest that *vocational* counseling is needed only by a relatively few students by the time they enter college?; (2) how might the appropriateness of a vocational choice be better determined than merely by the judged "feasibility" in terms of measured abilities, interests, etc., since "feasibility" of a goal does not necessarily imply a *best* choice; and (3) in view of developmental concepts regarding vocational choice, how long an experimental period or how many counseling interviews would seem to be a minimum of time before one might anticipate measurable changes in vocational choice as a criterion of counseling effectiveness?

A final implication that might be drawn from the results of this study deals with the differences observed between the two experimental groups in the counselee ratings of satisfaction. Inasmuch as Group I rated the counseling more highly than did Group II (regarding the "warmth of the relationship," "coverage and clarity of the test interpretation," and "value of the test interpretation") one might conclude that individual counseling may have provided a better "climate" or interview relationship than was felt by the counselees in the group session. However, the fact that the differences in satisfaction feelings of the two groups were not as great on the delayed questionnaire as on the immediate questionnaire raises a question regarding the extent to which the feelings of both groups might be even more congruent after a longer period of postcounseling incubation.

The differences in counselee satisfaction did not change the fact that both counseling approaches produced comparable amounts of learning in terms of improved self-knowledge. For this reason one wonders about the relative importance of counselee satisfaction as a criterion of counseling effectiveness. The findings on this criterion would seem to indicate that a counselee need not feel completely satisfied with, or highly positive about, counseling in order to benefit from the experience. On the other hand, when is the counselee's positive regard toward the interview or counselor a crucial factor in establishing rapport and effecting subsequent learning and change? In view of the importance currently being given to the "relationship" in counseling, additional investigation is suggested regarding the nature and evaluation of relationships developed in multiple counseling sessions which are devoted to more extensive counseling goals than merely the dissemination and interpretation of general information and test data.

Received November 20, 1962.

REFERENCES

1. Bailey, B. "A Comparison of Multiple and Individual Counseling in Terms of Self-knowledge." Unpublished manuscript, Univer. of Calif. (1955).

2. Baymur, F., & Patterson, C. H. "Three Methods of Assisting Underachieving HighSchool Students," *J. Counsel. Psychol.* (1960), **7**, 83–90.

3. Bilovsky, D., et al. "Individual and Group Counseling," *Personnel Guid. J.* (1953), **31**, 363–365.

4. Broedel, J., Ohlsen, M., Proff, F., & Southard, C. "The Effects of Group Counseling on Gifted Underachieving Adolescents," *J. Counsel. Psychol.* (1960), **7**, 163–170.

5. Caplan, S. W. "The Effect of Group Counseling On Junior High School Boys' Concept Of Themselves in School," *J. Counsel. Psychol.* (1957), **4**, 124–128.

6. Cartwright, D., & Zander, A. *Group Dynamics Research and Theory* (Evanston, Ill.: Row, Peterson, 1956).

7. Cronbach, L. J., & Gleser, G. C. "Assessing Similarities Between Profiles," *Psychol. Bull.* (1953), **50**, 456–473.

8. Crutchfield, R. S. "Social Psychology and Group Processes," *Ann. Rev. Psychol.* (1954), 171–202.

9. Driver, Helen I. *Multiple Counseling: A Small Group Discussion Method for Personal Growth* (Madison, Wis.: Monona Publications, 1954).

10. Driver, Helen I. "Small Group Discussion," *Personnel Guid. J.* (1952), **30**, 173–175.

11. Failor, C. W. "Group Activities in Guidance Services," *Personnel Guid. J.* (1954), **32**, 411–414.

12. Festinger, L. "Cognitive Dissonance," *Scientific American* (1962), **207**, 93–102.

13. Froehlich, C. P. "Multiple Counseling: A Research Proposal." Unpublished manuscript, Univer. of Calif., Berkeley, Calif., 1953.

14. Froehlich, C. P. "Group Guidance Approaches in Educational Institutions," *Rev. Educ. Res.* (1954), **24**, 147–155.

15. Froehlich, C. P. "Must Counseling Be Individual," *Educ. Psychol. Meas.* (1958), **18**, 681–689.

16. Hewer, Vivian H. "Group Counseling, Individual Counseling, and a College Class in Vocations," *Personnel Guid. J.* (1959), **37**, 660–665.

17. Hoyt, D. P. "An Evaluation of Group and Individual Programs in Vocational Guidance," *J. Appl. Psychol.* (1955), **39**, 26–30.

18. Hoyt, K. B., & Moore, G. D. "Group Procedures in Guidance and Personnel Work," *Rev. Educ. Res.* (1960), **30**, 158–166.

19. Katz, E., & Lazarsfeld, P. F. *Personal Influence* (Glencoe, Ill.: Free Press, 1955).

20. Ohlsen, Merle M. "Counseling Adolescents in Groups." A address delivered to the Minnesota counselors association conference, Highland Park Junion High School, St. Paul, Minnesota, February 3, 1961.

21. Pepinsky, H. B. "The Role of Group Procedures In the Counseling Program. In R. F. Berdie, *Roles and Relationships in Counseling* (Minneapolis: Univer. of Minn. Press, 1953).

22. Richardson, H., & Borow, H. "An Evaluation of a Technique of Group Orientation for Vocational Guidance," *Educ. Psychol. Measmt.* (1952), **12**, 587–597.

23. Shostrom, E. L., & Brammer, L. M. *The Dynamics of the Counseling Process* (New York: McGraw-Hill, 1952), 47–61.

24. Super, D. E. "Group Techniques in the Guidance Program, " *Educ. Psychol. Measmt.* (1949), **9**, 496–510.

25. Volsky, T., & Hewer, Vivian H. "A Program of Group Counseling," *J. Counsel. Psychol.* (1960), **7**, 71–73.

26. Wrenn, C. G. Editorial comment. *J. Counsel. Psychol.* (1960), **7**, No. 4.

27. Wright, E. W. "Multiple Counseling? Why? When? How?" *Personnel Guid. J.* (1959), **37**, 551–557.

Chapter IV

GROUP COUNSELING IN ACTION

Many activities have been carried on under the general heading of group counseling, as previous chapters have indicated. The various attempts to delimit group counseling through definitions have not made clear just what does go on in a counseling group. The selections in this chapter have been chosen because they offer the reader some detailed, albeit incomplete, explication of group counseling in action. By studying a collection of articles each of which reports in some detail at least one aspect of the process, the reader may acquire some of the flavor of a group counseling experience. Among the elements which might be highlighted in an individual article, other than the design for research which may be the author's main concern, are the participants, the purposes, the content, the counselor role, and the member roles. A further differentiation may be discovered by comparing and contrasting group counseling at different age levels of group members.

In preparing this section of the book, the editors desired to present articles which would illustrate clearly some unique features of group counseling with younger children, with preadolescents, with high school youth, and with adults. However, the search of the literature for appropriate articles failed to disclose many materials that would lend themselves well to this purpose. This may be due to a style of writing among scholars which treats rather casually the description of the group process. On the other hand, the limited supply of literature illustrating aspects of a process peculiar to certain age groups may indicate there are no uniquenesses. As more experience is gained and reported about group counseling, it will be helpful to have the possibilities of age-related elements explored more fully. It is also to be hoped that a wider range of goals will be sought through group counseling. In the present collection of articles "under-achievement" appears by far the most popular problem which has been attacked through group counseling. Ten of the projects reported here are attempts to reduce under-achievement while several are concerned with other student inadequacies. How about some studies of group counseling to help achievers find deeper meanings and broader goals than success in courses?

As long as group counseling is employed primarily as a tool with which to take corrective action with students who are not accomplishing minimum goals, the power of the tool will not be fully appreciated. Personnel workers should be encouraged to attempt group counseling with students who are functioning well according to traditional criteria. Through the stimulation of the group process, such students can explore questions which go beyond mastery of subject matter. They can discuss the interrelationships among subjects, express the joy of mastery, share the suspense of posing questions which threaten the alleged certainties of subject matter. They can struggle with an effort to draw from their knowledge guiding principles for application in living beyond today and beyond the school. In short, group counseling with students who are coping will with traditional school demands may enhance creativity and independence.

In reading the following articles, one might ask these questions: (1) Are there elements in the group counseling process which are unique to work with a certain age group? (2) What purposes and goals are relevant for group counseling? (3) How are participants selected? (4) What behavior is to be expected from members? (5) What is typically discussed by the group in counseling? (6) How does the counselor function during the sessions? (7) What adjunctive activities may be included within a group counseling experience?

12

Mechanisms and Practical Techniques in Group Counseling in the Elementary School*

Manford A. Sonstegard

The problems of our children are primarily social. Each child tries to find his place in society. His behavior expresses his social orientation and intention [2]. In this light, behavior is a movement toward a goal. It is not sufficient to know what a teacher "feels" toward a child, or the child toward the teacher. It is more important to discover what the pupil *does* to the teacher and how she responds to his misbehavior. Usually her reactions are in line with his intentions, which she does not recognize [4]. The counseling approach must serve to clarify and if necessary, improve the nature of interaction. We need to deal with a problem common to both teacher and student, i.e., their relationship [10,13].

The recognition that the problem of all children is essentially social gives group counseling its special significance both for diagnosis of the child's problems and for their solution. In the action and interaction between group members, each expresses his goals, his social orientation, and his intentions. Looking for deep psychological processes in the child and his parents is not only unnecessary, but even discouraged, as such "introspection" usually loses sight of real problems.

The concept that man is an indivisible, social, and decision-making being, whose actions have a social purpose is not always easily grasped. Behind us is a history of mechanistic approaches to behavior, explaining it either by physiological functions and hereditary endowment or as a result of environmental influences. It is not surprising that behavior, at first, was understood to be based on habits, mechanistically developed through responses to stimulation. One assumed an interplay between hereditary endowment, physiological processes, and environmental stimulations. The controversy raged as to which played the more dominant role in determining behavior, heredity, or environment. In an autocratic society the first was considered as decisive; man was born good or bad, high or

*Reprinted by permission of the author from a paper read at the American Personnel and Guidance Association Convention, Washington, D.C.., April 6, 1966.

low. With the democratic evolution, the emphasis shifted to environmental influences. But in either point of view, man was considered a
passive victim between forces within him and around him. Personality was
thought of as a product of the struggle between hereditary and environmental forces. Later modifications of this concept pictured either biologi-
cal drives being in constant conflict with the demands of society, or
physiological processes distinguishing each organism.

In contrast to these concepts, teleo-analytic psychologists [4] see man's
behavior not as a result of the impingement of environment upon his
psychophysical makeup; but rather as his way of perceiving his hereditary
endowment and environmental experiences, his interpretation of what he
sees and the conclusion which he draws. Man formulates his own individual goals and purposes in life and molds both his hereditary makeup
and environmental experiences according to his self-created "private logic."

The concept that maladjustment means uncertainty about one's
place among fellowmen replaced the deterministic explanation of
maladjustment as a consequence of pathological processes within the individual. It was Adler who postulated an "Ironclad Logic of Social Living,"
and "the unity of personality" which became the basis for what he called
Individual Psychology. This new psychology is in tune with the forward
surge of democratic principles recognizing man's ability to decide for himself [1]. It has provided a formula for democratic living by accepting social
equality as the basis for cooperation and social harmony. In this light, the
tremendous intrinsic power and strength of each individual becomes
recognized. A child may appear weak and deficient when he becomes discouraged and loses his self-confidence. Actually, he is merely using wrong
methods to find his place. The teleological perspective of Individual Psychology permits recognition of the creative ability of every individual,
be he good or bad, "strong" or "weak," as he determines his actions toward
self-directed goals. This holistic socioteleologic concept of man is the basis
for our counseling as an educational and correctional approach toward a
change of behavior and personality [5].

In an autocratic society, all human relationships are those of
superiority and inferiority, dominance and submission. In a democratic
society everybody reaches a state of equality [6]. In the development of
democracy, the power to "make" a student perform, behave, or study decreases [3]. As the individual achieves a status of equality, inner motivation becomes more important than pressure from without. When the
authority of adults diminishes, the group of peers gains in importance.

Group counseling is a natural tool for dealing with relationships.
Through group counseling we can experiment with interactions and produce
changes in the mistaken goals which the student is pursuing. Heretofore,
the element of privacy has been an indispensable requirement of counseling.

Willingness to air intimate feelings and conflicts in front of others was considered a sign of exhibitionism or other abnormal needs. It has been our experience that this need for privacy is often a neurotic reaction, prevalent in a highly competive era. "People live a life of quiet desperation," Thoreau stated. They reside in an atmosphere of emotional isolation, ever fearful that deficiences will be discovered. It is this fear that clamors for privacy. It is the lack of mutual trust, of the all-important feeling of belonging, which keeps people at a distance. It has been observed that this is less true of young children, but becomes more pronounced as they advance through the grades.

The spread of group counseling is not only the consequence of a lack of sufficiently trained counselors, it also reflects public interest in and a request for new and more effective methods. The social values promulgated in group counseling are in line with man's search for equality and cooperation. Group counseling teaches each member to deal with one another as equals. This implies more than assistance to individuals; it becomes a social force in a culture which is in a transitional stage from an authoritarian to a democratic society. Thus, it is more than counseling, more than education. Group counseling is a product of the democratic evolution and a tool to meet its needs.

The impact of the group on each child is readily observed whenever he participates within it. The use of the group to influence the child not only constitutes an effective way to teach, but also an effective means of exerting corrective influences. Group techniques are more imperative in a democratic society where the authority of the individual has been replaced by the authority of the group. The group is the reality in which the child operates.

What are the dynamics of group counseling? Any attempt to formulate a theory for the effectiveness of group counseling is encumbered by historical antecedents. Counseling is still looked upon in many circles as a form of dealing with individual problems. The educational feature of group counseling is one of its unique mechanisms. Group counseling is learning. If learning is to take place, there must be action.

Kelly [8] points out, in the Hanover study, that a subject could look upon objects in a compartment but was unable to "see" what he was looking at until he took action by touching one of the objects with a pointer or stick. Then everything fell into place and he could "see" the object. In the group, participation is the action that is necessary for "seeing." Without participation by group members, no therapy can result. The participation may be of a non-verbal nature. The writer has experienced group sessions when a youngster who is extremely withdrawn would have withdrawn still further and perhaps left the group if pushed to interact verbally. Permitted to participate more passively on the nonverbal level as by a smile, movement of the lips, twinkle of the eye, or other reactions to the interaction of the other group members, the with-drawn youngster, after a period of time, forgot himself and began to participate verbally. Most people have observed that talking to someone about a problem is often beneficial. Even though the other person may merely listen, without any comment, the one who talked may go away with some clarification of his problem. Disclosures in a group are similar ex-cept for the added advantage of the benefits of "feedback" from group members, guided and stimulated by the counselor. The effectiveness of this procedure is sometimes expressed by, "What you say is nothing new but I had never thought of it that way before."

Insight, and thereby an understanding of our own problems through listening to someone discussing his, is another phenomenon of group counseling. For example, a parent came for individual counseling. It be-came clear, after a number of interviews, that the necessary reorientation was going to be slow. It was suggested that the mother attend the parent group counseling sessions. During the second group session, she interrupted the discussion with, "Now I know what I am doing wrong." A remark by the other mother struck a chord which the counselor, in individual sessions, was unable to achieve. From that point on, the counselor actually counseled two mothers simultaneously, with the other parents in the group participating and benefiting. The group member identifies with others, comes to understand their feelings, accept their ideas, and encourages participation. Universalization is the cementing element in achieving group cohesiveness. This is true for adults as well as for children.

Some youngsters develop negative concepts of themselves which no amount of effort on the part of teachers or counselors can eliminate. The group, as an educational medium, appears to have two unrelated influences in such cases. The group increases one's receptiveness to different ideas, to new facts or concepts. It is a frequent defense mechanism for an individual to deny or reject these. Perhaps a more important outcome of the group process goes beyond the intellectual acceptance of ideas. The interactions in the group tend to help each member to integrate certain ideas previously unacceptable to his own thinking. Learning and the growing of insight are facilitated by group discussion. Children and parents are often more influenced and encouraged by their peers than by the teachers or counselor. As an example: Bruce, a bright boy, made little progress in school, despite the efforts of both his teachers and his parents. Bruce was invited to join a peer group for counseling. One day, after at-tending a number of sessions, he remarked, "Before I joined this group, I thought I was dumb." Another youngster who was a member of a group said to his mother, "You know, I am not stupid." "What makes you say that?" she asked. "The kids who meet with Mr. ———— to talk about things think I am smart." "We have told you this before," the mother answered. "Yeh, but these guys mean it."

Group counseling not only helps the individual parent or child to help himself, but the members begin to help each other, for participating in a group almost automatically evokes mutual help. The majority of the classrooms are competitive with each student interested, for most part, in his self-evaluation. Under these conditions, there is little possibility to assume responsibility for one another to counteract the social isolation in which each lives. It is generally assumed that children in the same classroom know each other. On the contrary, many are as socially isolated as a hermit. This was brought to our attention in a conversation with Karen who was interested in horses and riding. Karen did not own a horse and, therefore, had no opportunity to ride. "Well, Karen, if you are interested in learning, Alice would be happy to let you ride her horse and even teach you to ride. Why don't you talk with her about it?"

"Oh! I couldn't do that."

"Why not?"

"I don't even know her."

"I thought Alice said you were in the same class with her."

"Yes, I am, but I don't know her."

These were not isolated or rejected youngsters. What must life in the classroom be like for them? Group counseling helps to dissolve social walls within which most children live. When a group member says, "I'll help you with it if you like," we immediately know two things: (1) the group member who has offered help has found his place in the counseling group and is most likely on his way to finding his place in a large group—the classroom, and (2) the help will be offered to a peer because of social interest and not merely to elevate the helper.

The group provides a social situation with real meaning. Some youngsters have never had an opportunity to test themselves in a real social situation. They may never have adequately found their place in the family group and have never been assured of their place in the school group. In group counseling each member feels soon that he has a place, despite the various ideas and attitudes he encounters from his peers. Under the guidance of the counselor he learns how to contend with them, and develops coping devices which are to his advantage when he returns to the family and classroom group. The problems of each youngster reveal themselves in the group in which he attempts to interact. Therefore, they must be solved in a group. It is in group counseling that the youngster finds he is equal with others. In the counseling groups, deficiencies lose their stigma. Paradoxically, deficiencies may be the necessary qualification for membership in a counseling group; for example, group counseling for under-achievers. Thus, in the group, deficiency does not lessen social status, but serves as a basis of equality for all members of the group.

In a democratic society, as contrasted with an autocratic society, an atmosphere of equality is necessary to obtain the cooperation of all participants [4]. Their integrated efforts help all individuals attain greater fulfillment of their potentialities. It has been pointed out above that the potentiality of establishing socially positive attitudes is not found in the community or the school, only in a well directed counseling group. The group becomes a value-forming element. Individual counseling does not lend itself to bringing about necessary value changes. Group counseling cannot avoid dealing with values. All human values are of a social nature; and social participation in one way or another affects the value system of the students. The normal family and classroom experiences of a youngster are usually not conducive to shaking his already well established value systems. They usually fortify his wrong values. The impact of social experiences in group counseling is bound to have a beneficial effect on the value systems of each participant.

This can be illustrated by the interaction in a group of third graders. Larry did not get up in the morning to have breakfast with his parents. He would not eat solid foods. None of these facts were known to the counselor. The group interaction went something like this:

Larry: This morning I woke up at the sound of the mixer.

1st Child: The mixer?

Larry: Yes, my mother was making my milkshake for me.

2nd Child: A milkshake for breakfast?

Larry: My mother always fixes a milkshake for me. Then she brings it to bed for me.

1st Child: You eat in bed?

Larry: While I am drinking the milkshake, my mother draws the water for my bath. She is a regular servant to me.

Counselor: How many of you have breakfast brought to you in bed?

3rd Child: Oh, I haven't eaten in bed since I was a baby. I always get up for breakfast.

4th Child: I always get up.

5th Child: I never heard of milkshake for breakfast. I take my own bath, usually before going to bed, now that I am big.

The exchange went on for a short time concerning responsibilities of getting up in the morning, getting dressed, and what the family had for breakfast. Larry listened silently. After awhile the discussion turned to other topics. Shortly thereafter, Larry's mother related in the parent group that he was now getting up in the morning, and for the first time ate the same kind of food as the rest of the family. Larry's family experiences maintained the faulty goals he was pursuing, and reinforced the goal of getting service. The counseling group became a means for effecting a change of a positive nature [11].

Counseling must have structure. This is easily discernible in individual counseling. In group counseling, because of the interaction of the members, the structure which the counselor provides is not always so easily observed. It is there, nevertheless. Without structure, group interaction becomes confused and chaotic. In keeping with the dynamics of the group counseling process: (1) the establishment and maintenance of proper counseling relationships; (2) an examination of the purpose of the group members' action or behavior; (3) revealing to the individual the goals he is pursuing, called psychological disclosure; and (4) a reorientation and redirection [5].

Developing an effective counseling relationship requires more than mere good relationships [12]. The counselor has to establish himself as the leader of the group even though a democratic atmosphere must prevail. An effective group counseling relationship is based on mutual respect. This does not mean that each member may do anything he pleases. Firmness and kindness are necessary in all group counseling as illustrated by the following incident. Jeff, a fifth grader, attempted to maneuver the counselor into a power struggle during each group session. Although the counselor recognized what Jeff was trying to do and refused to become involved in a fight, it became evident that Jeff's disturbing behavior would disrupt the entire group. The counselor asked the group, "Do you see what is going on?" The members pointed out that Jeff wanted to be the boss. His behavior, they said, disrupted discussion. They indicated their disapproval of his behavior. The counselor made it clear that he did not intend to fight with Jeff. But Jeff continued to disturb. The counselor then told Jeff he would either have to go along with the group so the discussion could continue, or he would have to leave. Jeff persisted. The counselor then asked Jeff if he were leaving by himself or if he had to be removed. Jeff made no move to leave. The counselor then insisted, firmly but kindly, that Jeff leave the room with the understanding that he could return when he felt able to participate. Jeff returned to the group after an absence of one session. The change in his behavior was dramatic, not only in the counseling group, but also, as reported by the parents, at home and in the classroom. The redirection of Jeff's mistaken goals could not be attributed to this one action alone. The parents had been counseled in a group with other parents, and the teacher attended a teachers' seminar. They began to understand Jeff's behavior and what to do about it. However, the counselor established himself as a leader of the group and a man of his word.

The goals which the child is pursuing are the purposes of his behavior [2]. The method of examining, of discovering these goals, can be applied in individual counseling as well as in a group situation. However, the child's goals and movements become more obvious in the interaction with the group members in contrast to the limited interaction between him and the counselor in individual counseling. Secondly, the counselor no longer depends exclusively on the student's verbal reports of his interactions with others outside of the counseling session. He sees him in action during the session. Often the child acts differently in a group than when alone with the counselor. Much of the veneer which the child uses as a cover up may be stripped away in the group, and his true personality openly revealed. As an appropriate illustration let us take Gale, a bright, charming, fourth-grade girl. Most of the teachers were impressed with her; she was aggressive, but she caused no trouble. In Gale's group and from the same classroom, was Jim, who was a bright boy also, but a disturbing element in the classroom. At the beginning of one group session, with Gale and Jim present, the school principal came into the room. Gale immediately invited him to participate in the group session. He accepted, but had to leave to answer a phone call. Gale informed a late arriving group member that the empty chair beside her was reserved for the principal and that he should locate another chair. The group discussion shifted immediately after the principal returned. Gale took the initiative and began subtly to push Jim down, and to put herself in a favorable light. This disturbed Jim and be began to act up. Whereupon other boys also began to act up. Gale had achieved her goal and could sit back with a feeling of "see how badly they behave and see how good I am?" The expression on her face vividly revealed her triumph. The principal indicated his disapproval of the boys by his nonverbal reaction. Gale had given the principal the most adroit "snow job" imaginable. The group was well on the way to getting out of hand when the counselor began to change the course of the session with, "I wonder how many of you know what happened to get the boys started acting up?" The technique which Gale used to push the boys down and build herself up, thus creating a classroom disunity, couldn't have been discovered by counseling Jim and Gale individually. It could only be revealed in the group situation.

The group helps more effectively than individual counseling to gain insight and to redirect each child's mistaken goals. The group facilitates the process of insight. Many would not be able to learn about themselves without the interaction taking place in the group. The child comes to see himself in others. Thus the psychological disclosures and the interpretations during the group sessions are not only valuable for the child to whom they are directed, but to other members of the group who learn from these disclosures. A sixth grade girl recognized herself when we counseled one of her peers. "I used to be like that, always helping the teacher, being good and doing the right things, not because I wanted to, but because I would get in good."

Mistaken goals and erroneous motives among members of the group are similar enough for each member to see himself in others. It appears that this factor should be considered in selection of group members. In other words, the more similar the group, the greater the mirror effect. Thus, there is the greatest possibility of learning from each other when members are selected on the basis of their common problems; for example, groups of under-achievers, parents, teenagers, or dropouts.

The statements and opinions of group members often carry more weight than anything the counselor tells them. In a parent group, a father was relating how neither he nor the mother could make their son, Butch, a sixth grader, come home after school to change from school to play clothes. Butch had been spanked, had privileges removed, and been subjected to numerous punitive actions. He still persisted in going with the boys right from school to play, rather than coming home first to change clothes. The father said, "I told him tonight that the next time he goes to play with the boys without first coming home to change, I am going to take his model airplanes from the ceiling in his room and trample them to bits."

The counselor, being human first and professional second, reacted in a characteristic manner, but fortunately not too soon. Another father fairly shouted, "You can't do that! That's just being revengeful." Another member pointed out that there was good reason for Butch's behavior. "How would you like being left out just because you had to go home to change clothes?" The counselor had recovered sufficiently, professionally, to say, "What do you think of that?" The father admitted that he had not thought of it that way before, but that it made sense because Butch had been having trouble making friends. The counselor recommended what the father could do and asked him what he thought of the recommendations. "Well, if they (the parents in the group) say it will work, then it will work."

The reactions of the group members and what they told the father was much more significant than what the counselor might have said. Group members accept each other more in redirective efforts because they sense the equality which exists among them. In the above case, the counselor was able, later in the session, to develop more insight and exert more corrective influence because he had won the active support of the group.

The insight which a counselor helps to develop in the group sessions is not always a matter for the individual alone. Very few, if any, human beings understand their own behavior. Even though Socrates admonished people to "know thyself" centuries ago, man still does not "know himself" and may never in reality be able to understand himself. But he can and will likely learn about human behavior in general. So children and parents in groups learn something about themselves, but more about people. With the understanding of human nature, they begin to understand themselves. Group counseling is in reality a learning process. Research indicates that the group enhaces learning and that group counseling as a learning process is enhanced by the group.

The development of insight often becomes an end product in individual counseling. It could also become an end product in group counseling as well. However, insight is not an end in itself—it is merely a means to an end. It is not often a basis for behavioral change, but always a step in that direction. The end product is reorientation and redirection. The children are helped to redirect their mistaken goals, and the parents to give up erroneous concepts about dealing with children and to make a change in their approaches and relationships. The change becomes evident in the child's improved relationship with his peers, with his teachers, with his siblings and parents, and a more realistic concept of self [11]. The group becomes an agent in bringing about these changes because of the improved interpersonal relationship in the group, a greater possibility for each group member to see himself as he is, and the realization that his concept of himself and the goals he is pursuing are faulty.

BIBLIOGRAPHY

1. Ansbacher, H. L. and Ansbacher, R. R. *Superiority and Social Interest* (Chicago: Northwestern University Press, 1964).

2. Dreikurs, Corsini, Lowe, and Sonstegard. *Adlerian Family Counseling* (University of Oregon: University Press, 1959).

3. Dreikurs, Rudolf, and Soltz, Vicki. *Children: The Challenge* (New York: Duell, Sloan & Pearce, 1965).

4. Dreikurs, Rudolf. *Group Psychotherapy and Group Approaches.* Collected Papers (Chicago: Alfred Adler Institute, 1960), pp. 95–105 and 127–155.

5. Dreikurs, Rudolf. *Psychodynamics, Psychotherapy and Counseling.* Collected Papers (Chicago: Alfred Adler Institute, 1963), pp. 37–43 and 137–150.

6. Dreikurs, Rudolf. *Equality: The Challenge of Our Times* (Chicago: Alfred Adler Institute, 1961).

7. Johnston, Edgar G.; Peters, Mildred; and Evraiff, William. *The Role of the Teacher in Guidance* (Englewood Cliffs, New Jersey: Prentice-Hall, 1960).

8. Kelley, E. C. *In Defense of Youth* (Englewood Cliffs, New Jersey: Prentice-Hall, 1963).

9. Kemp, C. Gratton. *Perspectives on the Group Process* (Boston: Houghton Mifflin Co., 1964).

10. Ohlsen, Merle M. *Guidance Services in the Modern School* (New York: Harcourt, Brace, & World, Inc., 1964).

11. Stormer, G. E. *A Demonstration of Group Counseling Procedures to Help Talented Underachievers in the Elementary School.* Quincy Public Schools, 1965.

12. Sonstegard, Manford. *Interaction Processes and the Personality Growth of Children.* Psychotherapy, American Society of Group Psychotherapy and Psychodrama, Vol. XI No. 1 (March 1958).

13. Torrance, E. Paul. *Rewarding Creative Behavior* (Englewood Cliffs, New Jersey: Prentice-Hall, 1965).

13

Group Counseling as a Method of Modifying Attitudes in Slow Learners*

Francis J. Lodato

Martin A. Sokoloff

Lester J. Schwartz

Many American public school systems in recent years have been inaugurating special programs to provide education and training for the seriously retárded, the emotionally disturbed, and the academically talented. Little, however, has been done for a relatively large group of students who, although they present difficulties in learning, do not fit into any of these categories. They are the youngsters who are limited in intelligence, though not retarded, and who are unable to adjust their behavior, either academically or socially, to the demands of a school. In many schools it is these youngsters who pose the most difficult curricular and administrative problems. They do not fit into either regular classes or special classes for the retarded. Their achievement is below the standards of the school. In addition, they frequently misbehave, engage in acts of delinquency, play truant, or drop out of school. Their behavior is notable for frequent acting-out, lack of impulse control, short attention span, hyperactivity, and distractibility. They do not relate well to their peers or their teachers.

Upon examining the records of these youngsters, one usually finds a long history of poor school adjustment, frequently beginning as early as kindergarten or first grade. Many, because of difficulty in the area of abstract learning, are extremely slow in their reading development and limited in their ability to respond to the usual educational approaches. Because of their failure to keep up, they are often characterized as "lazy" or "stupid" by their teachers, peers, and sometimes parents. Failing to achieve any real satisfaction from the learning situation, they become bored, withdrawn, aggressive, or resistive. Because of the consistently negative reactions of others to them, their own self-concept is extremely poor;

°Reprinted by permission of the authors and publisher from *The School Counselor*, 12 (1964), 27–29.

many of them give up trying to succeed, and simply wait out the time until they are legally able to drop out of school.

Estimates vary as to the relative numbers of these students among the total school population. The experience of the authors would tend to indicate that they comprise about 10 to 15 per cent of the population.

PURPOSE OF PROJECT

The authors undertook the study in order to determine whether group counseling could produce changes among these "slow-learning" students in the following areas: attitude toward school, the learning situation, their peers and teachers; development of more adequate self-concept; reduction of truancy and dropout frequency; reduction in acting-out behavior; and changes in attitude toward these students on the part of faculty members and other students.

SUBJECTS

Six groups of students were selected, four on the elementary school level and two on the junior high level, varying in numbers from 7 to 11 students per group, with a total of 49.

GROUP I was composed of 11 students, five boys and six girls, ranging in age from 14 to 16 years. All but one were in the middle socioeconomic bracket. These students were in a class called grade 7-8 special. They spent three periods a day with a core teacher who was interested in them and who usually had a high tolerance for them. Placement in other classes was not as satisfactory until after the inauguration of the group counseling program. It appeared that faculty interest was heightened because of the fact that the Special Service Staff found time to spend one period a day with these students. Four students withdrew from school and entered other schools. One girl improved sufficiently in her attitude and behavior to be taken from the group and returned to regular classes.

GROUP II was composed of seven students also on the junior high school level, five boys and two girls. Three students were repeats from Group I. Three were new students to the junior high school, and the seventh was a student who had a history of poor school adjustment. Four of the seven students were borderline retardates whose academic achievement was extremely low. Of all the groups, this was the least successful, and it appears that the reason for the lack of success can be found in the make-up of the group. First, the repeating students set the tone for the rest of the group in terms of acting-out behavior and resistance to the group leader. Second, many of the new students were functioning at too low an achievement level for the group counseling to produce any significant change in their functioning. Unless there was drastic curriculum revision, these four students (three boys and one girl) seemed to be misplaced.

GROUP III was composed of seven boys in grades four and five. These boys were in constant competition with each other and were frequently disciplined by their teachers for fighting, swearing, and making indecent remarks or gestures. Two were on the verge of being expelled. Of this group, one boy moved out of the school district. Of the remaining six, five showed considerable improvement. One appeared to have made progress in the early part of the year and then showed signs of regression. This was worthy of note, since in spite of what the group leaders considered a loss in strength, some teachers were more accepting of this boy at the end of the year than they had been earlier. Group psychotherapeutic treatment was recommended for this boy. The other students each achieved sufficiently to be advanced to higher learning groups.

GROUP IV was a group of seven boys from a second-grade class. Each student in this class was placed in it because of poor achievement. These students were chosen for group counseling because of notable lack of impulse control, short attention span, and lethargy toward learning. Of the seven boys in this group, all but one had achieved sufficiently to be promoted to the next grade.

GROUP V was a group of nine boys, from a third-grade class, who were so placed educationally because of extremely retarded academic performance. There were three boys in this group who were virtually non-readers. Each had been left back once. One of these three children was recommended for special evaluation and was diagnosed as brain damaged. Of the original nine boys, one was promoted out of this class grouping, since he began to achieve at a faster rate. Of the remaining seven (excluding the brain damaged boy), there was a marked increase in academic achievement, and it was the judgment of the teacher that these boys were on their way to adequate (for their tested abilities) achievement.

GROUP VI was composed of eight girls of the same third grade class as the boys of Group V. There was considerable rivalry existing among the girls. Four girls attempted to dominate the entire group proceedings. One began to gain some insight into her behavior, while another developed stronger masculine identification. In the teacher's judgment, the attitude of the girls became more conducive to the learning situation, and in general they were more receptive to learning. One child in this group was academically misplaced. Although she had a tested I.Q. on the Lorge-Thorndike of 87, she functioned in a manner which was superior to her peers. On the administration of a WISC, her I.Q. score was found to be 110. She was removed from the class placement and advanced. She continued to function in a satisfactory manner.

With groups V and VI, the teacher was given a major role in the group counseling procedure. There were frequent conferences with the teacher who was both interested in, and capable of receiving and handling the information and insight given to her by the group leaders.

PROCEDURE

Criteria for selection included I.Q. above 75, achievement one year or more below actual grade placement in at least two major subjects, and history of poor school adjustment.

The groups met from three to five times a week with one or more of the authors for a period of one year. Activities for the groups included pantomime, role playing, psychodrama, structured and unstructured group discussion, puppetry, and individual counseling.

RESULTS

1. Positive changes in attitudes toward learning and toward authority figures were observed in a large majority of the students as judged by teacher ratings on a behavior and attitude rating scale.
2. Increase in self-concept of most of the students as indicated by figure-drawing projectives. (Karen Machover, consultant to the pilot project, evaluated the pre- and post-test figure drawings.)
3. Significantly improved attendance record of the students in the study.
4. Satisfactory integration of many of the students into regular classrooms following the study.
5. Increased tolerance, insight, and understanding by classroom teachers of students who present these kinds of difficulties.

CONCLUSIONS

1. Group counseling as defined in the study is successful in modifying negative attitudes among slow learning students toward their studies and school in general.
2. Group counseling provides an effective means of utilizing time of professional personnel.
3. The changes in attitudes of the students enable them to function more effectively in the school setting.

14

Group Counseling for Slow Learners*

Frances J.Lodato
Martin A.Sokoloff

In recent years the American secondary school has made special provisions for the academically talented, the seriously retarded, and the emotionally disturbed. Little has been done, however, for a relatively large group of students who do not fit into any of these categories. These are the youngsters who are limited in intelligence, though not retarded, and who are unable to adjust their behavior to the demands of a school, though they are not seriously ill.

In order to explore the suitability of group counseling as a method of helping students in this category a pilot study was undertaken at The Fox Lane School during the 1961–1962 academic year. In general the objectives of the group counseling project were to assist slow-learning students in adjusting to their teachers, the curriculum, and to other students. This adjustment was to be assisted by helping these students to increase their self-understanding and by specific assistance in making realistic vocational choices. It was also considered desirable to develop an increased awareness of the realistic intellectual limitations of these students, both by their teachers and by themselves. It was thought that this latter objective might lead to the establishment of an in-service program which would assist the teachers to serve these pupils more effectively.

METHOD

Ten students were selected from among students in a special, nongraded class in the seventh and eighth grades of the junior high school. The students selected were characterized generally by an IQ range of 77–90. They also failed to meet achievement goals set for the particular classes they ordinarily would be attending. Their behavior was characterized by lack of impulse control, negativistic attitudes, hyperactivity, lethargy, stealing, and the malicious damaging of property. These characteristics manifested themselves in the classroom situation by short attendance spans, excessive

*Reprinted by permission of authors and publisher from *Journal of Counseling Psychology*, 10 (1963), 95–96.

distractibility, daydreaming, and other escape mechanisms. Further, these students appeared to have an unrealistically low self concept as well as extreme feelings of inadequacy. These feelings coupled with inadequate sexual identification and feelings of hostility made it impossible for them to adjust to their peers and to teachers.

The students were evaluated initially, during, and at the conclusion of the project, both by their classroom teacher and by staff members participating in the project. Test materials included the House-Tree-Person test, Human Figure drawings, Bender Gestalt test, and a Rating-Scale measuring observed personality traits.

Counseling sessions were held three times a week for the first half of the school year and were increased to five times a week for the remainder of the year, after the completion of the scheduled remedial reading program. Group activities included: directed and nondirected group discussions, role playing, pantomimes, athletics, field trips, parties, dancing and record playing.

While the approach used was essentially persuasive, certain limitations were consistently imposed by the staff participants. Students were required to attend all group sessions unless excused from a particular session by the group leader. Students were prevented from exhibiting behavior which might be disruptive to other phases of the school program (excessive noise, destruction of school equipment). Physically aggressive behavior toward the group leader—or any other member—was prohibited.

RESULTS

Three students, originally members of the group, left the group early in the year because of their families' moving from the community. Of the remaining group:

One student, a girl, was sufficiently adjusted to be transferred to regular class sections after half the year had elapsed. She was offered the opportunity to receive supportive counseling on an individual basis.

The six remaining students (five males and one female) were originally characterized by frequent acting-out behavior, hyperdistractibility, lack of impulse control, low self-esteem, and poor academic achievement. By the end of the school year, it was the consensus of the counseling staff, classroom teachers, and the administration that four of the six had shown marked improvement in behavior, in their attitudes toward school work, and in their relationships with school personnel; one had shown no change; and one appeared to be regressing.

DISCUSSION

That positive changes in the behavior patterns of these children had taken place was concluded by all who observed them—staff working directly with these children, teachers, and administrators. The most significant gains were in the areas of self-confidence, social confidence, and the appropriateness of expressions of nonverbal agressions. Less significant gains were made in areas such as responsiveness to educational approaches and in attempts to be self-directing. It is interesting to note that the attendance of the members of the group, after the initiation of the program, was significantly better than the attendance record of the over-all school population.

The over-all language patterns of these students are limited, uncommunicative and characterized by poor articulation. These qualities did not appear to show any improvement.

It appears to the staff that some of these children could function in an academic setting providing that there was sufficient self-respect developed to keep them functioning effectively.

15

An Experiment with Underachievers*

Pearl Harris

Frank Trotta

It is quite common for group therapy to be undertaken with children who have behavior problems. This experiment, however, sought to work with bright children who were not living up to their potential in their school work, i.e., with underachievers. Too frequently, relatively normal children's problems are overlooked until they become more serious. The trend toward dealing with social problems right in the community and toward making the most of intellectual resources led us to consider setting up the project after obtaining permission from the psychiatric directors of our children's clinic where traditional child guidance is carried on.

THE PURPOSE AND THE GROUP

Our aim was to meet with a group of pre-adolescents averaging 12 years of age, to explore difficulties in the way of their getting passing grades, and their ability to do the work. This proposed plan was immediately and favorably accepted in a meeting with school officials, even though it was a new and experimental venture. The generously co-operative principal, counselor, and teachers of the school chosen enabled us to form a group in a relatively brief period of time.

They presented us with thirty-two potential candidates who met the qualifications of being rather bright according to their past school ability tests and/or earlier classroom performance, of not presenting any marked problem of discipline or personality disturbance, (with one exception), and of course, currently getting poor grades. They were seventh-graders.

From these thirty-two children we selected three girls and five boys, from two classrooms, for a once-weekly "Group Discussion," as we came to call it. Each session lasted one hour and fifteen minutes.

Originally we intended to run with a twelve-week time limit, but found we had time for only nine sessions in that particular semester. The total time required of two psychologist co-therapists was four hours

*Reprinted from the February 1962 issue of *Education*. Copyright 1962 by The Bobbs-Merrill Company, Inc., Indianapolis, Indiana.

weekly. The clinic investment of time was actually less, since this was also training for one psychologist who was inexperienced in group therapy.

We emphasized from the beginning the crucial matter of time involved for all concerned. Therapeutic intervention entered the students' lives at an important point, primarily to help them make a decision.

In junior high school they could not, as in elementary school, continue along the same course and pattern of under-achievement without concern about consequences, because if they did poorly they would not be permitted a choice of curriculum (i.e., Academic, Vocational, etc.). The choice was to be made in the latter half of the seventh grade. This fact enabled us to put pressure on the children and to point out that they could not afford to procrastinate about living up to their academic potential.

HOW THE GROUP WORKED

The many anticipated obstacles proved less formidable in actuality. Once the plan had been worked out, the group was quickly and easily set up. An interview with each of the students, and written parental permission, brought about voluntary participation from the first eight students. (They were each given the option not to participate.)

The first group meeting got off to a strong start. After brief reviewing remarks by the leaders about the nature and purpose of the group and the commonness of their academic problem, the children discussed their various problems.

Their individual personality symptoms ranged from stuttering to disrupting classes, and to greater disturbance shown by one girl who made mouthing sounds and faces. This girl was taken on, with full awareness of her marginal adjustment, to determine if the group could "carry" one such member.

SOME FINDINGS

After several sessions the members of the group divided themselves into two types: those with obviously and consistently serious intent, and those who giggled, joked, and cut up most of the time. It was felt that a longer period of time and more sessions might have furthered these trends with some of the students. The serious faction might eventually have gained sufficient strength to counteract the disruptive tactics of the other.

The main point, however, is that it soon became evident what, if anything, each child wanted to do about his problems. This is true despite the fact that the group never evolved into a smoothly organized, cohesive unit.

In the nine sessions held our efforts were directed toward having the children explore their attitudes and desires toward school work and future goals. The discrepancies between their words and their marks and be-havior in the school and group itself were pointed out.

When it became clear to them that this was their group to shape and direct, without criticism or forced direction by adults, they became freer in assuming their usual orientation to peers and authorities. In effect, their personality patterns were brought right into group and could be pointed out and related to their underachievement problems.

While our ostensible aim was to deal with underachievement, we followed this to the more personal aspects of the children's personalities. In this matter we found extremes once again, such as the girl who took the sessions seriously but could not bring herself to speak up against those "too immature" peers who played around, and the boy who denied problems while kicking others under the table. In the final session this boy said he would have liked more serious discussion of school problems but felt he could not be consistently serious unless all his peers were.

We found a few members of the group about whom we could not make accurate predictions even to the very end. While they showed little change in group behavior, their classroom attitude and/or grades improved. Others whose attitudes we felt had changed were not yet reflecting the change in their grades.

EVALUATION OF PROJECT

In an evaluation of the project with school officials, the changes in grades and/or behavior were found to be sufficiently substantial, in view of the newness of the project and the limited time invested, to make it worth-while to continue the project.

Four students had improved their grades; two more showed minor improvement. Two showed no improvement or change of behavior. The most disturbed girl was one of these.

At the close, the children regretted that they had not had more serious discussions about their problems, but they recognized that the failure was their responsibility. They felt that common problems like daydreaming, laziness, and inability to be serious might well have been explored further.

They were well aware that many good suggestions arising out of the group had been followed. For example, one boy confessed to his parents a secret he had kept for fear of punishment and thereby eliminated the anxiety that had prevented him from concentrating. Another boy was helped to recognize the greater importance of longer range goals and quit two out-side jobs he was holding, so that he could get more sleep and do his home-work.

Finally, as therapists, we learned several important things from this first attempt at short-term group therapy with pre-adolescent underachievers. First, we learned that the children found it difficult to talk with sustained, serious focus about personal problems, because they had not thought of themselves as having serious problems. Thus, much time was spent by therapists in making the children aware that they had a problem.

We learned that, committed as we were to a time limit, we should have supported the serious members more actively and strongly. We found that a group of this kind cannot tolerate even one severely disturbed individual; we would not include one again.

We also learned—and it should have come as no surprise—that the girls of the same age were more verbal and expressive than the boys, and tended to lead the group in discussion.

Finally, as with group therapy generally, we felt that the presence of a group of peers enabled the group members to relax and display their typical behavior more quickly than in individual counseling or therapy.

16

A School Report on Group Counseling*

Benjamin Cohn

A. Mead Sniffen

Early in the year 1961, a local high school asked the Board of Cooperative Educational Services for assistance in dealing with a group of underachieving seventh grade boys who were demonstrating acting-out behavior. These boys lacked interest in school and contributed generally to
the disruption of classes in which they were placed. A request was made
that the senior author consider a pilot project directed toward investigating
the possibilities of helping these pupils in a group situation. The basic
purposes of the project were threefold:

1. To learn more about this type of pupil.
2. To assist these pupils toward a better school adjustment by effecting
   a change in attitude.
3. To study the techniques of group counseling as it applies to eight
   seventh grade boys who were underachieving and demonstrating
   acting-out behavior.

WHY GROUP COUNSELING

Group counseling was chosen as the medium for this project because
it offered an opportunity to work with the maximum number of pupils and
involved a minimum amount of counselor time. It was hoped that, by
studying the effects of this process, group counseling might be shown to
have promise for those counselors pressed for time. Although many
counselors had used the group guidance technique effectively for imparting information to students, the senior author felt that this technique was
not adequate for this particular problem population.

In addition to the fact that group counseling involves fewer students
than group guidance, it has more rigid requirements for success. For
example, Lifton [1] indicates that group counseling has its major emphasis on providing group members with opportunities to explore their
own feelings and attitudes. It requires that the members experience some

*Reprinted by permission of the authors and publisher from *Personnel and Guidance
Journal*, XLI (1962), 133–138.

anxiety about a problem which they wish to resolve and that they possess the willingness to share their concerns. Group counseling implies a permissive atmosphere where an individual can explore his negative feelings or ideas without fear of losing status within the group and where the potential authority figure conveys a feeling of real concern and acceptance. For the students this process offers an opportunity: (a) to express themselves both verbally and actively on any number of topics without the usual limitations set by school or society; (b) to test reality by trying out new methods of handling situations without fear of punishment from authority figures; (c) to help others and discuss common feelings without losing their individual identity; and (d) to investigate and evaluate their past experiences in light of their present behavior so that they can make the decision for change in a more positive direction.

THE PROJECT

Members of the group chosen for this pilot project were selected from the lowest section of the seventh grade and were boys who demonstrated underachievement and acting-out behavior. Of the 14 potential members, eight were selected on the basis of their ability and willingness to verbalize their feelings as well as to attend meetings on Mondays and Thursdays. An attempt was made to balance the group by giving preference to pupils with varying degrees of emotional difficulty. Thus pupils with personality strength were selected to offset those demonstrating hostility and less control.

In structuring for the group, pupils were informed that they would have an opportunity to take part in a pilot project that would help the school gain information about boys like themselves and, at the same time, increase their understanding of themselves and possibly improve their overall academic achievement. Although membership was, of course, not compulsory, all 14 boys wanted to participate.

Prior to the group sessions, all boys in this lowest section of the seventh grade were administered the Wechsler Intelligence Scale for Children, the Machover Draw-a-Person Test, and the Combs Sentence Completion Test. Although these tests were to be used in a pre-post testing evaluation, time unfortunately did not allow for the post testing.

The sessions ran for one hour, two afternoons per week, for a total of 20 meetings. At the beginning of each session, each member was given a sheet of paper and a pencil for doodling, and all but two sessions were tape recorded. (During two sessions the recorder did not function properly.) These tapes were reviewed by the Board of Cooperative Educational Services Guidance Center Staff, which served as a control on the techniques used.

ROLE OF THE COUNSELOR

The first concern of the counselor was to structure the group counseling sessions. The students were told that they would have the opportunity to talk about anything they liked, in any way they liked, as long as they kept in mind the goals of the group. These were defined as an effort to help other members and to gain better understanding of their own feelings. Talking about things that concerned them would give the group and the counselor an opportunity to learn more about each person and help each one work through some of the problems that might be interfering with school achievement. The members were told that all information brought out during the session would be kept strictly confidential within the group and that each member had the responsibility of protecting the "sense of privacy" of every other member. The only other limits placed on the group at this time were that their actions could not be destructive of school property and that there was to be no physical violence or harm to any other member of the group. Although the counselor tended to play a permissive role with these members he always reserved the right to suggest and, if necessary, enforce limits that might enable the group to work more efficiently. For instance, when the students seemed to lack enough self-discipline to control a member who physically annoyed others, the counselor, with the consent of the other members, took an authoritarian position.

The counselor saw his role as being primarily permissive, accepting, and reflective. The students were encouraged to select their own topics and express any feelings they felt important. At all times the counselor attempted to convey to the students the feeling that he understood how they felt and that, to him, they had a great deal of personal worth.

The counselor felt that it was not his role to give information during these sessions. When the students asked specific questions, underlying feelings were reflected and discussed. The goal was to encourage the student to take the initiative and to inquire from other sources when necessary.

The counselor found it very difficult to achieve closure because of the time limitations. The group, because of its emotional make-up, was slow getting started and the students felt a certain amount of incompleteness in their experience to the point of demonstrating hostility toward the counselor. The technique which served to solidify the experience was to investigate with the group the possibility of using school resources such as the Guidance Office and the Reading Clinic. The counselor role-played some situations for the purpose of assisting the student in approaching teachers with some of their problems.

After the close of the last session the counselor held a staff meeting with guidance and reading personnel, as well as with the teachers involved, and offered them general information obtained from the group sessions. These staff members then discussed with the counselor possible ways of reinforcing results obtained in the group.

TOPICS DISCUSSED

The first topic discussed, and possibly the least threatening, was that dealing with the school curriculum. As a group these pupils felt that they preferred more shops or more activities that would involve manipulative skills. They seemed to dislike the primarily verbal courses and felt they should be given the opportunity to choose their program in the same way as pupils who have moved on to high school.

The second topic discussed was their teachers. Although this topic was somewhat threatening, it offered them the opportunity to test the limits of the group's ability to keep this material confidential. After venting their hostility toward certain teachers, they began to settle down and indicated their resentment of negative attitudes expressed by teachers toward them. They seemed to cry out for more understanding and sensitivity to their feelings and often found it very difficult to accept the teacher who made facetious remarks about their ability to achieve. It was interesting to note that these boys always seemed to side with the "underdog" whenever a conflict occurred between a pupil and teacher. However, it was not uncommon for these pupils to be on the teacher's side when the pupil was obviously wrong.

Another indication of the pupils' strengths was demonstrated by the fact that, after discussing their negative feelings about different teachers and how unsympathetic and insensitive they were, they would invariably add, "But he's a nice guy, though." They seemed to dislike the teacher for his attitudes in class but showed a basic desire to like him.

These pupils were very sensitive about their intellectual capacity. They all demonstrated a very poor impression of themselves and resented any negative reference to their intellectual level being made or implied in front of the class. It seemed acceptable for the group members to call each other "retards" but not acceptable to use the word "dumb." This latter term had been used by their parents and, as a result, was highly charged.

After discussing the school curriculum and their teachers, the boys began to express their feelings about themselves and their peers. Physical contact was a major means of expression outside the group, and exploits were quite often discussed with a great deal of pleasure as signs of personal worth. After some time in the group, this physical aggression toward others was displaced by verbal aggression, called "chopping." This is a process of degrading an individual or individuals through the use of words. A "chopping" session usually involved two or more boys using vulgar expressions to cut down another individual or group. In the group this technique served as a form of resistance against discussing sensitive topics as well as a kind of "baptism of fire" for the other members. If a member could take "chopping" and still come back without holding any grudges, the other members felt they could trust him and that he was worth having around. If, however, he began to fight physically, ran to an outside source, or broke down emotionally, he was considered weak and not to be trusted. It was interesting, however, that after a vicious session of "chopping" and the intermittent "chopping" that followed, the group structure began to disintegrate. New pairings developed which seemed much healthier. It was also at this time that positive developments began to appear. Certain members requested remedial reading help; some began talking more freely about their personal feelings outside of the group; and the discussion in the group became less critical, more supportive, and more greatly loaded with feeling.

Frequently, it seemed that after the most discouraging sessions with the group the most marked progress was made. For example, after an incident that threatened the survival of the group (the group went beyond the limits set by the counselor), the members talked about their feelings of inadequacy, being left back, their need for support and understanding, and the tremendous influence of peer attitudes on their present behavior. They felt that the school forced them into undesirable social groupings which they themselves would not have chosen. They had a serious fear of failure in school, but refused to compete for better grades. Thus they could say that they really didn't try, rather than take the chance of facing the possibility that they lacked the intelligence needed for success. After this critical incident, the group developed a firm ability for self-discipline. The discipline was confined to the group only. When the members discussed their lack of self-discipline outside of the group, they indicated that they felt neither the school nor society had done anything to deserve their support.

The next general topic discussed was that of their parents. Here the group members verbalized negative and hostile feelings. They indicated that their parents were inconsistent as far as discipline was concerned and that they lacked the understanding need by most typical adolescent children. The members seemed to be pleading for more warmth and acceptance, which they felt they could not get.

Because time ran out, the last topic discussed was their difficulty with their siblings. Here again they reflected lack of parental understanding.

RESULTS

This pilot project was considered to have been successful in view of the purposes suggested originally. Below are some of the facts obtained from the counseling sessions about these eight seventh grade boys:

1. These boys in general seemed to have a very poor concept of themselves. On the one hand they felt they were "dumb" and lacked personal worth, and on the other hand they craved patience and understanding so that they could test their ability. Although they feared they lacked intelligence, they still held out hope that they were at least average. They felt the school contributed to this poor self-concept by placing them in the lowest section of their grade group, thereby labeling them.

2. These boys, by being placed in the same section of the seventh grade, were forced into groupings with each other that they would not have made for themselves. These pupils would much rather have chosen peers on a higher level. When they were thrown together, the common element seemed to be hostility and aggression toward the school. This anxiety usually vented itself in physical acts against others.

3. Their over-all academic achievement suffered because most of their energies were spent competing for peer group status. When this point was discussed, the students indicated that the school did not understand how they felt and "no one cares, anyway."

The following tend to indicate changes in the pupils' attitudes which should result in better school adjustment:

1. Some members of the group arrived at a more realistic picture of themselves. They saw the need for remedial help, and, although they had had very few experiences with the Guidance Office, at least five of the boys sought interviews, requesting information about tests, occupations, and help with their personal problems. One boy requested referral to an outside agency for help with his problem as a result of the group experience.

2. As far as relationships with their peers were concerned, these boys seemed to become more sensitive to the feelings of others. They also tended to rely less on physical aggression as a sign of personal worth. As counseling progressed the members took on more responsibility for disciplining their own group. By the end of the total process, teachers' comments indicated that the individuals were demonstrating greater self-discipline and had suggested higher standards of behavior to pupils who had not been involved in the sessions.

3. Their attitude toward school also changed. It was much less critical and seemed to reflect a more positive acceptance of authority. This was also apparent in their attitudes at home as well as in school. Their teachers felt that a conspicuous change was visible in the attitudes of some of the members toward better academic achievement. They seemed to have a more serious attitude toward their lessons and were more concerned about their future.

The group counseling technique worked very well with this particular group of boys. Here are some of the outstanding considerations for this type of process:

1. It seemed important to these pupils that they not be involved in any kind of activity that would place them in a position of being any more different from their peers than they felt they already were. In this group, structuring was used to convey the feeling that these students were chosen because of their better-than-usual ability to verbalize and talk about themselves. They were told that this group was very selective and that not everyone would be allowed to participate. This in itself tended to strengthen their self-concept and sense of personal worth.

2. Establishing rapport with this group was a highly sensitive process. The pupils' acceptance of the counselor was facilitated by a purposeful use of vocabulary. It was necessary to incorporate many of the slang terms and vulgar expressions into the counselor's vocabulary when dealing with this group. It seemed that after the counselor broke the language barrier by reflecting their feelings in terms that were common to the group, many resistances disappeared and the group spoke more freely.

3. Each session in this process ran for one full hour. During the earlier meetings the full time was used constructively. However, as the problems became more sensitive and the pupils more defensive, the 60-minute period seemed too long. The more defensive members became more resistive and blocked the group process. This would seem to suggest the feasibility of a classroom period of approximately 40 to 50 minutes for a group session. On the other hand, however, this blocking attempt by the more defensive members presented a problem which was important for the group to learn to handle. By working with this type of problem, the group learned self-discipline.

4. The group process continued for 20 sessions, beginning in February and ending in May. There were two one-hour sessions per week. Although the pupils were in the same section and class and "palled around" together, they did not trust each other. Many sessions were utilized in creating an atmosphere of trustfulness and confidentiality. Other sessions were spent testing the limits of the counselor. Because of the types of problems represented in this group, the amount of hostility and aggression, and the familiarity among the members, 20 sessions were not enough.

5. As mentioned earlier, the pupils were given paper to doodle on during each session. They were asked to sign their names, date the papers, and turn them in at the end of each session. Although nothing was done to evaluate this material, the subjective information was very interesting. The drawings indicated an increase or decrease in hostility and aggression during the sessions; they reflected positive or negative changes over a series of sessions; and they occasionally offered clues to topics causing anxiety but not yet discussed by an individual. This technique provided the boys with a manual task while they were verbally involved in the group process. Because these boys tend naturally to work better with objects and symbols

than with words, the material produced was very often subjectively significant.

6. Because the members of this group needed and wanted support from adults and because the total number of sessions was not adequate to solve their problems, closure was difficult. The pupils resented the counselor's inability to give them concrete answers to their problems and to influence their environment both in school and at home. They had not yet achieved the readiness needed to take personal responsibility for dealing with the difficulties of which they had become more realistically aware.

RECOMMENDATIONS

Below are some specific recommendations suggested for consideration by the school personnel when dealing with seventh grade boys who are underachieving and demonstrating acting-out behavior.

1. Teachers' attitudes with respect to these pupils should lean more toward a sincere concern for their welfare. There should be a more conspicuous effort toward honesty and integrity in all contacts with these boys. Male teachers could establish a good relationship by putting an arm around the boy's shoulder or making other friendly gestures toward him of a physical, personal contact nature.

2. Teachers should offer and even create for these pupils as many opportunities for success as possible.

3. The school administration should consider doing away with grade numbers and possibly classify grade sections as "Grade 7, under Teacher _____."

4. The school personnel should do whatever is possible to include these pupils in group projects outside of their "chosen" group relationships. In other words, the school should try to break up their cliques by giving them different lunch periods and by catering to their different interests.

5. The reading specialist could provide individual reading sessions for these pupils with suitable books or stories that could be used as a springboard for discussion of some of their more personal feelings and attitudes.

6. The last point, but far from least in importance, is that the school should be aware of the dangers inherent in the "preconceived label." This label serves as a convenience for the school, but may result in a disservice to the pupil.

REFERENCE

1. Lifton, Walter M. *Working with Groups* (New York: Wiley, 1961).

17

*A Project in Group Counseling in a Junior High School**

S. Theodore Woal

This project attempted to determine whether or not group counseling could be used successfully to help selected students to (1) reduce failures in subject matter, (2) improve work habits, (3) improve behavior. It was planned so as to ascertain the possibility of accomplishing these purposes without bringing the parents into conferences, actually without contact between parents and school, except for the initial consent for pupil participation in the activity. Another goal of the project was to explore the opportunities through the group process to reduce tensions through improvement in school attendance, citizenship, peer-group, and student teacher relationships.

The group consisted of six students selected by the school counselor who were active counseling cases when the group started or were carried as cases for the duration of the school year. Throughout the period of the project individual counseling was available when requested by the student. Each student used this service between two to five times during that period.

These students were retarded up to three years although each one possessed the potential ability as measured by individual and group intelligence tests to perform at grade level. They lacked the ability to establish friendships among the peer-group and acceptable relationships with teachers. In general, interpersonal relationships were poor both in and out of school. Truancy was, in some cases, an interrelated factor.

Analysis of the counseling records of the group members revealed several additional characteristics, (1) instability within the home, (2) a generally poor environment, (3) negative experiences with teachers and school administrators.

The name "club" was given to the group. The use of the words "counseling" and "guidance" was avoided. Meetings were held once weekly during school hours for a period of 45 minutes for 28 weeks.

The purpose of the club was indicated to the members at the first meet-

*Reprinted by permission of the author and publisher from *Personnel and Guidance Journal*, XLII (1964), 611–613.

ing. "You are a member of this club because you are having problems in school. You are not getting along with your teachers and/or other students. You are not doing acceptable class work.

"I know you want to get along better in school. The club will give you an opportunity to talk about your problems and to do something about them. Try to get some ideas about your behavior by listening to what other members are doing. In this way, perhaps, together, you can help yourself and each other to become better school citizens.

"You should feel free to 'gripe' about your school and your teachers, your schoolmates or anyone or anything else. Get help in your school work if this is what you need. Suggest to your clubmates how they can help themselves to do better, or anything else you want to talk about."

The statement of purpose was acceptable as the goal of the club. The members agreed that they needed this assistance and expressed a desire to join the club.

The initial club sessions, after the boys got to know each other, consisted of a series of gripes about the school and the treatment by the teachers. "Unfairness" was the theme. Club members reinforced each other in many areas of "grievance." Nothing very kind was said about the school or staff.

There followed a period of disagreement among the club members, particularly in connection with specific teachers. One saw the teacher as punitive and unfair, another characterized the teacher as "right" and "fair" in a particular situation. This led to a series of suggestions from one or several members on how to act to avoid the disapproval of the teacher.

It was part of the procedure for the counselor to initiate a review of the past week for each member by asking a question such as, "What happened to you during the past week?", or "I understand you were detained by Mr. _____."

This was usually sufficient to start the group going. Each club member had an opportunity to talk about himself and listen to the comments and suggestions of the other members. As time progressed the suggestions were more constructive and less reinforcing of the complaining member.

Reduction in total number of failures, subject matter, work habits, and behavior of each student on the last report card in June, 1961, the first report card of the 1961–1962 school year (November, 1961) and the final report card (June, 1962) were utilized as measures of adjustment.

An examination of the records revealed that the greatest rate of improvement was in subject matter and work habit marks. Thus a reduction in subject failures from 13 to 3 and in failing marks in work habits from 16 to 4, about 75 per cent improvement, shows good progress. Since the subject matter mark is cumulative from the beginning of the term, the rate of improvement is significantly greater than the above reduction in failure indicates.

The behavioral category indicated a lesser improvement as failing marks lessened by 33 per cent. The smaller reduction in behavior failures appears to suggest that these students can function in classroom work even though behavior is below the standards set by the teacher. The teachers' increased sensitivity to the attempts of these students to improve may be a significant factor.

It is significant that the greatest reduction in failures came during the period when these students were very active in the club. It is suggested that they were becoming more secure in their feelings about themselves and the school, developing and strengthening their ability to cope with problems and gaining insights into their behavior, thus enabling them to adjust with greater satisfaction to the school milieu.

The question, "Has the club helped you?" was asked of each member toward the end of the school year, during an individual conference period. The reactions of the members are given below:

I feel I'm not the only one that does things wrong—so I try to do better. I have improved.

You talk to us, I take it seriously and try to do right. It helped me to settle down.

I am not truant anymore.

Kept me out of trouble; I know I have someone to come to when I'm in trouble.

Helped me to settle down.

Two club members, now in high school, have come in to see the writer several times since leaving the school, "just to talk." One of these estimated that about 75 per cent of the reduction in his failures while he was in our school was due to being in the club. He continued, "We used to make bets as to who would show the best record of reduction in failures."

These statements, supported by the record of improvement, suggest that with proper motivation and interest on the part of school personnel and with the easing of tension and anxiety made possible by the club association, considerable improvement in subject matter, work habits, and behavior can be anticipated.

A significant outcome of the experiment centered around the fact that the club members reduced appreciably the number of failures on their report cards. While it is difficult to assess what part of this achievement was due directly to the group experience there would appear to be some relationship between their success and membership in the club.

The group approach appears to give the members a certain sense of belonging, of security in the realization that (1) they are not alone in their situation, (2) they have an opportunity for a sympathetic and understanding hearing, (3) the counselor is always available for help, if needed, and (4) each club member, in some way, is helping the others.

One question asked by the club members revealed the fear of dismissal or elimination from the club if they improved. Each member was assured of continuation as long as he felt the need to come and as long as the club could be helpful to him or he could be helpful to the other club members.

Another outcome appears to be a warmer, more understanding desire to help on the part of the teacher. Teachers who considered these students problems in the classroom began to see the club members as students with problems. The focus of the teacher was sharpened; attitudes became more sympathetic and tolerant, more information about the student was sought by the teacher. The teachers were enabled "to take" the behavior of these youngsters more calmly and with more understanding. One teacher developed special work for a club member to bring out his particular capability in English; another used a club member in a class position to help him gain status with his peers. Several teachers have asked for a continuation of the club and are prepared to suggest potential members.

Frequent short informal conferences between counselor and teacher resulted in an exchange of ideas, methods, and hopes and more insights for teacher and counselor pertinent to the club member.

A particular aim of the experimental group program was to determine whether club members would improve their school adjustment by utilizing the resources within the school only. In keeping with this objective no contact was made with the home when discipline or other situations arose which normally would have required parental conferences in the school. This appears to have reduced one sensitive area in the student-school relationship, enabling the student to feel a little more relaxed in the school atmosphere. The fear of reprisal or punishment by parents was diminished.

The sympathetic forum presented by the club in which problems could be discussed, the realization that others had similar difficulties, the growing ability to use the club period and the counselor for working out these problems, coupled with the increased alertness of teachers to the problems of these students, and the willingness of teachers to provide additional assistance to the club members—all these factors helped to reduce hostility toward school and the frustrations of attending school. As a result energy was directed into the patterns of behavior that resulted in achievement, gratification, and success.

The outcomes of the project appear to suggest that the methods and techniques of group counseling can be utilized to help individuals within a group acquire the additional insights and inner resources necessary to effect improved adjustments to school living; and group methods can facilitate the counseling of a larger number of students, thereby extending this service to a greater proportion of the student body.

18

The Effect of Group Counseling on Junior High School Boys' Concepts of Themselves in School*

Stanley W. Caplan

School counselors are faced with ever increasing demands upon their skills and time.

It has become essential to reexamine their techniques of dealing with youth and to try out and evaluate new techniques which seem promising.

One such new technique is called group or multiple counseling [1, 2]. Froehlich, who calls this technique multiple counseling, defines it simply as counseling with more than one individual at a time, but with each on a co-ordinate basis. This technique, whether called group or multiple counseling, is a challenge to the widely held "one to one" counseling method.

Group counseling emphasizes a permissive relationship in which an individual can evaluate himself and his opportunities, can choose courses of action, and can accept responsibility for those choices. It overlaps with group guidance (emphasis on imparting facts) and with group psychotherapy (emphasis on treatment).

As group counseling is thought to be a real social situation, it seems particularly appropriate for work with adolescents, many of whose problems are social in nature.

THE PROBLEM

This investigation attempted to study group counseling within the framework of "self" psychology. The investigation is related in design to experiments carried on at the University of Chicago under Carl Rogers [5] for the evaluation of nondirective therapy. It was felt that research on new techniques should attempt to discover whether the techniques fit with existing research and theory.

Group counseling was assumed to effect measurable changes in self

*Reprinted by permission of the author and publisher from *Journal of Counseling Psychology* (1957), 4, 124–128.

concepts of the counselees and further was assumed to effect changes in school achievement and behavior.

METHOD

This study utilized regular staff school counselors of a large junior high school in San Francisco, California. The boys counseled were 12–15 years of age. The boys were selected by records of long-term, frequent conflict with school authorities and regulations. Typically, the boys had been referred by teachers as unruly, anti-social, unteachable, or incorrigible.

Within each of the low 7, low 8, and high 9 grade groups, two groups of such boys were picked as experimental and control. (Low 7 and low 8 groups had six boys each, the high 9 group, five.) The groups were roughly matched for economic status, intelligence, age, and school record.

The Q-technique was used to measure the self and ideal-self concepts in school of the boys at the beginning and end (pre- and postcounseling) of the one-semester experimental period. Fifty self-referent phrases describing various aspects of the self in school were selected from student autobiographies and were typed on cards (i.e., "get my school work done on time," "like school"). These cards were presented to the boys to be sorted into eleven piles in a forced normal distribution from those which described him most to those which described him least; first, as he thought he really was in school and second, as he would like to be in school if he could. The sorts were intercorrelated and studied. In addition, records of academic and citizenship marks were analayzed.

Between the pre- and postcounseling periods the three experimental groups each met separately with their counselors weekly for ten 50-minute interviews. Regular individual counseling facilities were equally available to control and experimental boys during the semester.

The meetings were conducted on a permissive basis and only minimal limits necessary to protect property were established. The counselors attempted to get the boys themselves to identify the reason for the formation of the group. This the boys quickly accomplished. One group called itself "The Goof-Off Club." Much of the time in the early meetings was spent in testing the counselor by relating lurid stories of their real and fancied misdeeds. Once the boys appeared to be satisfied that the counselor could be trusted, a long period of violent verbal release of hostile feelings against school in general, particular teachers, and parents, occurred. The counselor served as a nonevaluating sounding board for these feelings. It was noted that the boys in all the groups seemed to enjoy knowing and being with others with like problems. Minor successes in school progress were related in the group, and considerable group approval of these achievements was evident—"I only got kicked out of class twice last week" was a typical announcement made with considerable pride.

Discussion of in-school behavior increased over the counseling period. The boys seemed to come closer to grips with their school problems as the interviews proceeded. The boys in all groups evidenced considerable anxiety when a group meeting was canceled or when the time was changed. One of the counselors expressed his role as that of a "benevolent father," and this seemed to express the attitude of all the counselors toward their role in the groups. The counselors attempted to help the boys release and to deal with their hostile feelings about school. They attempted to use the advantages of group disapproval and approval as a major tool. It was felt that the strong relationship built up between the boys and the counselors accounted for many of the changes that occurred.

Frequent staff meetings with consultants were held to aid the counselors in their work.

RESULTS

Q-SORT

The self and ideal correlations for the pre- and postcounseling testing periods were computed and tranformed to Fisher's z scores. These z scores were averaged, and the mean differences between the two testings, their standard errors, critical ratios of these standard errors, and confidence levels are presented in Table 1.

Table 1

Analysis of Changes in Self and Ideal-Self Correlation

Group	N	Mean z pre-counseling	Mean z post-counseling	Diff. M	SE	CR	P
Experimental							
L-7	6	−.053	.165	.218	.064	3.41	.05
L-8	6	.165	.318	.153	.054	2.83	.05
H-9	5	−.074	.401	.405	.107	3.79	.05
Total	17	.071	.291	.220	.051	4.31	.01
Control							
L-7	6	.234	.143	−.091	.054	1.69	NS
L-8	6	.060	.119	.059	.024	2.46	NS
H-9	5	.003	.081	.078	.420	.019	NS
Total	17	.108	.116	.008	.148	.054	NS

1. In order to test whether the total experimental and the total control groups, when considered together as one larger group, had been drawn from a random population, a Chi Square test for association based on the precounseling self/ideal-self correlations was used. The Chi Square of .31 obtained was not significant, indicating that the proposition that the group had been drawn from a random population was tenable.

2. The data in Table 1 indicate that a significant change took place within each experimental subgroup (and within the total experimental group) and that no such significant change took place within any control subgroup (or within the whole control group).

A total of fifteen boys in the experimental group showed an increase in self and ideal-self correlations as opposed to two boys who showed a decrease in such congruence. The difference in the number of boys showing an increase over the number showing a decrease is significant at the 1 per cent level of confidence by nonparametric sign test. Within the control group seven boys showed an increase in congruence and ten showed a decrease. This difference was not significant by the sign test.

3. An analysis of change present in each experimental subgroup was made. No significant difference in the amount of increase in self and ideal-self sorts was registered for any subgroup when compared to any other subgroup. It did not appear that the influence of any particular counselor on his group was a factor.

4. It was evident that nonrandom increases in the congruence of the self and ideal-self sorts took place during the semester within the experimental groups and did not take place within the control groups. In order to test whether the measured increase in the total experimental group was significantly greater than that of the whole control group when the groups were directly compared, the t-test was used. The mean difference in change in congruence between the groups in terms of z was .212. The ratio of this mean difference to its standard error of .071 was 2.986 which was beyond the 1 per cent level of significance. Thus, it may be said that the measured change in the experimental group was significantly greater than that of the control group and that the difference found in increases was not due to chance factors. It was inferred that the changes in the experimental group were consequent upon the group counseling interviews.

ACADEMIC RECORDS

Analysis of academic records was based on Honor Point Ratios. These ratios were computed by numerically weighting A—F marks, given on a five-point scale ($A = 4$, $B = 3$, etc.). Mean Honor Point Ratios for the groups were then computed.

In the total experimental group the mean Honor Point Ratio increased from 1.8 precounseling to 2.0 postcounseling. The standard error of the mean difference of .20 was .097. The ratio of the mean difference to its standard error by t-test was 2.1 which was barely significant at the 5 per cent level of confidence. However, the increase was small, and analysis of the experimental subgroups did not disclose any significant changes. The total control group registered a small decrease in Honor Point Ratio. No significant change took place in any control subgroup.

When the total groups were directly compared, the ratio of the mean difference, .30, to its standard error of .18 was by t-test 1.67—a nonsignificant t-ratio. Therefore, no clear-cut conclusion can be made regarding the effect of multiple counseling on Honor Point Ratio.

CITIZENSHIP RECORDS

The results of the analysis of the citizenship records are presented in Table 2. Due to the nature of the grading system, study of citizenship marks

Table 2

Analysis of Changes in Number of Classes
in which Poor Citizenship Marks were Given

Group	N	Mean no. classes pre-counseling	Mean no. classes post-counseling	Diff. M	SE	CR	P
Experimental							
L-7	6	1.3	0.2	1.1	.17	6.5	.01
L-8	6	4.5	2.3	2.2	.17	13.9	.01
H-9	5	1.0	0.3	0.7	.24	2.9	.05
Total	17	2.4	0.9	1.5	.30	5.0	.01
Control							
L-7	6	1.8	1.8	.0	.00	.0	NS
L-8	6	2.0	1.8	.2	.50	.4	NS
H-9	7	.8	.8	.0	.00	.0	NS
Total	17	1.6	1.7	.1	.14	.71	NS

could only be approached negatively; that is, through the number of classes in which warning or unsatisfactory citizenship marks—both regarded as poor—had been given. The mean number of classes in which poor citizenship marks were given appears for both precounseling and postcounseling periods. The mean difference (in terms of decrease), the standard error of the mean difference, the critical ratio of the mean difference to its standard error (t-test), and the level of confidence also appear.

It is evident that significant decreases in mean number of poor citizenship marks was present in each of the experimental subgroups and in the total experimental group. A total of thirteen boys in the experimental group had improved (in terms of decrease) citizenship records as opposed to four who did not improve. None had poorer records. The difference in the number improved over those who did not was significant at the 1 per cent level of confidence by nonparametric sign test. No such significant decreases were present in any control subgroup nor in the total control group (five improved, seven remained the same, five had poorer records).

When the difference in the mean number of decreases in poor citizenship marks for the total experimental and total control groups was directly compared, the ratio of the mean difference, 1.4, to its standard error of .44, was 3.18, which was above the 1 per cent level of confidence.

It was possible that the noted decreases in poor citizenship marks resulted from a desire on the part of the teachers to please the counselors by marking the experimental boys somewhat easier than usual. The marks given were, however, from about sixty different teachers, and almost no publicity had been given to the project. The teachers were accustomed to having youngsters out of their classes for counseling, and the teachers had no way of knowing which boys were receiving the group counseling unless the boys themselves revealed the fact. In short, teacher desire to please the counselors did not appear to have been a factor.

It was concluded that positive changes in citizenship marks took place within the experimental but not within the control group. These changes were inferred to be a result of multiple conseling.

SUMMARY

The changes after a series of group counseling interviews in the self concepts of a group of adolescent "problem" boys has been investigated by Q-technique. The nonrandom increases in self and ideal-self concepts found within the experimental but not within the control group were inferred to be a result of the interviews.

If a more integrated self structure enables one to be less tense, less disturbed, and more accepting and understanding of others, then it might be reasonably hoped that positive changes in behavior might also occur. It was found that nonrandom decreases in the mean number of classes in which poor citizenship grades were given did take place within the experimental but not within the control groups. Certain changes in academic records also occurred although the findings were not clear-cut.

It was probable that the changes represented only temporary progress. The lack of follow-up was one of the limitations of the study. However, Rogers [5] found that similar increases in self and ideal-self concepts remained relatively constant. The changes in classroom behavior were certainly to be desired, and it is to be hoped they might continue.

The results indicate that group counseling is a promising method for dealing with many of the problems of adolescents and warrants serious consideration and further investigation.

REFERENCES

1. Driver, H. I. *Multiple Counseling: A Small Group Discussion Method for Personal Growth* (Madison, Wisconsin: Monona Publications, 1954).

2. Froehlich, C. P. "Multiple Counseling—A Research Proposal." Unpublished manuscript, Univer. of California, Berkeley, not dated.

3. Froehlich, C. P. "Must Counseling Be Individual?" *Educ. & Psychol. Measmt.* (in press).

4. Mowrer, O. H. "Q-Technique—Description, History and Critique." In O. H. Mowrer (Ed.), *Psychotherapy: Theory and Research* (New York: Ronald Press, 1953), pp. 316–377.

5. Rogers, C. R., & Dymond, R. F. *Psychotherapy and Personality Change* (Chicago: Univer. of Chicago Press, 1954).

6. Stephenson, W. *The Study of Behavior: Q-Technique and Its Methodology* (Chicago: Univer. of Chicago Press, 1953).

19

Multiple Counseling with Underachieving Junior High School Pupils of Bright— Normal and Higher—Ability*

Oscar G. Mink

Broedel, Ohlsen, Proff, and Southard [1], used multiple (group) counseling as a treatment method with underachieving adolescents. Their study illustrated well the difficulty that can ensue in treating academic underachievers. They applied an accepted therapeutic method to students with underachievement problems. The investigators apparently operated on the assumption that successful remediation would involve the modification of the antecedents of current behavior. They found significant changes in acceptance of self as well as increased acceptance of others by the gifted underachievers but they failed to produce evidence ". . . that group counseling improves underachievers' academic performance in school" [1, p. 169].

One of the significant factors in underachievement might well be the influence of significant others, e.g., parents, peers and teachers, in the underachiever's environment. Failure of an investigator to describe and analyze the contemporary behavior of the subjects in interaction with their environment might lead to an incomplete picture of the variables influencing underachievement. Change in the direction of increased self and other acceptance as a result of the learning experience of multiple counseling may have little or no effect upon their present academic performance, because the attitudes and expectations of parents and teachers alike may not allow for any change in observable behavior. This problem is illustrated by Trow, et al., [6] where they point out that students cannot modify behavior because of "inhibition blindness." The student is afraid to behave in unaccustomed ways. This feeling can be relieved by use of a "cultural island." It is a group method whereby the instructor places the student in a situation where he will be influenced by his peers who are

*Reprinted by permission of the author and publisher from *Journal of Educational Research* (1964), LVIII, 31–34.

being affected by the same causes determining his inhibitions. Just as a "cultural island" is necessary for modification of one's attitudes so must one be placed in a new behavioral field where he can experiment with using these new attitudes. Assuming that by modifying the individual's attitudes one can modify his behavior seems to imply that changes in one's self-concept necessarily make it possible for him to respond differently to his environment. However, by definition, interpersonal interaction involves action and reaction by both elements in a dyad. Therefore, it would seem that one could not be certain that a significant change in underachievement behavior would be brought about by change in self-concept without any changes in the nature of expectations directed towards underachievers by parents, peers, and teachers.

Culbertson [3, p. 99] in summarizing a series of studies dealing with drop-outs, discusses the major areas of neglect by most investigators studying drop-outs. His remarks are apropos to underachievement if Mullin's [4] findings[1] are to be considered. Culbertson's conclusions were: 1) multiple factors are associated with drop-outs; 2) these factors are complex and interrelated; 3) research has not validly defined the dynamics of these interrelationships. He later lists agreement by investigators as to two major reasons for drop-outs: 1) inadequate curriculum, and 2) unsatisfactory student-teacher relationships. Both of these reasons would be discovered and remediated by dealing with the dynamics of the contemporary behavior of the underachiever.

Sears, *et al.*, [5] give substantial theoretical and experimental evidence to indicate that significant parental attitudes are transmitted to children through the identification process provided a reasonably healthy parent-child relationship exists. Brookover and Paterson [2] in a study designed to predict academic achievement using self-concepts of ability as an additional independent variable to IQ in a regression equation, found that they could approximately double the variance accounted for by the multiple R. However, an additional finding of their study was that substantial correlations existed between the student's self-concept of his general ability and the images that he perceives each of four significant persons hold of his ability. These correlations were: 1) mother's image—.50, 2) father's image —.52. 3) teacher's image—.55, and 4) peer's image—.47. It would appear that a fruitful effort towards remediation of underachievement in students centered around inadequate self-concepts of achievement might well be made in the direction of raising the expectations of parents.

[1]She found that superior attenders came mostly from middle class homes. They also were more intelligent as a group and ranked higher in school interest, industry, and responsibility than poor attenders.

DESCRIPTION AND PURPOSE OF THE STUDY

The project was designed to test the applicability and effectiveness of multiple counseling with eight talented underachievers selected from a pool of such individuals initially identified through a testing program which encompassed the entire 7th and 8th grades. There were three purposes for conducting the project: 1) To identify talented underachievers, 2) to determine the effectiveness of multiple counseling as a guidance tool in stimulating academic achievement among talented underachieving adolescents, and 3) to determine the effectiveness of multiple counseling as a guidance tool in developing a higher level of expectations on the part of parents towards their talented underachievers.

SELECTION OF THE SAMPLE

The entire seventh and eighth grades were tested with the Lorge-Thorndike-Level 4, Nonverbal, and a total of 23 students identified whose true score IQ's were 116 or higher and who were doing below average or failing work in three or more subjects. In the judgment of their teachers these students were not consistently performing academically at a level of performance commensurate with their capabilities. Out of this group, four eighth graders and four seventh graders were paired with members of the same class group in order to compose an experimental group and a control group of underachievers. There were two girls in the eighth grade in each group and one girl in the seventh grade in each group, leaving two eighth-grade boys and three seventh-grade boys in each group. Pairings were based on IQ and sex.

THE SAMPLE

The subjects were from middle SES families in a rural-urban community. The major industry is farming with many of the urban dwellers employed by a nearby university and a nearby state mental hospital. One boy was a first generation American with parents of German lineage who operated a local grocery store. The father of one boy operated a successful automobile dealership. Another boy's father was president of the school board and a dairy farmer. His mother taught in the high school. One girl's mother was a divorcee who was employed as a registered nurse in a nursing home.

PROCEDURE

The experimental and control groups were pretested and posttested, using the Guidance Test—HGU—ETS Guidance Inquiry. (This was an experimental edition of a test devised to be used in conjunction with *You: Today and Tomorrow*, 3rd Edition, by Martin R. Katz[2]), *The Allport-Vernon Study of Values* and the *Brown-Holtzman Survey of Study Habits and Attitudes*[3] It was decided that the school psychologist would be the counselor for the students and that the guidance counselor would work primarily with the parents. As the study progressed, the psychologist worked exclusively with the students and both the psychologist and the guidance counselor worked with the parents. All the counselees had had previous contact with the psychologist and the guidance counselor for educational planning or personal-social counseling. Each group member had expressed interest in joining the group when asked during individual counseling interviews. Seven of the eight counselees appeared to be more inhibited in the group situation than in the individual counseling sessions. The one exception was a seventh-grade boy who seemed to take special responsibility to keep the group in a state of verbal interaction. The experimental students had eleven 45-minute group sessions with the psychologist, and two two-hour testing sessions.

CONTENT OF INTERVIEWS

By orientation, the psychologist was client-centered in his group approach. However, the frequency of interaction between group members was regarded by the psychologist as law and primarily cognitive. Thus, the psychologist changed his approach to the group and increased the amount of lead and the frequency of his contributions. At least twenty-minutes of each session with the students were taken by the counselor in presenting content from *You: Today and Tomorrow* and short illustrated talks on topics relating to study skills such as SQ3R, note-taking, and listening. There were discussions which centered around parental relationships, school studies and activities. Some of the discussions of aptitude, values, interests, and future plans produced conative statements and self-references from the counselees. The conative and self-reference statements involved less than 5 percent of the session content, by the psychologist's estimate.

The students were told that the psychologist wanted to meet with their parents but that the guidance counselor would also meet with their parents. When asked if they approved of the "counselors" meeting with their parents, the group responded with characteristic apathy.

The sessions with the parents were most lively. After 15- to 20-minute presentations on "Your Child and College" and "Your Childs' Intelligence" the parents became involved in a discussion containing statements that were

---

[2]Published by Cooperative Test Division, Educational Testing Service, Princeton, New Jersey.

[3]It was necessary to define several terms used in these tests for both groups.

composed of approximately 80 percent self-references. These expressions were primarily conative and indicated a good deal of parental misunderstanding regarding college costs, scholarships, academic aptitude, curriculum and similar topics related to educational-vocational planning.

One two-hour session and one one-hour session were held with the parents of the experimental group. No contacts were made by the investigator with the control students or their parents, other than the pre- and posttesting sessions with the students. However, all students were told that the school was involved in a talent search project.

As a result of the group meetings, two sets of the parents were seen on a volunteer basis several times by the psychologist in follow-up interviews.

FINDINGS

On the variables measured, the only one to show any significant difference was the increase in knowledge of materials pertaining directly to educational and vocational guidance as measured by the Guidance Test. The difference between the before and after tests was significant at the .01 level of confidence using a T-test for correlated data [7, p. 418].

Clinical impressions of the meetings with the parents were that the parent discussions were qualitatively more affective in content than the student discussions. It seemed to the investigator that he would have accomplished more by working almost entirely with the parents. In follow-up interviews with the two sets of parents, the investigator found these parents to be seeking specific advice as to how they could help their sons. They were highly motivated to resolve their problems. The psychologist was client-centered in his counseling with those parents. In the February 1962 follow-up, neither of those boys could have been classified as underachievers.

The most progress definitely seemed to be made with the parents in terms of an increased interest on their part in their children and their activities as well as increased understanding of their offspring—a factor which is estimated only by clinical observation. The long-range effects of this study on all the subjects involved may yet prove to be positive.

A one-year follow-up of the achievement of the two groups as measured by teacher grades indicates no significant changes in the total group. However, it should be noted that three of the members of the experimental group were each failing a subject when the study started. In the February 1962 follow-up, not one of these subjects was failing a course. All of the experimental subjects were doing satisfactory work, with the two boys previously mentioned achieving at a level predicted by their ability.

One of the control subjects was failing a course when pretested, with borderline grades in all subjects. At posttesting, his grades were all passing with three grades definitely on level with his ability. The remaining controls had maintained a status quo with the exception of their English grades as already mentioned. Both the experimental and control groups made significant increases in English achievement levels as measured by teacher grades. It is assumed that this change is due to some factor not related to the study such as change in teachers or curriculum or both.

DISCUSSION

This study suggests that counseling with parents of underachievers may be fruitful. Meetings with parents should begin after the children have been studied and after the counselor has been able to prepare a report on each student's aptitudes, etc., for purposes of the parents' consumption. The investigator suggests that topics suitable for parent conferences are college costs, meaning of interests, values, attitudes, aptitudes and intelligence, different curriculums, and similar topics that will give parents an accurate picture of their child's characteristics and potential. Even though the junior high-school student may be indifferent and possibly hostile towards counselor-parent contacts, this investigator believes that parent sessions have great potential value.

For future studies, it would be interesting to work with significant peers and teachers of underachievers in an effort to modify their perceptions and expectations of the underachiever to ones that are in line with the underachiever's true potential if discrepencies exist between the true picture of an underachiever and their perception of him.

It wouldn't do for the investigator to leave the reader with the impression that the sessions with the students were of no value. The causes that contributed to what improvement in academic performance that was observed are confounded by the many possible independent variables. The investigator is left with the conviction that the treatment effects in future studies should encompass the use of several matched groups of underachievers with whom various combinations of variables can be tested in an effort to determine the relative effectiveness of different treatment procedures such as multiple counseling with peers, parents, teachers, and students as opposed to multiple counseling with parents and underachievers or underachievers or parents alone. Another study might well be done in an effort to ascertain the relative effectiveness of counseling with individual students and groups of students as well as a combination of individual and multiple counseling. Certainly enough evidence exists regarding the influence of significant others on a student's self-perceptions and subsequent behavior to suggest that these significant others need to be considered as composing a significant part of the treatment situation.

Note: This project utilized funds from the New York State Education Departments' *Project Talent.*

REFERENCES

1. Broedel, John; Ohlsen, Merle; Proff, Fred; and Southard, Charles. "The Effects of Group Counseling on Gifted Underachieving Adolescents," *Journal of Counseling Psychology*, VII (1960), pp. 163–170.

2. Brookover, Wilbur B. and Paterson, Ann. *Self-concept and School Achievement of Seventh Grade Students*. Paper presented at February 1962 meeting of American Educational Research Association in Atlantic City.

3. Culbertson, Jack. "School Attendance," in *Encyclopedia of Educational Research*, 3d ed. (New York: The Macmillan Company, 1960).

4. Mullin, Margaret M. "Personal and Situational Factors Associated with Perfect Attendance," *Personnel and Guidance Journal*, XXXIII (1955), pp. 438–443.

5. Sears, R. R.; Maccoby, E. E.; Levin, H. *Patterns of Child Rearing* (White Plains: Row, Peterson and Co., 1957).

6. Trow, William C.; Zander, A. F.; Morse, W. C.; and Jenkins, D. H. "The Class as a Group: Conclusions from Research in Group Dynamics," *Journal of Educational Psychology*, XLIV (1950), pp. 322–338.

7. Wert, J. E.; Neidt, C. O.; and Ahmann, J. S. *Statistical Methods in Educational and Psychological Research* (New York: Appleton-Century-Crofts, Inc., 1954).

20

The Effects of Group Counseling on Gifted Underachieving Adolescents*

John Broedel
Merle Ohlsen
Fred Proff
Charles Southard

Counseling psychologists operating in schools have become increasingly interested in group counseling. Accompanying this interest, however, is an appalling lack of experimental evidence to support training practices, utilization of staff, and the application of therapeutic techniques in groups [10]. These conditions, combined with an interest in gifted youth, led several of us at the University of Illinois to undertake a long-range project to investigate the application of group counseling[1] in treating gifted youth. The present paper [3] is a partial report of a study growing out of the first phase of this project.[2] It is concerned with the extent to which group counseling improves the mental health and academic performance of gifted underachieving adolescents.

Group counseling is particularly appropriate for adolescents. So often they are made to feel that they are culprits, and that whatever the difficulty is they are the ones who should be expected to change their behavior [2]. Most also believe that few adults will listen to them and try to understand them; many question whether adults can understand them. On the other

°Reprinted by permission of the author and publisher from *Journal of Counseling Psychology* (1960), 7, 163–170.

[1]The authors use the terms counseling and psychotherapy to describe the same process. However, they prefer the term group counseling to indicate that clients within the normal range of adjustment were treated in a non-medical setting.

[2]This study was conducted in Evanston Township High School. Funds for the initial phase of this project were provided by Evanston Township High School, College of Education at the University of Illinois, and the University of Illinois Research Board. Funds for the second phase of this project were provided by U. S. Office of Education under the provisions of Public Law 331, 83rd congress. The writers are indebted to the following school counselors who served on the two four-man observer teams: Edward Adamek, Jean Cantelope, Floyd Cummings, Edward Curry, Barbara Garrison, Colleen Karavites, Joseph Kanitzi, and Marilyn Meyers and to the assistant superintendent, Lloyd McLeary, and the television engineer, Frank Bullard.

hand, they believe that their peers can and want to understand them. Because they often use peers as models and they want to win peers' acceptance, adolescents appreciate the opportunity to exchange ideas with peers in a permissive and accepting group. Inasmuch as they are struggling for independence from adults, they also prefer peers' assistance in solving their problems. Moreover, they are genuinely reassured when they discover that their peers have problems similar to their own. Ackerman [1] reported that while members of a counseling group, adolescents not only came to feel better understood by others, but that they also learned to empathize with others and to increase their tolerance for others' idiosyncrasies.

THE PROBLEM

The previous paragraph makes the case for treating adolescents in groups. To the extent that underachieving gifted adolescents are like other adolescents it applies to them too. Gifted underachieving adolescents have a number of unique characteristics that makes group treatment especially appropriate for them. Shaw and Grubb [12], Gowan [6], and Kirk [8] found underachievers to be hostile. Gowan also described them as indifferent to their responsibilities, unsociable, self-sufficient, and hard to reach and Shaw and Grubb reported that others' demands on them for better quality of work tended to produce negative results.

Generally, these descriptions agreed with our observers' descriptions of our clients. Our observers also concluded that most of our clients questioned whether they were gifted. Apparently they felt that academic promise had been used against them so often that many of them had to deny it. In other words, these youths are not the type that one would expect to seek counseling. Furthermore, when caused to look at their problems, one would expect them to deny that they had problems and to withdraw from counseling. Supporting evidence for the previous point is reported by Katz, Ohlsen and Proff [10]. From Caplan's [4], Gersten's [5], and Paster's [11] work with hostile people and Ackerman's [1] and Berman's [2] experiences with adolescents, *we concluded that group counseling would increase our clients' acceptance of themselves and improve their ability to relate to others.* We also assumed that these changes were necessary conditions for motivating them to accept and to use their untapped resources.

METHOD

This study was conducted in a four-year high school which provided better than average counseling services. In short, this was not a setting in which one would expect any added personal attention, regardless of type, to account for client improvement.

The counseling was provided in an ordinary classroom which was furnished with movable arm chairs. These were arranged in a circle. Three microphones were placed in the center of the circle. Two remote-controlled television cameras were mounted on opposite walls. Usually one or the other kept the entire group in view. The other was focused on behavior which was judged to be clinically significant. All the counseling sessions for all four groups were, with subjects' awareness, electrically recorded and observed by four-man observer teams by closed-circuit television. The two groups which were treated last also were kinescoped. For these latter groups, the observer teams received the same stimuli which were recorded on kinescopes. An experienced clinician decided what video material should be sent to the observer teams and be recorded on kinescopes.

The sample was composed of ninth grade students who as eighth graders ranked in the top ten per cent of their class on the California Test of Mental Maturity and at the ninth decile or below in terms of their grade-point average earned in the eighth grade. Of the 34 pupils identified by this method, 29 actually participated in group counseling. The parents of one child refused to grant permission for their child to participate. For another, his mother asked that he be dropped from the project because his work improved significantly during the first six weeks grading period. Scheduling problems prevented the other three from participating in counseling.

Originally the entire population of 34 was divided into four groups—assigning proportionate numbers of boys and girls to each group by random numbers. The 29 who actually participated in the project were divided into two experimental and two control groups as follows: E_1—2 girls and 4 boys; E_2—3 girls and 5 boys; C_1—2 girls and 6 boys; and C_2—2 girls and 5 boys.

After the sample had been selected every prospective client was interviewed for three purposes: (a) to acquaint him with what he might expect from group counseling and to inform him what would be expected from him; (b) to answer his questions about the experience, and (c) to appraise the seriousness of each client's problems. This was followed by a meeting of the parents where the project was described in detail, their questions were answered, and written permissions for pupil participation were obtained. Though the investigators stressed the point that they wanted only those pupils who themselves recognized the value of group counseling and elected to participate, they learned from the pupils' comments during counseling that every counseling group except C_1 contained some pupils who participated as a consequence of parental pressure.

While E_1 and E_2 were counseled C_1 and C_2 served as the control groups. Following the posttesting, group counseling was provided for C_1 and C_2 by the same counselor. These latter clients were used as their own control for the purpose of evaluating growth during two periods: the second period in which they received counseling and the first when they served as control groups for themselves as well as E_1 and E_2.

During the first treatment period, clients were excused from their study halls for counseling. Each group met for one class period twice each week for eight weeks.

An effort also was made to control the educational and guidance experiences during the experimental period. In most instances the members of one experimental group and one control group were assigned to the same sections for English, social studies, study hall, and homeroom.

The same was done for the other experimental group and control group. During the course of the experiment, none of these pupils were referred either for assistance with study skills or for counseling.

Originally the plan called for the members of the control group also to be excused from study hall and to be assigned some special activity while the members of the experimental groups were in group counseling. None of the activities suggested for the control groups met the criteria defined by the school administration: an educational experience that is sufficiently worthwhile to justify excusing the pupils from a study period.

Growth of clients was evaluated and compared with members of the control groups in terms of three variables: (a) academic performance as measured by the California Achievement Test Battery and grade point averages earned in high school; (b) acceptance of self and of others as revealed in responses to the Picture Story Test; and (c) behaviors in interpersonal relationships reported on the Behavior Inventory by the pupils themselves and such significant others as the members of each observer team, the clients' parents, and the counselor.

RESULTS

Originally these were two separate studies: the first dealt with the results obtained from E_1 and E_2 and the second with results obtained from C_1 and C_2. Except for those instances in which the *t*-test was used, the same statistical tests were used in both studies. In the latter the *t*-test for correlated means was used in certain instances to determine whether chance could account for differences between pre- and post scores during treatment period and control period. In each instance the E_1 and E_2 data will be presented first.

ACCEPTANCE OF SELF AND OTHERS

Attitudes of acceptance of self and of others were evaluated by content analysis of clients' written responses to the Picture Story Test. Five pictures were selected for the test: Card 1 of the Michigan Picture Story Test; Card

2 of Murray's TAT; and Cards 1, 4, and 5 of Alexander and Cronbach's adaptation of the TAT.

The scoring procedure devised by Ohlsen and Schultz [9] was used to classify the clients' responses. For our purposes here 20 questions were used in the content analysis. In each instance the story was read with a particular question in mind and when the client discussed the content of the question either a positive or negative sign was assigned to that content. Each client's score was the algebraic sum of these signed numbers (not more than 1 for each question) for the 20 questions on all five pictures. Actually, by the very nature of the questions two subscores (one for acceptance of self and one for acceptance of others) and a total score was obtained.

For E_1 and E_2 the mean gain in acceptance of self and of others was significantly greater than the mean gain demonstrated by their control groups over the pre- to posttesting period. In stories elicited in response to the Picture Story Test, the clients, after group counseling, demonstrated an increased ability to project affectivity into their stories. Not only was more affect introduced into the stories, but Identification Figures as well as others were described in more positive terms than previously. In stories produced after counseling, clients also tended increasingly to depict Identification Figures as demonstrating more warmth and affection for others, as well as being more willing recipients of affection.

With only one exception, an inspection of the scores for C_1 and C_2 also showed increased acceptance of self and of others. However, these differences were not significant. On the other hand, it should be noted that while these same students were serving as their own controls, and waiting for counseling, most of their scores shifted in the opposite direction. Moreover, clinical evaluations of the members of C_1 clearly suggested for three clients increased acceptance of others, for three clients increased acceptance of self, and for two clients substantial improvement in their total scores. In C_2, which was judged by observers to be unproductive [7], substantial improvements were noted for one client on self score, for three clients on acceptance of others' scores, and for three clients on their total scores.

Unfortunately, a problem arose in the administration of the follow-up testing which could have invalidated the responses. Therefore, they were not scored. Nevertheless, even a cursory analysis of these data suggested that the gains achieved were maintained.

ACADEMIC PERFORMANCE

Grades were given every six weeks. The school used five numerical grades in addition to the F which was given as the failing grade. Since 1 was the top grade, an F was assigned a value of 6. Gain in academic performance, therefore, was demonstrated by a decrease in grade-point average.

Group counseling was begun for E_1 and E_2 immediately following the first grading period. The second grading period occurred during the experimental period and the third occurred four weeks after the termination of counseling (counseling was terminated for E_1 and E_2 just prior to Christmas vacation).

While some improvement was demonstrated between the first and third grading periods by control subjects, experimental subjects' grades grew gradually worse. The differences between the mean grade-point average earned by experimental subjects at the first grading period and that earned at the third was equal to .54. The comparable difference for control subjects was equal to .26. The discrepancy between these two differences was demonstrated by an analysis of variance test to be significant at the .05 level. Changes in the second semester grades for E_1 and E_2 also were compared with the grades they earned prior to counseling. None of these differences was significant. Though there was a slight improvement in grades between the third and fourth grading periods, this improvement was not maintained. Despite their giftedness, and their increased acceptance of self and of others, they failed to improve their grades significantly even in the eighteen-month follow-up.

For C_1 and C_2 counseling began just one week before the third grading period. No significant improvement in grade point average was obtained. However, it is interesting to note that when one compares grades earned in ninth grade with those earned in the tenth grade, these clients improved their grades every grading period except one.

With reference to improvement in scores on the California Achievement Test Battery, we found that whereas the scores for E_1 and E_2 decreased slightly during the treatment period, their control groups remained almost constant. However, analysis of variance tests indicated that these differences could be accounted for by chance. On the other hand, when we compared pre-, post-, and four-month follow-up performance for E_1 and E_2, we found that the difference between the mean raw scores earned at each of the three testing periods was significant at the .01 level. Thus, the impaired performance on this standardized test was only a temporary effect. A further statistical analysis indicated that there was no point in giving this achievement test again in the eighteen-month follow-up—the form of the test used lacked adequate ceiling for these clients to make further significant improvements in their scores.

INTERPERSONAL RELATIONSHIPS

The Behavior Inventory was designed for this study to ascertain the ways in which subjects perceived their own behavior and the ways in which the subject's behavior was perceived by others. The instrument was a forced-choice rating schedule consisting of 66 pairs of statements describing 12 classifications of behavior.

A Rank Profile of Behavior was obtained for each record by ordering the behaviors in terms of the frequency with which each of the twelve behaviors was selected by the rater as more typical of a subject than another. Although the Rank Profiles provided summary descriptions of subjects' behavior, a criterion was needed with which the profiles could be evaluated quantitatively. A Model of Adjustment was constructed to serve this purpose.

The combined judgments of 13 counseling psychologists were utilized in formulating the Model of Adjustment. These psychologists were provided with comprehensive definitions of the 12 classes of behavior included on the Behavior Inventory. They were then instructed to think of some individual they knew or had known who came closest to approaching their concept of the ideally adjusted person and to describe that person by ranking the twelve behaviors in terms of the extent to which each was characteristic of him. The 13 sets of ranks obtained from the psychologists yielded a coefficient of concordance of .82 which was demonstrated by an F test to be significant at the .01 point. In the computation of the W coefficient, the mean rank of each behavior was determined; it provided the basis for establishing the order of the behaviors in the Model of Adjustment.

Three of the behaviors had a mean rank of six when rounded to the nearest whole number, so the 12 behaviors were reduced to ten ranks in the model. The order given the classes of behavior in the Model of Adjustment was as follows:

1. Behavior indicates acceptance of self
2. Behavior indicates acceptance of others
3. Gives information
4. Gives action-oriented suggestions
5. Agrees with others
6. Gives opinions
7. Asks for information
8. Asks for opinions
9. Disagrees with others
10. Asks for action-oriented suggestions
11. Behavior indicative of rejection of others
12. Behavior indicative of rejection of self.

The clients' parents, members of the observing teams, and the counselor provided their judgments of clients' behavior on the Behavior Inventory both before and after the counseling period. The behavior of clients was quantitatively expressed by computing rank correlation coefficients r' between the Model of Adjustment and each Rank Profile obtained from judges' responses to the Behavior Inventory. To ascertain whether judges perceived positive changes in client behavior after group counseling, each r′ coefficient resulting from a single judge's precounseling description of a subject with the Model of Adjustment was compared with the r′ obtained from the same judge's description of that client after counseling. The significance of the differences between such pairs of r′ coefficients was determined by making Fisher z′ transformations.

A total of eighty-five pair of r′ coefficients was obtained for E_1 and E_2. In only 8 of the 85 were the r′ coefficients based on a description of precounseling behavior more highly correlated with the Model of Adjustment than the r′ coefficients based on postcounseling data. In none of the 8 cases were the differences significant at the .05 level. The remaining 77 pair of r′ coefficients indicated cases where judges reported clients as acting in a manner more congruent with the Model of Adjustment after counseling than before. In 41 of these 77 cases the improvement was demonstrated to be statistically significant: 18 at the .01 level; 23 others at the .05 level. It was concluded, therefore, that behavioral changes were manifested by clients participating in group counseling and these changes were in a healthy direction.

The clients' perceptions of their own behavior before and after counseling were obtained by use of a self-report form of the Behavior Inventory. The method for determining differences between pre- and posttesting was the same as that used in evaluating changes in behavioral descriptions provided by parents, observer teams, and the counselor. No significant changes in the clients' reported perceptions of their own behavior were revealed.

Unlike the precounseling ratings of others, clients from E_1 and E_2 described themselves before counseling in a way that indicated moderate to high correlation with the Model of Adjustment. While not significant at the .05 level, 8 of the 14 clients described themselves in a more negative manner after participating in group counseling. These less idealized self-reports obtained after counseling more closely concurred with the descriptions made by others than did the precounseling self-reports. If, as seems likely, others were more objective and less biased in their ratings than clients themselves, it is suggested that the self-reports obtained after counseling were more reality-oriented than the initial self-reports. Further investigation would be required to determine whether group counseling does result, in fact, in participants formulating more accurate perceptions of their own behavior and/or are more able, because of reduced anxiety, to admit to others those aspects of themselves of which they are acutely aware but reluctant to admit to others.

Analysis of the data collected during the eighteen-month follow-up indicated that little change occurred during the period between the first follow-up four months after termination of counseling and the last. The descriptions of subjects' behavior by parents remained significantly more positive than precounseling ratings, but the clients' own descriptions of themselves still showed no significant changes.

Those who observed C_1 and C_2 by closed-circuit television agreed that the members of C_1 improved, but that C_2 did not improve significantly. These conclusions also were supported by the rank order correlation with the Model of Adjustment. Inasmuch as kinescopes also were made of these two groups, it was possible to have four postdoctoral research associates use a revised form of the Behavior Inventory to re-appraise the growth achieved by these two groups of clients. The differences in their descriptions of these clients revealed that the members of C_1 made significant growth. Every one of these observers of the kinescopes reported changes, based upon independent judgments, which were significant at the .07 level or better. For C_2 three of the four judges reported no significant changes in clients' behavior between the beginning and termination of counseling. The fourth judge reported changes in the clients' behavior which could be accounted for by chance only seven times in a hundred.

The data obtained from self-reports failed to indicate significant improvement in interpersonal behavior for either C_1 or C_2. However, certain individuals from both noted significant changes in their own behavior. For example, one client from C_1 noted significant improvement within his behavior between pre- and posttesting and two other clients noted significant improvement between pre- and follow-up testing.

DISCUSSION

Shaw and Grubb [12] were right when they said that underachievement is not a surface phenomenon which is easily modified. Though three of the four groups (E_1, E_2, and C_1) were judged to have made significant growth, we concluded that it is expecting too much to complete treatment for this type of client within an eight-week period.

Results obtained with C_2 were disappointing. However, this was not a surprise. From the beginning the group showed little promise for growth. This nontherapeutic climate was created largely by two hostile boys who consistently attacked those who tried to make the group therapeutic. Their influence on this group, and on each other, and the ways in which the counselor attempted to cope with them is discussed in a paper by Katz, Ohlsen, and Proff [7].

Two interesting sidelights are worth noting: (a) certain clients may impede or inhibit the therapeutic process for others and still profit from counseling themselves; and (1954) group counseling, in contrast to individual counseling, affords an opportunity for nonverbalizers to participate vicariously through the verbalizations of others, and thereby achieve significant growth.

Picture Story Test protocols, as well as the opinions of members of the observer teams, indicated that prior to counseling the underachievers had negative attitudes toward themselves and others which would have interfered with any program specifically designed to help them improve their academic efficiency.

Although this study failed to produce evidence that group counseling will improve underachievers' academic performance in school, it may nevertheless make it possible for improved scholastic performance to be attained. Further investigation is needed to determine whether the replacement of negative attitudes by attitudes of acceptance of self and of others permits the underachiever to benefit from a remedial program specifically designed to help him improve his academic efficiency and his study skills.

Had not the Picture Story Test and other indicators pointed to an increased acceptance of self and of others in experimental subjects, the negative movement in school grades might have been interpreted as an indication that the subjects had in fact become more self-rejecting. The occurrence of growth in acceptance of self and of others accompanied by poorer achievement, however, deserves special consideration. Initial retardation in school performance may have been a result of increased independence and assertiveness, both products of increased acceptance of self. Since participation was the parents' idea for some, it was not necessarily an indication that the underachievers say their performance as a serious problem. The underachievers' new sense of well-being after counseling may have been directed to areas more important to them. These perhaps caused them to focus more of their energy on interpersonal relationships, which had not been satisfactory to them in the past, to such an extent that they gave less attention to their academic work.

It also can be hypothesized that increased assertiveness and independence in students who have already created problems in the classroom may not have been recognized by the teachers as an indication of growth. Teachers were perhaps as baffled as the parent who noted, "A manner of conversation has developed among him and his friends to say the most horrible things and insults to one another—and nobody seems to resent it!" If a failure to understand changes in behavior was communicated by the teachers to the underachiever, it would create feelings of rejection in the student, which, in turn, would result in increased hostility toward the teacher. Implicit in this proposed explanation is the further suggestion that group counseling *per se* is not adequate in bringing about better school performance unless it is accompanied by closer cooperation between the counseling staff and the teaching faculty in order to achieve in teachers greater awareness of the needs and dynamics operating in the underachieving group and to interpret for them the changes which they may observe in the classroom.

Finally, we should like to give our clinical explanations of what we think happened to our clients. With varying degrees of depth each client discovered: (a) that expressing his own real feelings about people, things, and ideas helped him to understand himself and the forces that disturbed him; (b) that at least one adult could accept him and this this adult, the counselor, wanted to understand him; (c) that his peers had problems too; (d) that, in spite of his faults which his peers wanted to help him correct, his peers could accept him; (e) that he was capable of understanding, accepting, and helping others; and (f) that he could learn to trust others. When a client discovered that others accepted him, he found that he could better accept others, and eventually, that he could better accept himself. After he began to accept himself, then, and only then, could he accept the fact that he was gifted, and make plans which required him to use his great potentialities. All of this takes time—these changes come ever so gradually—yet they must precede substantial improvement in grades. What is more, each client must learn to live with his new self, communicate this new self to important others, and teach these important others to understand, to accept, and to live with the new self. For example, it is difficult for the average teacher to believe that these hostile and uncooperative students have really changed and for the distressed parents to believe that these youngsters are willing to take responsibility for their work, and without nagging.

SUMMARY

Four groups of underachieving ninth graders were treated in small groups. All of the sessions were electrically recorded for the four groups; kinescopes were made of all 16 sessions for each of two groups. Growth of clients was evaluated in terms of grades earned, scores on an achievement test battery, responses to a Picture Story Test, and observations made by the clients, their parents, and the members of observer teams.

We concluded that three of the four groups achieved significant growth. Positive changes in clients were noted in improved scores on the achievement test, increased acceptance of self and of others, and improved ability to relate to peers, siblings, and parents.

REFERENCES

1. Ackerman, N. W. "Group Psychotherapy with a Mixed Group of Adolescents," *Internat. J. Group Psychother.* (1955), **5**, 249–260.

2. Berman, S. "Psychotherapeutic Techniques with Adolescents," *Amer. J. Orthopsychiat.* (1954), **24**, 238–244.

3. Broedel, J. W. "The Effects of Group Counseling on Academic Performance and Mental Health of Underachieving Gifted Adolescents." Unpublished doctoral dissertation, Univer. of Illinois, 1958.

4. Caplan, S. W. "The Effect of Group Counseling on Junior High School Boys' Concepts of Themselves in School," *J. Counsel. Psychol.* (1957), 4, 124–128.

5. Gersten, C. "An Experimental Evaluation of Group Therapy with Juvenile Delinquents," *Internat. J. Group Psychother.* (1951), 1, 311–318.

6. Gowan, J. "The Underachieving Gifted Child—A Problem for Everyone," *J. Except. Child.* (1955), 21, 247–249.

7. Katz, Evelyn W., Ohlsen, M. M., & Proff, F. C. "An Analysis Through Use of Kinescopes of the Interpersonal Behavior of Adolescents in Group Counseling," *J. Coll. Student Personnel* (1959), 1, 2–10.

8. Kirk, Barbara. "Test Versus Academic Performance in Malfunctioning Students," *J. Consult. Psychol.* (1952), 16, 213–216.

9. Ohlsen, M. M., & Schultz, R. E. "Projective Test Response Patterns for Best and Poorest Student Teachers," *Educ. Psychol. Meast* (1955), 15, 18–27.

10. Ohlsen, M. M., Proff, F. C., & Roeber, E. C. "Counseling and Adjustment," *Rev. Educ. Res.* (1956), 26, 292–307.

11. Paster, S. "Group Psychotherapy in an Army General Hospital," *Ment. Hygiene* (1944), 28, 529–536.

12. Shaw, M. C., & Grubb, J. "Hostility and Able High School Underachievers," *J. Counsel. Psychol.* (1958), 5, 263–266.

21

Themes in Group Counseling
with Adolescents*

Marilyn Bates

A group of counselors met in seminar over a period of a year, critiquing
tapes of their group counseling sessions. It was found through analysis of
these recordings that certain themes could be identified which occurred
and reoccurred in the content of group counseling with adolescents. These
themes were entitled: "My Vices," "Outwitting the Adults," "Problem
Parents," "My Brother, the Brat," "My Public Image," "Nobody
Loves Me," and "Let's Change the Rules." Illustrative material is presented that was transcribed from the recordings, after all identifying data
were removed.

Since the unexpected confrontation is the expected encounter in group
counseling, even the seasoned group counselor approaches each session
with an edge of anxiety, knowing he needs all the professional skill he can
muster to deal with the complex nuances of the group's dynamics. The
inexperienced group counselor may approach his first session naively confident that his individual counseling skills will carry him through the com-
plexities of the group process, but it only requires a few grueling sessions to
raise his panic level to the red button stage. Unfortunately, there are no
panic buttons in the group counseling room. There is only a small group of
students putting trust in the professional skills of the group counselor.

It was in an effort to improve their professional skills that one group of
counselors critiqued tapes of their group counseling sessions, recorded over
a period of a year, in a university seminar. A facet of professional compe-
tency that grew out of the seminar was an awareness that a group counselor
could anticipate certain patterns of thought in the group process. The element of the unexpected will never be removed from human dynamics, of
course, but nevertheless it was found through listening to many taped
recordings that there was a reservoir of themes that arose in the counseling
content of group after group. Hopefully, a delineation of these reoccurring
elements will be of help to other counselors as they work with groups. The
themes have been somewhat facetiously. entitled: "My Vices," "Out-

*Reprinted by permission of the author and publisher from *Personnel and Guidance
Journal* (1966), XLIV, 568–575.

witting the Adults," "Problem Parents," "My Brother, the Brat," "My Public Image," "Nobody Loves Me," and "Let's Change the Rules." Other themes emerge occasionally, such as "Fear of Mental Illness," "Concern over Academic Ability," "Dating Problems," "Fascination for the Macabre and Death," but these did not appear consistently. The seven major themes which are developed here seem to account for much of the group counseling content when the counselees are adolescents. Obviously, all identifying data have been omitted from the extracts of recordings which are presented as illustrative material, necessarily out of context.

MY VICES

Generally speaking, no particular sequence of themes was noted but the "My Vices" theme tended to appear early in the sessions, and then, once worked over, was given little further attention by the counselees. While at times this verbal "muscle flexing" consisted of efforts to top each other's tales (often severely taxing the counselor's credulity), most usually a serious discussion of values evolved. In the nonjudgmental atmosphere of the group counseling situation the students were able to turn to an examination on the reasons for their "Vices," analyzing with each other possible consequences, working through rationalizations to the true reasons for their behavior. The following example is fairly typical of the kind of discussion that can be expected in a group counseling situation:

Mavis: If you're going to smoke and your parents don't let you, you're just going to smoke behind their backs anyway.

Counselor: You feel it's better to tell them and be honest than sneak behind their backs.

Jean: I do. I mean, I can see how your parents wouldn't want you to smoke around their friends, but I think it's better to smoke in front of them than behind their backs.

Counselor: Implying that if a son or daughter smoked in front of their friends, parents might be embarrassed?

Jean: Yeah.

Bill: My parents don't feel that way. I asked my dad whether he wanted me to smoke in front of him or behind his back and he said he didn't want me to smoke at all!

Gary: Does your dad smoke?

Bill: Yeah, but they try to tell me it's a bad habit. "I'd sure like to get off it, Son. You'd better not start." But they keep right on smoking.

Counselor: I hear you questioning whether it's right for parents to smoke and not let their kids smoke.

Bill: No, I don't think it is. If they don't want you to smoke, then they should set the example and not do it. If they don't want you to drink and run around, then they shouldn't drink and run around, 'cause you usually go by what your own parents set before you.

Counselor: That there should be one standard for all ages?

Mavis: I disagree with that! I think you should do as you're told by your parents. When you're young, you're not old enough to do all the things you can do when you're grown up.

Jean: I agree with you, Mavis. Part of the enjoyment of smoking is the sneaking around. When my mom told me I could smoke, I didn't enjoy it any more and I stopped.

Counselor: Part of the fun was the feeling of getting away with something. . .

As the students elaborate on their "Vices," comments on drinking frequently follow a discussion of smoking. Ordinarily the drinking problem is not developed as thoroughly, although it patterns into the same general attitudes:

Mary: The only reason kids drink is to think they're big.

Joe: Yeah, you can't have it, so that's why you do it.

The groups usually capsulate the "My Vices" theme into a conclusion that the main attraction involved is the lure of forbidden fruits, yet seldom do they suggest seriously that teen-agers be allowed more freedom in these areas.

OUTWITTING THE ADULTS

In group counseling, the getting-away-with-it idea occurs over and over in many guises. Indeed, the pervasive theme "Outwitting the Adults" seemed to occur in one form or another in almost every session. "Outwitting the Adults" is an activity that apparently occupies a great deal of a teen-ager's time and energy and, consequently, is a ubiquitous topic in group counseling. The adults may be teachers, parents, juvenile authorities—the "who" was not as important as the process of playing the game. Interestingly enough, the "Outwitting the Adults" game is not taken particularly seriously and the teen-ager seems to expect to be on the losing side as often as not, taking his wins or losses quite philosophically:

Cliff: This dope sitting here cried his way out of a ticket for speeding. I'm not kidding. He told the cops such a big sob story about how he'd try to do better, and didn't mean to be going so fast, and the cop believed him and let him off. He really put on an act!

Joe: Well, I'm proud of it. The dumb cop believed me, so I must have made it good. And I didn't have to pay, did I?

June: In the cafeteria we had the most fun. When the teacher wasn't looking, we would flip peas on our spoons over onto the other kids, and then when the teacher would look around, we would look innocent-like, like something was hitting us. Boy, did we ever fool that teacher.

Roger: Yeah, and then you got caught and got in trouble.

June: Sure, but we had fun first.

John: When we needed eggs for an egg fight, we would go from house to house and pretend to be on a scavanger hunt, and tell the people we needed two things—a green tomato and a rotten egg. So they would say, "All we have is a good egg," and we would say, "Okay," and that way we'd get enough eggs for our egg fight. Almost everyone gave us eggs.

It is the "Outwitting the Adults" and "My Vices" themes which place the greatest pressures on any "teacher-trace" that may remain in the counselor. The urge to make "tut-tut" noises may be hard to resist, but if the counselor steadfastly reflects and clarifies, he can be almost sure that group members will themselves present society's views of right and wrong. For example, after a group had griped at length about how the juvenile authorities picked on teen-agers, a rather silent member spoke up:

Judy: Now I want a chance to talk. You guys have a pretty dim view of life—you really do. Jill, you asked for trouble in the stupid way you snuck out of the show.

Jill: (*downcast voice*) Yeah, I suppose so.

Judy: And Dave, the way you run from the cops—common sense would tell you. . . Me, I've gotten busted at so many parties. I've got a record bigger than Abraham Lincoln's right arm. (*Laughter*) I mean it. But common sense tells you a kid, a teen-ager, don't go out in public with beer. You show a cop a little bit of respect and he'll show you respect. You get smart with a cop and he's going to get smart right back.

Maria: Yeah, half the kids who get in trouble are just asking for it. If they wouldn't talk to the cops like they do, they wouldn't get in half the trouble they're in. Sneaking isn't the right thing.

At times, as a member verbalizes his actions and reactions, the awareness of individual responsibility appears through a student's own self-analysis, rather than another group member's reaction:

Bob: I guess I just don't have a conscience. I didn't take into consideration of how my mother would feel when I ran away. I didn't think of calling her and telling her I was okay. I guess I just thought about myself 'cause I guess maybe I'm selfish or something.

PROBLEM PARENTS

The theme of a student's relationship with his parents has appeared in tape analysis almost as frequently as "Outwitting the Adults," but the latter is usually a maneuvering, manipulative sort of game which is not taken too seriously. The parental relationship theme usually appears with overtones of pathos, and involves the adolescent's struggle for identity. It also involves deep feelings and often deep pain. Groups return to the "Problem Parents" theme over and over throughout the course of the group counseling sessions.

Avis: You might not show it, basically right out. But deep down you may think you despise your parents and might tell everybody you hate them, but deep down you actually know you really love your parents. Kids under 18 have to have someone over them, and they actually are afraid of losing that, but they don't really know it.

Counselor: Afraid of losing the security of having someone responsible for you.

Avis: Yeah. Everybody wants to be wanted. If you do something wrong and your parents put you on restriction, it proves they love you.

Jim: But parents will love you—no matter what you do.

Greg: You might not lose their love, but you lose their respect and then you lose your freedom.

The students seem almost desperate at times as they explore the parent-child relationship, but the process of talking about their feelings and problems in the safety of the group counseling situation seems to lessen tensions, even though the problem is insoluble for the time being:

Bill: Parents seem to be afraid to let you go out on your own. They don't want to lose their little baby. My mother's afraid I'll move out. I'm just her little boy. I work, pay my own bills, my car, all my clothes, but I'm still supposed to rely on her.

Counselor: She wants you to lean on her a bit.

Bill: Yeah, she just won't let go. She just can't realize I'm big enough that maybe I can support myself now. Sure, I don't pay for my food or the bed I sleep in yet, but. . .

Two sub-categories of the "Problem Parents" relationship theme appear consistently. The first is an irritated resentment with being told what to do. Since the teen-ager feels that he is old enough to do what is expected without constant reminders (the unfortunate fact that this usually is not true is beside the point), he finds the parental prompting that earlier was taken in good grace now an intolerable "nagging."

Greg: I have an hour after I get home from school before I go to work and the minute I walk in that house I get nagged at—nothing but complaints. I get woke up in the morning with, "Your room's a mess." "Get up, you're going to be late for school." But never anything else, never anything good.

Counselor: You feel like you just can't do anything right.
Greg: You can't. No matter what you try to do, it's always wrong.

The second sub-category concerns parental relationship within the framework of peer relationships, usually centering around resentment over not being able to make plans with friends because parents reserve the right to make last-minute changes:

Ruth: If your parents make plans and they want to do something and the dishes aren't done, they say, "Oh, let them wait until tomorrow." But if the kids make plans, the dishes have to be done *right now*, no matter what! Because the kids have to grow up to be RESPONSIBLE PEOPLE.
Nancy: So when we get older we do the same thing—we're not responsible. We let the dishes wait, just like our parents do.
Counselor: One rule for parents and another for kids.
Jean: Yeah, but our parents must have had the same trouble we have when they were kids with parents.
Counselor: It's kind of a circle then, that goes on and on. . .
Nancy: Yeah, but I'm going to change it. I don't want my kids to go through what I have. I want them to be self-reliant, but not to the point where they have no affection for their family.

Sometimes amateur psychiatry gets into the act:

Jim: I'll get ready and my mother knows I have a date and want to leave, but she keeps thinking up little things I have to do first—and she does this just to irritate me.
Lila: No, it's not to irritate you. It's just to keep you so you won't go out and leave. She wants you to stay with her. She's jealous of your girl friend.

MY BROTHER, THE BRAT

The examination of the "Problem Parent" often involves a discussion of sibling rivalry, sometimes long and bitterly developed. The "My Brother, the Brat," theme does not seem to involve as deep a feeling as does the parental relationship theme. This theme, however, is usually developed with many expressions of hostility:

Joan: And that's another thing. I get $3.00 a week for lunch and I have to go without lunch and save my money for clothes. My little brother has lots saved up, but when *he* wants clothes, he gets all he wants.
Jean: Maybe because he's younger.
Joan: No, it's because he gets straight A's in school.
Jean: Well, that does it. That makes them proud of him. He's a model kid. He's the one who will get the car and everything else.
Joan: Yeah, anything my little brother wants, he gets.

Since the group process presents an opportunity for members to interact—and learn how to interact—in the "substitute family" group, the "My Brother, the Brat" theme may occur as heated interchanges between group members:

Ronda: Shut up! You think you know everything and you don't. You can't smoke on a school campus.

Eric: I think I know everything!

Ronda: You just said—"When you're 18 they can't do nothing," and you're so positive, so sure, and you're wrong. So don't blab out like that.

Or the "My Brother, the Brat" theme may be reflected in a student's value system:

Joe: It's all right to pick on little kids cause when you were little everybody picked on you.

Or it may be expressed as resentment against a silent member:

Martin: Why doesn't she ever talk? She just sits there the whole time.

Counselor: Mattie's silence bothers you?

Martin: Yeah, she never says a thing. She just sits there and looks at you.

Mattie: I like to just listen. It makes me nervous to talk.

Martin: Yeah, but it makes me nervous when you don't. I want to know what you're thinking.

The group will find that one of the values of the group process lies in the opportunity it presents for members to learn social relationships within the small, controlled environment of the group situation. And time spent on practicing these skills is time will spent—whether it takes the form of venting hostilities caused by sibling rivalry, as in the "My Brother, the Brat" theme, or the form of seeking a clarification of self-concepts.

MY PUBLIC IMAGE

The adolescent's struggle to clarify a value system, which parallels and permeates his developmental task of seeking to discover "Who am I?" seldom emerges as a clear-cut theme, but will thread in and out of the sessions as the students examine the behavior of both adults and young people. This theme has been labeled "My Public Image." The intense preoccupation with self, particularly the physical self of the teen-ager, makes this topic a very sensitive one for both boys and girls. At times it takes the form of trying to determine the "proper" way to behave in public:

Sue: I don't think either girls or boys should fight. It doesn't prove anything.

Counselor: The boys have been saying that boys should fight, but this is not acceptable behavior for girls.

Pam: But if someone walks up to you and calls you a filthy name you have to defend yourself.

Counselor: That somehow the name rubbed off on you and you had to fight to get rid of it.

Pam: That's right.

Steve: It would be better for a girl to ignore it. If you fight you're on the same level as the person who called you a name.

Sue: When someone calls you a name, they're putting themselves so low for even trying to start a fight.

Counselor: In other words, why sink to their level?

Sue: Yeah, that's it.

The varying standards of different age groups seem well understood and accepted (with resignation, albeit) as part of the struggle for a suitable "Public Image."

Vince: Yeah, my mom tells me not to invite my friends over when she has company. My friends aren't bad, they just look bad. They just have a jerky appearance.

Counselor: Your mother doesn't approve of the way they look.

Vince: If she's going to have company, she tells me, "Tell your friends to stay away today." They're just guys from the pool hall.

Counselor: You seem to resent this.

Vince: No, they look like jerks, and I don't want her embarrassed. I think she's right about their dress.

Marvin: Well, I mind it. If my parents don't like my friends, they don't have to like me.

In line with the frankness of a real family situation, group members often pass candid comments about the appearance of group members and the "My Public Image" theme gets very personal at times:

Terry: You mean you paid $6.00 to have your hair styled?

John: Yeah, I had it styled a week ago, and look at it—it looks so much better. . .

Bob: And if you'd comb it right, it'd look even more better.

Terry: (*To counselor*) What do you think about boys getting their hair styled?

Counselor: The thing that matters most—is what do *you* think?

Terry: I think it's a waste.

John: Just 'cause you're a surfer.

Terry: Yeah, man, everybody's going back toward women. I don't like it.

Counselor: I hear you saying you think it's sissified.

Terry: I sure do.

John: It isn't sissified. It keeps your hair in place. They have hair spray for men now.

Counselor: It's all a matter of getting used to?

Bob: What about perfume? Women had perfume first and men wear perfume now.

Besides a discussion of personal appearance, the "My Public Image" theme may delve into personality characteristics:

Rick: I think you're a leech. You borrow money and don't pay it back and make a big joke out of everything. You invite yourself everywhere.

Rob: What do you mean, leech? You're talking about yourself when you said that about me.

Counselor: You seem to feel, Rick, that since you share money when you have it, you kind of expect others to do the same.

Rick: Sure. If I borrow a dime, I don't expect to pay it back, but a dollar is different.

Rob: Well, I think that's being a leech!

The degree to which the "My Public Image" theme contributes to a change or clarification of self-concept is difficult to assess. Silent members may be gaining as much as the more vocal members. As much development may take place between sessions as during sessions. Of this we can be certain: The "Public Image" theme constitutes an important part of group counseling.

NOBODY LOVES ME

An elaboration of attitudes toward school in general is, of course, a frequent topic in discussions; but as a group progresses and feelings are revealed, a common reaction which can be identified is the student's feelings of helplessness, his feeling of being an insignificant cipher in a world which belongs to the adults. The "Nobody Loves Me" theme usually develops after groups have been together for some time and members have learned to feel comfortable with each other—and with the counselor.

Richard: Some teachers get a first impression of you and they keep that all the time and actually, you're not that way. Sometimes you're judged by the way you dress, or the way you look. A kid can walk in the first day and they'll look at you and you can just see them say, "You and I aren't going to get along!" They sort of seem to have a grudge against you like they knew you all your life.

Counselor: Are you saying they jump to conclusions because of your hair or your dress. . .

Richard: That's about it, about it.

Counselor: You seem to feel there's no solution.

Richard: Well, parents take the part of the teacher before they take the part of the student, so you haven't anyone who will help you.

Brenda: I don't see why grownups have the right to jump to conclusions about kids. And I don't see why they think they have the right to tell you how horrible you look and how horrible you are and we have to stand there in front of the whole class and take it or we get in more trouble.

Richard: Yeah, just be criticized and not say a word!

Brenda: We ought to have the right to speak—even to adults—in the right way, of course.

Counselor: You're saying then, that you are expected to respect adults and they should treat you with the same respect and courtesy.

Sandra: Yeah, just because you're young doesn't mean you're inferior. Adults think they're better than us—we're only students—just little grades in a book.

Brenda: Well, some teachers do care. They don't all feel that way. If you do the right thing and do your work, you don't have trouble.

Counselor: Sort of the idea that people bring their troubles on themselves?

LET'S CHANGE THE RULES

As feelings about school and being a student are explored, groups will usually spend time devising "better" ways of doing things and will seem to enjoy the game of "Let's Change the Rules." Some groups perform this as a purely academic exercise, knowing full well that existing conditions are not likely to be changed. And at other times a press for action may develop. Individual members may require the counselor's subtle support as they advance highly impractical suggestions which are met by the well-expressed derision of the group. The "Let's Change the Rules" theme may also hold a trap for the unwary counselor as the groups try to maneuver him into defending and justifying school rules. Or they may seek to make the group counselor their "front" man with the administration, rather than submit their suggestions themselves:

Tom: Suspension is stupid. That's what a lot of people want. Just a vacation—so they can go home and goof off. They don't want to go to school anyway.

Carla: Yeah, when I got suspended my mother was mad at me for one day. Then she let me go to the beach and stuff the rest of the time. She didn't care.

Jerry: Yeah, detention doesn't help either. Everybody turns around and does the same thing over.

Counselor: What do you suggest?

Jerry: Well, pick up papers—or something.

Ronald: I don't see why we don't have open campus. Other schools do. This makes us feel like we're in jail. Colleges don't make their students stay inside a fence like prisoners.

Bill: I don't see why we can't have a smoking room. Other schools do. Why can't the counselors do something about it?

At times the "Let's Change the Rules" theme can be the springboard for sensible action, but, again, the counselor must be alert that he is not drawn into a commitment for action, but that the initiative is left in the hands of the students:

Carl: Well, I think that's one thing the school needs—a car club. We had one last year and the year before that we had one too, but this year it was discontinued and it was closed to only mostly the auto shop and the school just didn't get behind it at all. They never put our name in the bulletin or anything and, well, that's really a boss thing for a school to have is a car club. You'd be surprised how a car club . . . that's almost like a continuation school for high school dropouts. It's really the socializing part of it—a car club is really the thing, you know. It speaks well for your school just like a good football team speaks well of your school.

Dick: It doesn't speak well of your school if half the guys in it are ding bats and. . .

Carl: Man, you're not going to fool around with anyone who gets tickets—in fact, that's the biggest rule.

Counselor: You'd like to see the car club started up again.

Carl: Yeah, I think we should do something.

Frequently, as the "Let's Change the Rules" theme progresses, group members verbalize a preference for law and order.

Tod: I don't like teachers that let kids do anything they want.

Rodney: Yeah. I like a teacher that can control the class, make them be quiet when they want to, but who is real cool, you know, laughs every once in a while because—I don't think a teacher should just go in there and go right by the book, day after day.

IN CONCLUSION

The process of group counseling is a fascinating one and one which makes great demands on the counselor, both inexperienced and experienced.

It is hoped that this teasing out of themes from the many tape recordings of one group of counselors will contribute to the professional skills of other group counselors. The light titling of the themes: "My Vices," "Outwitting the Adults," "Problem Parents," "My Brother, the Brat," "My Public Image," "Nobody Loves Me," and "Let's Change the Rules," is not intended to imply that the group counseling process is to be taken lightly. The world of the adolescent is a very real world and the rules are for keeps. Your entree of trusted counselor that permits you to enter this world carries with it the responsibility to understand and to accept. If you dare judge or moralize, the masks will be assumed and politely but firmly the doors to this world will be closed. If you can enter into this world, reflecting, clarifying, summarizing, in the group but not *of* the group, functioning as a counselor and not a member, then through the group process the counselees can clarify their value system as they struggle with their search for identity. You, as counselor, may even do a little of the same.

22

A Project in Group Counseling with High School Underachievers*

John A. Schulz

INTRODUCTION

The purpose of this project was to demonstrate the techniques of conducting group counseling sessions with adolescents. Emphasis was placed on the identification of both the verbal and non-verbal clues as expressions of interpersonal behavior.

The basic hypothesis in conducting these group counseling sessions was that underachievement in academic subjects is one way in which adolescents react to stress situations. Therefore, the goal in the group counseling sessions was aimed toward helping each individual identify his own reaction pattern to stress situations, describe his pattern, and offer alternative patterns for change.

Other areas of concern as part of the group process involved the observation of the participants as to their quality of performance in the group. Was there an improvement in the quality of performance? When conflicts arose in the group, was there a move toward tension reduction? Is an experience in tension reduction helpful to a participant in a group situation in understanding why he is underachieving?

METHODS

The sessions were observed by the twenty-five enrollees in the Counseling and Guidance Training Institute at the Portland Center of the General Extension Division. The demonstration sessions were part of the program organized for the enrollees during their counselor training under the National Defense Education Act.

For an hour prior to the demonstration of group counseling, discussions were held with the enrollees on the identification of clues in counseling. After each demonstration, a further discussion evolved around the processes at work that day.

*Reprinted by permission of the author and publisher from *Counselor Education and Supervision* (1963), III, 24–28.

The adolescents who participated in the group counseling sessions were from two high schools. It was requested that the students chosen be under-achievers. Other than indicating that six group counseling sessions would be held, no additional information was given to the high schools. In each case the selection of the students was left to the high school counselor.

Prior to the first group counseling session, a brief letter was sent to the parent of each participating student asking parental permission for attendance at the group sessions. No attempt was made to discuss group counseling concepts with the parents. No records of these participating students were analyzed because it was desired that the group counselor should demonstrate how pertinent information may be solicited from participants.

The group counseling sessions took place in a private room. In an adjoining room the twenty-five enrollees observed the sessions through a one-way window. Microphones made it possible to hear the group counseling session and a recording was made of the sessions.

RELATED RESEARCH

Much has been written on how counseling groups differ in certain ways from other groups [1]. Other studies illustrate that there is a decreasing interest in verbal content and an increasing interest in the nonverbal behavior [3]. The attempt was made in this study to combine both elements: the analysis of verbal content and the observation of nonverbal behavior.

The observation of the non-verbal behavior pattern of the group was conducted by nine of the counselor enrollees. Joel and Shapiro [2], have indicated that such an analysis may be called "pseudo-objective" as descriptive of a highly complex area. In this study the non-verbal clues reported by the counselor enrollees formed the basis of descriptive behavior for each session. The verbal clues were checked by replaying the recording of the session. Each counselor enrollee followed the same student in the group counseling session for six weeks.

DIAGNOSIS OF THE GROUP COUNSELING SESSIONS

The high school students who participated were: C, D, JA, T, S, J, B, P and TR.

First Session. By moving the session quickly into a discussion of underachievement in school work, the group leader was able to keep the members of the group involved in the discussion. The group leader enhanced the group process by not opening up questions which would have had to pull the group toward himself. Such questions as "what is group counseling," or "what are the possible results from attending six group sessions," were not raised. However, near the end of the session reference was made to these areas by the members of the group but the group leader made no attempt to spell out the answers, leaving the discussion in areas which were more familiar to them. What happened to each of the members of the group during this first session? C withdrew within herself. This was the only session attended by C, though she did return for the second session but became ill before coming into the room. D and B isolated themselves from the group but were able to follow along with the discussion. P responded in the group but at a level which would not show any inner feelings. T not only dominated the session but did so in such a way as to draw resentment against himself. The content of his discussion was varied and self-centered. The ideas presented were in no particular pattern nor were the ideas inter-related. The listener was merely pulled through a wide variety of verbiage. When the discourse became personal by way of attacks on other members of the group, resentment was apparent. JA tried to find a place in the group by describing his mode of conduct. T took exception to everything JA said and blasted JA's adherence to traditional forms of behavior. Nevertheless, JA continued to search for a place for himself in the group. S was deeply involved in the group process. Constant attempts were made to find out more about what statements meant. J followed the group process closely but hid his feelings until near the end of the session. His remarks brought forth an attack from T. TR was perhaps more involved in the group than any other student. Deep concern and thought was given to the area of underachievement and how this might be resolved.

Second Session. The second session opened with some evidence of tension. Though C had come with her classmates, she did not appear in the session. Perhaps an attack would come against T for excessive domination of the first session. The group leader insulated T by throwing questions back to the whole group. T was ready to attack throughout the session, for T had learned in the first group session that he had the better command of language. T made no attempt to understand himself better; he merely reacted in an antagonistic manner to statements made by others in the group. J, TR and P became involved in these attacks. J tried to become a member of the group but T swarmed over him easily with words. P talked freely, revealing problems in her own home life. TR began to open up by discussing the problems she had to face. These students began to move into areas of importance in their lives. TR and P seemed to be more involved than others in the group. D withdrew from the group by identifying himself with his own classmates. JA withdrew to a greater extent by reacting only to the general discussions. B and S stayed out of the general discussion, though interest was shown in what was going on.

Third Session. Tension appeared to be mounting in the group, but it was more of an internal factor than an open attack, as evidenced in the previous sessions. C and D have now dropped out of the group. Though the group leader tried to shield out the most talkative member of the group, T, the attempt was far from successful. T discussed at length a proposed European tour, marriage, and ways of dealing with complex financial problems in married life. When this material became tiring, he sat back and coughed. He borrowed a book from a nearby desk, read it from time to time, and on occasions read portions of the book to the group. TR took the lead in this session and it may well be called her therapeutic session. She discussed her parental relationships in a highly emotional manner. When the group leader attempted to assist her in understanding a relationship between home conditions and high school grades, she resisted momentarily and then returned to the original vein of her story. TR's ability to look at her own problems and willingness to discuss them openly showed a real movement forward in the counseling process and perhaps even a readiness at this point for individual counseling.

Fourth Session. The fourth session saw a further movement in the group by other members who had not been participating freely. The group leader made no attempt to be protective of anyone. T was wide open for attack. He had no book and no cough to hide behind. However, he withdrew from the group from time to time by writing notes back and forth with S and by writing poetry and drawing pictures. Verbally he discussed college plans with the group, almost forgot about Europe and marriage, and made a desperate attempt to become friendly with the group leader. At the close of the session he handed some of his poetry to the group leader and asked for a reaction. S formed the sub-group with T. She was unable to communicate with any other members of the group. P came in cool and aloof at the beginning of the meeting. However, since TR had been so successful in discussing her problems in the previous session, P was now willing to make a similar try. Her complex home situation was so clearly stated and her understanding of her own pattern of withdrawal was so open that it was obvious P was facing a real need for alternative plans for dealing with these problems. P showed a readiness for individual counseling. J made the mistake of laughing during P's discussion of family problems. His attempts to explain the laughter evoked verbal attacks from the group. J withdrew. JA clowned throughout the session and the superficial remarks from time to time kept the group away from him. TR was so successful at the last session that there was more confidence exhibited by her behavioral pattern. The role taken today was one of prodding other members in the group to participate. B stayed withdrawn from the group.

Fifth Session. The fifth session opened on a note of T's demand for the group leader's attention and the session remained pretty much on that level. T wanted the group leader to express a liking for him. Almost one-half of the entire session was spent by T telling the group leader how much better his own world now is just because of the group leader. T launched a verbal attack at J for laughing at P in the previous session. The group was with T, for J was unable to explain his laughter in a satisfactory manner. J tried to apologize over and over again for laughing at P the week before. The more he said the worse the situation became. However, instead of withdrawing as he had been doing in the previous four sessions, he made an attack on the organization of the high school program. P did not seem to move forward out of the previous session as had TR following the discussion of her personal problems. This may have been caused partially by the interchange of attacks over J laughing at her. S and B withdrew from the group.

Sixth Session. There seemed to be a genuine spirit among the members of the group that it had been profitable to participate in these group sessions. The participation seemed to be freer in this session. When the group leader told the group that provisions had been made for individual counseling for those who would like to continue, there was a note of appreciation throughout the group. T was well organized. He was confident that in the hour remaining in this group session the everlasting affection of the group leader could be won. P and TR had both made sincere analysis of their own problems in previous sessions. They appeared willing to discuss other modes of responding to stress situations than those on which they had previously leaned so heavily. Both responded positively to the fact that further counseling was now available. J expressed concern about his problem. He was less withdrawn than in previous four sessions. He had learned not to withdraw completely when a verbal attack is made on him. He perhaps is becoming ready for individual counseling. S remained indifferent to the group process. Near the end of the session she indicated that she did not discuss her problems because people are not trustworthy. She indicated that she has considered suicide a more satisfactory answer to problems than counseling.

SUMMARY

The purpose of this study was to demonstrate the techniques of conducting group counseling sessions with adolescents. Observation and discussion of these group counseling sessions illustrated techniques for conducting successful meetings. Even though participation in the group was strictly voluntary, and even though the composition of the group was not identical each week, the group leader was able to keep the group discussing the central theme of high school underachievement.

Was anything accomplished toward solving the problem of underachievement? Though one student reported that his grades were going up and another student reported that all of his problems were now solved, verification would have to be made over a longer period of time before any credence could be given to such statements.

The underlying hypothesis of this demonstration was that underachievement in academic subjects was one way in which adolescents reacted to stress situations. During the six sessions three students began the process of analyzing the way in which they reacted to stress situations. A test of the hypothesis would be to follow closely the progress of these three students in their future academic work.

BIBLIOGRAPHY

1. Bion, W. R. "Group Dynamics: A Re-view," *International Journal of Psychoanalysis* (1952), 33, 235–247.

2. Joel, W. and Shapiro, D. "A Genotypical Approach to the Analysis of Personal Interaction," *Journal of Psychology* (1949), 28, 9–17.

3. Katz, E. W., Ohlsen, M. M., and Proff, F. C. "An Analysis of the Interpersonal Behavior of Adolescents in Group Counseling." University of Illinois (1960).

23

Group Counseling at the Eleventh-Grade Level*

Harold H. Metcalf

Challenged by the problem of meeting individual needs, the high-school counselor, now more than ever before, must plan ahead lest he become so entangled in detail that he find himself the slave rather than the master of circumstance. Attention must always be given to the needs of the moment. Truancy, discipline, out-of-school jobs, family discord, war neuroses, and all related problems must be dealt with intelligently and sympathetically as they occur. Running through the maze of guidance activities, however, there must be an underlying plan that carries the students nearer to meeting the responsibilities of adult living. The purpose of this article is to explain how well-planned group counseling may promote general welfare.

BACKGROUND OF THE STUDY

Oak Park and River Forest Township High School is a school of approximately thirty-five hundred students. However, it is organized under the superintendent into what could be compared to four small schools, each having a man to head the counseling activities for the boys and a woman to head these activities for the girls. The Freshman counselors, called "deans," direct the orientation of Freshmen to their new and expanded environment. The superintendent, the members of the Student Council, the Monogram Club, and the Girls' Club—all have a part in helping acquaint the group with the activities, traditions, and responsibilities of high-school citizenship. Then, too, home-room study of the school handbook and the program-of-studies booklet aids in planning, and the challenge of more formalized school work in an organization in which "acting one's age" is expected, results in rapid development for most students. Both the Freshman and the Sophomore deans hold personal conferences with pupils wishing or needing individualized attention.

ASPECTS OF THE ELEVENTH-GRADE PROGRAM

Rapid physical growth and the emotional disturbances characteristic of adolescence bring the students to their Junior year with many questions

°Reprinted from *School Review* by Harold H. Metcalf by permission of The University of Chicago Press. Copyright 1946 by the University of Chicago Press.

pertaining to their futures. The war accentuated the diversity of these problems. When they were in Grade VIII, most of our pupils completed projects in which they read about the requirements of a vocation, interviewed successful workers in the field, visited an operating business or unit, and submitted an illustrated booklet on "My Vocational Plans." By the time they reach Grade XI, some of them have further explored the vocation and have become interested in pursuing it even further, but many are ready for rethinking their relationship to their vocational futures.

In order that the counselors may more intelligently assist the students in this planning, all the data accumulated during the first ten years of each student's school life are made available to the counselors. The elementary schools send to the high school a measure of intelligence, a brief record of achievement in studies, and an appraisal of the student's stability. Shortly after entering high school, the Otis Self-administering Test of Mental Ability is used to obtain another measure of intelligence, and the Iowa Silent Reading Test is administered. Each student is given help over any hurdles that he may meet, but a discipline file is kept only on those who persist in overt acts of disrespect to school responsibility. The marks earned in the various subjects give an index to achievement.

The two individuals working as deans at the Junior level aim at a program which will enable every boy and girl to feel the pride and satisfaction which come from achievement in school and from happy social adjustment. To acquire such satisfaction, students must assume a full share of responsibility and realize that habits of industry and co-operation are indispensable. The dean's office has become a place to go for help rather than a spot to shun; a place in which intelligent questions receive sympathetic answers; and a place in which long-time, co-operative planning is done on a friendly basis.

The activities through which this purpose is achieved consist, in part, of counseling individual students; working with club advisers and students to obtain broader club participation; planning individual programs of study that lead to work or college; making friendly but persistent endeavors toward punctual and regular school attendance; conferring with parents on many kinds of problems; giving up-to-date and reliable information about the armed services; working with home-room teachers on programs of study for individual students; working with home-room teachers in promoting an awareness of general pupil responsibility; assisting students to plan and elect a council of representatives; working with the Junior council in the planning of assemblies, parties, a "prom," and other activities that promote general welfare; and acting immediately and intelligently to meet any emergency that may arise. In all these activities the superintendent of the school is always at hand to give help, direction, and advice.

Shortly after the beginning of the Junior year, each student is given the American Council on Education Psychological Examination for High-School Students. The Iowa Placement Examinations, Mathematics Aptitude, are made available to all but are not compulsory; about 40 per cent of the boys and 5 per cent of the girls took this test in 1944–45.

GROUP APPROACH TO COUNSELING

An announcement is made in home rooms that pupils may take the Kuder Preference Record either in study-hall time or after school. A short explanation is given of the significance of this inventory and of the follow-up conferences that are held.

Students who have taken the Kuder Preference Record are called in for conference in groups of approximately fifteen. Each is given a Kuder profile sheet and asked to study with the dean the nine areas of interests. Then each is asked to check at the top of the columns two or three high-interest areas and at the bottom of the columns two or three low-interest areas. Each is then given the answer pad, with his scores shown in each area, and is asked to make a profile of his own interests. These profiles become the basis for chalk talks and explanations of Kuder's interpretation of the occupation in each of the nine areas or area combinations. In some cases the expressed interests indicated by the checks on the columns are not in agreement with the measured interests and thus call for challenging thought.

Does the pupil have capacity for the fields of interest? To help him think through this question, a previously prepared profile is given to him, on which is shown his percentile rank in the class in intelligence, in marks earned in the first two years of high school, in linguistic and quantitative aptitude as measured by the American Council test, and his age in relation to other Juniors. In addition, data from the Iowa Mathematics Aptitude Test and any other tests he may have taken are included. The ensuing discussion and questions center in an understanding of the profile. Students are encouraged to become so thoroughly aware of its meaning that they can take the forms home and explain them to their parents. In all the explanation the dean gives direction and meaning, but the student does the thinking in terms of his fitness for the occupational interests that showed up in the Kuder Preference Record. For example, a student who plans to enter the medical profession and who stands in the lowest quarter of his group in scholastic achievement and aptitude obviously must change either his goal or his approach. In such a case the pupil usually comes in for help, or his parents come for a conference. The dean must then skilfully interpret all available data so that new and better direction is given to the student's life. Any change of direction, however, must be made by the student as a result of his own thinking rather than by the counselor or by the parents.

The students are led to study the opportunities in the fields of their occupational choices and the resources necessary to obtain the college or other training essential for success in the occupation chosen. At this point military service and its effects on boys' lives are brought up for discussion. A few skilfully placed remarks on the part of the dean can do much to undermine the feeling: "What's the use, Uncle Sam will put his finger on me, and I'll land in the infantry." Landing in the infantry may indeed be the probability, but landing in the infantry also may help toward the goal. Expert, up-to-the-minute advice on the programs of the armed forces must be available at all times. Military service and its effects are seriously considered, but an attempt is made to bring the boy to see the whole picture and not a single view or a few segments. Government information and advice is of great help to the dean in successfully meeting the problem of service in the armed forces. Statistical evidence of the opportunities or the lack of opportunities in both general vocational fields and specific occupations is of value and should be briefly presented.

Personality traits are important also, as is shown in a study made by Frank S. Endicott. Questionnaires regarding desirable qualities of employees were returned by seventy representative business concerns. The following statement taken from the report of this study serves as a basis for discussion with the group.

> The tabulation of responses shows clearly that ability to get along with people and to meet and talk with others is fundamental in the broad area of personality. It seems clear that business and industry attach a great deal of importance to human relationships with special emphasis upon those qualities essential to meeting and working with people.[1]

Since personality traits can usually be developed or controlled to some extent, it is possible for each pupil to make progress in this area.

At the close of the conference the students are again urged to take the profiles home and interpret them to their parents. Not a small number of students come in for further help, and many parents telephone or come in for conferences. The group conference answers general questions and helps many students on their way to making satisfactory vocational adjustments. The individual follow-up may divulge the need for further testing; it may indicate a need for helping the pupil make a satisfactory social adjustment; it may be directed toward choice of college; or it may answer more fully some question that grew out of the group conference.

---

[1]Frank S. Endicott, "An Analysis of Factors Relating to the Employability of College Graduates in Business and Industry: A Survey of Policy and Practice in Seventy Major Corporations," p. 7. Evanston, Illinois: Frank S. Endicott (c/o Northwestern University), 1944.

EVALUATION OF THE PROGRAM

Strang has said: "Each technique may be used to serve three purposes: to get information, give insight, and establish friendly relationships."[2] The group-counseling technique serves all these purposes. It is suspected that a study of accomplishment, as measured by school marks, would show significant differences in favor of those taking advantage of the plan. Resulting motivation is illustrated by the following student reactions.

I thought engineering was to be my field. Accountancy now seems a natural for me.

I've always wanted law, but I think I'll investigate mechanics. Lawyers need a more extensive vocabulary than I am interested in developing. Besides, I tested very low in linguistic aptitude.

I'm in need of more advice and information. I have many interests but no real choice of an occupation.

My folks want to send me to college, but these tests and interviews convince me that I'll not make good there. Will you talk with them about it?

I've been worried because I have no occupation in mind. I'm glad to know that many other boys are in my shoes. May I come in to see you again?

The parents' reactions have also shown their appreciation of the program.

John tried to explain those charts. May I come over to talk with you?

Henry has a great deal more interest in school since he took those tests. He says he can see something to what the teachers are trying to do now that he knows what he wants to be.

Wish I had had some of that kind of help when I was in school. I would have got into a field I could enjoy.

Sam got more out of your interview than he did out of the test which he took downtown and which I paid $25 for. I guess it's because you know him better.

Weaknesses in this counseling plan have shown up. The Kuder Preference Record seems to place too many boys high in mechanics. Whether it is the effect of the war or the peculiarity of the group taking the inventory is a question. The boys in this school fall too far below the norms in art, music, and literature. This finding may indicate intellectual immaturity; it may result from war pressure; or the norms may be of questionable significance. Not enough boys from the lowest quarter of the class come in voluntarily, but this indifference is characteristic of that group in every volunteer activity.

CONCLUSIONS

It may be asserted, on the basis of trial to date, that the group-guidance technique 1) permits the dean to meet many students in a personal way;

[2]Ruth May Strang, *Counseling Technics in College and Secondary School* (New York: Harper & Bros., 1937), pp. 8–9.

2) gives the students the benefit of group interaction and brings more questions into focus, for the group *stimulates* its members; 3) leads to further conferences with individual students and parents; 4) makes more time available for individual attention to exceptional problems by answering many questions in groups; 5) promotes general interest in the *whole class group*; and 6) results in an understanding that the dean is present as a friend and helper.

Choosing an occupation is a process rather than an event. Hamrin and Erickson, in their book *Guidance in the Secondary School*, state: "[The pupil] must be assisted in thinking through the relationship of his abilities and interests to the educational and vocational opportunities open to him."[3] The group technique assists many pupils another step along the way toward a final choice of their life work. The superintendent of our school and the dean's staff consider such a program a necessary integral part of the service of a modern high school which prides itself on meeting pupil needs.

[3]Shirley A. Hamrin and Clifford E. Erickson, *Guidance in the Secondary School* (New York: D. Appleton-Century Co. Inc., 1939), p. 69.

24

A Comparison of Three Methods of Assisting Underachieving High School Students*

Feriha B. Baymur

C. H. Patterson

Academic failure is one of the major problems confronting counselors in schools and colleges. Not all failures are a result of lack of academic ability or aptitude. Mental or intellectual ability is not the exclusive determinant of academic achievement. The discrepancy between potential and achievement identifies a group of students who are known as underachievers. Underachievement is both a problem to the individual, who may suffer from the sense of failure, and to society, which loses the full potential contributions of unestimated numbers of its members.

It follows that anything which can be done to reduce the incidence of underachievement will contribute to individual and social accomplishment and well-being. The present report describes an attempt to reduce underachievement in a group of high school students by three methods, which are compared with each other and with a control situation .[1]

THE PROBLEM

The present study investigates the hypothesis that if emotional factors are involved in underachievement, then therapeutic counseling should be effective in reducing such underachievement. The study further investigates the relative effectiveness of two different methods of counseling, and in addition compares such counseling with an attempt to increase motivation in what might be considered a common or traditional way. The three methods used are individual counseling, group counseling, and what is designated as one-session motivational group counseling. If it were found that group counseling, or one-session motivational counseling, were as

*Reprinted by permission of the author and publisher from *Journal of Counseling Psychology* (1960), 7, 83–89.

[1] From a thesis submitted by the senior author for the Ed.D. degree, College of Education, University of Illinois, completed under the direction of the junior author, August, 1958. Members of the committee included J. T. Hastings, W. M. Lifton, R. H. Simpson, and W. O. Stanley. Henry Kaiser was helpful in the statistical analysis of the data.

effective as individual counseling, this would be important, since these methods are less expensive or time-consuming to use, and thus more students could be reached by the limited number of counselors available.

DESIGN AND PROCEDURE OF THE STUDY

SUBJECTS

The design of the study called for the identification of a group of under-achievers at the high school level. The 220 members of the junior class of a midwest high school were selected as a source for such subjects. Of this group, 209 students had been given the Verbal and Abstract Reasoning tests of the Differential Aptitude Test at the beginning of the school year. Grades for the first semester of the junior year were available at the start of the study.

A student was designated as an underachiever if his percentile rank based on grades was 25 or more points below his percentile rank on the DAT score. In order to obtain a sufficient number of subjects for four matched groups of at least 8 members each, 2 students with differences of 24 percentile points were included.[2] The differences ranged from 24 percentile points to 67 percentile points. There were 9 girls and 23 boys, a sex difference which has frequently been observed among underachievers.

ASSIGNMENT TO EXPERIMENTAL GROUPS

Since four groups (three experimental and one control) were required, the subjects were matched four at a time on the following variables: discrepancy between grades and DAT score, potential scholastic capacity (DAT score), academic achievement (grades), socio-economic status, chronological age, and sex. Economic status was based upon classification of the subjects by the deans of boys and girls into middle, lower-middle, and upper-lower status. Although this is a rough measure, based on judgments of the deans, it appeared to be sufficient as a control. Three of the four groups consisted of 6 boys and 2 girls, while the fourth included 5 boys and 3 girls. The success of the matchings on the other variables was indicated by the fact that analyses of variance indicated no significant differences in under-achievement, DAT scores, grades, or age among the groups. The ranges within the groups for the first three variables were quite large.

The groups were assigned, to the extent possible, randomly to the treatment conditions. It was, however, necessary to select the students for group counseling on the basis of the entire group having the same period free for the counseling session. The resulting groups are designated as follows:

Group I: individually counseled experimentals

[2]While percentiles are unequal units, the matching procedure described in the next section assured that the groups were equivalent in degree of underachievement.

Group II: group counseled experimentals
Group III: one-session motivational counseled experimentals
Group IV: noncounseled controls.

TREATMENT CONDITIONS

Group I: This group was provided individual therapeutic counseling at weekly intervals for a maximum of twelve weeks. One student who proved to be rather seriously disturbed was seen twice weekly during the latter part of the period, for a total of 16 interviews for the experimental period. The remainder were seen from 10 to 12 interviews. Interviews lasted from 35 to 55 minutes. All interviews were conducted by the investigator (the senior author) in a client-centered manner. The counselor had been trained in this approach, including a practicum course under the junior author. Interviews were recorded, and counseling was supervised.

Group II: Group counseling was conducted weekly, but because of holidays and other unavoidable conditions, only nine sessions were held. The counselor attempted to conduct the group sessions in a client-centered manner also. The students in both Group I and Group II were informed of the nature and purpose of the study. This was done to equate the information-motivational factor with Group III. In both situations, however, students were not restricted to discussing academic problems.

Group III: Group III met only once during the first week of the experiment. Members were informed of the fact that they were underachievers, and were encouraged to work to reduce the gap between potential and achievement. The importance of good grades for further education and employment was pointed out. They were told that some other students would receive special help, but that such help could not be given to all the underachievers in the class.

Members of all three experimental groups were also given copies of *Study Your Way Through School* [9].

Group IV: The control group had no contact with the counselor. The deans and counselors were given the names of the students in the control group and asked to refrain, if possible, from providing counseling for the duration of the experiment. This they were able to do, limiting their contacts to discussion of curriculum choices for the next year.

INSTRUMENTS USED

Three different instruments were used to provide criteria for the study since it was anticipated that the outcomes might be related to three different areas: (a) improved personal adjustment, (b) improved study habits and attitudes, and (c) improved academic performance. While the last is the most pertinent area for the evaluation of achievement, the other two might also be affected, and it is possible that results might show here prior to the improvement of academic performance. The following instruments were selected:

1. Q-sort. As a measure of personal adjustment, a Q-sort was used. Fifty statements were selected from Hilden's [12] pool. A criterion against which the self-perceptions of the students could be compared was developed by having seven experienced counselors and psychologists sort the items into nine piles (yielding a normal distribution of statements) as they thought they should be sorted by a well-adjusted 17-year-old adolescent. Five items were eliminated because of lack of agreement among the judges in their placement. The remaining items were ordered by sums of the placement categories assigned by the judges, and placed in nine categories to form the distribution required in the sorting instructions. Thus a criterion sorting of 45 items was available with which individual student sortings could be correlated. The correlations among the independent sortings of seven judges ranged from .42 to .83, while the range of correlations of each judge with the criterion sort (which included his own data) was from .72 to .91.

2. Study Habits and Attitudes. The Brown-Holtzman Survey of Study Habits and Attitudes was selected to measure the area of study habits and attitudes.

3. Academic Achievement. Grade-point average was used as the measure of academic achievement. The differences between the first semester averages and the second semester averages (the experimental period) constitute the criterion scores.

In addition to these instruments, a questionnaire was administered at the conclusion of the experimental period to determine what information and attitudes the students had about the study, etc.

STATISTICAL ANALYSIS AND RESULTS

The statistical (null) hypotheses to be tested may be stated as follows:

1. Subsequent to the experimental period, no significant differences will be found among the groups in regard to
   a. Positive changes in self concept
   b. Improvement in reported study habits and attitudes
   c. Increases in grade-point averages.

2. Subsequent to the experimental period there will be no significant differences between the combined individual and group counseled groups and the other two groups.

3. Subsequent to the experimental period there will be no significant gains on the criterion measures in any of the groups.

The hypotheses were tested by analyses of variance and the *t*-test. Prior to the analyses, the subjects in the groups were ranked and paired on the basis of pre-counseling scores. A two-way analysis of variance was applied. Results will be presented under the three criteria used in the study.

Q-SORT

The data for analysis were the correlations of the Q-sorts of each student in each group with the criterion sort before and after the experimental period. The differences between these correlations were subjected to analysis of variance. The differences were not significant at the .05 level. While the mean for Group I was the highest, the Group IV (control) mean was next highest, and Group III showed a decrease in relationship to the adjustment criterion.

When the two counseled groups were compared with the other two groups (one-session motivated and control) by means of the t-test for matched samples, the resulting t of 2.41 is significant beyond the .05 level. This difference is due to Group I, however, since Group II showed less improvement than the control group in this respect.[3]

A comparison of pretest with posttest scores for the noncounseled groups indicates that the difference (which is slightly negative) is not significant. The pretest and posttest means of the counseled groups are not significantly different ($t = 1.72$); for Group I the difference approaches significance, however ($t = 2.11, .10 > p > .05$).

BROWN-HOLTZMAN SSHA

The result of the analysis of variance of differences between pretest and posttest scores was not significant. While the means of the two counseled groups were higher than the means of the two noncounseled groups, the t-test of the differences was not significant (.20 level).

The pretest and posttest means of the counseled groups do not differ significantly, nor do the means of the noncounseled groups.

GRADE-POINT AVERAGES

The analysis of variance of differences in grade-point averages was not significant. A t-test of the difference between the two counseled groups and the two noncounseled groups was significant, however ($t = 2.35, p < .05$).

The gain in grades by the counseled groups is significant ($t = 2.25, p < .05$). While most of the gain is apparently in Group II, the gain for this group alone does not reach significance ($t = 1.55$). The difference between pretest and posttest grades for the noncounseled groups is negative.

For Group I, the counselor ranked the students for degree of improve-

---

[3]While the t-test is not ordinarily appropriate following an analysis of variance (even when F is significant), in the present instance it is appropriately used to test an *a priori* hypothesis.

ment during individual counseling. This rank order correlated .93 with the ranks of the students on the Q-sort ($p < .02$), but the correlations with rankings on the Brown-Holtzman SSHA and grade-point average were insignificant.

Analysis of the posttest questionnaire suggested some possible differences among the groups. Group I students appeared to have clearer ideas about the nature of the study. Approximately equal numbers of students stated that they had worked harder; however, only one or two students in Groups I, II, and III stated they had read the book given them, while none of Group IV had read it. Few students reported that their parents had tried to help them. A question about handedness was included in the questionnaire because of the observation that several were lefthanded. Of the 30 students answering the questionnaire, 7 (23 per cent) stated they were lefthanded, while another 8 of the remaining 23 stated they could use their left hands equally well in things other than writing. This incidence of lefthandedness and ambidexterity suggests further investigation of this characteristic in underachievers.

DISCUSSION

While the results of the over-all analyses of variance were not significant, the comparisons of the counseled versus noncounseled students yielded positive results on two of the criteria. This occurred as a result of the pooling of consistent trends and increasing the N's in the comparisons. The results are not, however, highly encouraging. There are a number of factors which should be considered in the interpretation and evaluation of the results.

1. The period and extent of counseling were quite limited, particularly for those receiving group counseling. Perhaps it is too much to expect immediate and extensive results under such conditions. Also it is possible that results may appear later than the semester in which the counseling occurred.

2. The counselor felt that the group counseling was not a successful experience. Several factors may have contributed to this. The group was selected on the basis of having the same period free, and had little in common except underachievement the degree of which was variable. They were heterogeneous in aptitude and achievement as well as amount of underachievement. The counselor felt that her limitations of experience in group counseling and her foreign background, resulting in feelings of lack of assurance in the group, prevented her from developing a therapeutic rather than a teaching attitude. The students did show progress in becoming a group, and had some serious discussions of the problem of underachievement as well as of more personal problems. In spite of this impression that the group counseling was ineffective, this group ranked first on improvement

in grades and tied with Group I on change in study habits and attitudes. It was third in change on the Q-sort, however. Possibly group counseling can be effective when directed to the problem of underachievement, without affecting personal adjustment.

3. Students in the counseling groups had not volunteered for or requested counseling, or assistance in improving their academic achievement or personal adjustment. Many apparently were not even aware that they were underachievers. Some were not interested in doing anything about it. For example, one student in the individual counseling group, who was planning on going to college to study engineering, was getting C grades. He stated that he was not concerned about this, that he was confident he could "get by" in college. The thought that he might have difficulty in being accepted in college did not seem to bother him. The problem of so-called "anti-intellectualism" among students is perhaps important here. To some students, high achievement is undesirable from a social point of view.

Although motivation or desire for change is no doubt important in counseling, the conditions of the present study are the conditions under which the high school counselor operates and in which he is expected to achieve results. Some students become motivated when they become aware of a problem, such as a discrepancy between capacity and achievement. The results of this study offer some encouragement to counselors faced with doing something for underachievers.

4. It is possible that during counseling which involves deep problems of personal-emotional adjustment, the student's academic achievement might even decline. Tyler (1953, pp. 271–293), among others, recognizes this possibility. It is interesting in this connection that Group I, in which there were several students with such problems, while showing the greatest improvement in the Q-sort adjustment score, did not improve in grade-point average as much as Group II. It is also possible that, during the course of counseling, a student will evidence a decline in adjustment, or in his concept of himself, prior to showing improvement. The student who presented the most serious personal maladjustment in Group I declined slightly in Q-sort adjustment score during the experimental period, but retained the same grade-point average, and showed a gain in study habits and attitudes score.

5. It is possible that being involved in the experiment to the extent of taking the tests (control group), may have positive effects. One student in Group II remarked: "Just taking the tests was something that helped me to think about my study habits and gave me ideas of what to do or not to do in order to improve my school work." However, the control group showed no improvement in grades or reported study habits and attitudes, though there was some gain in Q-sort adjustment score. Nor did Group III, which had the tests, show any improvement.

6. The levels of aptitude or ability, and the degree of underachievement, varied greatly within each group. It is possible that different approaches are required for effectiveness with different levels of ability and/or underachievement.

In addition to suggestions implicit in the above discussion, two other points may be made:

1. It appears that selecting students on the basis of a criterion of underachievement leads to the identification of students having personal-social-emotional problems. Most of the students in Group I, and several in Group II, revealed such problems during counseling. This supports the hypothesis that underachievement is related to general problems of adjustment. However, some underachievers appear not to have such general problems. It is possible that a student may accept academic underachievement in order to assure social acceptance, or in order to concentrate his time and efforts in other areas, such as extra-curricular activities.

2. The apparent failure of one-session motivational counseling is interesting. This group (Group III) declined in all three measures employed in the study, falling below the control group in all the posttest measures. The approach used with this group is perhaps the one commonly used by parents and teachers who attempt to raise the achievement of students. It is suggested that it may be better to leave underachievers alone, rather than pointing out their failure to achieve adequately and exhorting them to do something about it.

SUMMARY AND CONCLUSIONS

Thirty-two underachievers were identified in a group of 209 juniors in high school. Four groups of 8 students were matched on aptitude (sum of DAT Verbal and Abstract Reasoning subtests), achievement (grade-point average), underachievement (difference in percentile rank in aptitude and achievement), socio-economic status, age, and sex. Group I received individual counseling, Group II group counseling, Group III a one-session motivational experience, while Group IV constituted the control group. Three measures were obtained prior to and following the 12-week experimental period: (a) a Q-sort of 45 items selected from Hilden's [12] pool; (b) the Brown-Holtzman Survey of Study Habits and Attitudes; (c) grades in the four major courses taken in the first and second semesters. Correlations of individual Q-sorts with a criterion Q-sort based on sortings by 7 psychologists constituted the Q-sort adjustment score.

Two-way analyses of variance indicated that the four groups did not differ significantly on any of the criteria. A comparison of the two counseled groups with the two noncounseled groups indicated that they differed significantly in Q-sort adjustment score change (attributed to the change in Group I), and in increase in grade-point average.

The results are considered to be encouraging in view of the factors tending to attenuate differences among the groups. While it may be suggested that individual counseling is more effective with personal problems, and group counseling is better with cognitive problems such as improving academic achievement, the nature of the group counseling situation would not make such a conclusion justifiable. The counselor felt that the group did not develop into a therapeutic unit, for reasons suggested earlier.

Other limitations of the study, some of which have already been pointed out, include the lack of a follow-up beyond the experimental period, limitations of the counselor, the small size of the sample, the brief period of counseling, and the fact that the counseled students had not requested counseling. This last factor is one which perhaps might be present in the usual high school program, however. That underachievers will accept and apparently benefit from counseling is encouraging. However, some of the students would perhaps not have continued with counseling if they had not been aware of, and influenced by, the importance of their continuing for the sake of the experiment.

REFERENCES

1. Bradt, K. W., & Duncan, C. P. "Degree of Personal Relationship Between Instructor and Student as a Factor in Course Grade Improvement," *Amer. Psychologist* (1951), **6**, 368. (Abstract)

2. Briggs, L. J., & Roe, R. M. "Morale as a Function of Opportunity to Register Complaints." Technical Report HRRC-TR-53-4. Human Resources Research Center, Lackland Air Force Base, Texas 1953.

3. Brown, W. F., & Holtzman, W. H. "Use of the Survey of Study Habits and Attitudes for Counseling Students," *Personnel Guid. J.* (1957), **35**, 214–218.

4. Brown, W. F., & Holtzman, W. H. *Survey of Study Habits and Attitudes* (New York: Psychological Corp., 1956).

5. Calhoun, S. R. "The Effects of Counseling on a Group of Underachievers," *Sch. Rev.* (1956), **64**, 312–316.

6. Drasgow, J. "Underachievers," *J. Counsel. Psychol.* (1957), **4**, 210–211.

7. Drews, E. H., & Teahan, J. R. "Parental Attitudes and Academic Achievement," *J. Clin. Psychol.* (1957), **13**, 328–332.

8. Feyereisen, K. "Eliminating Blocks to Learning," *Leadership* (1948), **5**, 527–535.

9. Gerken, C. D'A. *Study Your Way Through School* (Chicago: Science Research Associates, 1953).

10. Gersten, C. "An Experimental Evaluation of Group Therapy with Juvenile Delinquents," *Int. J. Group Psychother.* (1951), **1**, 311–318.

11. Guthrie, G. M., & O'Neil, H. W. "Effects of Dormitory Counseling on Academic Achievement," *Personnel Guid. J.* (1953), **31**, 307–309.

12. Hilden, A. H. *Manual for Q-sort and Random Set of Personal Concepts* (St. Louis: Veteran Administration Regional Office, 1954).

13. Hoehn, A. J., & Salts, B. "Effects of Teacher-Student Interviews on Classroom Achievement," *J. Educ. Psychol.* (1956), **47**, 434–435.

14. Kimball, Barbara. "The Sentence Completion Technique in a Study of Scholastic Underachievement," *J. Consult. Psychol.* (1952), 16, 353–358.

15. Kirk, Barbara. "Test Versus Academic Performance in Malfunctioning Students," *J. Consult. Psychol.* (1952), 16, 213–216.

16. Lecky, P. *Self-consistency, a Theory of Personality* (New York: Island Press, 1945).

17. Richardson, LaV. H., & Perry, J. D. "Counseling for Academic Recovery," *J. Counsel. Psychol.* (1956), 3, 136–139.

18. Serene, H. F. "An Experiment in Motivational Counseling," *Personnel Guid. J.* (1953), 31, 319–324.

19. Shaw, M. C., & Brown, D. J. "Scholastic Underachievement of Bright College Students," *Personnel Guid. J.* (1957), 36, 195–199.

20. Sheldon, M., & Landsman, T. "An Investigation of Nondirective Group Therapy with Students in Academic Difficulty," *J. Consult. Psychol.* (1950), 14, 210–215.

21. Sherrifs, A. C. "Modification of Academic Performance Through Personal Interview," *J. Appl. Psychol.* (1949), 33, 339–346.

22. Schoenhard, G. H. "Home Visitation Put to a Test," *Personnel Guid. J.* (1950), 36, 480–485.

23. Tyler, L. E. *The Work of the Counselor* (New York: Appleton-Century-Crofts, 1953).

25

Group Counseling with Students Unable to Speak in Class*

Stephen J. Golburgh

Edward C. Glanz

This study was undertaken to investigate the effectiveness of a short period of group counseling in helping college freshmen overcome difficulty in verbalizing during classroom discussions. Boston University College of Basic Studies places considerable emphasis upon active discussion of course material by students. Individuals who find self-expression in a group situation difficult are therefore at somewhat of a disadvantage educationally.

Experimental and control groups were selected from a larger population of 100 students who represented a random sample of a freshman class of 500. The 100 students were asked to rate themselves on how easy or difficult it was for them to participate in classroom discussion. A five point scale was employed, one representing very easy, five representing very difficult. The 25 highest ratings were extracted and two matched groups were formed on the basis of these ratings and College Entrance Examination Board Verbal Scores. Selection of which subjects were to fall in the experiemental or control group was done randomly. The present study included an experimental and control group of 9 subjects each.

Each student in the experimental group was approached individually by the counselor and told of the group counseling sessions. Subjects were informed that the decision to enter the group was theirs entirely but if they decided positively they would be expected to come to each weekly meeting for the duration of the counseling, an eight week period.

During the preliminary individual interview some orientation to the group counseling procedure was offered. Students were told that talking about this difficulty in a group setting could sometimes prove useful in easing the problem or its effects. Each student was given the opportunity to ask questions and these were answered briefly and honestly. No pressure was exerted on any subject yet all but one of the originally selected members of the experimental group decided to enter counseling.

*Reprinted by permission of the author and publisher from *Journal of College Student Personnel* (1962), 4, 102–103, 128.

Four methods were employed to assess the possibility of change in quantity of verbalization in classroom discussion:

1. student self-rating before and after the counseling period,
2. mean rating by the student's four faculty members before and after counseling,
3. mean peer rating[1] before and after counseling and
4. change in self-attitude in a positive direction as measured by a Self-Attitude Scale. The Self Attitude Scale was administered prior to the experiment and after its completion.

The experimental group of students was involved in 8 weekly group counseling sessions for one hour. Attendance at the sessions was excellent[2] probably a partial result of this having been presented as a condition for entering the group. The counselor structured the group counseling sessions on a eclectic basis. Neither client centered nor interpretive techniques were avoided. Reflection, ventilation, interpretation, questioning, and providing information, reassurance and explanation were employed when appropriate to the presenting problem.[3] A typescript of a part of one group session may be found in *Groups in Guidance*, Glanz.[4] During the first meeting the group situation was presented as an opportunity to talk about the common difficulty the students were experiencing. It was further explained that such an opportunity sometimes helped in better understanding the problems of speaking in class and that an individual might develop better methods of dealing with such issues. The counselor employed an accepting, clarifying, interpretative, and supporting function seeking increased self-understanding on the part of the group members as the goal of the process.

After the counseling period, the students in both the control and experimental group, were asked to re-rate themselves on the basis of the original 5 point scale. The Self-Attitude Scale was also re-administered. Faculty

	Control		Experimental	
	Before	After	Before	After
Mean self-ratings	4	4.1	4.05	3.0
Mean Teacher ratings	3.6	3.8	3.39	2.7
Mean Peer ratings	3.4	3.49	3.2	3.1
Mean Attitude Scale score *	98	95	108	113

* Increased score indicates improvement in attitude toward the self.

[1] Each student is a member of a section (class) made up of approximately 25 students. The section is composed of the same students for all courses. The peer ratings were attained by having each student in the section rate every other student in the section on the basis of the previously described 5 point scale. This same scale was also employed for the faculty ratings.

[2] Two students were absent one session each.

[3] S. J. Golburgh, J. F. Penney, "Sector Counseling with Underachieving College Students," *Journal of Counseling Psychology* (in press).

[4] E. C. Glanz, *Groups in Guidance* (Allyn and Bacon, 1962).

post-ratings were obtained two weeks after the last counseling session. This was done in order to allow possible changes to become somewhat more obvious. Faculty members did not know of the composition of the experimental and control groups. At approximately the same time, the faculty were completing a second rating of the students, all students of the section were again asked to rate every other member of the class section.

RESULTS

The data were analyzed statistically in order to determine the significance of differences between experimental and control groups before and after the group counseling experience, on each of the four criteria of change.[5] These results follow:

Criteria	t
Self-ratings	22.33*
Mean Instructor ratings	2.76*
Self Attitude Scale	2.38**
Mean Peer rating	—

*Significant at the 1% level of confidence.
**Significant at the 5% level of confidence.

Significant changes in the improved direction were evidenced in the self-ratings, the mean instructor ratings and the scores on the Self-Attitude Scale. The t's were significantly at the 1% level of confidence for the self-rating differences and for the instructor rating differences. The t was significant at the 5% level of confidence for the scores on the Self-Attitude Scale. There were no significant differences between the mean peer ratings.

DISCUSSION

The results of this study support the contention that a relatively short period of group counseling has potential for being useful to students who have difficulty in verbalizing in the classroom situation. Three out of four of the evaluative measures showed significant results.

The fourth measure, peer ratings, showed no improvement after the counseling period. It is possible to speculate that this may be related to the fact that the peers who did the ratings were aware by the time of the second ratings which students were in the counseling group. Because of this, they perhaps anticipated glaring changes. They may have been less sensitive to subtle changes than were the instructors who were not aware of which students were in the specific groups. Furthermore, students perhaps form an

[5]The authors express their appreciation to Miss Sylvia Fleisch for her invaluable assistance with the statistical analysis of data.

opinion early in the academic year with regard to an individual's class participation and hold this opinion throughout the year with little re-evaluation.

Because of the small number of subjects in the present study, the results had best be looked upon as tentative and suggestive of the need for further research on the effectiveness of group procedures with college students experiencing difficulty in verbalizing during classroom discussion as well as other adolescent adjustment areas.

SUMMARY

College students often are handicapped by an inability to participate in class discussions. From 100 students the poorest twenty-five were selected on a basis of self-ratings. Two groups of nine matched on College Entrance Examination Board Verbal scores and self-ratings were established. After group counseling the experimental group surpassed the control group on three of four measures of change. Self-ratings and faculty ratings were significant at the .01% level, the Self-Attitude Scale showed changes significant at the .05% level, and peer-ratings did now show significant differences.

26

Group Counseling and the Academic Performance of Anxious College Freshmen*

Charles D. Spielberger

Henry Weitz

J. Peter Denny

College upperclassmen with high manifest anxiety scores have been found to earn lower grades and to have a higher dropout rate due to academic failure than non-anxious students with comparable ability [11, 12]. These findings suggest that the full contributions of many able students are being lost to society through under-achievement or academic failure stemming from emotional problems. Similar findings obtained for college freshmen using other indices of emotional adjustment [3] suggest that measures of anxiety or adjustment may be used to identify potential underachievers early in their college careers. The goals of the present study were to attempt to demonstrate that the academic performance of anxious college freshmen who were likely to be underachievers could be facilitated through the early application of group counseling procedures.

Most counselors who work with college students usually concentrate on those who seek assistance *after* they have developed emotional or academic difficulties [4, 7]. Where counselors have attempted to identify and work with "underachievers," it has been found that although counseling may facilitate the personal adjustment of such students, it has little demonstrable effect upon their academic performance [2, 5]. That improvement in personal adjustment does not directly facilitate academic achievement is not surprising. There is little evidence that emotional problems are the immediate causes of poor academic performance. But for many students, emotional problems predispose them to develop maladaptive study habits and poor attitudes towards academic work which, in turn, lead to underachievement. The "therapeutic prevention" [13] of emotional problems in

*Reprinted by permission of the author and publisher from *Journal of Counseling Psychology* (1962), IX, 195–204.

college students, and of maladaptive academic habits and attitudes which may stem from such problems, would enable more students to attain the education necessary for them to make the contributions to society of which they are capable. Preventive measures offered at the beginning of the freshman year of college would come at a time when the potential for maladjustment, especially for the more anxious freshmen, is increased by special environmental stresses. The college freshman, in addition to adjusting to demands for academic achievement under conditions of increased complexity of subject matter and heightened competition from peers, is also frequently confronted with the task of establishing a new set of social relationships in a strange environment.

The results of two previous studies with preventive features suggest that emotional adjustment can be facilitated through group counseling. Arbuckle [1] found that college freshmen who attended compulsory orientation classes consisting of lectures and group discussions showed changes in personality inventory scores indicative of better adjustment. Rosenberg and Fuller [9] found that a "Human Relations Seminar" for beginning nursing students reduced the withdrawal rate to less than half of what it had been in previous years. They also found that faculty and supervisors reported fewer expressions of anxiety in the classroom and noted a pronounced decrease in tension in students' relationships with patients and ward personnel. These studies, however, have limitations which make them difficult to interpret. (1) Comparisons with appropriate control groups were not provided; hence it was not possible to differentiate between the effects of the intervention procedure and of other factors such as normal personality development. (2) In Arbuckle's study, no measures of the effects of the group experience were obtained outside of the orientation classes themselves. (3) In the Rosenberg and Fuller study, the seminars appeared to have profound effects on the entire school environment since all first-year nursing students participated in them. Changes in the environment may well have produced the changes in the students' behavior.

The present study has five important features, several of which were designed to avoid the shortcomings noted in the previous investigations with preventive features. (1) College freshmen whose anxiety test scores indicated that they might be underachievers or academic failures were identified shortly after their arrival on campus. (2) Group counseling with therapeutic prevention goals was initiated during the first semester with those anxious freshmen who volunteered to participate. (3) Group counseling was provided for only half of the students who volunteered, thereby permitting the comparison of the performance of counseled students with a control group of noncounseled volunteers. (4) Since less than two per cent of the total student body were participating in group counseling at any given time, it was unlikely that the college environment was greatly influenced by the counseling program. Thus, inferences concerning the effectiveness of the counseling procedures could be made on the basis of objective criteria of academic adjustment external to the counseling situation. (5) Counseled students were compared to noncounseled students with respect to a number of uncontrolled variables which might be related to academic performance and which could serve, in the place of counseling, as alternative explanations for any obtained differences in academic performance.

METHOD

SELECTION INSTRUMENTS

The American Council on Education Psychological Examination, 1949 Edition, (ACE) and a modified form of the Minnesota Multiphasic Personality Inventory (MMPI) were administered to all freshmen entering Duke University in the fall of 1959. These tests were given during the week prior to the beginning of classes as parts of the university's regular placement testing program. The MMPI had been shortened from 566 to 398 items so that it could be completed in the limited time available ($1\frac{1}{4}$ hours). The modified MMPI included all of the items comprising the three validity scales, *L*, *F* and *K*; the nine original clinical scales; the Taylor Manifest Anxiety Scale [14]; and the Welsh Factor A Scale [18]. A biographical information card, which provided data on the type of high school attended and whether or not the student had declared his major area of study, was also completed during the placement testing period.

IDENTIFICATION OF ANXIOUS COLLEGE FRESHMEN

Previous research had indicated that anxiety scores for male college students may not have the same intellectual correlates [10] and may not be related to nonintellective factors in the same way as those of female students [16]. Therefore, the sample to be offered group counseling was limited to entering male freshmen enrolled in the liberal arts curriculum. Since the original relationship between anxiety and academic performance had been obtained with the Taylor Manifest Anxiety Scale (MAS), scores on the MAS were given the most weight in determining which students would be offered counseling; but to insure the inclusion of students who were consistently high in maladaptive anxiety, the Welsh Factor A Scale (A-Scale) was also employed. The criterion established for the identification of anxious students required an individual to score in the upper 30 per cent of the MAS raw score distribution (16 and above) and in the upper 50 per cent of the A-Scale raw score distribution (10 and above). Of the students satisfying the anxiety criterion, those who scored below the fourth stanine on local ACE norms (raw scores of 104 and below) were eliminated from the sample since previous research had indicated that students with low ability performed poorly regardless of their anxiety level [11]. Of an entering class of 565 male liberal arts freshmen for whom data were available, 112 met the combined anxiety and intellectual criteria.

ASSIGNMENT OF STUDENTS TO COUNSELING AND CONTROL GROUPS

All students who met the selection criteria were invited by letter to participate in a voluntary "academic orientation program." They were told that the purpose of the program was to assist entering freshmen adjust to college life so that they might more effectively utilize their educational opportunities. It was further explained that the program would be carried out through small discussion groups meeting once a week in which students would be encouraged to raise questions related to their own academic, vocational, personal, and social interests. Students wishing to take part were asked to return a completed schedule card and to commit themselves to participation for a minimum of four weeks. The latter requirement was instituted because it was expected that mounting pressure from academic work coupled with possible arousal of anxiety in early sessions might cause some students to drop out before they recognized any of the possible benefits of the program. Of the 112 students invited, 56 volunteered and were assigned in equal numbers to an experimental-counseled group (E) and a non-counseled-control group (C) which were matched on factors found previously to relate to academic performance in the university population. These included: ACE scores; type of high school attended [17]; and declaration of a major field of study [15].

The present study was concerned exclusively with the effects of group counseling upon the academic performance of students who volunteered for the special orientation program. Therefore, two students assigned to the E group who did not attend a single counseling session and one student in the C group who dropped out of school early in the semester were eliminated from the final sample.

The results of the matching procedures, excluding the data for the three students who figured in the matching but who were subsequently eliminated, are presented in Table 1. There were no statistically significant differences between the E and C groups on any of the matching variables. Although it was planned that the counseling sessions would begin shortly after classes commenced, administrative and scheduling problems prevented their meeting until the sixth week of the semester. The assignment of midterm grades two weeks later afforded the opportunity to check the adequacy of the matching procedures directly against a criterion of academic performance. It may be noted in Table 1 that the midsemester grades for the E and C groups were well matched.

Table 1

Mean Scores on the Matching Variables for the Experimental and Control Groups

Variable	Expt. Group		Control Group		Difference[a]
	Mean (N = 26)	SD	Mean (N = 27)	SD	(Control-Expt.)
% Private School	15.4	7.0	11.1	6.0	−4.3
% Declared Major	19.2	8.4	25.9	8.4	6.7
ACE	130.8	16.2	132.2	15.1	1.4
Midterm GPA	2.12	.45	2.20	.59	.08

[a] When evaluated by the appropriate t test or chi-square, none of the differences approached statistical significance.

COUNSELING PROCEDURES

Students in the E group were assigned to four counseling subgroups, each consisting of six to eight students, and notified by letter of the time and place that their counseling groups would meet. The C group was told by letter that more students had volunteered than could be worked with during the current semester, and that they would be offered an opportunity to participate in the program during the second semester. The group counseling was conducted within the administrative framework of the Duke University Bureau of Testing and Guidance. The two counselors were members of the university faculty; both had extensive previous experience in counseling and clinical work with college students. Each of the counselors worked with two counseling groups. Students were encouraged to bring up problems of any sort about which they were concerned. Topics most favored by the students included methods of study, individual academic difficulties, vocational goals, dormitory life, relations with professors in class and on the campus, and to a lesser extent, matters relating to nonacademic difficulties and problems of personal identity. The counselors attempted to stimulate group discussion, to facilitate the utilization by the group of ideas presented by individual students, to provide relevant factual information, and to summarize and clarify what was said.

The number of counseling sessions with the four groups ranged from 8 to 11. One group terminated prior to the Christmas vacation period; the other groups met until the end of the semester. During the fourth group session, the students were given the Survey of Study Habits and Attitudes [6] and the Kuder Preference Record, Vocational. These tests along with the students' placement tests were discussed during the fifth group meeting. All sessions were recorded on magnetic tape. A graduate student observer, who kept attendance and made behavioral observations, met regularly with each group.

CRITERION MEASURES OF ACADEMIC ADJUSTMENT

Academic achievement provided the principal objective criterion against which the effects of group counseling were evaluated. Midterm and first semester grade-point averages (GPA's) were obtained from university records for students in the E and C groups. The students's GPA is the weighted average of his academic performance in course work where 4 points are credited for each hour of A, 3 for B, 2 for C, 1 for D, and 0 for F. Data were also collected on factors which might relate to academic performance and thereby provide alternative explanations for any obtained effect of group counseling. The measures examined were class attendance, scores on the Survey of Study Habits and Attitudes (SSHA), and on the personality scales of the MMPI. Students in the E and C groups were interviewed as soon as possible after the end of the semester to gain information about their adjustment to college life.

RESULTS

THE ACADEMIC PERFORMANCE OF COUNSELED AND NONCOUNSELED STUDENTS

Because of the limited number of subjects, data for the four counseling sub-groups were pooled. The academic performance of the total E group was then compared with that of the C group. Since the counseling groups did not begin meeting until just prior to midterm and had comparable GPA's at that time, improvement in GPA from midsemester until the end of the semester served as the principal criterion of the effects of counseling upon academic performance. The improvement in GPA obtained by the E group is compared to the improvement of the C group in Figure 1 in which

Figure 1

The Mean Improvement in GPA from Midterm
to the End of the Semester for Students in the
Counseled Group (E) and the Noncounseled Control Group (C).

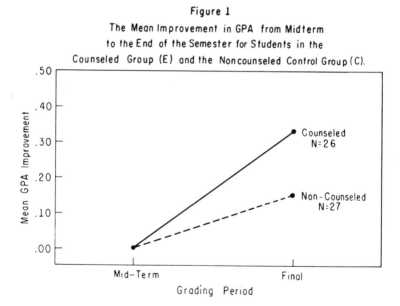

the groups have been equated for midterm GPA's. Both the E and C groups showed improvement in GPA.

The statistical significance of the obtained improvement was evaluated by means of an analysis of variance [8] (Type I Design). The difference between midterm grades and end of semester grades for both groups combined was found to be highly significant ($F = 23.37$; $df = 1/51$; $P < .001$). This improvement would appear to be attributable to university grading practices which regularly produce lower grades at midterm than at the end of the semester. Although slightly below the C group at midterm (see Table 1), the E group showed greater improvement in GPA and by the end of the semester was performing at a higher level. The statistically significant interaction between groups and grading period ($F = 6.63$; $df = 1/51$; $P < .05$) when considered along with Figure 1 indicated that the counseled students showed greater improvement in academic performance than the noncounseled students.

THE RELATIONSHIP BETWEEN NUMBER OF SESSIONS ATTENDED AND IMPROVEMENT IN ACADEMIC PERFORMANCE

The finding of greater GPA improvement for the E group is consistent with the hypothesis that counseling led to the obtained improvement, but more confidence could be placed in this interpretation of the data if students who attended more counseling sessions showed more gain than those who attended fewer sessions. When change in GPA from midterm to the end of the semester was used as the index of improvement, a Pearson r of .63 ($P < .01$) was obtained between number of sessions attended and GPA improvement. This positive relationship between attendance and grades was further evaluated by dividing the E group into three subgroups according to the number of counseling sessions each student attended. The number of counseling sessions attended by students in the E group ranged from 2 to 11; the mean number of sessions attended was 6.7. Students who attended 2–5 sessions were designated Low Attenders; those who attended 6–7 sessions were designated Middle Attenders; those who attended 8–11 sessions were designated High Attenders. The Low, Middle and High Attender groups consisted of eight, nine, and nine students, respectively. The means and SD's of the GPA's obtained by these groups for the two grading periods are presented in Table 2. The amount of improvement in GPA from midsemester to the end of the semester for the three attendance groups is compared with the improvement of the control group in Figure 2 in which the midterm GPA's for the four groups have been equated. The evaluation of these data by analysis of variance (Type I Design) yielded a statistically significant interaction between groups and grading period ($F = 7.69$; $df = 3/49$; $P < .01$), which when considered together with Figure 2 indicates

Table 2

Mean Midterm and Semester Grade Point Averages* for the
Experimental and Control Groups

Group	N	Midterm GPA		Semester GPA	
		Mean	SD	Mean	SD
Control Group	27	2.20	.59	2.35	.63
Experimental Group	26	2.12	.45	2.43	.54
High Attenders	9	2.16	.41	2.75	.44
Middle Attenders	9	1.95	.44	2.13	.55
Low Attenders	8	2.27	.65	2.39	.48

*A student's GPA is the weighted average of his academic performance in course work where 4 points are credited for each hour of a, 3 points for B, 2 points for C, 1 point for D, and 0 for F.

that the High Attenders showed significantly greater improvement than the other groups.

Although regular attendance at group counseling sessions was related to improvement in academic performance, this improvement cannot be attributed to the effects of counseling unless it can be demonstrated that factors which might account for regular attendance do not, in fact, also account for the obtained GPA improvement. Therefore, the High, Middle, and Low Attenders were compared on available measures which might be related to academic performance. The measures included the variables on which the E and C groups had been originally matched, and, in addition,

Figure 2

The Mean Improvement in GPA from Midterm to the End
of the Semester for High, Middle, and Low Attenders in the
Counseled Group and for the Noncounseled Control Group.

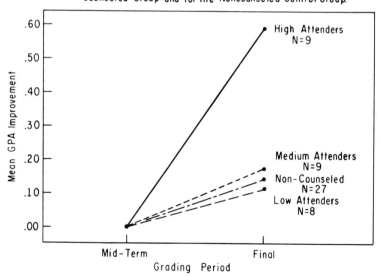

class attendance, scores on the SSHA, and scores on individual MMPI personality scales. The means and SD's for the three attendance groups on these measures are presented in Table 3. Analyses of variance [8] (Simple Randomized Design) for each of these measures failed to yield a single significant difference among the attendance groups.

Table 3

Mean Scores for the Three Attendance Groups on Variables
Possibly Related to Academic Improvement

Variable	High Attend. Mean	SD	Middle Attend. Mean	SD	Low Attend. Mean	SD	F
	(N = 9)		(N = 9)		(N = 8)		
Ace	131.9	17.2	132.8	14.1	127.4	18.7	.25
% Private School	11.1	10.4	11.1	10.4	25.0	15.3	*
% Declared Major	22.2	8.1	11.1	10.4	25.0	15.3	*
Class Absences	5.2	4.7	11.1	9.4	5.5	4.4	2.23
SSHA	33.2	11.1	34.6[a]	8.8	32.3[a]	4.4	.08
MMPI Scales[b]							
Hs	57.5	9.6	57.3	7.1	58.4	14.4	.04
D	57.2	11.7	63.3	12.8	60.3	11.1	.30
Hy	63.0	7.6	61.2	8.2	59.2	5.9	.26
Pd	58.1	11.2	64.3	8.1	57.9	8.7	1.13
Mf	64.5	9.3	70.0	13.6	66.3	8.3	.58
Pa	58.5	8.5	72.5	7.8	58.2	9.9	.65
Pt	65.0	4.9	64.8	8.2	66.4	14.6	.12
Sc	62.7	10.4	63.0	13.2	63.0	14.1	.04
Ma	64.4	10.4	60.0	7.3	59.7	8.9	.07
MAS	20.3	3.2	20.9	3.1	22.4	6.8	.39
A-Scale	15.7	6.7	19.7	4.9	17.8	6.6	.60

* Cell frequencies were too small to permit meaningful statistical analysis.

[a] Data were available for only 4 Low and 7 Middle Attenders.

[b] Data are reported on T scores for all MMPI scales except the MAS and A-Scale where raw scores are reported.

COMPARISON OF HIGH ATTENDERS WITH PERSONALITY-MATCHED CONTROLS

Although no single personality measure was found to be related to attendance at counseling sessions, it was still possible that the High Attenders were characterized by a personality syndrome which determined their regular attendance at counseling sessions as well as their improvement in academic performance. To evaluate this alternative interpretation of the data, it was first necessary to demonstrate that a personality pattern which uniquely characterized the High Attenders could be isolated. The academic performance of High Attenders could then be compared with a group of noncounseled anxious volunteers who possessed these same personality characteristics.

The personality characteristics of High Attenders were isolated in the following manner: 1) K-corrected T scores for each of the nine MMPI clinical scales were obtained for the students in the E and C groups; 2) personality profiles which consisted of a student's three most highly elevated scales were determined for each student; 3) personality criteria which differentiated the High Attenders from the Middle and Low Attenders were derived through comparisons of the profiles of students in the three attendance groups. It may be noted in Table 3 that scales *Ma* and *Hy* are the only MMPI clinical scales whose means tend to show a linear, albeit nonsignificant, relationship with attendance. For 8 of the 9 students in the High Attender group, either scale *Ma,* or scale *Hy* but not scale *Mf,* appeared among the students' three most elevated scales. Only 2 of 9 Middle Attenders and 3 of 8 Low Attenders had these profile patterns. Although this procedure for determining the personality patterns of High Attenders is admittedly *post hoc* and capitalized on chance factors, it served to isolate empirical personality criteria which were relatively unique for the High Attenders.

There were 9 students in the control group whose MMPI profiles fitted the personality criteria established for the High Attenders. The mean GPA's at midsemester and at the end of the semester for these noncounseled students who were personality-matched with the High Attenders were 2.19 and 2.43, respectively. In Figure 3 the amount of GPA improvement of the

Figure 3

The Mean Improvement in G PA from Midterm to the End
of the Semester for Students Who Regularly Attended
the Counseling Sessions and for Students
Selected from the Control Group (Matched Controls)
on the Basis of Personality Measures Which
Tended to Uniquely Characterize the High Attenders.

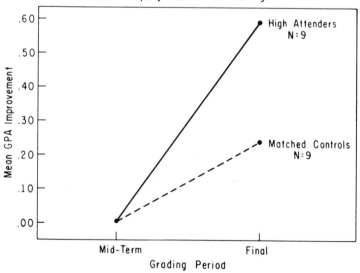

High Attenders is compared with that obtained by the personality-matched controls after these groups were equated for midterm grades. When these data were evaluated by analysis of variance (Type I Design), the finding of a statistically significant groups by grading-period interaction ($F = 6.87$; $df = 1/16$; $P < .025$), when considered together with Figure 3, indicates that students who regularly attended group counseling sessions showed greater improvement in GPA than personality-matched noncounseled controls.

DISCUSSION

The results of the present study indicated that anxious college freshmen who volunteered for and regularly attended group counseling sessions showed significantly more improvement in academic performance than anxious freshmen who either did not regularly attend group counseling or who were not offered this opportunity. The greater improvement in academic performance of High Attenders could not be accounted for in terms of scholastic ability, study habits and attitudes, class attendance, type of high school attended, or declaration of a major area of study. Nor did High Attenders differ from Middle and Low Attenders on any of the MMPI clinical scales. It was possible, however, to isolate personality patterns which tended uniquely to characterize High Attenders. But when the academic performance of High Attenders was compared with noncounseled students who possessed these same personality characteristics, the latter did not show academic improvement comparable to that obtained by the High Attenders. Therefore, it would seem reasonable to conclude that although personality characteristics of High Attenders may have accounted for their regular attendance at group counseling sessions, participation in group counseling provides the best explanation for the improvement in their grades.

Interviews with 23 of the 26 counseled students were conducted at the beginning of the second semester. These students were asked what benefit, if any, they had derived from the group sessions. Their most frequent responses were that the "discussion groups" had helped them to improve their study habits and to learn to use their time more effectively. The students also felt that it had been useful and interesting to hear views expressed by peers, and to learn that other students had problems similar to their own. On one topic there was nearly complete agreement; the students felt that the counselors' interpretations and the group discussion of the aptitude and interest tests had been worthwhile and helpful in contributing to a better understanding of themselves. Participation in the group discussions was also felt by some of the students to have contributed to a better understanding of their own personal problems.

Since students who participated in the counseling groups had been invited to do so on the basis of high anxiety scores, it was expected that a significant portion of the counseling sessions would focus upon experiences which had induced anxiety in these students prior to their entering college. But this did not occur despite the counselors' biased expectations and their overt encouragement of the students to discuss their personal problems. Instead the students were concerned almost exclusively with anxiety-arousing aspects of their present environmental circumstances, e.g., difficult course work; inability to study; low social status of freshmen; attitudes of professors; aggressive and noisy roommates. Although there was ample observational evidence of a high level of manifest anxiety in the behavior of these students, either they did not feel the need to discuss precollege antecedents of their anxiety or they did not feel the counseling groups a safe enough place to do so. In any event, group discussions with anxious college freshmen about the anxiety-arousing aspects of their academic environment appeared to facilitate the academic performance of those who regularly participated in the counseling sessions. But only half of the students invited to participate in the counseling groups volunteered to do so, and only a third of those who volunteered attended a sufficient number of sessions to benefit from the program. These facts clearly indicate that, for most anxious college freshmen, group counseling may not be a generally applicable procedure for the therapeutic prevention of underachievement or academic failure. Group counseling may be of value only for those students who possess personality characteristics which make it possible for them to participate fully and thereby benefit from such counseling.

Suggestive information bearing on the personality characteristics associated with being helped by group counseling was available in the MMPI data obtained in the present study. The High Attenders may be tentatively described as "active-repressive" on the basis of their MMPI profiles. The *Ma* scale was the single most frequently elevated scale for students in this group; *Hy* followed in terms of the frequency of occurrence among the three most elevated scales in individual student profiles. The MMPI profiles of the High Attenders were consistent with observations in the counseling sessions that these students tended to repress disturbing feelings and antisocial impulses, and appeared to seek solutions to their problems through active interaction with the environment. Markedly different profiles were obtained for the Middle and Low Attenders. The Middle Attenders were labeled "passive-rebellious with concern about rebellious tendencies" since scales *Mf*, *Pd*, and *D* were most frequently found among the elevated scales for individual students in this group. For the Low Attenders, scale *Mf* was most frequently elevated, followed by *Sc* and *Pt*, a pattern which was called "passive, withdrawn and ruminative." The personality descriptions applied to the Middle and Low Attenders were also consistent in a general way with the behavior of these students in the counseling groups and their attendance patterns.

SUMMARY

College freshmen with high anxiety scores were invited to participate in counseling groups designed to help them make more effective adjustments to college life. Of the students who volunteered, half were seen weekly in group counseling sessions during their first semester; the other half served as a control group. Improvement in academic performance from midterm to the end of the semester was the principal criterion of academic adjustment.

Those anxious freshmen who regularly attended group counseling sessions showed more improvement in their academic performance than students who were not counseled or who did not regularly attend counseling. Although it was possible to isolate a personality pattern which relatively uniquely characterized the students who regularly attended the counseling sessions, participation in group counseling appeared to be the most likely explanation for the improvement in grades obtained by these students.

Received July 24, 1961.

REFERENCES

1. Arbuckle, D. S. "A College Experiment in Orientation," *Occupations* (1949), **28**, 112–117.
2. Baymur, F. B., & Patterson, C. H. "A Comparison of Three Methods of Assisting Underachieving High School Students," *J. Counsel. Psychol.* (1960), **7**, 83–89.
3. Berger, I. L., & Sutker, A. R. "The Relationship of Emotional Adjustment and Intellectual Capacity to the Academic Achievement of College Students," *Ment. Hyg.* (1956), **40**, 65–77.
4. Blaine, G. B. Jr. & McArthur, C. C. *Emotional Problems of the Student* (New York: Appleton-Century-Crofts, 1961).
5. Broedel, J., Ohlsen, M., Proff, F., & Southard, C. "The Effects of Group Counseling on Gifted Underachieving Adolescents," *J. Counsel. Psychol.* (1960), **7**, 163–170.
6. Brown, W. F., & Holtzman, W. H. "A Study-attitudes Questionnaire for Predicting Academic Success," *J. Educ. Psychol.* (1955), **46**, 75–84.
7. Funkenstein, D. H. (Ed.) *The Student and Mental Health: An International View* (Cambridge: The Riverside Press, 1959).
8. Lindquist, E. F. *Design and Analysis of Experiments in Psychology and Education* (Boston: Houghton Mifflin, 1953).
9. Rosenberg, Pearl P., & Fuller, Myrtice. "Human Relations Seminar," *Ment. Hyg.* (1955), **39**, 406–432.
10. Spielberger, C. D. "On the Relationship Between Anxiety and Intelligence," *J. Consult. Psychol.* (1958), **22**, 220–224.
11. Spielberger, C. D. "The Effects of Manifest Anxiety on the Academic Achievement of College Students," *Ment. Hyg.* (1962), **46**, 420–426.
12. Spielberger, C. D., & Katzenmeyer, W. G. "Manifest Anxiety, Intelligence, and College Grades," *J. Consult. Psychol.* (1959), **23**, 278.

13. Stevenson, G. S. "The Prevention of Personality Disorders." In J. McV. Hunt (Ed.), *Personality and the Behavior Disorders*, Vol. 2 (New York: Ronald Press, 1944).

14. Taylor, Janet A. "A Personality Scale of Manifest Anxiety," *J. Abnorm. Soc. Psychol.* (1953), **48,** 285–290.

15. Weitz, H., Clarke, Mary, & Jones, Ora. "The Relationship Between Choice of a Major Field of Study and Academic Preparation and Performance," *Educ. Psychol. Measmt* (1955), **15,** 28–38.

16. Weitz, H., & Colver, R. M. "The Relationship Between the Educational Goals and the Academic Performance of Women, A Confirmation," *Educ. Psychol. Measmt* (1959), **19,** 373–380.

17. Weitz, H., & Wilkinson, H. Jean. "The Relationship Between Certain Nonintellective Factors and Academic Success in College," *J. Counsel. Psychol.* (1957), **4,** 54–60.

18. Welsh, G. S. "Factor Dimensions A and R," In G. S. Welsh & W. G. Dahlstrom (Eds.), *Basic Readings on the MMPI in Psychology and Medicine* (Minneapolis: Univer. of Minnesota Press, 1956).

27

A Program of Group Counseling *

Theodore Volsky

Vivian H. Hewer

Most counseling research and discussion deals with outcome variables relevant only for the more seriously disturbed, long-term client in need of some rehabilitative treatment. To the researcher and theoretician, the appeal of the "deeper" problems and the need for techniques for understanding and dealing with them, are certainly understandable and desirable. However, the need for similar understanding and techniques for dealing with the healthy individual requiring counseling for a short time, is obvious also. In a recent survey of large counseling centers throughout the country, Berdie [1] found that most counselors spend the majority of their time with such clients.

This paper describes a program of group counseling directed toward the problem of efficiently and effectively aiding the students usually seen two to three times by a counselor. These may be students who need new or additional information in planning tentative life goals, who may need assistance in integrating new learning or experiences into on-going behavior patterns, or who may wish a more objective appraisal of themselves as they approach important decision points in their lives.

If one looks at research with small groups, one finds little information about techniques for dealing with the usual clientele of a college counseling center. Most research has been concerned with problems found among emotionally disturbed patients [3] or problems of leadership and democratic living [5]. The social psychologists have studied groups also, but their concern most often has been with group interaction and process, not outcomes.

Dealing with the average counseling center client from what we believe to be a realistic point of view, we have become concerned about the quality of service offered these students. We do not believe we are best meeting their needs or expectancies by using techniques designed for the long-term client. It is also our belief that criteria used for assessing outcomes of long-term therapy are not appropriate for evaluating counseling effectiveness

*Reprinted by permission of the author and publisher from *Journal of Counseling Psychology* (1960), VII, 71–73.

with the short-term client. Hewer [2], investigating outcomes in individual and group counseling, used a criterion which may be appropriate when counseling these individuals. Her criterion was realism of the student's vocational choice as related to counseling. The present paper is an extension of experiences and ideas developed following Hewer's experiment. More specifically, it is concerned with the expanding group counseling program at the Student Counseling Bureau of the University of Minnesota.

PURPOSES OF THE PRESENT GROUP PROGRAM

The purposes of the group counseling program can best be understood in terms of the clientele. The majority of students coming to counseling centers are seen two or three times. A recent survey of the Student Counseling Bureau case load demonstrated about 60 to 70 per cent of the client population sought help on vocational or educational problems.

Several reasons can be hypothesized from the large number of one, two, and three interview cases: (1) the student wanted information, which he got quickly; (2) the help offered did not conform to the student's expectations, so he did not return; (3) the student was discouraged by the long wait between interviews caused by counselors' crowded calendars; (4) there was a lack of empathy and understanding on the part of the counselor for the student's educational or vocational problem; (5) interviews concerned with vocational choice were so structured by the counselor that they were terminated quickly (6) the demands for the counselor's time was so great that no more than two or three interview hours were available. Whatever are the reasons for the large number of short-term contacts, the authors believe group techniques have potential for minimizing some of the problems.

Early attempts at group counseling in our setting raised questions of whether too much time within a given school term would be lost in establishing rapport or increasing group cohesiveness so that little time would be left for dealing with students' problems. Leaders of early groups also felt problems were so specific to individual students that they were doing little more than carrying on five to ten individual interviews at once with the disadvantage of loss of confidentiality. Subsequent experience, however, led us to believe that if the major goals of a group counseling program are understanding of self and understanding of self in relation to the educational and occupational world, the group situation has advantages over short-term individual contacts.

For the student there are several benefits of group counseling, not possible in individual counseling. He is in a counseling situation with a professional person for ten hours rather than two or three; he has an opportunity to study his own problems as others explore theirs; he can compare his problems to those of others; he can gain a more sophisticated view of the occupational world as the vocational choices of others are examined; and the counselor can obtain a better understanding of him by observing him in a broader and more active social setting.

Although understanding of self and understanding of self in relation to a specific problem is the primary purpose of the group program, there is a secondary goal, to improve counseling center efficiency. If a counselor spends two and one-half interview hours with each client in individual counseling, he would have to spend 25 hours to see ten students, exclusive of time needed for preparation and record-keeping. If the same ten students were seen as a group, a minimum of ten hours of counselor time would be required (again exclusive of preparation and recording time). Even if more time were allowed the group leader than the individual counselor for preparation, there would be a substantial saving of counselor time.

Thus, more efficient use of counselor time may be a desirable outcome of a group counseling program, even though the major concern is to provide better services for those individuals having short-term contact with the counseling center.

In summary, the program undertaken at the University of Minnesota had three purposes:

a. To explore clinically the values and shortcomings of group procedures in dealing with students' problems of vocational and educational choice.

b. To evaluate experimentally such a program and compare its effectiveness and efficiency with other counseling methods.

c. To develop new techniques for dealing with individual student problems in the group situation.

PROCEDURES USED IN ORGANIZING GROUPS

In the Student Counseling Bureau at the University of Minnesota, approximately 25 groups have been conducted to date, involving more than 200 students. The earliest groups, formed from the membership of a class called Choosing a Vocation, already have been described by Hewer [2]. This past year two types of groups were formed from students voluntarily seeking help from the Counseling Bureau: groups with constant membership, and groups with shifting membership.

The first problem in forming these groups for educational and vocational counseling was to inform students and staff that this service was available. A description of the services offered by the Counseling Bureau (the class, individual, or group counseling) was circulated to residence counselors, college advisors, administrators and faculty. A story also appeared in the student newspaper. Students were offered the opportunity of joining a group upon first contact with the Bureau, or were referred to the groups by the staff.

The groups with constant membership were formed at the beginning of the academic quarter and the same students met with the group through-out that quarter. Groups with shifting membership were formed in an at-tempt to take care of the scheduling problems of the many students who worked and had few available free hours. A group was offered at a given hour at the beginning of the quarter and began with whatever number of students had agreed to meet. If another student later wanted counseling and could meet at that hour, he entered the group. Similarly, if a student felt he had received the help he needed, he left the group. Obviously, the more groups available, the more easily students could be scheduled.

SELECTING GROUP MEMBERSHIP

With both group and individual counseling available, some selection was necessary to determine who was to be seen individually, who entered a group, and who received both individual and group help. A screening interview was used to make this determination. When a student requested counseling, the Bureau receptionist scheduled (within a week) a short ap-pointment with a screening interviewer. A counselor can handle three to five such screening interviews in an hour. At the time of this interview, the counselor has all available information, e. g., tests, grades, and reports of previous counseling. Based on the student's description of his problem, the other data available, and his clinical impressions, the counselor makes a judgment as to whether the student could benefit from the group counseling procedures. He may also assign additional testing before the student enters the group.

In general, we believe students with emotional problems requiring pro-longed psychotherapy, those with premarital or marital problems, and those with adjustment problems deriving from physical handicaps can best be served by individual counseling or at least groups with different objec-tives. Also, precollege students and noncollege clients are not referred to groups because of scheduling difficulties.

SELECTION OF GROUP COUNSELORS

We are are uncertain as to the criteria for judging which person would be a good group counselor, just as we are unsure which person will make a good individual counselor. Our experience thus far has led us to believe that counselor judgment of his own skill in the situation has to be the primary criterion as to whether he should undertake group counseling.

COUNSELING PROCEDURE IN THE GROUP

The method currently being used in group counseling can best be des-cribed as the case conference approach. Previous attempts at group voca-tional counseling, however, have utilized other methods [4].

In the current program, at least one group meeting (50 minutes) is devoted to the discussion of educational and vocational plans of each member. A group of eight has worked out best in our experience.

Specifically, the goals in the group discussion are: defining the problem, characterizing the individual under discussion, suggesting various courses of action, assessing probabilities of success of various choices, balancing potentialities of satisfaction of various actions against probabilities of success, and reaching some compromise solution where necessary. The group members realize it is their responsibility to learn as much as they can about the member under discussion, and to make as many suggestions as possible. In effect, they become counselors with the responsibility of making vocational suggestions. Ideally, some acceptable recommendation for a tentative course of action should be reached at the conclusion of each case discussion.

The group leader assists the discussion by constructive criticism, pointing out instances in which conclusions were reached without sufficient information, or were inconsistent with information, or in which a goal was recommended without concern for the probabilities of success or satisfaction. After some experience, group members themselves become quite critical, allowing the leader to take a less active role. The leader also has all available test data about the individual being discussed and supplies information as the group members request it. The leader thus can exercise control and withhold information to protect the student under discussion.

As the groups developed, we were concerned with whether the person under discussion should be dealt with anonymously, or whether he should be identified. In the earliest group experiment, the students were dealt with anonymously. This was done to make the group more comfortable and to help students over the initial discomfort of discussing their personal problems. Only the person himself was aware of the identity of the individual under discussion. This method of discussion was continued until the group demanded that the one being discussed identify himself because only he could provide information necessary for the discussion. When identification was made only when the need arose, this seemed to contribute to effective group operation.

Some counselors felt more comfortable in this situation than in the one where the students were identified at the outset, because they had more latitude in the information they supplied to the group and the group began to operate more quickly. However, students soon announced they would receive more help if they identified themselves, since they could supply information about themselves which the leader could not, and they would be able to react to suggestions offered them. Because of this experience, some counselors allow the students to identify themselves as soon as the case discussion begins; others have a few sessions dealing with students anonymously.

CONCLUSION

In general, our impressions of this program are favorable as far as the effectiveness of the group technique is concerned in meeting student needs. We trust, in addition, the efficiency in the use of counselor time will increase.

At present, only Hewer's [2] initial appraisal of the group program is available. Student reports following group participation have been positive. Of approximately 200 students involved, no more than 5 have dropped out at inappropriate times.

Some students have sought additional individual counseling during or after participating in the group program, but we have viewed this as a positive reaction. The group may have served to make the student aware of, and accepting of a problem which should be discussed individually with a counselor. Also, counselors seeing students who have had group experience report a readiness for counseling that accelerates the counseling process.

We hope that the group counseling program now underway can be developed to the point where a rigorous evaluation can become the focus of our attention.

REFERENCES

1. Berdie, R. F. Unpublished survey of counseling centers.

2. Hewer, Vivian H. "Group Counseling, Individual Counseling, and a College Class in Vocations," *Personnel Guid. J.* (1959), 37, 660–665.

3. Hinckley, R. G., & Hermann, Lydia. *Group Treatment in Psychotherapy* (Minneapolis: Univer. of Minnesota Press, 1951).

4. Hoyt. D. P. "An Evaluation of Group and Individual Programs in Vocational Guidance," *J. Appl. Psychol.* (1955), 39, 26–30.

5. Woolf, M. D., & Woolf, Jeanne A. *Remedial Reading—Teaching and Treatment* (New York: McGraw-Hill, 1957).

Chapter V

RESEARCHING GROUP COUNSELING

While for most counselors the reason to engage in group counseling is to use a promising tool to provide a needed service in support of the growth potential of individuals, there are many counselors who also are challenged by the search for "truth"—to expand knowledge of the group counseling process itself. In most situations the service and research functions will probably be combined, with selection of participants determined primarily by the former purpose, The remarks which follow, however, are addressed to those for whom the research function has a high priority.

THE RESEARCH PROBLEM

Ohlsen points out that the definition of a problem in research goes beyond simply stating what the researcher expects to do and the reasons for doing it. The importance of precise definition of research problems is very important. As Ohlsen states:

> The researcher must state precisely what service he hopes to evaluate, under what conditions, and for what subjects. To communicate effectively with his colleagues he must try to avoid professional jargon and any words that mean different things to different people. Where he cannot avoid the use of such words, he must define the terms as he uses them [2, p. 443].

Once the researcher has clearly defined what he intends to do, he must also list appropriate objectives for the research project. What are the expected outcomes? Does the researcher expect that group counseling in some way will change the behavior of the clients? Is the study primarily an investigation of process in group counseling or is the researcher more concerned with the outcomes of group counseling? Is he, perhaps, interested in both process and outcome? Such basic questions must be answered in the initial planning stages of any research project. Many counseling studies fail to do this. The results of such research have often produced rather vague generalizations of results that have less than adequate meaning.

A review of the literature related to group counseling and group psychotherapy reveals that a wide range of topics has been studied by researchers. Some of the more common areas of investigations are :

1. Changes in individuals who have benefited most and least from group counseling.

2. Amount and type of client verbal behavior as it relates to change in attitude, self acceptance, etc.
3. Content analysis of the interaction in counseling.
4. Nonverbal aspects of group counseling.
5. Studies correlating physiological reactions (galvanic skin responses) with other types of client reaction.
6. Investigations of "counseling" and "therapy" groups as they compare to "problem solving," "task oriented," and other groups.
7. Survey investigations of counselor techniques in counseling, materials used, methods of determining outcome, etc.
8. Projects attempting to discover the effects of "counselor style" on group interaction and outcome.
9. Role structure in counseling groups.
10. Studies attempting to compare group and individual counseling success.
11. Investigations where the treatment process has been of different duration to determine if the number of group counseling sessions affect such factors as interaction and outcome.
12. Investigations of laboratory or artificial groups as they compare with "real" or field groups.
13. Studies designed to test certain counseling theories.
14. Research involving outcomes in which "group" counseling was used with specified subjects such as teacher, minority groups, racial group, "neurotics," and alcoholics.
15. Studies of "symptom reduction" in which the group members were given pre- and post measures to determine if they were less anxious, less hostile, etc.

Numerous investigations, of course, combine several of the listed categories into one design. The list presented here is far from exhaustive; other investigations have focused on other areas of study, but the researcher in group counseling may wish to use some of these catagories as a starting point in developing his own research project.

ASSESSMENT OF THE NEED FOR A STUDY

The group counseling researcher, once he has identified and defined the problem to be studied, must decide whether or not the project is sufficently worthy of investigation. The most elaborate and well-controlled research designs are of little value if the data that is gathered and the results of the study have no meaning. The question of just what constitutes a worthy design is an open one and involves such factors as the competence of the researcher, the probability of shedding new light on a given problem area, and the practicality of the obtained results.

In determining the need for a given study, the group counselor can formulate his own reasons for need—for example, he may wish to test his effectiveness as a group counselor by designing a study to show how he has been effective. The determinants of effectiveness will depend on the objectives of the study, the measured outcomes, counselor philosophy, and similar related factors. Regardless of how the counselor arrives at determining the need for a given research project, one of his basic steps should be a careful review of similar studies that have been reported in the literature. The articles included in this chapter are representative of the types of investigations already reported on which new studies may be built. Information on counseling methods, instruments employed to assess change, and statistical analysis can also be gathered from a review of such periodicals as *The Personnel and Guidance Journal, Journal of Counseling Psychology, International Journal of Group Psychotherapy, Psychological Abstracts, Review of Educational Research, Encyclopedia of Educational Research*, and other professional publications concerned with counseling research.

OBTAINING THE SAMPLE

The researcher in group counseling must identify the subjects involved in the study. To simply state that "high school students will be used" is not sufficient. Many factors, including age, sex, educational level, socioeconomic background, rural or urban residence, and occupation are a few of the common areas that researchers have attempted to control in the planning of an investigation.

Ohlsen identifies five problem areas of selecting subjects for treatment in a school setting, but his identification of problem areas would seem to be appropriate to the counselor-researcher in a variety of settings. According to Ohlsen, the common problem areas are:

1. obtaining enough subjects who understand and see value for the service for them;
2. being able to define the population from which the population was drawn and having enough information on the subjects to determine the extent to which the results of the study can be generalized;
3. securing enough information on the subjects to obtain data on the relevant variables prior to assigning subjects to experimental and control groups;
4. obtaining an adequate amount of the subject's time for pre, post, and follow-up testing; and
5. enlisting the cooperation of teachers and administration in order to provide adequate control of the subject's experiences outside of the experimental conditions [2, p. 456].

Since obtaining appropriate subjects for a study is an important early step in the development of an effective design, these problem areas should be carefully considered *prior* to the start of the study. It is not uncommon for clients to terminate counseling after a few sessions, or to be unavailable for post-testing. In addition, lack of teacher and administrator cooperation can bias the results of the study. Complete control of the subjects in the sample is not always possible. There will be many instances when unforseen happenings disrupt a carefully planned project. The best that the counselor-researcher can do is to study the possible problem areas involved in the study, consider alternate plans if certain subjects cannot be utilized, and prepare himself for the possibility that factors beyond his control may influence the subjects under investigation.

SELECTION OF THE STATISTICAL TECHNIQUE

The numerous statistical procedures available for use with different designs are too broad in scope to be considered here. The researcher should, however, decide how he is going to analyze the data before he starts to gather them. A basic knowledge of statistical theory is vital to the researcher in group counseling since the use of statistics enables the counselor to conduct either simple or complex investigations. In some studies the counselor may want only to describe the characteristics of a group in individuals he observes and use percents, averages or measures of variability. In other investigations he may wish to search for principles which have a degree of generality and apply to a much larger domain than the actual cases observed. In such cases, he must be familiar with various techniques of statistical inference. Excellent texts are now available to help the researcher with the selection of an appropriate test to fit his design [2, 3, 4, 5, 6, 8, 9].

ASSUMPTIONS AND LIMITATIONS

Most research projects make a number of assumptions that should be identified. For example, the counselor-researcher may have to assume that his selection of a sample was the most logical way to approach a study of group counseling, or he may have to assume that a selection of one instrument to measure change in a group of clients is more appropriate than another for his particular design. This is not to indicate that assumptions are made in a haphazard manner; on the contrary, a given assumption is generally made after careful consideration is given to the overall plan of the study and all possible approaches have been considered.

The counselor-researcher must also be aware of the limitations of his investigation. Small samples, data gathering devices of questionable reliability and validity, and the restrictions that may be imposed by the methods and procedures used for conducting the study are common limitation problems in counseling research. Since there are limitations involved in most research, it is important for the counselor to be aware of them in designing his own projects and reviewing the works of others.

DEFINITION OF TERMS

One of the major problems in much reported research is that the experimenter does not define adequately what he is doing and how. The term "counseling," for example, has been used in a variety of ways and one may find studies in "pre-college counseling," "vocational counseling," "personal counseling," "therapeutic counseling," "group counseling," and numerous others. Merely placing an adjective before the word counseling does not inform the reader of exactly what the counselor was doing when he was conducting the study. Other terms in counseling research such as "self," "anxiety," "dogmatism," and "underachiever" are commonly used with less than adequate definitions.

In studies of counseling the counselor must carefully define all words and phrases that may be vague or unclear to others. Unless the researcher can refer to a definition of terminology that is commonly accepted by those who read research, he may have to explain terms in enough detail to insure adequate reader understanding. This would seem to be especially true in group counseling since the relative newness of the approach as a whole can be confusing to the uninitiated reader. To date some researchers in group counseling have been less than clear in providing adequate definitions of the terminology utilized in their experiments.

COMMON INSTRUMENTS UTILIZED IN GROUP COUNSELING RESEARCH

Valid and reliable measuring instruments to test adequately experimental hypotheses are not readily available. In an effort to bring together some of the common devices used in both process and outcome studies in group and individual counseling, a list of some of the ways in which counselors have gathered data for counseling research is presented. No attempt will be made to classify the various data gathering devices as "good" or "bad" for counseling research since the use of any or all of them would depend upon the particular design and the type of data the researcher would like to gather. In addition complete evaluations of some of the data gathering devices are available in Buros' *Mental Measurement Yearbooks*, in various professional journals, and from the publishers of the instruments. The instruments listed in this section were gathered from an examination of over one hundred fifty research projects in group counseling and group psychotherapy. The reader will note that certain devices such as the *Rorschach* require special training and the counselor-researcher who has not had specific preparation in their use should not, of course, attempt to employ them in any project. Many devices in the following list, however, are available for counselor use.

1) *The A-S Reaction Study.* Boston: Houghton Mifflin Company.
2) *Study of Values.* Boston: Houghton Mifflin Company.
3) *The 16 Personality Factor Questionnaire.* Champaign, Illinois: Institute For Personality and Ability Testing.
4) *Edwards Personal Preference Schedule.* New York: The Psychological Corporation.
5) *California Psychological Inventory.* Palo Alto, California: Consulting Psychologists Press.
6) *The Guilford-Zimmerman Temperament Survey.* Beverly Hills, California: Sheridan Supply Company.
7) *Minnesota Multiphasic Personality Inventory.* New York: The Psychological Corporation.
8) *Kuder Preference Record—Personal, Vocational.* Chicago: Science Research Associates, Inc.
9) *Mooney Problem Check List.* New York: The Psychological Corporation.
10) *Rorschach.* New York: The Psychological Corporation.
11) *Thematic Apperception Test.* Cambridge, Massachusetts: Harvard University Press.
12) *California Test of Personality.* Monterey, California: Test Bureau.
13) *Thurstone Temperament Schedule.* Chicago: Science Research Associates.
14) *Barron Preference For Complexity Scale.* Barron, F., "Discovering the Creative Personality" In *The Behavioral Sciences and Education.* Princeton, New Jersey: College Entrance Examination Board, 1963, pp. 79–85.
15) *IPAT High School Personality Questionnaire.* Champaign, Illinois: Institute for Personality and Ability Testing.
16) *Rating Scale for Pupil Adjustment.* Chicago: Science Research Associates.
17) *SRA Youth Inventory.* Chicago: Science Research Associates.
18) *The Rotter Incomplete Sentences Blank.* New York: The Psychological Corporation.
19) *Bales Interaction Analysis.* Bales, Robert F., *Interaction Process Analysis: A Method for the Study of Small Groups.* Cambridge: Addison-Wesley, 1950.
20) *Child Behavior Rating Scale.* Los Angeles: Western Psychological Services.

Obviously this list is not all inclusive. Other studies have employed a variety of unpublished instruments. Investigations utilizing Q-sort techniques, client-self-reports, and researcher devised scales appear frequently in professional literature. Many of these hold promise for the counselor-researcher and a careful review of investigations in group counseling can uncover numerous other devices that may be appropriate to a particular design.

The readings presented in this chapter were selected to provide the reader with samples of both process and outcome research. The reader is invited to refer back to the principles of research discussed in the preceding pages as he reads and evaluates the articles which follow. The lead article by Walter Foley and Warren Bonney is somewhat different in that it suggests a developmental model that may be applied to counseling groups. Other selections deal with such questions as: What topics are discussed by children in group counseling? Are these topics likely to vary in different groups? Is it possible to evaluate and quantify some of the aspects of the group process? Are there recognizable themes in counseling discussions? Do client roles play a part in productive and unproductive counseling groups? Hopefully the readings will provide the prospective researcher with some knowledge of group counseling research and help him to plan and conduct projects on his own.

REFERENCES

1. Buros, O. K. *The Fifth Mental Measurements Yearbook* (Highland Park, New Jersey: The Gryphon Press, 1959, other editions were published in 1938, 1940, 1949, and 1953).

2. Edwards, A. L. *Experimental Design in Psychological Research* (New York: Rinehart, 1960).

3. Garrett, H. E. *Statistics in Psychology and Education* (New York: David McKay, 1962).

4. Hays, W. L. *Statistics for Psychologists* (New York: Holt, Rinehart and Winston, 1963).

5. Lindquist, E. F. *Design and Analysis of Experiments in Psychology and Education* (Boston: Houghton Mifflin Company, 1953).

6. Meyers, J. L. *Fundamentals of Experimental Design* (Boston: Allyn and Bacon, 1966).

7. Ohlsen, M. M. *Guidance Services in the Modern School* (New York: Harcourt, Brace and World, 1964).

8. Siegel, S. *Nonparametric Statistics for the Behavioral Sciences* (New York: McGraw-Hill, 1956).

9. Walker, Helen M., and Lev, J. *Statistical Inference* (New York: Holt, Rinehart and Winston, 1953).

28

A Developmental Model for
Counseling Groups*

Walter J. Foley

Warren C. Bonney

Students taking a course in Group Guidance participated in group counseling as an adjunct experience to the course. The counseling sessions
were tape recorded and later analyzed according to an affect-topic classification. This paper presents a theoretical discussion of the development
of one of the counseling groups. and the results of the analysis of the recorded group sessions.

This paper has two objectives: (a) to examine behavior in a group setting in terms of a theoretical model of group development and change; (b)
to present a method of analysis that delineates the developmental stages
of small groups.

SUBJECTS AND PROCEDURE

During the second semester of the 1962–63 academic year, students in
the group guidance course at the University of Illinois were given an opportunity to participate in group counseling. Participation in the counseling
groups was presented to the students as of value in itself as well as a prag-
matic corollary to the didactic presentation of group theory and technique.
The class was divided into three groups of six persons each. Since the three
groups followed very similar developmental patterns, the discussion and
analysis presented in this paper will be restricted to one of the groups.

The six members of the counseling group were students in the counselor
training program. There were three males and three females. One of the
students (male) was a doctoral candidate, while the other five members
were master's degree candidates. The counselor was a second-year doctoral
candidate and was supervised by a faculty member experienced in group
work. In the context of the group, the counselor was attempting to accomplish two goals: first, to create an atmosphere that would allow freedom of
interaction among the group members and provide an opportunity for

*Reprinted by permission of the author and publisher from *Personnel and Guidance
Journal*, XLIV (1966), 576–580.

therapeutic gain; second, to present a teaching experience, defined as play-back, to the group members. To accomplish this, each counseling session was tape-recorded. The playback was intended to be and was structured as that hour of the two-hour time period when significant portions of the tape of the preceding group session would be discussed in terms of group dynamics and counseling technique. This was to be done during each of the group meetings. In practice, two of the 11 playback periods were spent administering and analyzing the group-rating scale and a sociometric device discussed in this paper.

THE DEVELOPMENT OF THE GROUP

The development of the group will be discussed in terms of concepts derived from equilibrium theory [10] and the dynamic theory of George Bach [3]. The early meetings of the group follow a pattern best described as stages. The group members during the first stage, the *establishment stage,* reveal individual characteristics through verbal and nonverbal expression and receive feedback from other group members. By the end of this stage, usually one to four meetings, the role and status relationships at the top and bottom have polarized [9].

A counseling group, once through the establishment stage, enters into a *transition stage* that is climaxed by the members' acceptance that the goal of this group is unique. Early in this stage, they realize that the purpose for their existence as a group is to develop a situation that will allow for ther-apeutic experiences. This realization carries with it a negative connotation about discussing personal problems in groups based on past social exper-ience. There ensues a period characterized by a lack of involvement on the part of the group members for fear of violating the perceived social norm inhibiting the discussion of personal problems in groups. The incongruency is eventually resolved through the acceptance of a new norm that demands the discussion of personal concerns. In an earlier paper by the junior author [4], the transition period, Stage 2, in group counseling was described as an example of the operation of equilibrium theory.

The early socialization in therapy groups as described by Bach [3] and here called the establishment stage was, for the most part, nonexistent in the counseling group under discussion. Students in the group began to talk of problem areas and attitudes without the expected socialization period. They also discussed freely the personal meaning of the group and of signifi-cant people in their lives. While this was deemed highly desirable, it was also surprising in view of the theoretical development of groups. Since the group described in this paper did not experience the establishment period as the first stage, the transition period did not occur in the usual manner. In this sense the group process and development did not follow the expected stages of development.

THEORETICAL EXPLANATION

The first objective, that of providing an explanation for the nonoccur-
rence of the expected sequential periods in the early phase of group formation, is presented in terms of group pressures and group standards toward
conformity [5]. The concept of conformity in group counseling is dealt with
at greater length in another paper [4]. It was concluded that group members
understood and accepted the standard presented by the course instructor.
Support for this conclusion was found in the pre-group self-rating scale in
which "willingness to discuss personal concerns" was central to the group.
There was also evidence based upon the members having experienced: (a)
similarity of background in course work (the group guidance course occurs
late in the counselor-training sequence), (b) the nature of the group (counselors in training, (c) the initial contact with the group counselor (administration of the pre-counseling rating scale). These data led to the conclusion that the group analysis that did not show an establishment stage was
correct and also consistent with group development theory.

Counseling groups formed under more usual conditions (i.e., not as an
adjunct to a course in a counselor-training program) are presented with
essentially the same standard by the counselor, "discussion of personal
concerns," as were the trainee groups discussed here. Nevertheless, these
groups characteristically develop through the establishment and transition
stages. The difference found appears to be that the perceived authority of a
course instructor coupled with conditions (a) and (b) are not operant in the
more usual counseling situation. Festinger and Aronson [6] present a position
on group norms and standards that supports the conclusions stated and was
reflected by the data. The members were influenced by prior information
relating the aspiration and goal of becoming a counselor with the performance and relationships in the group situation.

The effect of group pressure to conform to the norm of discussing personal matters in the group context (shown in the analysis that follows) is
also consistent with the findings of Asch [2], as the situation had little ex-
trinsic structure in terms of the group members' past experiences and the
counselor offered little in the way of structure for the group situation. The
"majority effect" (following the behavior of other group members) described by Asch was seen to occur under these circumstances. The verbal
reports of the participants in the group presented during the playback portion of the experience supported this inference. The students reported that
they found themselves talking about personal concerns, even when their
desire was not to exhibit this verbal behavior.

ANALYSIS OF THE RECORDED INTERVIEW

In keeping with the second objective of the paper, a method of analyzing group tape material on the basis of content is presented as the vehicle

for delineating stages in the group. The method noted by Antenen [1] may be most briefly described as a sequential content-affect classification and yields acceptable interjudge reliability. Agreement among pairs of four judges for topic ranged from 76 per cent to 88 per cent; for affect from 74 per cent to 90 per cent. The sequential aspect of the analysis will identify the developmental stages of the group and will help to illustrate more clearly the dynamics discussed earlier in this paper.

SOURCE OF THE DATA

The topics classified were "self," "group," "significant others," and "things and ideas." "Things and ideas" are relatively superficial discussions at an intellectual rather than an affect level. The discussions may represent sincere problem-oriented concerns or, more likely, a defensive avoidance of personal involvement. The topic "group" mostly involved the discussion of group goals, processes by which the goals may be accomplished, and the norms or rules necessary for the group to develop in the desired direction. Talk about "self" is the expression of personal feelings, attitudes, and concerns. Talk about "significant others" usually involves the client's relationship with the significant others and is often as personal as talk about self. "Self" and "significant others" are the topics that most counselors believe contain the potential for therapeutic gain [8].

A frequency count of the verbal output of each group member was obtained from the tape recording of each session, and an affect-topic rating of each of the verbalizations of the group members was made and defined as: positive affect (the subject expresses positive feeling when discussing a topic), negative affect (the subject expresses negative affect when discussing a topic), no affect (the subject does not show a classifiable affect when discussing a topic). This material was treated in two ways for the group as a unit: the total classification of topic discussed across sessions and the affect classification by topic across sessions. The matrices were then pooled to obtain the total classification parameters.

TREATMENT OF THE DATA AND DISCUSSION OF RESULTS

The data on the group, in terms of total group parameters, consisted of the classification of verbalization for the four topics classified. A tabulation of these data is shown in Table 1.

The group members spent approximately 50 per cent of their verbalization on "self." This was taken as a gross indication of the relevance of the topic for the group. The second largest percentage of the group's verbal output was concerned with the "group" itself. This was followed by "significant others" and the least frequent, in terms of percentage of total talk, was "things and ideas."

Table 1

Verbal Output Tabulated by Significant Topic

Topic	Per Cent
Self	47.5
Group	29.3
Significant Others	18.9
Things and Ideas	4.2

The other classification of the group data of interest was the analysis of topic, stated as a percentage of the total use of the topic, over the course of the sessions. Figure 1 shows the topic "self" as it was classified with reference to affect classification.

The figure describes graphically the tendency of the group members to describe themselves positively at the beginning of the sessions, negatively during the middle sessions, and positively toward the termination of the group meetings. The pattern of talk about "self" throughout the sessions was consistent with the findings of the analysis of individual client-centered therapy reported by Rogers and Dymond [8].

An analysis of the affect classification showed that the topic "self" was discussed with positive affect 61 per cent of the time, and negatively 30 per cent of the time. The remaining 9 percent was classified as either no affect or as no describable affect.

An analysis across sessions of the relationship between topics clearly demonstrates the stage effect of a group's development. In Figure 2 the topics "self" and "significant others" are combined and compared with the topic "group." The percentages are total percentages without regard to sign, since the nature of the affect is not important for this purpose.

An inspection of Figure 2 reveals a median-level discussion of the topics "self" and "others" from Session 1 through 6, and a relatively high level of discussion of topic "group" from Session 2 through 5. This suggests that the topics "self" and "others" remained restricted and perhaps somewhat forced

Figure 1

Classification of the Use of the "Self" During 10 Group Sessions*

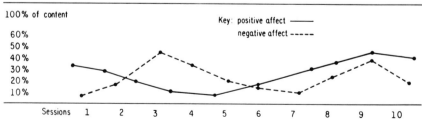

*Bernoulli's theorem based on total probability distributions shows differences greater than ±8% significant at .05 level [6]. The n's in Figures 1 and 2 are the number of topics discussed.

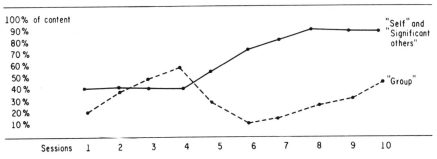

Figure 2
Classification of the Use of the Topic "Self" Plus "Significant
Others" Compared with the Use of the Topic "Group."

until the concerns about the group were resolved. The peak of "group" discussion at Session 3 represents a kind of transition period involving discussion of goals and procedures. But the high anxiety level that characterizes the transition stage following the usual establishment stage was not present. In a theoretical sense, the transition stage under the unique circumstances of the training situation involved group goals and norms, but was not typical of what has been presented as the transition stage in other writings.

SUMMARY

This analysis method and theoretical discussion are presented to aid in the structuring of group guidance courses in terms of the evidence on group development and to assist the counselor in understanding the behavior that occurs in groups under these unique circumstances through a topic affect classification system. Also, it was felt that students who participated in groups would be better able to cope with the dynamics of the group situation. The outcomes of a process analysis of group development in a training setting were most parsimoniously explained in terms of the operation of group standards and group pressures toward conformity.

REFERENCES

1. Antenen, Wayne. "Changes in Topic and Affect During Group Counseling: Its Relationship to Outcomes of Group Counseling." Unpublished dissertation, Univ. Illinois, 1963

2. Asch, S. E. "Effects of Group Pressure Upon the Modification and Distortion of Judgements." In D. Cartwright and A. Zander (Eds.), *Group Dynamics, Research and Theory* (Evanston, Ill.: Row, Peterson, 1962).

3. Bach, G. R. *Intensive Group Psychotherapy* (New York: Ronald Press, 1954).

4. Bonney, W. C. "Pressures Toward Conformity in Group Counseling," *Personnel Guid. J.* (1965), 43, 970–973.

5. Bonney, W. C., & Foley, W. J. "The Transition Stage in Group Counseling in Terms of Congruity Theory," *J. Counsel. Psych.* (1963), *10*, 136–138.

6. Festinger, L., & Aronson, E. "The Arousal and Reduction of Dissonance in Social Contexts," In D. Cartwright and A. Zander (Eds.), *Group Dynamics, Research and Theory* (Evanston, Ill.: Row, Peterson, 1962).

7. Hays, William L. *Statistics for Psychologists* (New York: Holt, Rinehart and Winston, 1963).

8. Rogers, Carl R., & Dymond, Rosalind F. (Eds.) *Psychotherapy and Personality Change* (Chicago: Univ. Chicago Press, 1954).

9. Sherif, M., & Sherif, C. W. *An Outline of Social Psychology* (New York: Harper, 1956).

10. Zojouc, R. "The Concepts of Balance, Congruity, and Dissonance," *Publ. Opin. Quart.* (1960), *24*, 280–296.

29

Behaviors in Group Guidance (Socio Process) and Group Counseling (Psyche Process)*

C. Gratton Kemp

Hypotheses are: (a) responses in group guidance will be superior (more in accord with its purposes) to those in group counseling; (b) responses in group counseling of open-minded will be superior to those of closed-minded. Criteria by Coffey were used in making comparisons. Subjects with scores on Dogmatism Scale Form E [2] of 120 and below, were considered "Open," of 150 and above "Closed." Ninety graduate students participated for 15 class sessions in groups of six. Ratings were made by three adults and one student observer. Student leaders described process. Results of comparisons gave significant support to each hypothesis. Responses in group guidance were superior (more in accord with the purposes of the activity) in all groups. "Open" subjects recognized problems; made more progress in group counseling.

Training in group methods presents several persistent problems, including those of definition, process, evaluation. Frequently asked are such questions as: What is the difference between group guidance (socio process) and group counseling (psyche process)? Should a practicum similar to that in individual counseling be required in group counseling?

Equally disturbing is the lack of experimental evidence of the cause and effect relationship of the leader and group in either group guidance or group counseling. Does a discussion group interested in the preparation for various occupations require a different kind of process and leadership than a group concerned with dislike of school and fear of failure? If so, what are the distinctive characteristics in process and functioning of the leader? Does the character of the belief systems of the members and leaders influence the progress of the group toward its goals?

These problems are explored in this study and some tentative conclusions formulated.

HYPOTHESES

1. That the responses in socio process would be superior (more in accord with its purposes) than those in psyche process.

*Reprinted by permission of the author and publisher from *Journal of Counseling Psychology*, X (1963), 373–377.

2. That the psyche process responses of those with "open minds" would be superior to those with "closed minds."

THE STUDY

A total of 90 graduate college students in three sections participated in the study in regularly scheduled courses in group process. Each section of approximately 30 was divided into groups of six students on the basis of the scores on the Dogmatism Scale Form E [2]. In the study those with low scores, 120 and below (Open Belief Systems) will be referred to as Group A, and those with high scores, 150 and above (Closed Belief Systems) as Group B. Eash six-student group met as a unit for a total of fifteen 50-minute periods.

Plans were made to use the first three meetings to become acquainted and accustomed to observers (their peers) and judges in each group. For the following six meetings a problem was chosen requiring a socio process, and for the remaining six meetings it was planned to use the psyche process in discussing personal concerns.

The socio process (group guidance) and psyche process (group counseling) as described by Coffey [1] were discussed. Descriptions of each process were formulated to act as a guide in determining progress (Figure 1). As a means of quantifying the degree and direction of change in the process a rating scale was developed (Figure 2).

Three judges observed and rated the members and leaders of each of the sub-groups of Group A and Group B. Through comparison and evalua-

Figure 1
Description of Socio Process and Psyche Process Indices.

Socio Process Behavior Indices

1. Establish the goal.
2. Supply relevant information.
3. Stimulate thought related to goal.
4. Listen to understand expressed ideas.
5. Encourage expression of problem-solving ideas.
6. Link together ideas associated with goal.
7. Reflect and clarify ideas when necessary.
8. Summarize as required.
9. Endeavor to reach a consensus.

Psyche Process Behavior Indices

1. Leave situation unstructured.
2. Listen to understand the meaning to each individual of his expression.
3. Link together expressions of feeling for further consideration.
4. Reflect and clarify feelings expressed, as necessary.
5. Avoid any attempt to reach a consensus.
6. Endeavor to further feeling-oriented responses rather than idea-oriented responses.
7. Proceed at members' rate without encouragement or reward for verbalization.
8. Expect differences on both the ideational and feeling levels.
9. Accept strong expressions of personal feeling as acceptable material and useful in the process.

Figure 2
Group Process Rating Scale.

Response No.	Kind		Category*		Unable to Determine
	Socio	Psyche	Socio	Psyche	
....	....	....	....	....	....
....	....	....	....	....	....
....	....	....	....	....	....

*Category refers to those listed on the Behavior Indices Sheet.

When response does not correspond to any of the categories, list in the column under "Unable to Determine."

tion of ratings during the first three sessions, the judges' ratings reached a correlation of .92.

A student also observed and rated each group using the same criteria as the judges, and made notes regarding the progress of each group. Student observers and student leadership rotated from member to member. Each leader, following his session, made a report in writing on what took place with reference to the members and himself. Neither the judges or the students knew the rationale for the establishment of the subgroups.

A comparison was made of the judges' ratings of the character of the members' responses of Group A and Group B. A second comparison was made of the judges' ratings in the character of the leaders' responses in Groups A and B. A third comparison was made of the behavior indices of the two groups in each category of the socio and psyche process, as given in Figure 1. A content analsysis was made of the written observations of the observers and leaders in each of the subgroups.

RESULTS

1. In socio process or group guidance discussion there was no significant difference between those with Open and Closed Belief Systems with reference to the number of socio process and psyche process behavior indices (Table 1).

Table 1

Comparison of the Number of Socio and Psyche Process Behavior Indices of Groups with Open and Closed Belief Systems Engaged in Socio Process or Group Guidance (N = 60)

Behavior Indices	Belief Systems	
	Open	Closed
Socio	171	175
Psyche...	5	2
Undetermined	4	3

.01 = 9.21
X^2 = 1.60

2. In the psyche process or group counseling there was a significant difference at the .001 level between those with Open and Closed Belief Systems with reference to the number of psyche-process behavior indices. Those with Open Belief Systems had a larger number of psyche-process behavior indices (Table 2).

Table 2

Comparison of the Number of Socio and Psyche
Process Behavior Indices of Groups with Open
and Closed Belief Systems Engaged in Psyche
Process or Group Counseling (N = 60)

Behavior Indices	Belief Systems	
	Open	Closed
Socio	79	90
Psyche..	91	33
Undetermined	10	2
X^2 = 25.76		
.001 = 13.82		

3. In group guidance discussion there was no significant difference in the number of socio and psyche behavior indices of the leaders (Table 3). In group counseling the leaders with Open Belief Systems had significantly more (.001 level) psyche-process behavior indices than the leaders with Closed Belief Systems (Table 4).

Table 3

Comparison of the Number of Socio and Psyche
Process Behavior Indices of Leaders with Open
and Closed Belief Systems Engaged in Socio
Process or Group Guidance (N = 60)

Behavior Indices	Belief Systems	
	Open	Closed
Socio	48	52
Psyche	8	6
Undetermined	4	2
X^2 = 1.12		
.05 = 5.99		

Table 4

Comparison of the Number of Socio and Psyche
Process Behavior Indices of Leaders with Open
and Closed Belief Systems Engaged in Psyche
Process or Group Counseling (N = 60)

Behavior Indices	Belief Systems	
	Open	Closed
Socio	12	28
Psyche..	35	10
Undetermined	3	2
X^2 = 19.41		
.001 = 13.82		

4. A comparison of the number of responses in each category in socio process or group guidance discussions indicates no significant difference between those with open and closed minds (Table 5). The largest single difference was in category 7, (reflect and clarify ideas when necessary). More activity was shown by those with open minds.

Table 5

Comparison of the Number of Behavior Indices in Each Category for Groups with Open and Closed Belief Systems Engaged in Socio Process or Group Guidance (N = 60)

Belief Systems							Categories		
	1	2	3	4	5	6	7	8	9
Open	14	16	18	19	17	15	27	23	22
Closed	18	20	16	18	21	17	17	22	27
$X^2 = 1.58$									
$.05 = 5.99$									

5. A comparison of the number of responses for the open and closed-minded groups under each category for the psyche process or group counseling indicates a significant difference at the .01 level between those with open and closed minds (Table 6). The closed-minded groups felt the need for more structure (Category 1). They did not listen as frequently to get the

Table 6

Comparison of the Number of Behavior Indices in Each Category of the Psyche Process for Groups with Open and Closed Belief Systems Engaged in Psyche Process or Group Counseling (N = 60)

Belief Systems							Categories		
	1	2	3	4	5	6	7	8	9
Open	12	14	10	8	7	11	6	8	15
Closed	2	2	5	2	3	5	5	6	3
$X^2 = 9.67$									
$.01 = 9.21$									

covert meaning of responses (Category 2), and much less frequently accepted strong expressions of personal feeling of other members (Category 9).

OBSERVER REPORTS

The observer-members in Group A (Open Belief Systems) described in their written observations the difficulties that were encountered in trying to become a psyche group. They concluded that the members frequently discussed ideas in the third person safely removed from the exploration of their own feelings. However, they agreed that gradual progress was made in the overcoming of their inhibitions which made it difficult to enter into group counseling.

The observer-members in Group B (Closed Belief Systems) apparently perceived the members as engaging in psyche process. Their written observations disagreed with the judges who decided that most of their comments were of a socio-process character. The observers were of the opinion that the difficulties of the members focused on the better sharing of time.

LEADER REPORTS

The leaders in Group A in their written observations expressed difficulty in resisting the inclination to motivate the members toward some conclusions, in trying to perform the linkage function, in clarifying comments and especially in enduring the ambiguity of the situation and the lack of a definite goal.

The leaders of Group B in their written observations indicated no concern about achieving a psyche-process group. They expressed some uneasiness that the discussion "got out of hand," and that everyone didn't have an opportunity to contribute.

DISCUSSION

1. In socio process (group guidance) all members' responses were more useful in the attainment of the purposes of the activity than in group counseling.

2. In psyche process (group counseling) the responses of those with Open Belief Systems furthered the purposes of the activity significantly more than the responses of those with Closed Belief Systems. The open-minded apparently experience less difficulty in expressing their personal feelings and in relating to one another in a manner which induces release of emotion and insight concerning personality dynamics. In the group counseling, those with Closed Belief Systems changed very little the kinds of responses they used in group guidance.

3. Attitudes and beliefs of members and leaders influence the form and content of interaction. Those with Open Belief Systems were apparently more aware of the inability of the members and themselves to relate fully on a psyche-process level. They also tried to create for one another a more accepting permissive climate. Those with Closed Belief Systems did not apparently question the character of their interaction but assumed that they were relating on a psyche-process level. Their concerns resembled those of members engaged in a socio-process interaction.

It might be reasoned that since engaging fully in psyche-process interactions requires the endurance of ambiguity both in means and goals, and also carried with it an unpredictable degree of threat, those with Closed

Belief Systems avoid this type of involvement by various means such as withdrawal, disregard, or the assumption that it does not differ from any other form of discussion.

IMPLICATIONS

In socio process (group guidance) members respond more in accordance with the demands of the situation than in psyche process (group counseling).

In psyche process those with "open minds" can be expected to benefit more than those with "closed minds."

Those with "closed minds" apparently avoid the necessary personal involvement for beneficial results from group counseling.

REFERENCES

1. Coffey, H. S. "Socio and Psyche Group Process: Integrative Concepts," *J. Soc. Issues* (1952), **8**, 65–74.

2. Rokeach, M. *The Open and Closed Mind* (New York: Basic Books, 1960), Chapter 4.

30

Problems Discussed by Underachievers in Different Treatment Groups*

Betty J. Bosdell

John Teigland

Adolescence is usually described as a period with unique problems resulting from the physical changes of puberty, the increased expectations and different demands placed upon the adolescent and his actions by society, as well as the adolescent's changing expectations of himself.

Problems of adolescence are frequently seen as typical or idiosyncratic. Gardner suggests that the majority of the problems of adolescents are normal reactions or phases without any serious emotional maladjustment arising from the problem situation. These normal problems faced by all adolescents in their striving for adult status provide a basis for observation of the specific adolescent's problems.

Bell [1] in one of the early studies on adolescent problems reported that young people not attending school viewed economic security, educational, vocational, home, personal, and social problems as being important.

Carlson and Sullenger [3] and Garrison and Cunningham [5] among others found that problems concerning school, future plans, home life, social relations, boy-girl relations, health, and religion were of importance to high school students.

Frankel [4] and Phelps [9] in their study of high ability high school boys found that the underachievers were less interested in school, had fewer problems in the social relations area, and were less active and less interested in future educational plans. Bresse [2] reported that underachievers manifested greater feelings of insecurity, expressed greater hostility, and were more concerned with physical characteristics. Kimball [6] and Morrow and Wilson [8] studied the home atmosphere of underachievers. Kimball found that underachievers often had negative relationships with their father. Morrow and Wilson suggested that the home atmosphere of underachievers did not foster academic achievement.

*Reprinted by permission of the author and publisher from *The School Counselor,* 4 (1965), 222–227.

In terms of self-perception, Shaw, Edson, and Bell [11] found differences in self-concept between achievers and underachievers. Male underachievers had more negative feelings about themselves while female underachievers tended to have ambivalent feelings about themselves.

The identification of the concerns of underachievers in the above studies was approached through studying their responses to personality instruments and questionnaires.

This study was concerned with ascertaining the types of problems that underachievers discussed in interview situations. Statistical comparisons were utilized to determine: (1) if different types of problems were discussed in different treatments (individual counseling, group counseling, and study skills groups) and, (2) if the frequency with which problems were discussed differed between treatments.

PROCEDURE

For this study tapes were randomly selected from a pool of tapes. They were analyzed for five males and five females who had received individual counseling, three counseling groups, and three study skill groups. Individual counseling sessions were twenty-five to thirty minutes long. Group counseling and study skill sessions were for fifty-five minutes, the length of the class period. Eighteen interview hours were analyzed for each treatment: individual (boys), individual (girls), group counseling, and study skills instruction. The results of this study are based on seventy-two hours of tape analysis. For each counseling group and for each study skills group an average of six tapes was analyzed; for individual clients an average of seven tapes was analyzed.

Ten different counselors served as the counselors for the individual and group sessions with eight of these counselors having both individual and group sessions.

Judges (project research assistants who had had secondary school coun-

Table 1

Frequency of Problems Within Treatments

Treatment	Problem Categories									
	SP	FR	RO	PP	FP	AP	TOT.		df	P
Study Skills	49	5	0	0	18	0	72	157.16	5	.001
Group Counseling	63	8	5	2	14	14	106	171.23	5	.001
Individual Girls	33	25	16	17	13	13	117	24.44	5	.001
Individual Boys	52	16	12	20	20	20	140	42.27	5	.001
Total	197	54	33	39	65	47	435			
Total	= 100.31 with 15 df, P			.001						

SP School Problems   PP Personal Problems
FR Family Relations   FP Future Problems
RP Relationships with Others AP Activity Problems

seling experience) listened to the tapes. When a problem was discussed by the student, whether it was introduced by him initially or whether it followed a counselor lead which the student picked up and discussed, the problem was listed by the judge. After all tapes had been analyzed in this fashion, the problems were tallied according to their area and specific sub-topic. The frequency of a specific problem was determined by the number of times that problem was brought up in the treatment condition. The categories used for classification were ascertained from the tapes and the related research. The Mooney Problem Checklist [7] and the S R A Youth Inventory [10] served as guidelines for the classification of problems. The classification system used for the problems of underachievers is as follows:

I. School Problems
  1. Teachers
  2. Other Students
  3. Course Work
  4. Tests
  5. Grades
  6. Studying Habits
  7. School Activities
  8. Problems with Memory
  9. Interest and Motivation
  10. School Regulations
II. Family Relations
  1. Father
  2. Mother
  3. Siblings
  4. Home environment
  5. Parental Control
III. Relationship with Others
  1. Peers
  2. Adults
  3. Popularity
  4. Social impressions
  5. Relatives
  6. Dating and sex problems
IV. Personal Problems
  1. Insecure and nervous
  2. Unhappy
  3. Behavior problems
  4. Self-concept
  5. Lazy

6. Shyness
7. Physical appearance
V. Future Problems
1. College
2. Vocational choice
3. Service (Military)
4. Marriage
5. General outlook
6. Uncertainty of future
VI. Activity Problems
1. Car
2. Social Activities
3. Working
4. Having money

RESULTS

The results of the analysis of tapes for problems areas and frequency with which the problems were discussed was analyzed using chi-square. The chi-squares for each treatment across all problems are found in Table 2.

Table 2

Frequency of Problems Across Treatments

Problem Categories	Treatment Conditions							
	GC	SS	IG	IB	TOT.	X^2	df	P
School Problems............	49	63	33	52	197	9.36	3	.05
Family Relationships	5	8	25	16	54	17.85	3	.001
Others – Relationships....	0	5	16	12	33	18.51	3	.001
Personal Problems...........	0	2	17	20	39	32.07	3	.001
Future Problems..............	18	14	13	20	65	2.01	3	.80
Activity Problems	0	14	13	20	47	37.78	3	.001
Total	72	106	117	140	435			

GC Group Counseling   IG Individual Counseling (Girls)
SS Study Skills   IB Individual Counseling (Boys)

The significance of the main chi-square indicates that the types and numbers of problems brought up is significantly different (P.001) for the various treatment conditions.

Individual chi-square analyses for each treatment across all problems involving school experience with some discussion of problems related to future plans. It was the only experimental treatment condition in which students did not discuss problems relating to activities.

Similarly, those underachieving adolescents in group counseling spent the majority of their time discussing school problems. Future problems and activity problems were secondary problems, with problems in other areas being discussed infrequently.

The types of problems discussed in individual counseling by the under-achieving girls were more evenly distributed, although the results were still significant. School problems arose most frequently, followed by family re-lationships. Personal problems and relationships with others were discussed slightly more frequently than were future problems and activity problems.

Boys in individual counseling stressed their school problems, discussing with less frequency their problems related to personal matters, the future, and activities. Relationship problems with family or others received less emphasis than other problem categories.

The chi-square analyses for each problem area across all treatment groups indicated some significant differences.

Future problems were considered to the same extent by counselees in all treatment conditions. Although school problems were discussed significantly more than any other category of problems by all counselees, it was con-sidered to a slightly greater extent by those in the group treatments (coun-seling and study skills) than by those in individual counseling.

Problems in family relationships were considered proportionately more times by the individual counselees, particularly by the girls, with group treatment counselees discussing this problem area with less frequency.

Greatest concern in the area of problems with relationships with others was shown by the girls in individual counseling. The study skills group did not discuss problems in this area.

Personal problems were discussed frequently by the individual coun-selees and rarely by those students in the group treatments.

Problems relating to working, social activities, having a car and money were discussed more frequently by boys in individual counseling than by students in the other treatment conditions.

DISCUSSION

It is quite apparent on the basis of the chi-square analyses that students participating in different treatments discuss different kinds of problems. Whether it can be assumed that the treatment condition evoked different responses is not determinable from the data. However, the data do indicate that students in the counseling treatments discussed problems that were of a more personal nature than did students in the study skills groups. The goals of study skills groups, whether a class or a small group, usually tend to be oriented toward educational and vocational goals related to the present and future. This would probably account for the lack of the "per-sonal orientation" in the study skills groups and for the concentration on problems relating to school and future plans. Although there is an element of personal investment in these topics, discussion of them tends to be more topic oriented.

Students in group counseling tended to resemble more closely students in study skills groups than students in individual counseling. Although problems of the more personal nature were discussed, it was not with the same frequency as in individual counseling. It would appear that the underachievers in group counseling were reticent to discuss personal problems. From the tape analysis it can be postulated that the different levels of readiness on the part of the clients, as well as the proficiency of the counselors, were partially responsible for the topical emphasis in the counseling groups. Many references can be found concerning the values of group counseling in helping adolescents to discuss their personal problems; however, the present study would raise a question as to whether this might be from a more topical frame of reference than from an intrapersonal one.

Problems concerning school, teachers, grades, and other facets of the educational setting were the most predominant topic of discussion for all the treatments. The emphasis in these discussions usually was more "What's wrong with them?" than "How am I responsible for these school difficulties?" Since the students were told initially that the school felt they could be doing better in their school work, this undoubtedly influenced the preponderance of school problems discussion. However, since other problem topics were discussed in initial interviews and the students, not the counselors, usually initiated the topics relating to school problems, the investigators felt the results reflected a real concern on the part of the underachievers. Specific topics such as "lazy teachers' unfairness to individual students," "tests not covering material we had in class," "dull classes," "and subjects not related to my plans," were frequently discussed. The manuals and norm tables of the two inventories revealed that the majority of senior high school youth did not consider such things as predominate problems. The underachievers in this study reflected much greater concern with such topics.

Problems relating to future plans, checked frequently by the inventory's norm groups, were also of concern to the underachievers. The specific emphasis, however, differs somewhat with the underachiever's major concern being his ability to get into college, and finding a suitable vocation while the norm groups indicated concern with need for actual information concerning their future plans.

From the review of the literature and the data obtained in the present study it would appear that although underachievers have the same types of problems as other adolescents, they differ from other adolescents in intensity and emphasis.

SUMMARY

An analysis was made of a random sampling of tapes representing group counseling, study skills instruction, individual counseling (boys) and individual counseling (girls) to ascertain the type of problems and frequency with which these problems were discussed.

Chi-square analyses of the data indicated a significant difference (P .001) in the types of problems and frequency with which they were discussed between the various conditions. Individual chi-square analyses for all treatment groups across all problems were significant beyond the .001 level. Chi-square analyses also showed significant differences for the frequency with which problems in the areas of family relationships, relationships with others, personal problems and problems relating to activities were discussed in the different treatments.

Problems of a personal orientation were discussed more frequently by students in the counseling treatments as compared to study skills and more· so by those in individual counseling than in group counseling.

The investigators concluded that although types of problems are common for all adolescents, the underachiever differs in the intensity and emphasis with which he views some of these problems.

REFERENCES

1. Bell, H. M. "Youth Tell Their Own Story," *Amer. Council Educ.* (Washington, D. C.: 1938), 249–255.

2. Bresse, C. W. "Affective Factors Associated With Academic Underachievement in High School Students," *Dissertation Abstr.* (1957), 17, 90.

3. Carlson, M. B., & Sullenger, T. E. "A Study of Certain Areas in Which High School Youth Desire Counseling," *J. Educ. Sociol.* (1958), 31, 179–182.

4. Frankel, E. "A Comparative Study of Achieving and Underachieving High School Boys of High Intellectual Ability," *J. Educ. Res.* (1960), 53, 172–180.

5. Garrison, K. C., & Cunningham, B. W. "Personal Problems of Ninth Grade Pupils," *School Review* (1952), 60, 30–33.

6. Kimball, B. "Completion Technique in a Study of Scholastic Underachievement," *J. Consult. Psychol.* (1952), 26, 353–358.

7. Mooney, R. L., & Gordon, L. V. *Mooney Problem Check List* (New York: Psychological Corporation, 1950).

8. Morrow, W. R., & Wilson, R. C. "Family Relations of Bright High-achieving and Under-achieving High School Boys," *Child Develpm.* (1961), 32, 501–510.

9. Phelps, M. O. "An Analysis of Certain Factors Associated with Underachievement Among High School Students," *Dissertation Abstr.* (1957), 17, 306–307.

10. Remmers, H. H., Shimberg, B., & Drucker, A. J. *Examiner Manual, SRA Youth Inventory* (Chicago: Science Research Associates Inc., 1953).

11. Shaw, M. C., Edson, K., & Bell, H. M. "The Self-concept of Bright Underachieving High School Students as Revealed by an Adjective Check List," *Personnel Guid. J.* (1960), 39, 193–196.

31

*To What Extent Is Affect a Function of Topic and Referent in Group Counseling?** *

W. W. Wigell

M. M. Ohlsen

This paper presents a content analysis of the interactions within a counseling group of eight gifted, underachieving adolescents; the interactions were classified in terms of topic, referent, and affect. During the first few sessions these clients discussed authority figures, "doing things," and sex, and during the last few sessions they discussed peers, group members, self, and family, more than one would expect by chance.

It is not sufficient to demonstrate that some clients can be helped by group counseling.[1] The counselor also must try to understand why clients behave as they do during counseling. One approach to further understanding of their behavior is content analysis of the interactions. Until quite recently the interactions between a counselor and his clients were accessible only to the counselor. With the introduction of the electronic recorder all of this was changed. In addition to having an accurate record of the interactions for careful analysis, it is now possible to increase the objectivity of these judgments by having someone other than the counselor study and classify the interactions.

This paper presents a content analysis of the interactions within a counseling group of eight ninth-grade, gifted underachievers in terms of topic, referent, and affect. The senior author classified these interactions solely on the basis of tape recordings and transcripts of the recordings. He had no other contacts with these adolescents. None of the pre-, post-, or follow-up data were made available to him.

*Reprinted by permission of W. W. Wigell, M. M. Ohlsen, and the *American Journal of Orthopsychiatry*, 32 (1962), 728–735. Copyright, the American Orthopsychiatric Association, Inc. Reproduced by permission. The research reported herein was supported through the Cooperative Research Program of the Office of Education, U.S. Department of Health, Education, and Welfare. This paper summarizes a doctoral dissertation completed at the University of Illinois by the senior author under the direction of the junior author.
[1]The investigators chose the term group counseling rather than group psychotherapy to indicate that they were treating normal pupils in a nonmedical setting.

Pioneer work in the analysis of the recorded interview was done by Rogers [21], Covner [8], and Porter [19]. Since this early work, Rogers and his students have continued to make some of the most significant contributions to the study of the counseling process: Curran [9], Kaufman and Raimy [13], Peres [18], Raimy [20], Rogers and Dymond [22], Rogers, Kell, and McNeil [23], Seeman [24], Sheerer [26], Snyder [27, 28], and Stock [29]. A similar study by Gorlow, Hoch, and Telschow [11] also was a direct outgrowth of several studies by Rogers and his students.

About this same time Dollard and Mowrer [10] developed their Discomfort-Relief Quotient on the theory that responses are incited by drives and reinforced by drive reduction. They had hoped to measure the tension experienced by clients. Murray [15] developed a system for studying motivation and conflict during psychotherapy which included categories for classifying both the client's and the therapists' behavior. Since it is not the primary purpose of this paper to review the literature, only a few of the most relevant studies are cited. For a thorough review of the literature on content analysis of counseling and psychotherapy, the investigators recommend that of Auld and Murray [2]. On the basis of their review of 99 of the most important studies, they concluded that the content-analysis systems developed up to that time (1955) were not adequate to the task of marking out the main variables in therapy and that most of the studies relied too much on the opinions presented by clients and neglected the clients' unconscious motives. They also said: "Content systems are inevitably criticized for what they leave out. The practicing clinician often feels that the measured part of the therapeutic transaction is pitifully small alongside the complex of stimuli that he senses as a participant observer. Yet it seems unfair to expect any single content-analysis system to describe all of this complex situation."

For a study of interactions and for defining scoring units within a counseling group, significant contributions also have been made by Bales [3] and Cartwright and Zander [7] in their studies of the group process; by Berelson [4] and Lasswell and Leites [14] in their studies in communications.

Though some counselors and psychotherapists have said that it does not make any difference what clients discuss, many believe that it does. In fact, many believe that best results are achieved when clients talk about themselves and the topics that disturb them most. In general, Talland's and Clark's research [30] supports this notion. They found that their patients rated as most helpful the topics which were most disturbing. Winder and Hersko [31] also found that themes could be identified from the topics, attitudes, and feelings expressed and that certain themes were discussed significantly more often during the early phases of treatment, others during the later phases. From these studies the investigators concluded that it would be useful to study the relationship between referent, topic, and affect as they are revealed in counseling interactions.

The data for this paper were obtained from a larger study described by Ohlsen and Proff [17]. The present study was based upon tape recordings and typed transcripts of material from one of four groups of gifted, under-achieving ninth-graders included in the original study. It also was one of three groups that made significant growth during counseling, but not one of the two productive groups described by Noble, Ohlsen, and Proff [16].

METHOD

For classification purposes the data on the tape recordings were divided into grammatical clauses. Three steps were involved in the process of classifying the interactions for each tape: 1) the observer listened to the recording to obtain a global reaction to the counseling session; 2) he divided the interactions into scoring units and transcribed them; and 3) he classified all interactions in terms of affect, topic, and referent while listening to the recording and reading the transcriptions. In making transcriptions, articles and conjunctions that were judged to be unessential were omitted. Impressions obtained from such things as tone of voice and earlier interactions were added parenthetically to clarify meaning and feeling. The comments made by the counselor, though not a part of this study, were placed in context in capital letters to distinguish them from those made by the clients.

In general, the nine referent categories were based upon the first, second, and third person pronouns and the persons, places, and things that were used as subjects. The four affect categories were positive, negative, ambivalent, and no affect. After considerable revision, eleven topic categories were defined: 1) self; 2) self and others; 3) members of the counseling group, 3a) the counselor; 4) peers; 5) a client's family; 6) authority figures such as teachers and other members' parents; 7) other persons; 8) things, places, and ideas; 9) doing something or manipulating things; 10) sex, courtship, and dating; and 11) diversional activities—e.g., singing ditties. Though the topic categories were similar to the referent categories, they were different because they referred to the topic being discussed rather than to the actor (subject of the sentence).

Since identification of the speaker frequently was not possible from tape recordings, all the clients' interactions for each session were combined and analyzed as a group. In the fourteenth session this group became concerned about closure. They achieved closure by the end of the fifteenth session. Therefore, the sixteenth session was not used. The fifteen sessions utilized were placed in random order prior to the analysis to avoid preconceived judgments from listening to the tapes in sequential order. After the tapes were analyzed, they were returned to their original order and the coded data derived from them were placed in five groups of three sessions each. Progress was predicted in terms of these subdivisions.

A preliminary analysis of the material included a category for unclassifi-able data for each of the three dimensions. Interactions were so classified when they were garbled by mumbling or by several clients speaking at one time. In the final analysis of the data, these categories were ignored.

After necessary revisions were made in the directions and definition of the categories was improved, satisfactory percentages of agreement between judges were obtained. A tape recording from one of the other three groups was used to evaluate the reliability of the procedure. After the person who classified the interactions used the prescribed procedure for one recorded session, he provided two other judges with a written description of the procedure and answered their questions. When they completed their clas-sification of interactions, the investigators found that agreement between pairs of judges was not satisfactory (it varied from 72% agreement on referent to 22% on affect). Two revisions of the affect and topic categories produced some improvement, but not adequate reliability between judges. At this point the entire research staff (the two principal investigators, the four postdoctoral research associates, and two graduate assistants), employed on the project at that time, met as a group and discussed each instance in which the judges disagreed. As a result of this work, the categories were regrouped and redefined. With these new definitions for the categories three judges classified the interactions and obtained the following percent-ages of agreements between pairs of judges: referent: 89.8 to 94.2; affect: 75.8 to 78.8; and topic: 81.1 to 85.0.

The following hypotheses were tested: As counseling progresses 1) cli-ents talk increasingly about themselves and other group members and make fewer references to out-of-group persons, places, and things; 2) interactions reflect less negative and ambivalent affect and more positive affect; 3) clients discuss fewer topics; and 4) clients make more positive self-references (and positive references to other group members) and less negative self-refer-ences. In all the previous research, perhaps Gorlow, Hoch, and Telschow [11] contributed most to the development of these hypotheses.

RESULTS[2]

The way in which the interactions were distributed among the various categories would perhaps not be accounted for by chance more often than once in a hundred times (chi square test). When, however, the distributions of the interactions were compared with the predicted patterns, the investi-gators rejected most of the hypotheses stated above.

Though there were almost no categories showing a smooth pattern of increasing or decreasing use throughout counseling, the clients did come

[2]These results were summarized in thirteen tables which can be obtained from the junior author. They also can be found in reference 17 (pages 104–117).

to talk increasingly more about themselves and other members of the group and to talk less about doing things. The extent to which certain other categories were used is worth noting (and explains why chance did not account for some of the differences observed).

1. From the group of ten categories for referent, clients used one of the following about 60 per cent of the time: self, other members of the group, and peers. The sentence subject most commonly used was "I" or some other specific reference to self.
2. During the first few sessions authority figures, doing things, and sex received more attention than could be accounted for by chance. In the last few sessions clients focused significantly more of their attention on the topics peers, self, group members, and family.
3. Throughout the counseling period, these adolescents expressed primarily negative affect and discussed impersonal topics with which they associated little or no affect more often than one would expect by chance.
4. The analysis of the relationship between affect and referent produced few significant differences which were systematic and meaningful. Throughout the first twelve sessions, clients did discuss themselves with more positive affect than could be accounted for by chance.
5. Though examination of the relationship between topic and affect suggests the extreme unlikelihood that chance could account for the observed differences, few meaningful patterns stood out. The discussion of authority figures was an exception. In the initial counseling sessions the clients discussed authority figures with significantly more negative affect, later discussed them with both significantly more positive and negative affect, and finally discussed them with more positive affect than one would expect by chance. Whenever they discussed authority figures, they usually discussed them with affect. Except for the first few sessions, they also discussed the topic family with affect. Clients did discuss the topic self with more positive affect than one would expect by chance.

DISCUSSION

First, the point should be made that interactions can be classified, with satisfactory reliability, in terms of referent, affect and topic. Referent appeared to contribute very little to understanding the counseling process. The other two hold some promise for further research.

These investigators question the common procedure of combining the interactions from several counseling sessions. For example, some of the positive changes noted in the last half of the fourteenth session and in the fifteenth session were at least partially concealed within the block of the last three sessions. Moreover, the therapeutic climate within a group of young adolescents is very sensitive to changes in individual clients. It can be influenced markedly by the absence of one who impedes or inhibits the therapeutic process for others [12]. These investigators also concluded that the therapeutic process can be enhanced by the presence of a productive member or one who has experienced some unusual success which he perceives to be an outgrowth of counseling. Furthermore, they concluded that growth of clients is an individual matter and therefore should be studied as such. These clients' growth, which could be detected by content analysis of interactions, suggests that individuals grow at different rates and that behavior changes which mean growth for one may not mean growth for another. When, therefore, one combines the interactions for several sessions, one runs the risk of disguising significant data.

Shaw and Grubb [25] correctly concluded that underachievement is not a surface phenomenon which is easily modified. The high proportion of negative affect, even in the last few sessions, suggests that counseling was terminated too early. Broedel, Ohlsen, Proff, and Southard [6] concluded from their analysis of test data and observers' reports that at least some of the clients who had made substantial growth were still learning to live with the new self, learning to communicate this new self to others, and helping other persons important to them to live with this new self.

Broedel, Ohlsen, Proff, and Southard [6] also concluded that these adolescents were hostile youths who used poor school achievement as one way of expressing antisocial or nonconforming attitudes. Although they had a chance to refuse counseling when it was offered, they did not refuse it, and comments they made during counseling indicated that some of them had been coerced into participating by their parents. Perhaps this explains why at first clients often offered verbal assurances of their personal worth. Eventually, however, a climate was developed in which they learned to express their real feelings. Whether they enter counseling passive and seemingly compliant, or overtly hostile, many adolescents probably have misgivings about it, especially when the counselor, or some other adult, initiates counseling. The experiences of both Ackerman [1] and Berman [5] support this notion. Ackerman found that adolescents were profoundly vulnerable to criticism from without; Berman found that they were often brought to therapy against their will and made to feel that whatever was the difficulty they were the culprits.

Finally, the investigators question whether it is possible to identify and to classify accurately some of the most significant interactions without an accurate record of nonverbal as well as verbal behavior. They agree with Auld and Murray [2] that those who try to understand the main variables in counseling must take cognizance of the clients' unconscious motives as well as their opinions and verbal interactions. To do this requires an accurate video record as well as an audio one. Katz, Ohlsen, and Proff [12] concluded that raters who observe kinescopes or video tapes have many advantages over observer teams who are forced to make judgments while observing the actual counseling process. The primary advantages are that raters can work independently and can control the flow of stimuli. They can stop the flow of stimuli when they fall behind in classifying behavior of clients, and even replay parts of the record when too many things have happened at once for them to make and record judgments. For at least some research, this means that kinescopes or video tapes must replace tape recordings.

SUMMARY

This paper presents a content analysis of the interactions within a counseling group of eight ninth-grade, gifted underachievers in terms of topic, referent, and affect. These interactions were classified by the senior author solely on the basis of recordings and transcripts of these recordings.

Though chance rarely accounted for the way in which the interactions were distributed among the various categories, the distributions of the interactions usually failed to fall into the predicted patterns; consequently, the investigators were forced to reject their hypothesis that as counseling progressed the clients would: 1) talk increasingly about themselves and the members of the group and make fewer references to out-of-group persons, places, and things; 2) express less negative and ambivalent affect and more positive affect; 3) discuss increasingly fewer topics; and 4) make more positive and less negative self-references. However, these clients did come to talk increasingly about themselves and the other members of the group and to talk less about doing things. During the first few sesseions they talked more about authority figures, doing things, and sex, and during the last few sessions they talked more about peers, group members, self, and family than one would expect by chance. Their discussion of authority figures also followed a pattern that suggested growth: First, they discussed the topic with significantly more negative affect and finally discussed it with significantly more positive affect than one would expect by chance.

Interactions among clients within a counseling group can be reliably classified from tape recordings in terms of referent, affect, and topic. The evidence suggests that the relationship between topic and affect deserves further study. However, these investigators question the practice of combining the classification of interactions for either a group of clients or sessions. Clients grow at different rates and in their own peculiar and appropriate ways. Moreover, the therapeutic climate within a group of young adolescents is very sensitive to changes in individual clients. Consequently, when one combines the interactions either of all the clients in a group or of several sessions, one runs the risk of disguising significant data.

Finally, the investigators question whether it is possible to identify and classify the most significant interactions without a record of nonverbal as well as verbal behavior. At present this can be accomplished best with video tapes or kinescopes.

REFERENCES

1. Ackerman, N. W. "Group Psychotherapy with a Mixed Group of Adolescents" *Int. J. Group Psychother.*, 5, 249–260 (1955).

2. Auld, Frank, and E. J. Murray. "Content-Analysis Studies of Psychotherapy," *Psychol. Bull.*, 52, 377–395 (1955).

3. Bales, R. F. *Interaction Process Analysis* (Cambridge: Addison-Wesley Press, 1950).

4. Berelson, B. *Content Analysis in Communication Research* (Glencoe, Ill: Free Press, 1952).

5. Berman, S. "Psychotherapy Technique with Adolescents," *Am. J. Orthopsychiatry*, 24, 238–244 (1954).

6. Broedel, J., M. Ohlsen, F. Proff, and C. Southard. "The Effect of Group Counseling on Gifted Underachieving Adolescents," *J. Counsel. Psychol.*, 7, 83–90 (1960).

7. Cartwright, D., and A. Zander. *Group Dynamics* (Evanston, Ill.: Row Peterson, 1953).

8. Covner, B. J. "Studies in Phonographic Recordings of Verbal Materials: I. The Use of Phonographic Recordings in Counseling Practice and Research," *J. Consult. Psychol.*, 6, 105–113 (1942).

9. Curran, C. A. *Personality Factors in Counseling* (New York: Grune & Stratton, 1945).

10. Dollard, J., and O. H. Mowrer. "A Method of Measuring Tension in Written Documents," *J. Abnorm. Soc. Psychol.*, 42, 3–32 (1945).

11. Gorlow, L., E. L. Hoch, and E. F. Telschow. *The Nature of Nondirective Group Psychotherapy: An Experimental Investigation* (New York: Teachers College, Columbia University, 1952).

12. Katz, Evelyn W., M. M. Ohlsen, and F. C. Proff. "An Analysis Through Use of Kinescopes of the Interpersonal Behavior of Adolescents in Group Counseling," *J. College Student Personnel*, 1, 2–10 (1959).

13. Kaufman, P. E., and V. C. Raimy. "Two Methods of Assessing Therapeutic Progress," *J. Abnorm. Soc. Psychol.*, 44, 379–385 (1949).

14. Lasswell, H. D., and N. Leites. *Language of Politics* (New York: Stewart, 1949).

15. Murray, E. J. "A Case Study in a Behavioral Analysis of Psychotherapy," *J. Abnorm. Soc. Psychol.*, 49, 305–310, (1954).

16. Noble, F., M. Ohlsen, and F. Proff. "A Method for Quantification of Psychotherapeutic Interaction in Counseling Groups," *J. Counsel. Psychol.*, 8, 54–60 (1961).

17. Ohlsen, M. M., and F. C. Proff. *The Extent to Which Group Counseling Improves the Academic and Personal Adjustment of Underachieving Gifted Adolescents.* Cooperative Research Project No. 623 (Urbana: University of Illinois (mimeographed), 1960).

18. Peres, Haddassah. "An Investigation of Non-Directive Group Therapy," *J. Consult. Psychol.*, 11, 159–172 (1947).

19. Porter, E. H. "The Development and Evaluation of a Measure of Counseling Interview Procedures," *Educational and Psychological Measurement.* 3, 105–126 (1943).

20. Raimy, V. C. "Self Reference In Counseling Interviews," *J. Consult. Psychol.*, 12, 153–163 (1948).

21. Rogers, C. R. "Electrically Recorded Interviews in Improving Psycho-Therapeutic Techniques," *Am. J. Orthopsychiatry*, 12, 429–435 (1942).

22. Rogers, C. R. and Rosalind Dymond. *Psychotherapy and Personality Change* (Chicago: Univ. of Chicago Press. 1954).

23.———, B. L. Kell, and Helen McNeil. "The Role of Self-Understanding in the Prediction of Behavior," *J. Consult. Psychol.*, 12, 174–186 (1948).

24. Seeman J. "The Process of Non-Directive Therapy," *J Consult. Psychol.*, 13, 157–168 (1949).

25. Shaw, M. C., and J Grubb. "Hostility and Able High School Underachievers," *J. Counsel. Psychol.*, 5, 263–266 (1958).

26. Sheerer, Elizabeth T. "An Analysis of the Relationship between Acceptance of and Respect for Self and Acceptance of and Respect for Others in Ten Counseling Cases," *J. Consult. Psychol.*, 13, 169–175 (1949).

27. Snyder, W. U. "An Investigation of the Nature of Non-Directive Psychotherapy," *J. Gen. Psychol.*, 33, 193–223 (1945).

28.———. "A Comparison of One Unsuccessful with Four Successful Nondirectively Counseled Cases," *J. Consult. Psychol.*, 11, 38–42 (1947).

29. Stock, Dorothy. "An Investigation into the Interrelations between the Self-Concept and Feelings Directed toward Other Persons and Groups." *J. Consult. Psychol.*, 13, 176–180 (1949).

30. Talland, G. A., and D. H. Clark. "Evaluation of Topics in Therapy Discussion Groups," *J. Clin. Psychol.*, 10, 131–137 (1954).

31. Winder, A. E., and M. Hersko. "A Thematic Analysis of an Outpatient Psychotherapy Group," *Int. J. Group Psychother.*, 8, 293–300 (1958).

32

Evaluation of a Group Counseling Procedure*

William Ofman

In evaluating the effectiveness of a group counseling procedure five groups of 60 students each were compared. Results indicated that the groups, while comparable in ability, differed in initial gpa. As a function of counseling, the Experimental Group's gpa became comparable to the Baseline Group's, and significantly higher than the Control and Dropout Group's gpa. The Wait Group did not improve until after counseling. Gpas of the Control and Dropout Groups did not improve at all. Since this investigation stressed the control of relevant baseline, temporal (criterion measures were taken over eight semesters) and critical motivational variables, it was concluded that the group counseling procedure described was effective in improving scholastic behavior.

There is an increasing recognition among professional workers that the quality of work required for academic attainment is qualitatively different from that required in prior academic settings. As Robinson [18, p. 11] put it, "college requires higher level work skills." It is also recognized that lack of appropriate performance (performance consistent with the student's academic potential) is often a function of more than a mere lack of strategic study skills. Shaw [20, p. 465] aptly points out that ". . . students fail in their course work because of social and emotional disturbances. Therefore, an adequate how to study program must offer assistance to the individual student beyond the mere teaching of study techniques." This point is compellingly illustrated by one student's communication to us, "I know I can do it, I know what I have to do . . . I've read the study books, but I just can't seem to get myself to set down and do it now." There are, then, problems in areas of motivation, goal definition, commitment, personal difficulties and conflicts which impinge upon, mitigate, and interfere with the adequate utilization of time and ability [12, 19].

The group counseling experience with which this research deals, the Study Habits Seminar (shs), is based on the recognition of the complex variables of which scholastic performance is a function. It is addressed to students who feel they need an approach to their university experience

*Reprinted by permission of the author and publisher from *Journal of Counseling Psychology*, 11 (1964), 152–159.

which is more consistent with the higher level demands that exist there. It also concerns itself with the needs of students who have the capacity to perform in an academic setting where the demands for independent work are great and the competition keen, but who, for reasons not directly related to their ability, do not perform at a level consistent with their potential.

The aim of helping persons to fulfill their potential through the exploration and learning of new attitudes, values and skills has traditionally been within the province of individual counseling. That which is relatively new is the group or multiple aspect of counseling: a method wherein a trained psychologist works in a group setting with several counselees who manifest several common concerns. Goldman [8] cogently points out the confusion that exists in the group counseling field between the process and content dimensions, and the confounding of teaching, guidance, group or multiple counseling, and psychotherapy. Group counseling as we conceive of it "weds" the insights of group dynamics, group psychotherapy, and psychological counseling [14].

THE PROBLEM

Based on students' reports of their experiences in such a group setting, psychologists working with counseling groups as well as with individuals who had been participants, felt that the study habits seminar helped persons to deal with scholastic demands in a more satisfactory fashion. Students who participated in group counseling reported gains in grades, seemed to find more purpose in their work, felt that "it was more an important part of me," seemed to find their work more satisfying and less of a burden.

For many reasons it was important to assess the overall effectiveness of this group counseling procedure. An extensive review of the literature on the effectiveness, in scholastic settings, of group counseling revealed a dearth of clear-cut finding in the area, for as Entwisle [4, p. 246] points out, many of the studies ". . . express expert opinion rather than the results of empirical findings." Importantly, a variable of central importance, motivation, was not controlled in many of the reported studies. Some studies included no control groups at all. Hewer, for example, evaluated group and individual counseling on vocational problems, but decided, "no definite conclusion can be drawn . . . Should further experimentation . . . be undertaken, a control group should be used, drawn from the same population from which the class comes" [9].

The difficulty in evaluating the literature on outcomes in unequivocal terms stems in the main from its methodological deficits. One finds lack of good experimental design, failure to use the proper control groups for motivation or baseline factors [3, 7, 10, 16, 20, 22, 23, 24], or failure to use control groups altogether [1, 2, 6, 9, 11, 17, 25]. There is a heavy reliance upon "before-after" studies and an almost predominant use of immediate rather than long-term criterion measures.

Clearly the problem of assessing the effectiveness of a group counseling procedure has much in common with problems inherent in outcome research in psychotherapy. The important issues relate to control of variables which might covary with behavior change in order to "tease out" those changes which are a function of the treatment: in this case, the experience in the group [5, 15, 21]. Nevertheless, the majority of authors report that group procedures are effective in influencing behavior in a positive direction.

We might mention two critical issues. It has been pointed out and commonly noted that the motivation to improve—the person's recognition of a concern, a difficulty of a problem—can often stimulate his thinking in a constructive way about it so that this recognition can, on its own, be "therapeutic" in that it can lead to more effective behavior. Students who perceive their need for developmental work around their reading habits, study procedures, their resistive or unrealistic attitudes towards scholastic demands, may become more receptive to the utterances, advice and thoughts of others and may, via their increased motivation to improve, re-evaluate their position in such a manner as to constitute a substantial change in behavior. The treatment variable has to be effective, then, in light of the sources of motivation that are provided by the recognition of the problem alone and desire to improve.

Another relevant issue is students' tendency to improve without any expressed motivation or acceptance of the existence of a difficulty. A plot of grades for a random group of students over their undergraduate semesters indicates that, for a variety of reasons, their grades rise. A baseline control group is therefore essential to a well-controlled study. In effect, this research is concerned with the control of relevant motivational factors, with the aim of arriving at relatively unequivocal results.

METHOD AND PROCEDURE

We chose as our criterion for effectiveness the grade point average (gpa). It is held that the gpa earned during the semester in which the student is a member of the group, or the semester immediately following it (a criterion used in most of the investigations to date), is insufficient. Rather a better measure of the effectiveness of the shs is its effect, if any, over the total undergraduate stay.

CONTROL VARIABLES

Scholastic aptitude: The scores on the American Council on Education Psychological examination (ACE) for Ss in the various groups will act as controls for this variable [13].

Motivation: As was mentioned earlier, motivational factors must be controlled if unequivocal statements are to be made regarding treatment effectiveness. The control of motivational factors was accomplished by the selection of appropriate control groups which will now be described:

The Experimental Group consisted of the eight-semester gpa of a sample of Ss who volunteered for the shs and were accepted as participants. A number of Ss who volunteered for the shs had to be excused from participating on administrative grounds.[1] This group of excused volunteers—those who showed the desire to improve—served as the *Control Group* for motivation. Three other control groups were included. One group served as a *Baseline Control* and consisted of Ss, chosen at random, whose gpa was plotted for eight semesters at the university. Another group consisted of the gpa of Ss who volunteered for the shs and were accepted, but who dropped out from the shs before the third session. This Dropout Group permitted an evaluation of the shs in a quantitative fashion. The last group was in reality a subgroup of the motivation control, and constituted a *Wait Group*. It consisted of the gpa of volunteers who were refused admission to the shs but who became participants in the seminar two semesters later. It is held that these five groups helped to control most of the contingencies of which improvement might be a function.

THE SAMPLE

Group A: *Baseline Control.* Gpa of 60 Ss,[2] randomly selected, over eight semesters.

Group B: *Experimental Group.* Eight-semester gpa of 60 volunteers who remained in the shs for at least 80% of its duration.

Group C: *Dropout Group.* Eight-semester gpa of 60 volunteers who dropped out before the fourth session and did not re-enter.

---

[1]Students came voluntarily to "sign up" for the seminar, and all who wished were allowed to sign into the seminar. About twice as many students signed up as accomodations permitted. When all the sections were filled, those who could not be accomodated were told that due to space limitations, the sections were closed. There is no reason to suspect that any systematic factor affected the choice of students who were excused because of space limitations.

[2]Since the numbers in the several groups varied naturally, and it was desirable to have equal numbers in all the groups, the total number in the smallest group (Dropout group $N = 60$) was taken as the standard and the other groups were reduced (their data cards shuffled and the first 60 chosen) to 60 each.

Group D:| *Control Group.* Eight-semester gpa of 60 vulunteers who were
refused admission for administrative reasons and who did not
enter the shs.

Group E: |*Wait Group.* Eight-semester gpa of 60 volunteers who were
refused admission for administrative reasons to the shs, but who
re-entered and participated in the shs two semesters later.

HYPOTHESES

1. Volunteers should not differ from a random selection of students at the university in their initial grade point averages: gpa of Experimental Group is not different from gpa of the Baseline Group.
2. Scholastic aptitude as measured by the ACE should be comparable for
   the five groups.
3. The Experimental Group should show a significantly different pattern
   of grades during its eight semesters than the four other groups.
4. The Experimental Group will have higher gpa than the other groups in
   semesters following the shs.
5. Gpa of the Experimental Group will be higher than that of the Control
   Group over eight semesters.
6. Gpa of the Dropout Group will be higher than that of the Control
   Group over eight semesters.
7. Gpa of the Wait Group will show significant difference in gpa before
   and after the experience.
8. Gpa of the Wait Group will, in semesters seven and eight, be comparable to that of the seventh and eighth semester gpa of the Experimental Group.

RESULTS

The design of the experiment was such that it permitted the testing
of differences among the curves of the Experimental, Baseline and Control Groups.

Figure 1 presents a graph of the curves of gpa for the different groups
per semester for eight semesters. Volunteers participated in the shs in
their first year. It will be noted that the Baseline Group began its career
at a higher level than volunteers for the shs. The Control Group and Dropout Group curves are essentially flat. The Experimental Group, on the
other hand, began to improve its gpa in the second semester and by the
fourth semester the curve of its gpa departs from that of the Control and
Dropout Groups and approaches that of the Baseline Group. The curve
of the Wait Group is not different from that of the Control or Dropout
Groups during the first four semesters, but it rises to join the curves of the
Baseline and Experimental Groups in semesters seven and eight.

Figure 1

A Plot of the Mean GPA Per Semester for Baseline, Experiment Dropout, Control, and Wait Group.

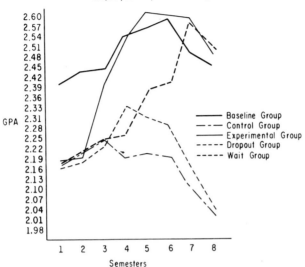

In evaluating hypothesis No. 1 (Table 1) it was found that there were significant differences between initial gpa of the Baseline Groups and that of the Experimental and Control Groups. There were no significant differences in the initial gpa among the volunteering groups. The initial gpa of the Experimental and Control Groups, while not significantly different from each other, are significantly lower than the gpa of the Baseline Group in the first semester of college.

Table 1

Critical Ratios of Initial Semester Gpas

Groups	CR	Significance
Base. – Exp.	2.01	.05
Base. – Control	2.08	.05
Exp. – Control	1.01	N.S.

Hypothesis No. 2 was upheld. (Table 2) Since an analysis of variance of ACE scores for the five groups yielded an insignificant F, it was concluded that scholastic aptitude was essentially comparable for the *five* groups. That is, while the volunteers for the shs began their academic career at a lower level of performance than the Baseline Group, they did not do so as a function of lower scholastic potential.

An analysis of variance of the gpas for each group per semester (Table 3) tested hypothesis No. 3. The highly significant Fs for Inter-

Table 2

Summary of Analysis of Variance of ACE Scores
for Baseline, Experimental, Dropout, Control, and
Wait Groups

Source	df	MS	F
Between Groups	4	192	
			0.362*
Within Groups	225	592.88	
Total	229		

*Not significant.

Table 3

An Analysis of Variance of Gpas of Baseline,
Experimental, Dropout, Control, and Wait Groups
for Eight Semesters

Source	df	SS	MS	F
Groups	4	35.68	8.920	5.304**
Semesters	7	10.48	1.497	
Interaction	28	51.28	1.830	4.800**
Within Cells	2360	815.22	0.345	
Total	2399	912.66		

**Significant at .01 level.

action and for Groups indicated that the curves of grades were neither
proportional nor parallel. It was therefore asserted that the differential
treatment had different effects upon the several groups.

In terms of hypothesis 4, the results indicated that the Experimental Group, while beginning significantly lower than the Baseline Group
in gpa, did not improve to a degree which significantly superseded the gpa
of the Baseline Group (Table 4). In effect, in the last semesters, the gpa
of the Experimental Group and the Baseline Group are comparable. However, hypothesis No. 5 was upheld: the Experimental Group's gpa was
significantly higher than the Control Group's and Dropout Group's gpa.

Hypothesis 6 was not upheld. The Dropout Group evidently did not
receive help from the four or fewer sessions of the shs in a manner sufficient to raise its gpa (Table 4). The gpa of the Dropout Group taken over
the last seven semesters is comparable to that of the Control Group
which did not participate in the shs at all.

Table 4

Critical Ratios of Gpas, Semesters 2-8 of Baseline, Experimental, Dropout, Control, and Wait
Groups

Groups	C.R.	Sig.
Base. − Exp.	1.00	N.S.
Exp. − Drop.	2.508	.05
Exp. − Control	3.438	.01
Exp. − Wait	1.312	N.S.

Table 5

Critical Ratios Between Gpa of Wait Group
Before and After the SHS

Groups	Gpa	s.d.	C.R.	Sig.
Wait (before)	2.222	.533		
			2.516	.05
Wait (after)	2.478	.568		

Hypothesis 7 was upheld. The results (Table 5) indicated that the gpa of the Wait Group during its wait period—before taking the shs—was significantly lower than its gpa in semesters after participation is the shs.

Further, hypothesis 8 was supported: there was no significant difference in the last two semesters between the gpa of the Wait Group and that of the Experimental Group (Table 4).

DISCUSSION

The findings indicated that those students who volunteered for the shs exhibited inappropriate performance in their first semester: their grades were significantly lower than those of the Baseline Group; but in the light of comparable ACE scores for all the groups, this was not a function of lower scholastic aptitude. It appears that those students who volunteered for the shs (it should be noted that they were not on probation at this point, nor had they been likely to have visited an academic counselor) perceived themselves correctly: they recognized their need for help, and this was a correct perception.

As a result of participation in group counseling, the Experimental Group's gpa became comparable to that of the Baseline Group's gpa and significantly higher than the gpa of the Control and Dropout Groups which, while comparable in other respects, were subjected to lesser amounts of the group counseling experience.

It might be interesting to note that the Experimental Group did not begin its improvement until the third semester. Evidently it takes some time before the results of the newly gained insights, as a result of the group counseling, are translated into action. This is one of the important reasons for the use of long-range rather than immediate criterion measures. Though some students do exhibit a "transference cure" and exhibit immediate marked behavior changes, most of them seem to do better in the "long pull" as a result of the counseling experience.

The improvement of scholastic behavior on the part of the inappropriately performing (underachieving) Experimental Group cannot logically be accounted for by the natural tendency to regress towards the mean. The Control Group, Dropout Group and the Wait Group do not indicate this phenomenon. Therefore, the change in behavior on the part of the Experimental Group (and later the Wait Group) can only be accounted for in terms of our treatment variable.

Further findings lend support to the effectiveness of the shs in influencing gpa. The Droupout Group evidently did not receive help from its limited participation in the shs in a fashion sufficient to significantly raise its gpa. The gpa of the Dropout Group taken over the last seven semesters is essentially similar to that of the Control Group which did not participate in the seminar at all. This is a useful finding. It is often said that students tend to gain as much from the "inspiration" of being stimulated by an ameliorative experience as by the process and content of the procedure itself. This is not the case in this investigation. The first three sessions of the shs are of this introductory, somewhat inspirational nature. Characteristically, there is a discussion of the basic reasons for being at the university, the commonly shared need for higher-level work skills, the basic goals and values consistent with university achievement, and the relationship between the student's goals, the aims of the university, and the aspirations that the student's relatives and parents have *for* the student [14]. The findings clearly indicate that such a process alone was not sufficient to significantly raise the Dropout Group's gpa. Evidently what is needed is, as McGowan [11], put it, ". . . therapy plus content."

More light is shed on the motivational variable by an inspection of the gpa curve of the Wait Group. It will be recalled that this group is comparable in gpa, semester of entry, and scholastic aptitude to that of the Experimental and Control Groups. The Wait Group was composed of Ss who volunteered for the shs, were refused admission and became participants two semesters hence. During the wait period, this group exhibits a curve of grades essentially similar to that of the Control Group. No improvement was exhibited during the wait period. After participating in the shs, however, its gpa became significantly different from that of the before period, and from the Control Group's gpa. In the last semester it becomes comparable to that of the Experimental and Baseline Groups. The implications of this finding lend further support to the fact that motivation to improve alone is not sufficient to change the scholastic performance of students who indicate a desire to change. This finding also sheds light on the "when is it too late?" question. Apparently students who are motivated to improve, if given the appropriate treatment, can improve rapidly—it took the Wait Group approximately two semesters to improve to a level comparable to that of the Experimental Group.

As a result, we can state with a high degree of certainty that in the findings of an investigation which concerned itself with long-range results, and which controlled ability and motivational variables, indicated that students of comparable ability who began their scholastic career with inappropriately lower grades, who recognized and expressed their need for help, and participated in group counseling were indeed aided to perform in a manner more consistent with their ability. In contrast, those Ss who were in the same circumstance, but were refused help, or dropped out of the group, continued to perform in a consistently inappropriate manner: they did not improve their grades even though they were motivated to do so.

The outcome of this investigation supports the results of many studies of the effectiveness of group procedures in academic settings. The critical issue to which this research was addressed was the establishment of controls and the manipulation of variables in a manner which was consistent with conclusions of an unequivocal nature—an aim which former studies accomplished only in small part. It dealt with, at once, a group procedure which focused on personality variables and scholastic skills simultaneously. It provided control for motivational variables, and it used an objective criterion for measurement over a prolonged period of time.

In the light of the design, the findings indicated that such group counseling procedures which take into account the whole person are effective in changing scholastic behavior in a positive direction.

SUMMARY

The effectiveness of a group counseling procedure concerned with students' adjustment to the university which dealt simultaneously with issues related to attitudinal, motivational and specific skills, was assessed in terms of its influence on the gpa of five groups of 60 students. These groups consisted of a Baseline Group of randomly chosen Ss, an Experimental Group of volunteers who participated in the seminar, a Control Group of volunteers who were refused admission to the seminar, a Dropout Group of Ss who participated in the seminar for less than three sessions, and a Wait Group of volunteers who were refused admission but who became participants two semesters later.

The grade point averages for each of these groups was plotted for each of their eight semesters.

The results indicated that students volunteering for the seminar, while comparable to the Baseline Group in scholastic aptitude, were significantly lower than the Baseline in first semester grades. As a function of group counseling, the Experimental Group improved its grades to a level comparable to that of the Baseline Group, and significantly above that of the Control and Dropout Groups. The Wait Group remained static during its wait period, but as a result of the subsequent counseling, improved its gpa to a level not different from the Experimental or Baseline Groups. Gpas did not improve for the Control and Dropout Groups.

It was concluded that the Study Habits Seminar as a group counseling procedure was effective in improving scholastic performance.

REFERENCES

1. Arbuckle, D. S. "A College Experiment in Orientation," *Occupations* (1949), **28**, 112–117.
2. Calia, V. F. "A Group Guidance Program in Action," *Junior Coll. J.* (1957), **27**, 437–442.
3. Charles, D. C. "College Reading and Study Improvement," *J. Higher Educ.* (1951), **22**, 265–267.
4. Entwistle, D. R. "Evaluation of Study Skills Courses," *J. Educ. Res.* (1960), **7**, 246–251.
5. Frank, J. D. Problems of controls in psychotherapy as examplified in the psychotherapy research project of the Phipps Psychiatric Clinic. In Rubinstein, E., & Parloff, M. (Eds.) *Research in Psychotherapy* (Washington: American Psychol. Assoc., 1959).
6. Froehlich, C. P. "Must Counseling Be Individual?" *Educ. Psychol. Measmt.* (1958), **18**, 681–689.
7. Gazda, G., & Ohlsen, M. "The Effects of Short-term Group Counseling on Prospective Counselors," *Personal Guid. J.* (1961), **39**, 634–638.
8. Goldman, L. "Group Guidance: Content and Process," *Personnel Guid. J.* (1962), **40**, 518–522.
9. Hewer, V. H. "Group Counseling, Individual Counseling and a College Class in Vocations," *Personnel Guid. J.* (1959), **37**, 660–665.
10. Hoyt, D. P. "An Evaluation of Group and Individual Programs in Vocational Guidance," *J. Appl. Psychol.* (1955), **39**, 26–30.
11. McGowan, B. "Group Counseling of University Students: Group Therapy Plus Content." Unpublished paper, University of Calif., Los Angeles, 1962.
12. Neugeboren, B. "Clinical Study of Academic Underachievers." In Wedge, B. M. (Ed.). *The Psychosocial Problems of College Men* (New Haven: Yale U. Press, 1958).
13. Ofman, W. "A Cross-validation of the Z-scale and a Further Exploration," *J. Educ. Res.* In press (1963) (a).
14. Ofman, W. "The Study Habits Seminar—A Statement of Viewpoint and Method," *Personnel Guid. J.* (1963) in press (b).
15. Parloff, M. B., & Rubinstein, E. "Research Problems in Psychotherapy." In Rubinstein, E., & Parloff, M. (Eds.). *Research in Psychotherapy* (Washington: Amer. Psychol. Assoc., 1959).
16. Ransom, M. K. "An Evaluation of Certain Aspects of the Reading and Study Program at the Univer. of Missouri," *J. Educ. Res.* (1955), **48**, 443–454.
17. Robinson, F. P. "Two Quarries with a Single Stone," *J. Higher Educ.* (1945), **16**, 201–208.
18. Robinson, F. P. *Effective Study* (New York: Harper, 1961).
19. Rust, R. "Personality and Academic Achievement: a Questionnaire Approach. In Wedge, B. M. (Ed.). *The Psycho-social Problems of College Men* (New Haven: Yale Univer. Press, 1958).
20. Shaw, J. G. "An Evaluation of Study Skills Course," *Personnel Guid. J.* (1955), **33**, 465–468.
21. Strupp, H., & Luborsky, L. *Research in Psychotherapy*, Vol. II (Washington: Amer. Psychol. Assn. 1962).

22. Stewart, C. C. "Attitude Change Following a Counseling Seminar," *Personnel Guid. J.* (1958), **37**, 273–275.

23. Tresselt, M. E., & Richlin, M. "Differential Prognosis in a College Methods Course," *J. Psychol.* (1951), **31**, 81–89.

24. Winborn. B., & Schmidt, L. G. "The Effectiveness of Short-terms Group Counseling Upon the Academic Achievement of Potentially Superior but Under-achieving College Freshmen," *J. Educ. Res.* (1962), **55**, 169–173.

25. Wittenborn, J. P. "Classes in Remedial Reading and Study Skills," *J. Educ. Res.* (1944), **37**, 571–586.

26. Wright, W. E. "Multiple Counseling: Why, When, How," *Personnel Guid. J.* (1959), **37**, 551–557.

27. Wright, W. E. "Group Procedures," *Rev. Educ. Res.* (1963), **33**, 205–213.

33

Effects of Group Counseling on Dimensions of Self-Acceptance, Dogmatism, and Preference for Complexity with Teacher-Education Students*

James J. Muro

Fred W. Ohnmacht

Numerous researchers [3, 7, 9, 12, 14, 16] have called the counselor's attention to the use of group procedures in counseling. Studies of counseling in groups have frequently yielded insignificant results [10]. Nevertheless, such writers as Gazda [15], Mahler and Caldwell [13], and Lifton [16] indicate that a group approach to counseling offers a solution to some problems that confront the counselor. The most obvious of these is the fact that the number of students who both need and desire counseling may make individual sessions an almost prohibitive task. The pressure to provide more counseling time is felt at all educational levels, and recently Tincher [19] suggested that group counseling should be extended to include work with teachers in an effort to help them clarify their attitudes toward children and the profession in general. The underlying rationale implied in Tincher's suggestion leads to the assumption that group counseling would provide teachers with added insights into their own behavior. The logic of Tincher's position would also seem to apply to those who are in the process of becoming teachers, and as such served as the basis of a pilot study in the teacher orientation program at the University of Maine.

Criteria for counseling success have been listed in the literature in a somewhat diverse pattern. Froehlich and Darley [8] and Dressel [6] list such factors as improved school work, attitude changes, placement, and within and between group change as common measures of evaluating the counseling process.

In general terms the current study explored the concept that group counseling would modify attitudes of counseled students by measuring between group change along the dimensions of dogmatism [17], self acceptance [4], and preference for complexity [2]. The direction of change in

*Reprinted by permission of the authors and publisher from SPATE, 5 (1966), 25–30.

the counseled groups would hopefully move the Ss toward becoming more self acceptant, less dogmatic, and exhibiting a greater preference for complexity.

The desired change was based on the underlying assumption that open-mindedness, self acceptance, and preference for complexity are positive attitudes and are in fact characteristics that should be possessed by an effective teacher.

METHOD

SUBJECTS

The original group of Ss consisted of 68 undergraduate freshmen enrolled in the Orientation Course of the College of Education at the University of Maine. An initial screening procedure and schedule conflicts reduced the initial participants to 28 from which the final sample of two experimental groups of eight students and a control group of 13 were selected. Post-treatment data for one experimental S was not obtained thereby reducing the total experimental group to 15. All Ss volunteered to participate in group counseling.

PROCEDURE

Prior to the experiment each S was administered the Dogmatism Scale [17], the Bills Index of Adjustment and Values (IAV), [4] and the Barron Complexity Scale [2]. Each S was interviewed individually for the purpose of explaining group counseling. An additional reason for the screening procedure was to determine if each S was willing to discuss himself in a confidential manner in a group. Of the 68 original volunteers, 25 were eliminated because of schedule conflicts and 15 decided not to participate in group counseling. The remaining 28 made up the final sample and were subsequently assigned to the experimental and control conditions through utilization of a table of random numbers. The sex composition of the groups was divided equally between males and females since no definite reason was apparent for like-sex grouping [5]. The age range was 17–20.

The counseled groups met under two experimental conditions for a period of 15 weeks. Group I met for an hour once a week, and Group II met for an hour twice a week. One of the authors, trained in counseling at the doctoral level, served as counselor for both groups. Group counseling as defined for the purposes of this study followed a pattern described by Gazda [10][1] in that the Ss were basically normal, were not institutionalized, and the involvement was primarily on a conscious level. Counselor behavior,

---

[1]Gazda, G. M., Personal communication, 1965.

after the establishment of rapport, could be characterized as eclectic in that the counselor served as reflector, interpreter, summarizer, and monitor. In addition, role playing and "going around" techniques were utilized [1].

At the end of 15 weeks, each S was readministered the three criterion instruments. The raw score difference between the pre- and post-test data for each criterion variable was taken as a measure of change. Change data were tabulated and analyzed through application of the Mann-Whitney U Test to evaluate the experimental hypotheses. The U technique was employed as the most useful alternative to the parametric *t* test since the measurement in the research (in this case raw change) is probably weaker than interval scaling [11]. It should be noted that the U test is conservative in that it is not as powerful as the parametric *t* test.

HYPOTHESES

The following hypotheses were tested in the study:

1. Counseled Ss will become significantly more self acceptant than non-counseled Ss as self acceptance is inferred from change scores on the acceptance of self scale on the IAV.

2. Counseled Ss will become significantly more open minded than non-counseled Ss as open mindedness is inferred from change scores on the Dogmatism Scale.

3. Counseled Ss will display a greater preference for complexity than non-counseled Ss as preference for complexity is inferred from change scores on the Preference For Complexity Scale.

RESULTS AND DISCUSSION

Table 1 shows the results obtained in the analysis.

An analysis of the data indicates that the scores of the counseled groups changed significantly over those of the non-counseled group on the self

Table 1

Mann-Whitney U Tests for Comparisons of Change Scores Between Pre- and Post-Test Measures of Counseled and Non-counseled Teacher-Education Students on the IAV, Self Acceptance Score, Dogmatism Scale, and Preference for Complexity Scale

Comparisons	Measure used to determine change scores	Obtained Z	p
Counseled Ss vs Non Counseled Ss	IAV Self Acceptance Score	2.71	< .05
Counseled Ss vs Non Counseled Ss	Dogmatism Scale	.90	n.s.
Counseled Ss vs Non Counseled Ss	Preference for Complexity Scale	.73	n.s.

Z test was calculated from U according to procedure outlined by Siegel.

acceptance scale of the IAV. The direction of the score change for counseled Ss was toward a greater degree of self acceptance. As a result of the significant change in scores, hypothesis one was supported (p < .05). It should be noted that the obtained results represent a score change and that actual change in self acceptance of the counseled Ss must be inferred from these scores.

A comparison of change scores between counseled and non-counseled Ss on the Dogmatism Scale and the Preference for Complexity Scale were non-significant. Thus hypotheses two and three were rejected, and we can infer that group counseling did not affect the dimensions of open mindedness and preference for complexity.

An additional note of interest was an attempt to discover if the "concept of self" scale on the IAV had undergone change since a significant difference was found on the "acceptance of self" scale.[2] Change scores on Column I of the IAV (concept of self) were also analyzed through use of the Mann-Whitney U Test to determine if the self concept scores of the counseled Ss had undergone change when compared with the controls. Results were non-significant (Z = .71), suggesting that group counseling in this study did not alter the "concept of self" score. In essence we can infer that counseled Ss did not change their self image during counseling. As previously noted, the procedure did help the counseled groups to become more self acceptant of that image.

Any interpretation of the results of this study must be made with caution since the authors realize the limitations of the instruments used to measure change and the smallness of the sample. Additional research in group counseling with prospective teachers is needed to substantiate the results of this study. Such research might profitably expand the criterion space to include measures of attitude toward children and the teaching profession.

REFERENCES

1. Bach. G. R. *Intensive Group Psychotherapy* (New York: Ronald, 1954).

2. Barron, F. "Discovering the Creative Personality," *The Behavioral Sciences and Education* (Princeton, N.J.: College Entrance Examination Board, 1963), pp. 79–85.

3. Bates, Marilyn. "Themes in Group Counseling with Adolescents," *Personnel and Guidance Journal* (1966), 44, 568–575.

4. Bills, R. E., Vance, E. L. & McLean, O. S. "An Index of Adjustment and Values," *Journal of Consulting Psychology* (1951), 15, 79–81.

[2]The IAV yields three measures of "self." The first is a measure of "concept of self," the second a measure of "acceptance of self," and the third a measure of "ideal self concept." In the original design of the study, the authors were concerned only with the "acceptance of self" scale. The decision to further analyze the data to determine change in the "concept of self" scale was made after the stated hypotheses had been tested.

5. Brammer, L. M., & Shostrom, E. L. *Therapeutic Psychology* (Englewood Cliffs, N.J.: Prentice-Hall, 1960).

6. Dressel, P. B. "Some Approaches to Evaluation," *Personnel and Guidance Journal* (1953), *31*, 284–287.

7. Foley, W. J., & Bonney, W. C. "A Developmental Model for Counseling Groups," *Personnel and Guidance Journal* (1966), *44*, 576–580.

8. Froehlich, C. P., & Darley, J. G. "The Evaluation of Counseling," *Purdue University Studies in Higher Education* (1951), *76*, 21–31.

9. Gaways, J., & Brown, O. B. "Group Counseling: More Than a Catalyst," *School Counselor* (1965), *12*, 206–213.

10. Gazda, G. M. "Group Counseling—a Growing Solution," *Catholic Counselor* (1963), *8*, 17–26.

11. Hays, W. L. *Statistics for Psychologists* (New York: Holt, Rinehart, & Winston, 1963).

12. Kinnick, B. C., & Shannon, J. T. "The Effect of Counseling on Peer Group Acceptance of Socially Rejected Students," *School Counselor* (1965), *12*, 162–166.

13. Lifton, W. M. *Working With Groups* (New York: John Wiley, 1966).

14. Lodato, F. J., Sokoloff, M. A., & Schwartz, L. J. "Group Counseling as a Method of Modifying Attitudes in Slow Learners," *School Counselor* (1964), *12*, 27–29.

15. Mahler, C. E., & Caldwell, E. *Group Counseling in Secondary Schools* (Chicago: Science Research Associates, 1961).

16. Ohlsen, M. M. "Adapting Principles of Group Dynamics for Group Counseling," *School Counselor* (1966), *13*, 159–162.

17. Rokeach, M. *The Open and Closed Mind* (New York: Basic Books, 1960).

18. Siegel, S. *Non-parametric Statistics for the Behavioral Sciences* (New York: McGraw-Hill, 1956).

19. Tincher, W. A. "Suggestions for SPATE Research," *SPATE Journal* (1965), *4*, 53–55.

34

Group Counseling with Parents of Underachieving Sixth Grade Children*

Robert S. Southworth

BACKGROUND

For years, counselors have spent innumerable hours working directly with secondary school students to elicit changes in academic achievement. Yet, it is possible that the efforts have been too late and with the wrong persons. That it is rather late to attempt to affect academic achievement in secondary school can be deduced from the fact that underachievement can be noted early in the school career of an individual. Barrett [1] found that a pattern of underachievement was noticeable in the fifth grade, while Schreiber [16] noted reading retardation in the primary grades. Meeks [13] stated that the prevention of underachievement called for early and continuous identification. Intertwined with underachievement are the problems of school behavior and the self-concept. McKenzie [11] brought in the factor of behavior while Roth and Meyersburg [15] and Kehas [8] wrote tellingly of the relationship of the self-concept and school achievement. However, identification of underachievers in elementary school presents the problem of what to do for a preventative or curative program. Chess [4] questioned verbal therapy with children, and, since Shaw [17], Roth and Meyersburg [15], Kirte [10] and others have indicated the responsibility of the parents in the problem of underachievement, it appears that significant changes in the school achievement of children might be wrought through working with parents. In the clinical setting, it is common practice to counsel with parents, therefore, why should it not be conducted in an educational setting?

A seemingly fruitful approach is that of group counseling. Cohn *et al.* [5], Caplan [3] and Broedel *et al.* [2] applied it to adolescents. Gazda [6] worked with fifth graders and their parents, while Sonstegard [19] did group counseling with parents. All of these studies appeared to have mixed statistical results with nonstatistical data in a more positive vein. Specifically, short-term group counseling was considered the best approach in this study

* Reprinted by permission of the author.

because of the possible difficulties of holding many parents together over a long period of time. Since Shlien, Mosak and Dreikurs [18] had found time-limited individual therapy to be satisfactory and Gazda and Ohlsen [7] had been fruitful with short-term group counseling, it was felt that limiting the number of sessions was feasible.

With the realization of parental influence, the early onset of problems and the value of group counseling, development of a study incorporating these factors appeared potentially useful. Therefore, the present study was designed to determine the effect of short-term group counseling with parents on the academic achievement, school behavior, and self-concept of their underachieving sixth grade students.

PROCEDURE

POPULATION

Underachieving sixth graders in two similar communities were identified on a school-by-school basis through a comparison of results of IQ tests and school marks. Students with averages that were two or more stanines below their IQ stanines were considered to be underachievers. This identification was verified by means of teacher conferences and analysis of school records. Eighty-three of the originally identified students remained as verified members of the population.

SUBJECT SELECTION

The identified students were paired on nine variables: (1) age, (2) sex, (3) IQ, (4) Stanford Achievement Test [9], (5) Stanford Achievement Test reading score, (6) siblings, (7) socio-economic status, (8) health, and (9) marital status of the parents. Their parents were then contacted seeking their agreement to participate in the project. The purpose of the project and what it entailed were explained. Some parents were unable to participate, while others refused; however, enough parents consented so that control and experimental groups of twenty-eight students each were established. These groups were compared on the nine variables by use of the t-test, using the .05 level of significance, and were found to be not significantly different on any of the variables.

GROUPINGS

The parents of the twenty-eight experimental group children were divided into eight subgroups, four composed of mothers and four of fathers. This separation by sex was done in order to facilitate better attendance and communication. It has been the experience of the researcher that parents were more apt to talk freely when the spouse was not present. Also, it was felt that in view of experience in mixed groups, male attendance would be poor in such group sessions. Furthermore, the separation was expected to provide points for home discussions, fostering greater growth.

COUNSELING PROCESS

There were two counselors involved, each counselor met with two subgroups of mothers and two of fathers, not in the same families. This further separation was to minimize the effect of counselor technique and personality. The group counseling with parents continued for twelve one hour sessions. During those sessions, the counselors fostered discussion of problems of significance to the parents, accepting their various points and criticisms and reflecting their feelings in order that insight could be developed.

INSTRUMENTS

The study necessitated the acquisition and comparison of data gathered on three occasions concercning the three areas of (1) school achievement, (2) school behavior, and (3) the self-concept of the individuals.

The threee occasions established for obtaining data were (1) prior to the beginning of the group counseling, (2) at the completion of the group counseling period, and (3) at the completion of a follow-up period of equal length as the counseling period.

School Achievement. School marks were used as the measure of change because they were readily obtainable from the teachers and because it was considered inadvisable to administer achievement test to students three times during one school year. The marks assigned for the five major subjects, arithmetic, reading, English, science, and social studies, were used because of the stated importance of these subjects by officials in the two school systems.

School Behavior. The effect of the group counseling with the parents on the school behavior of the students was determined by use of the Rating Scale for Pupil Adjustment [14], with copies completed by the teachers of the students in the study.

Self-Concept. A sixty item Q-sort, developed by the researcher, was used to determine the self-concepts of the students, and the parents' perceptions of those student self-concepts. The latter measurements were made to establish parental sensitivity for the child that might point to future gains, not detected at the time of the study.

RESULTS

Because of the nature of the study, it was deemed wise to compile subjective data as well as statistical data. With human interaction as the major process, it seemed possible that parental or teacher expressions might be indicative of change even if no statistical significance was evident.

STATISTICAL RESULTS

Data obtained about the two groups that remained at the completion of the study were analyzed according to statistical procedures given by Mc-Nemar [12]. The complex analysis of variance, comparing the control and experimental groups over the three times, was the specific procedure, with the .05 level of significance as the basis for acceptance or rejection of the null hypothesis.

Data analyzed about the variables, school achievement, school behavior, self-concept, and parental perceptions of those self-concepts, resulted in no significant differences between the two groups. However, line graphs of the mean scores provide another comparison of the control and experimental groups. That comparison indicated that on school achievement, self-concept, and both mother and father perceptions of the self-concept of their children, the experimental group appeared to have improved.

On the variables of school behavior, the line graphs of the scores were quite mixed, and a trend indicating improvement for the experimental group was not as apparent.

SUBJECTIVE DATA

Non-statistical data were collected from three sources, (1) the teachers, (2) the counselor, and (3) the parents, by means of personal conversations and written statements. The comments by the teachers indicating positive changes were more numerous for the experimental group than for the control group. The counselor impressions indicated that they felt the parents of the experimental group students discussed pertinent material, thoughtfully viewing their children and themselves, and, in some cases, effecting changes of potential benefit to their children. Parent comments that indicated recognition of problems were quite numerous as were statements that closer parent-child relationships were achieved and attitudes were changed. Specific comments were made about the helpfulness of the sessions because of the opportunity to interact with others.

CONCLUSIONS AND DISCUSSION

The analysis of statistical data indicated the following conclusions would have to be drawn about the experimental and control groups: (1) there were no significant differences between them on the variable, school achievement, as measured by teacher marks; (2) the groups were not significantly different on the variable, school behavior, as measured by the abbreviated and complete Rating Scale for Pupil Adjustment; (3) there were not significant differences on the variable, self-concept, as measured by the Q-sort; and (4) there were no significant differences between the two groups in terms of mother or father perception of the self-concept of their children, as measured by the Q-sort.

These were the conclusions from the statistical data; yet, the findings of the study were mixed, for the line graphs of the mean scores obtained from that data and the non-statistical data constituting the comments of the teachers, counselors and parents indicated positive gains for the experimental group as with the control group. That difference presented several questions for consideration.

What about the definition of underachievement used for the study? It was defined as academic work below expected according to indicated ability. More specifically, students with scholastic averages that were two or more stanines below that expected in relation to IQ stanines were identified as underachievers. Although such a definition is commonly used, perhaps there are many kinds of underachievement, identifiable by variables as yet undetermined, and which could be discerned only by a rethinking of the idea of underachievement and its many constituent parts. If there are other factors, it should not be deemed one problem, but a profusion of problems that cannot be dealt with by one procedure but which must be approached by a convergence of many methods in a total attack. In fact, it would seem reasonable that future studies attempting to cope with underachievement, particularly in elementary school students, should be designed to integrate the efforts of school personnel, teachers, students, and other persons important in the field of the students. It is possible that only in this way can significant results be obtained.

Allied with the above is the question about whether the variables used for matching the two groups of students were adequately sophisticated to determine the comparability of the two groups. The analysis of variance procedure had resulted in large variability in the Within Cells, meaning a great variability in individual differences. This occurred despite the fact that there were no significant differences between the two groups on the nine matching variables. It is possible that underachievement is a very individual thing, or it might be that there are other, still unidentified, variables involved in underachievement. It would appear that it should be re-examined, with the intent of uncovering other significant variables and of redefining it to establish its true nature.

Was the short-term feature of the group counseling sufficient to produce change? The changes in the experimental group evidenced by the line graphs and the subjective data might have indicated a beginning that could have been more fully developed by long-term counseling.

Were the instruments used in the study capable of measuring the changes possible in essentially normal persons? If underachievement is a multivariate problem, extremely sophisticated and total measuring techniques would be necessary—techniques that do not appear to be available.

Thus, the mixed results brought into the open several areas to be considered in determining and resolving the problem of underachievement. Yet, even with the questions being raised, there appeared to be positive implications from the study that opened several questions of relevance to school counselors.

Customarily, counselors have been centralized in the secondary schools, but is it too late to concentrate them at that level in view of indications that children can be helped while at the elementary school level? Should school systems acquire sufficient qualified counselors to be of value? Since many problems are evident early, are apt to "snowball" easily, and apparently can be dealt with when the children are in elementary school, it is reasonable to suggest that elementary school counselors are warranted.

What of the practice of the counselor? It is easy to spend time only with students, but it appeared from the study that involvement of everyone interacting with the student, including, teachers, counselors, and parents, would be justifiable, involvement of the parents appears particularly appropriate. Also, counselors usually prefer to meet with parents during the day; however, the time spent outside of regular hours appeared to be appreciated by the parents, and appeared to result in valuable benefits.

The group counseling process seemed to have several advantages. Included would be the saving of time and money, but more important factors were involved. The interaction among parents enabled them to recognize, comprehend, and, hopefully, change some practice and interrelations with their children. The parents, realizing that others shared similar problems with children, relaxed and discussed freely their problems and their children. They appeared to gain self-assurance and encouragement from the exchange of ideas.

Although mixed, some of the results pointed toward positive value in the study. As a consequence, it appears reasonable to give serious consideration to the questions herein postulated.

REFERENCES

1. Barrett, Harry B. "An Intensive Study of Thirty-Two Gifted Children," *Personnel and Guidance Journal*, XXXVI (November 1957).

2. Broedal, John, *et al.* "The Effects of Group Counseling on Gifted Underachieving Adolescents," *Journal of Counseling Psychology*, VII (Fall 1960).

3. Caplan, S. W. "The Effect of Group Counseling on Junior High School Boys' Concept of Themselves in School," *Journal of Counseling Psychology*, IV (Summer 1957).

4. Chess, Stella. *An Introduction to Child Psychology* (New York: Grune and Stratton, 1959).

5. Cohn, Benjamin, *et al.* "Group Counseling: An Orientation," *Personnel and Guidance Journal*, XLIV (December 1963).

6. Gazda, George M. "Group Counseling with Bright Underachieving Fifth Graders and their Parents." Paper presented at the American Personnel and Guidance Association Convention, Chicago, April 18, 1962.

7._____, and Ohlsen, Merle. "The Effects of Short-term Group Counseling on Prospective Counselors," *Personnel and Guidance Journal*, XXXIX.

8. Kehas, Chris D. "Underachievement as a Function of Self-Concept." Paper presented at the American Personnel and Guidance Association Convention, Boston, April 10, 1963.

9. Kelley, Truman L., *et al.* "Stanford Achievement Test, Intermediate Battery, Complete: Form J." (Yonkers: World Book Co., 1952).

10. Kirte, Barbara. "Test Versus Academic Performance in Malfunctioning Students," *Journal of Consulting Psychology*, XVI (June 1952).

11. McKenzie, James D., Jr. "The Dynamics of Deviant Achievement," *Personnel and Guidance Journal*, XLII (March 1064).

12. McNemar, Quinn. *Psychological Statistics* (New York: John Wiley and Sons, Inc., 1955).

13. Meeks, Anna. "What Can Be Done at the Elementary Level," *Guidance for the Underachiever with Superior Ability.* ed. by Leonard M. Miller, Bulletin No. 25 (Washington: U.S. Government Printing Office, 1961).

14. *Rating Scale for Pupil Adjustment* (Chicago: Science Research Associates, Inc., 1953).

15. Roth, Robert M., and Meyersbury, Arnold H. "The Non-Achievement Syndrome," *Personnel and Guidance Journal*, XLI (February 1963).

16. Schreiber, Daniel. "The School Dropout—Fugitive from Failure," *The Bulletin of the National Association of Secondary School Principals*, XLVI (May 1962)

17. Shaw, Merville C. "Definition and Identification of Academic Underachievers," *Guidance for the Underachiever with Superior Ability.* ed. by Leonard M. Miller, Bulletin No. 25 (Washington: U.S. Government Printing Office, 1961)

18. Shlien, John H., Mosak, Harold H. and Dreikurs, Rudolf. "Effect of Time Limits: A Comparison of Two Psychotherapies," *Journal of Counseling Psychology*, IX (Spring 1962).

19. Sonstegard, Manford. "Effects of Group Counseling of Parents upon the Performance of Underachieving Elementary School Children." Paper Presented at the American Personnel and Guidance Association Convention, Chicago, April 17, 1962.

35

Effects of Group Counseling on Role Behavior of Counselors in Training*

George M. Gazda

Warren C. Bonney

INTRODUCTION

Several authorities [4, 5, 10, 14, 18, 19] on the training of group psychotherapists have utilized and recommended the training technique of placing group psychotherapy trainees into psychotherapy groups with fellow trainees. Little has been done to investigate the application of a group counseling experience in the training of group counselors. However, with the increasing need for group counselors, methods of training them warrant investigation. In an earlier investigation by Gazda and Ohlsen [9], group counseling was found to be somewhat successful in increasing acceptance of self among prospective counselors. In addition, certain manifest needs were changed in the direction of increased adjustment.

In the study reported herein, the authors sought to measure pre- to post-counseling changes in the roles played by the counselors who participated in seven weeks of group counseling. The participants were twenty-four school counselors with at least a Masters Degree (major in guidance), and supervised counseling experience. These participants were enrolled in the NDEA Guidance Institute during the summer of 1962 at the University of Illinois. The Institute's emphasis was on group counseling, and prior to their acceptance, each member had volunteered to participate in a group counseling experience.

The use of role behavior in studying the effect of group counseling on the participants was employed because, according to Newcomb, it is "the unit par excellence from which we can draw conclusions *both* about individual personality . . . *and* about groups" [15]. Newcomb further contends that "persistence and change in personality are very closely

Reprinted by permission of the author and publishers from *Counselor Education and Supervision, 4* (1965), 191–197.

associated with persistence and change in roles . . ." and that the ". . . concept of role is as essential to the understanding of groups, as to that of individual personality" [15].

PROCEDURES

In order to study role behavior changes of the group counseling participants, it was first necessary to construct a Role Behavior Scale (RBS) of acceptable reliability and validity. For purposes of this study, Slater's definition of a role was adopted; he defines a role ". . . as a more or less coherent and unified system of items of interpersonal behavior" [16]. The descriptions of role behavior included in the RBS were adapted from Bales [2], Benne and Sheats [3], and Gorlow, Hoch and Teleshow [12], with modifications and additions by Ohlsen.[1]

The establishment of reliability for the RBS (nineteen descriptions of role behavior) employed in this research was of paramount importance to the entire study. (Content validity was assumed based on the role behavior descriptions.) We were fortunate to have two counseling groups in progress simultaneously with the experimental groups. The two groups which were used to establish the reliability of the RBS were composed of counselors and prospective counselors enrolled in a group counseling course taught at the Unversity of Illinois. The subjects in these groups matched very closely the subjects in the experimental group with respect to age, sex, education, and socio-economic levels. This group (reliability group) had met at least six sessions prior to the administration of the RBS. They repeated the test three days later—before they met again in their respective counseling groups.

The experimental groups had met for three one and one-half hour sessions prior to their completing the RBS. Three sessions were considered the minimum number necessary to avail subjects the opportunity to assume several types of role behavior. (Slater [16] had found that four sessions of forty minutes duration permits adequate differentiation of roles.) The post counseling evaluation was obtained at the termination of counseling—an experience which included fourteen sessions of approximately an hour and a half each twice a week extending over a seven week period.

The staff members who counseled the experimental subjects were experienced group counselors trained at the doctoral level. Hickley and Herman's [13] definition of group psychotherapy was acceptable to the group counselors as descriptive of the process they tried to emulate.

---

[1]M. M. Ohlsen. Personal communication. 1962.

RESULTS

Item and rater reliabilities were obtained from the ratings made by the control subjects on all nineteen items of the RBS for every person in their group but themselves. Each subject was rated on each role according to the following five point scale:

(a) never assumes this role in the group
(b) assumes this role less often than others in the group
(c) assumes this role about as often as others in the group
(d) assumes this role more often than most in the group
(e) assumes this role much more often than most in the group

To test the item and rater reliability, a two by two chi square table described by Garrett [8] with the accompanying coefficient of contingency C was computed for each item and each rater. Yates' correction was made in all cases and the coefficient of contingency was corrected for grouping in accordance with Garrett [8] by dividing the computed C by the maximum C for that classification, which in all cases of a two by two table is .707. For both item and rater reliability the expected frequency was arbitrarily established as one half of N even though the scale was a five point scale. This allowance was made to correct for the short time lapse of three days between the test-retest periods.

The data from the two non-experimental groups were combined in the computation of item reliability. The groups appeared similar enough to warrant this. Some items were retained and reported herein because of the exploratory usage of the RBS even though their reliability was questionable. A directional test of chi square was employed with the assumption that the raters' second rating would more often agree than disagree with their first rating. Hence, a $\frac{1}{2}$ P is used as the significance level of the item. The item reliabilities for those items which were retained and on which the role behavior changes were calculated are shown in Table 1. No item was retained for use in the analysis of role behavior

Table 1

Item Reliability*

Items	N	X^2	P	C
2. Opinion Seeker	98	2.30	.069	.21
3. Information Giver	98	1.72	.096	.17
6. Initiator	98	2.94	<.05	.24
8. Interpreter	98	2.94	<.05	.24
13. Passive-Resister	98	2.30	.069	.21
14. Non-Participant	97	2.02	.082	.33
16. Aggressor	98	12.50	<.05	.48
17. Recognition Seeker	98	18.86	<.05	.75
18. Help Seeker	98	9.80	<.05	.42
19. Dominator	98	48.6	<.05	.80

* df in all cases = 1.

change if ½ P was larger than .096. Because of the directional hypothesis, the retained items were items for which the number of exact agreements between the first and second ratings exceeded the number of disagreements.

The fact that nine items in the RBS could not be rated with satisfactory consistency suggests that the items may lack clairty or conciseness or that raters are unable to make nineteen independent reliable ratings. Carter [6] suggests that the latter explanation may be the answer. Carter demonstrated that even though semantic distinctions can be made among numerous behaviors, the actual number of independent dimensions which can be assessed for persons participating in small groups is about three or four. This explanation may also, at least partially, account for some of the poor reliability coefficients obtained for three or four of the ten items which were retained.

For the sake of brevity, only the ten roles which proved to have acceptable reliability for subjects in this study are reproduced in full below. The remaining nine are listed by number and title only.

2. Opinion Seeker: Asks not primarily for the facts of the case but for a clarification of the values pertinent to what the group is undertaking, or of values involved in a suggestion made or in alternative suggestions.

3. Information Giver: Offers facts or generalizations which are "authoritative" or relates his own experience pertinently to the group problem.

6. Initiator: Suggests or proposes to the group new ideas or a changed way of regarding the group problems or goal. The initiation may take the form of a proposed new procedure for the group or a new way of organizing the group for the task ahead.

8. Interpreter: Interprets feelings expressed by members of the group or interprets the significance of non-verbal behavior.

13. Passive Resister: Displays a lack of involvement in the group's work. Actions may take the form of cynicism, nonchalance, horseplay, and other forms of "out-of-field" behavior.

14. Non-Participant: Does not participate in the group discussion at all but shows no signs of active or passive resistance.

16. Aggressor: Exhibits hostile behavior toward others or attacks the topic of discussion. Deflates the status of others. Expresses disapproval of values, acts, or feelings of others.

17. Recognition Seeker: Calls attention to himself by boasting, monopolizing the conversation, or other forms of exhibitionistic behavior. Struggles to avoid being placed in an inferior position.

18. Help Seeker: Tries to evoke sympathy from others through expressions of insecurity, personal confusion, or depreciation of self.

19. Dominator: Tries to assert authority or superiority in manipulating the group or certain members of the group. The dominator gives directions authoritatively or interrupts the contributions of others.

Roles which did not prove to have adequate reliability were 1 (Information Seeker), 4 (Opinion Giver), 5 (Structurer), 7 (Clarifier), 9 (Reflector), 10 (Evaluater), 11 (Expeditor), 12 (Supporter), and 15 (Blocker).

Rater Reliability based on each of the ten items which were retained was obtained in the same fashion as the item reliability, but of course the group data could not be combined in this instance because each group member rated only those persons in his group. The reliabilities for each rater are shown in Table 2.

Rater reliability appeared to vary considerably between groups X and Y. An explanation for this phenomenon is unavailable.

Table 2

Rater Reliability*

Rater	N	x^2	P	C
x-1	60	20.42	< .05	.71
x-2	60	6.02	< .05	.43
x-3	60	8.82	< .05	.48
x-4	60	20.42	< .05	.71
x-5	59	27.2	< .05	.80
x-6	60	20.42	< .05	.71
x-7	60	8.82	< .05	.48
y-1	70	.064	N.S.	.13
y-2	69	.72	N.S.	.14
y-3	69	.72	N.S.	.14
y-4	69	.72	N.S.	.14
y-5	69	3.84	< .05	.29
y-6	70	.350	N.S.	.04
y-7	70	6.86	< .05	.40
y-8	70	2.06	N.S.	.24

*df in all cases = 1.

Table 3

Perceived Changes in Role Behavior

Items	N	Critical values for r*
2. Opinion Seeker	83	above 25%
3. Information Giver	85	1%
4. Initiator	86	25%
8. Interpreter	79	1%
13. Passive Resister	66	above 25%
14. Non-Participant	73	1%
16. Aggressor	78	1%
17. Recognition Seeker	68	15%
18. Help Seeker	96	above 25%
19. Dominator	69	above 25%

See Dixon and Massey (1957).

* Represents two-tail percentage points for the binomial for p = .5.

The Sign Test was utilized to test whether the group participants perceived role behavior changes at post counseling. The data for the three experimental groups were combined in this analysis. Although there were twenty-four experimental subjects, data from four of the subjects were incomplete leaving twenty on which the present analysis is based. Table 3 contains the results of the analysis.

DISCUSSION

Inspection of the data revealed that there was a significant increase in the assumption of the roles Information Giver, Interpreter, Non-Participant, and Aggressor. Before one attempts to account for these changes, it seems worthwhile to point out what these ratings mean. The reader is reminded that the results represent the cumulative perceptions of the participants of changes or shifts in roles made by the experimental group as a whole. Individual shifts in roles are of course hidden within the over-all change.

The increase in the roles Information Giver, Interpreter, and Aggressor appears to be consistent. The increase in the role Non-Participant, at first glance, may seem inconsistent with the other changes until one considers the possibility that some members may have decreased their participation near the end of the group sessions either because they had resolved the kinds of problems that they may have had in the beginning or because they were aware of the termination period and did not wish to open issues that could not be given adequate attention. Another hypothesis is that active role behavior in later sessions may be dynamically different from those same roles exhibited in earlier sessions because the individuals, in effect, have become different people.

Finally, the item does have questionable reliability and thus any change must be verified by further research.

An over-all increase in the Aggressor role may indicate that a significant number of group members became less inhibited. (There was agreement among the group counselers that this was in part the situation.) An increase in the role Information Giver may be represented in the lowered inhibitions of the participants and increased self confidence, as well as the over all increase in knowledge of group counseling techniques and dynamics which would be expected from the participants' class work and practicum experiences, or it may be the result of the item's questionable reliability. Increased assumption of the Interpreter role may also be tied to the new learning gleaned from the practicum experiences of the participants and/or to increased confidence as a result of the group counseling experience. Finally, any or all of the changes may represent some practices of the group counselors which were adopted by the participants as they themselves became co-counselors in the groups.

If one assumes as Bach [17] does that therapy groups go through growth phases and that various individual subjects go through the phases in the group at different times, our data may simply indicate that several individuals happened to be at the same stage or at a stage which caused others to see them as increasing in the use of a given role behavior.

One weakness of the use of subjects as raters, according to George [11] is that subjects will perceive patterns of behavior they have learned to expect in groups. The fact that these counselors who participated in the groups rated an increase in the Aggressor role suggests that they were not being influenced by what they expected to find in the group.

The fact that there were no significant decreases in role behavior may be an artifact of the role definitions. For example, an increase in the Non-Participant role would be a decrease in a participant role.

Repeated pre-post administration of the RBS to counselees in groups may help group counselors in the future better to predict what the effects of this experience will be for a particular group. Perhaps too, a group counselor will be able to evaluate his methods on the basis of the role changes his clients assume.

REFERENCES

1. Bach, S. R. *Intensive Group Psycotherapy* (New York: The Ronald Press, 1954).

2. Bales, R. F. *Interaction Process Analysis* (Cambridge: Addison-Wesley Press, 1950).

3. Benne, K. D. & Sheats, P. "Functional Roles of Group Members," *J. Soc. Issues* (1948), 4, 42–47.

4. Berger M. "Problems of Anxiety in Group Psychotherapy Trainees." In M. Rosenbaum & M. Berger (Eds.) *Group Psychotherapy and Group Function* (New York: Basic Books, 1963), pp. 555–557.

5. Berman L. "A Group Psychotherapeutic Technique for Training in Clinical Psychology," *Am. J. Orthopsychiat.* (1953), 23, 322–327.

6. Carter, L. F. "Recording and Evaluating the Performance of Individuals as Members of Small Groups." In P. H. Hare, E. F. Borgatta, & D. F. Bales (Ed.) *Small Groups* (New York: Alfred A. Knopf, 1955).

7. Dixon, W. J. & Massey, F. J. Jr. *Introduction to Statistical Analysis* (New York: McGraw-Hill, 1957).

8. Garrett, H. E. *Statistics in Phychology and Education*, 5th ed. (New York: Longmans, Green & Company, 1958).

9. Gazda, G. M. & Ohlsen, M. M. "Effects of Short-term Group Counseling on Prospective Counselors," *Personnel Guid J.* (1961), 39, 634–638.

10. Geller, J. J. "An Experience in Group Psychotherapy as a Teaching Device," *Group Psychother.* (1951), 7, 130–138.

11. George, C. E. *Research Memorandum: Some Determinants of Small-group Effectiveness.* (Revised Oct., 1962. (Fort Benning, Georgia: U. S. Army Infantry Human Research Unit, 1962).

12. Gorlow, L., Hoch, E. L. & Teleshow, E. F. *The Nature of Nondirective Group Psychotherapy* (New York: Bureau of Publications, Teachers College, Columbia University, 1952).

13. Hinckley, R. G., & Herman, Lydia. *Group Treatment in Psychotherapy* (Minneapolis: Univeristy of Minnesota Press, 1951).

14. Kugelmass, S. & Schossberger, J. "Problems of Initial Training for Group Psychotherapy in Israel," *Int. J. Group Psychother.* (1958), 8, 179–184.

15. Newcomb, T. H. "Role Behaviors in the Study of Individual Personality and of Groups," *J. Pers.* (1950), 13, 273–289.

16. Slater, P. H. "Role Differentiation in Small Groups." In P. H. Hare, E. F. Borgatta, & R. F. Bales (Eds.) *Small Groups* (New York: Alfred A. Knopf, 1955).

17. Talland, G. "Role and Status Structure in Therapy Groups," *J. Clin. Psychol.* (1957), 13, 27–33.

18. Warkentin, J. "An Experience in Teaching Psychotherapy By Means of Group Therapy." In M. Rosebaum & M. Berger (Eds.) *Group Psychotherapy and Group Function* (New York: Basic Books, 1963), pp. 555–557.

19. Wolf, A., Locke N., Rosenbaum, Hillpern, E., Goldfarb, W., Kadis, A., Abers, S., Milberg, I., & Abell, R. "The Psychonalysis of Groups," *Int. J. Group Psychother.* (1952), 2, 221–231.

Chapter VI

GROUP COUNSELING
OPERATIONALIZED: SOME
QUESTIONS AND
ANSWERS

This chapter is designed to provide the prospective and practicing group counselor with answers to some of the most common questions asked about group counseling. This is not to say that the intent here is to present a single method or "school" approach to group counseling. An extremely narrow parochial view of counseling in groups at a time when our knowledge is comparatively limited is neither possible nor practical. Research evidence in group counseling, though it continues to provide new data for bridging the gap between theory and practice, has not yet provided enough evidence to support a single approach to group counseling.

The editors' views presented here and the methods described in the readings selected for this chapter are not the final or only approaches to some of the practical problems of group counseling. The judge of their appropriateness for utilization in group counseling must be the counselor who may wish to apply the suggested techniques.

I. HOW DO I PROMOTE INTEREST IN GROUP COUNSELING IN A SCHOOL SETTING?

One of the most difficult problems that faces the group counselor is getting a group underway. If students are going to participate in group counseling, they must be able to see that participation will in some way be beneficial to them. The modern comprehensive high school places heavy demands on student time, and the teen age boy or girl who is burdened with a heavy academic load and numerous co-curricular activities is not likely to devote one or two hours a week to group counseling unless he can see that group participation is a valuable and worthwhile experience.

There are, of course, many factors that may work against a counselor who wishes to form a group. Foremost among these is the image of the counselor that the student body holds. If he is viewed as "the guy who helps me find a college," or the staff member "who gives the IQ tests," his task may become more difficult. In too many schools, counselors have assumed that the students know what counseling is when in reality they may have limited or distorted perception of the nature of counseling. Resistance to counseling is not uncommon and the initial role of the counselor in any school must be one of the provision of a proper climate for counseling both within the school and in the actual counseling process. This will require both administrative and faculty support, and in many cases this support must be earned. In addition the counselor must define for the student body how he can be of help to them.

The most obvious way to initiate counseling in groups is to communicate to students what group counseling is, how it will be beneficial to them, and what will be expected of them in a group. One effective way to accomplish this is to make a short presentation in those classes that are common to all students. In most schools, this can be done by securing teacher permission to speak to English, social studies, or physical education classes in each grade. By appearing in each English or social studies class at each grade level in the school, the counselor will be able to reach all students in groups that are small enough to provide time for the students to ask any questions they may have. Such presentations are also excellent opportunities to establish rapport with the student body.

The content of an oral presentation to the students may well vary with different counselors because of differences in counseling philosophy and methodology, but several specific topics should be discussed that are of importance regardless of counselor orientation.

(1) Students should be told in simple terms about the nature of group counseling. It may be helpful to inform prospective counselees that participants will be given an opportunity to learn more about themselves, their plans, and the ways that other students see them.

(2) Prospective group members should know that group meetings are confidential and the topics discussed in groups are not for general discussion outside the group meetings.

(3) Students should be informed that they are not joining a "therapy" group. Students frequently associate any type of counseling with an activity for those who are in some way "unhealthy."

(4) The counselor should prepare a schedule of the time he has available for working with groups. Within this limitation, the number of meetings a week and the duration of counseling should be a topic to be decided after the groups have been formed.

(5) The counselor should emphasize that a group counseling session is not a "class" and grades are not given for group participation.

(6) Students should know whether or not their volunteering to partici-

pate would mean that they would be selected as group members. It is best to inform class size groups of the number of students the counselor wishes to have in a group, and how the final selection will be made if the number of volunteers is too large.

(7) It is beneficial to inform the class size groups that students who wish to participate may be interviewed individually. This will give the counselor an additional opportunity to make decisions about placing the student in a group. In addition students may wish to ask the counselor certain personal questions about group participation that may be embarassing to ask in a class size group.

(8) A "sign up" sheet should be passed around following each presentation in order for interested students to place their names on a list for possible group participation. An additional "sign up" sheet should be maintained in the counselor's office or with his secretary.

Once a counselor has gathered a list of prospective members, he then must decide how to select the members of the groups. Scheduling problems, space limitations, and the goals of counseling may delimit the number who actually participate. For example, he may wish to conduct sessions with some students who need help in making career plans, or with those students who want to learn more effective ways of studying.

II. HOW DO I SELECT GROUP MEMBERS?

The problem of final group selection is one that frequently appears in the literature in both group counseling and group therapy. The most common problem is whether or not to use a homogeneous or heterogeneous group. What is important to remember is that a group is homogeneous only insofar as the factors that determine homogeneity can be controlled. Even groups that can be controlled on such factors as age, sex, and I.Q. may be diverse in socioeconomic background, maturity, and motivation. In essence a group will be homogeneous with regard to certain factors and heterogeneous with regard to others. Grouping by this criterion then may be simply a matter of counselor definition.

Some writers, Mahler and Caldwell [8] among them, suggest that definition of purpose sets the limits for determining group membership. They recommend that counselors start with groups of students who are concerned with educational and vocational problems or with students who are in trouble for minor misconduct problems. Although this sounds like a reasonable approach, the definition of purpose as perceived by the counselor and the purpose for participation as perceived by the student may be quite different. The counselor who wishes to use definition of purpose as a basis for group selection must be certain that *his* purpose and that of the student is similar unless of course the goals of group counseling are to be set entirely by the counselor.

Therapy groups are frequently formed on the basis of a clinical diagnosis, and this selection often varies because of the different theoretical orientations. Diagnostic grouping is also possible for the counselor who may wish to form groups of students on the basis of some measure of self-concept, or other personality dimension. In some cases groups are formed on such single factors as age, sex, maturity level or measured intelligence or some combination of these. The problem has also been attacked from the standpoint of exclusion, and some writers contend that almost any grouping is acceptable if certain "types" of individuals are excluded. For example Hobbs [6] and Bach [3] list such factors as psychological sophistication, extreme aggressiveness, and insufficient reality contact as factors for exclusion.

While all of these factors must be taken into account, the school counselor is generally not confronted with a psychologically sophisticated individual, and if no help is available he may have to guess at just what constitutes "extreme aggressiveness," and "insufficient reality contact." Until we have sufficient research evidence to support a given theory of grouping, counselor judgment and experimentation may be the best basis for group selection. There are, however, certain factors the counselor must consider in grouping.

GROUP SIZE

The key factor that the counselor must consider is his intended method of operation. The more task oriented the counselor is the more he may prefer a group approaching class size, although this would raise a question of whether the activity was in fact group counseling. If the counselor sees interaction among members as his method of operation, he may wish to reduce group membership to ten or less. Many counselors strive for maximum group interaction, and this dictates a smaller number of participants. As a general rule, a group consisting of eight participants in addition to the counselor seems to be a workable number.

GROUPING BY SEX

Counseling groups, like numerous social groups in the daily affairs of people's lives, should contain equal numbers of males and females unless there appears to be a definite reason for not doing so [4]. The fact that many high school and college functions are planned for members of both sexes and that topics concerned with boy-girl relations are common group themes lends support to the concept of mixed grouping.

AGE

The age factor is sometimes considered as important by group therapists, but this is generally not a problem in most high school or college groups since the age range of the student body is generally not extremely large. What the school counselor should consider, however, are factors of maturity. For example, a nineteen year old senior boy and a thirteen year old freshman may react quite differently to certain topics such as discussion of sex. The counselor must decide how mature an individual is prior to placing him in a group.

In the high school, class level must be considered along with age since classes tend to achieve certain status levels as they advance through the secondary school. Senior boys for example, often tend to dominate underclassmen. The captain of the football team or the head cheerleader may not care to be grouped with an "insignificant" freshman. Younger boys and girls are also not as likely to participate actively in counseling groups where most of the group members are at an advanced grade level.

GOALS

The goals of counseling must be considered both from the standpoint of the counselor and the members of the group. What are the expected outcomes of counseling? Who should determine the goal of the group, the counselor, the clients, or should this be a joint effort?

The counselor who selects a group of underachievers is probably hoping that they will achieve better, and the counselor who selects a group of "problem" children is probably hoping that counseling will result in improved behavior. In this sense the counselor has determined the goals and may "steer" the counseling group in ways that he feels will result in a predetermined outcome.

Much of the reported research done on group counseling has been done with underachievers, potential dropouts, or behavior problems. The counselor may wish to "counsel for college" with bright students who "have the ability and don't want to use it" or he may select children who "have problems" and counsel "to solve problems." If the goals of group members and the goals of the counselor are non-conflicting, the counselor who "counsels for" may achieve results that could be labeled "successful" counseling.

Related to the goals of counseling is the counselor's philosophy, his view of man, and his value system. The counselor might well heed Arbuckle who sees the goals of counseling in terms of client satisfaction and honesty toward self:

> A goal of counseling might be to help the individual attain a stage of development at which he can honestly look at himself and eventually derive some element of satisfaction in what he sees 1, p. 58 .

III. WHERE SHOULD I MEET WITH A GROUP?

In high school and college situations, the more appropriate question may be—Where can I meet? Double sessions, bell schedules, and administrative efforts to make maximum use of available building space give the counselor some unique problems that his therapist counterpart may not have to face with institutionalized persons. Even those counselors who have formed "after school" groups face bus schedule problems and the activities program. A group, however, must have a meeting place and some general rules of thumb should be followed:

(1) Select a room where there are as few distractions as possible. Gazda[1] describes the adverse effects of having other students peer in windows in a research study he conducted with elementary children. In his opinion student interruptions and the artificial environment caused by the use of television cameras were factors that worked against the development of a proper climate for counseling and contributed to the somewhat disappointing results obtained in the study.

(2) Groups who must "roam" from room to room seem to take a certain amount of time to get settled since different furniture, wall displays, and writing on the blackboards seem to distract their attention. Counselors who are forced to use different school areas for group sessions should try to select rooms that are as much alike as possible with regard to furniture, size, etc. For example, a counseling session conducted in a home economics room one week and in the gym bleachers the next week would be a poor practice.

(3) If the group is small enough the counselor's office or guidance conference room seem to be best suited for group counseling. Students generally perceive the counselor's office as being "different" than a classroom. Students tend to associate certain parts of a building with certain aspects of the school program. Evidence of this can be seen in situations where the school counselor and principal occupy adjacent offices. The counselor may well see himself as a "helper," but the students may see him as some sore of disciplinarian. If the school has had an effective guidance program and the students actively seek counselor help, the guidance office of a school may well be a place where students like to go. If this is true, then it represents an ideal locale for group counseling.

IV. HOW SHOULD A ROOM BE FURNISHED FOR COUNSELING?

There is much discussion in the literature related to group counseling about the arrangement and type of furnishing that promotes effective coun-

[1] Personal communication.

seling. McCann and Almada [9] conduct what they describe as round-table psychotherapy in which the table is an important aspect of the counseling process. Luchins [7] in his discussions of furnishings for group counseling discusses the use of hard and soft chairs and movable or immovable seats. The counselor, however, is more likely to find himself with furnishings that were primarily designed to be functional within the traditional concepts of formal education. In some of the more ancient school buildings in the land, he may get movable chairs only if the custodian has neglected to tighten the floor bolts!

Generally a circular arrangement with a round table seems to be effective for group counseling, especially if the counselor wishes to promote group interaction. Some writers, most notably Brammer and Shostrom [4] feel that certain furnishings such as a desk are authority symbols and actually hinder counseling. Care must be taken, however, if the counselor decides to use no furniture except chairs since one of the editors discovered in a recent research project that the elimination of a table from a counseling session decreased interaction. The apparent reason for this was the feeling on the part of some of the girls in the group that they could not "sit comfortably" and paid less attention to what was being discussed. The lesson to be learned from this is simply that the furnishings of a room for counseling may have some effect on the counseling process, but this effect cannot always be predetermined.

V. HOW OFTEN SHOULD A GROUP MEET? HOW LONG SHOULD EACH SESSION BE CONDUCTED? HOW LONG SHOULD A GROUP CONTINUE TO MEET?

The frequency of group meetings, the length of each session, and the number of sessions to be held are questions the counselor must consider. For example, some researchers in group counseling who have found little change in pre and post measures of students in group counseling seem to feel that they would have obtained better results if counseling had been continued for a longer period of time. Others have felt that if the frequency of the meetings had been increased their research efforts would have produced better results. Groups who meet twice a week tend to become more cohesive, do more self-exploration, and seem more willing to participate in counseling than those who meet once a week. In a recent study with college freshmen [10] noticeable differences were apparent in the group that met twice weekly when they were compared with the group that met once a week. The group which met more often explored more problems, interacted a great deal more, and seemed to derive more personal satisfaction from the counseling experience. There does not, however, seem to be much supporting evidence that increased frequency of meetings or counseling over a prolonged period will necessarily produce more "change."

In school situations the length of meetings, the number of sessions per week, and the ultimate number of sessions are more likely to be determined by the counselor's work load, the class schedule of the students, and the overall administrative framework of the school system. A counselor and a group may both agree that counseling during the summer months would be beneficial, but this is generally not practical since students often work during the summers, others take vacations with their parents, and the counselor himself may be unavailable during the summer. Thus factors beyond the control of the group or the counselor often dictate when counseling will terminate.

Group sessions can range anywhere from a half hour to two hours in length, but periods of an hour seem to work well for high school and college students, and generally this period of time approximates the time alloted to regular class meetings.

Children of elementary school age may not be able to participate in group sessions that are of an hour in length, especially if the counseling is primarily verbal in nature. The counselor who may wish to adopt play or activity techniques for "normal" children as suggested by Axline [2] or Slavson [13] may find that younger children may remain in counseling for an hour or longer.

The optimum number of sessions for counseling groups cannot be determined any more readily than can the determination of the optimum number of sessions for individual counseling. As previously noted, some researchers who have had disappointing results in getting little "change" or "improvement" in some aspect of the clients' behavior have suggested that better results would have been obtained if counseling had been prolonged. Such discussions are, of course, generally concerned with measureable change and the sensitivity of the instruments used to measure such change, and the inability to control many factors that determine the individual's behavior make the measuring of change extremely difficult.

In therapy groups, the therapist may make a subjective judgment that his group members are better or changed—perhaps by deciding that the group as a whole is less anxious, is better able to deal with reality or along some other clinical variable. In such cases he makes the decision to terminate counseling. Counselors also may make subjective judgments that will help them come to a decision about group counseling. Underachieving students may start to get better grades, "problem children" may be suspended from class less often, or the chronic absentee may attend school more often than he did before.

There is always the possibility, too, that students in a group or the group as a whole may wish to decide that counseling should be discontinued.

Since the questions when to meet, how often to meet, and how long to continue meeting are of importance to both the counselor and the group, the counselor should discuss these questions with the group at an early stage in counseling, preferably during the first meeting.

Final termination of counseling should be a flexible matter since the group as a whole may decide to discontinue counseling or specific individuals may wish to drop out. Such matters should be discussed in the group, since the group may wish to add new members to replace a student who has left, or they may wish to continue with a smaller number of members. It is important that the counselor, with the aid of the group, discuss and set up "group policy" at an early date in order that the counselor and the group are both aware of what procedures will be followed if several members decide to leave a group, or if an entire group decides to terminate counseling.

Students may wish to discontinue counseling for any number of reasons, but the counselor who feels that the group is for the benefit of the student will not be disturbed by group "dropouts" or group termination. The needs of the student, not those of the counselor are the ones that need be considered, and in the final analysis only the student can determine if he is deriving any benefit from group participation. In essence the counselor must be as flexible as he can be and allow individuals and groups to make their own decisions with regard to the frequency of meetings and duration of counseling.

VI. HOW SHOULD A COUNSELOR FUNCTION IN A GROUP

The counselor's functioning in a group is bound to be determined by his counseling philosophy, objectives that he has for the group, and his views on the nature of man. Counselors who feel that adolescents need advice, direction, and information will structure the group process in such a way that group members are directed to attend to authorities both within and without the group. The counselor who views counseling as a process that provides the student with a measure of self exploration and sees the goals of counseling in terms of greater self understanding will probably work with groups quite differently.

It is not the purpose of this book to present an argument for a certain "school" of counseling. Group counseling is no more a "method" or "bag of tricks" than is individual counseling. Counselors who differ as individuals must decide for themselves the "what" and "how" of group counseling. It may, however, be beneficial to provide counselors who have never worked with groups some of the suggestions of experienced group counselors.

Glanz sees the counselor working within the framework of six phases of the counseling process:

(1) rapport
(2) acceptance
(3) listening and observing
(4) promoting group and individual differences
(5) problem-solving skill development
(6) closing evaluation and procedures [5, p. 227, pp. 278–298]

Ohlsen calls for the counselor to function as a helper and to use the advantages of the group situation to provide maximum individual development:

> What does the counselor do in a group? He tries to understand how each pupil feels, to help each pupil tell how he feels, and help and discover what he can do to realize his own potential and to live more richly. The counselor also tries to sense how each person affects the others, and to help them help one another. Sometimes he helps them decide what they should try to do [11, p. 153].

Shertzer and Stone point out that the group counselor must be able to concentrate on both the *group* and the *individual*:

> The counselor's task is more complicated in group counseling. He not only has to understand the speaker's feelings and help him become aware of of them, but he must also observe how the speaker's comments influence the group members. The counselor must not only be aware of the discussion, he must be perceptive of the interplay of relationships among the members [12, p. 182].

Gazda (1964[2]) presents a rather eclectic position of the role of the counselor in a group and lists some techniques that the counselor may use. According to his views, the counselor:

(a) serves as group leader
(b) functions as a catalyst
(c) may have to protect some group members
(d) teaches skills needed by the group in order to make them function
(e) teaches techniques of problem solving
(f) facilitates group discussion
(g) looks for all things which interfere with group functioning
(h) looks for group assets
(i) may pull passive individuals into the group
(j) makes the experience meaningful to all in the group

The counselor does this by the use of such techniques as:

(a) reflecting feeling
(b) clarifying
(c) information giving
(d) role playing

[2]Personal communication.

Brammer and Shostrom [4] suggest several "techniques" that the counselor could employ including the going around technique, the psychodramatic or role playing technique, and the post session technique. The reader is referred to their text for a more detailed discussion of these approaches.

Waters [14] provides an overview of the role of the counselor and indicates how the group may be started, the importance of support and identification, reality testing, and discusses the evolutionary process in group work.

Bach in discussing the overt aspects of the therapist's role in groups lists eighteen "Do's" and ten "Don'ts" for group therapy. Some of these do's seem to be appropriate for group counselors and are printed in abbreviated form here:[3]

(1) Do try on the deepest emotional level to be an accurate reflector of the experience of patients.

(2) Do remember that you are a service rendering member, not a parasitic, "scientific" observer of the group.

(3) Do think of a group of patients as a basically constructive force, a manifestation for the capacity for mutual aid in man which can and will show.

(4) Do contribute to the group through your clinical helpfulness and democratic leadership, rather than through lecturing.

(5) Do share what you can of your knowledge and also of your personal feelings, experiences, and values with the group when such sharing can serve a useful stiulus.

(6) Do help patients in a group to increase their tolerance for individual differences.

(7) Do always attempt to gauge correctly and reflect the majority group consensus concerning any topic.

(8) Do acknowledge being puzzled.

(9) Do in your selection procedures, recognize the principles of the social interdependence of human personalities.

(10) Do engage in research.

The reader who is interested in full presentation of the "Do's and "Don'ts" of group psychotherapy as presented by Bach is referred to pages 204–209 of his text, *Intensive Group Psychotherapy* [3].

Counselors conduct groups in many different ways. Each counselor must find the methods that best fit him, capitalize on his own personal strengths, and accommodate to his limitations. Reading about the experiences and recommendations of others, as in the following articles can be a start towards developing a personal style. Two articles, one referring to group psychotherapy and one concerned with group size, are included because the

[3]George R. Bach, *Intensive Group Psychotherapy.* Copyright 1954 (New York: The Ronald Press Company).

editors believe such reading, while not directly transferable to the practice of group counseling, is an important stimulation to which the counselor should open himself. In the final analysis the counselor must experience group life both as a group member and counselor to complete the formulation of his unique approach to group counseling subject to a concept of professional ethics. Ethical considerations in group counseling are discussed in Chapter VII.

REFERENCES

1. Arbuckle, D. S. *Counseling, Philosophy Theory and Practice* (Boston: Houghton Mifflin, 1965).

2. Axline, Virginia. *Play Therapy* (Boston: Houghton Mifflin, 1947).

3. Bach, G. *Intensive Group Psychotherapy* (New York: Ronald Press, 1954).

4. Brammer, L. M. and Shostrom, E. M. *Therapeutic Psychology* (Englewood Cliffs, New Jersey: Prentice-Hall, Inc., 1964).

5. Glanz, Edward. *Groups In Guidance* (Boston: Allyn and Bacon, 1962).

6. Hobbs, N. "Group Centered Psychotherapy" in C. Rogers' *Client-Centered Therapy* (Boston: Houghton Mifflin, 1951).

7. Luchins, A. *Group Therapy: A Guide* (New York: Random House, 1964).

8. Mahler, Clarence A. and Caldwell, Edson. *Group Counseling in Secondary Schools* (Chicago: Science Research Assoc., 1961).

9. McCann, W. H. and Almada, A. A. "Round Table Psychotherapy: A Technique In Group Psychotherapy," *Journal of Consult. Psychology,* 14 (1950), pp. 431–435.

10. Muro, J. J. and Ohnmacht, F. W. "Effects of Group Counseling on Dimensions of Self-acceptance, Dogmatism and Preference for Complexity with Teacher Education Students." *SPATE* (1966), 10, 25–30.

11. Ohlsen, Merle M. *Guidance Services in the Modern School* (New York: Harcourt, Brace and World, 1964).

12. Shertzer, Bruce and Stone, Shelley. *Fundamentals of Guidance* (Boston: Houghton Mifflin, 1966).

13. Slavson, S. R. *An Introduction to Group Therapy* (New York: The Commonwealth Fund, 1943).

14. Warters, Jane. *Group Guidance* (New York: McGrawy Hill, 1960).

36

Homogeneous Versus Heterogeneous Groups*

William Furst

This presentation represents the opinion of my associates, Doctor Lewis H. Loeser, Mrs. Thea Bry and myself and is derived from the experimental work and experience we have gained in group therapy during military service and in private practice.

The problem of the homogeneous versus heterogeneous group has interested us from the onset of our work. In using these terms we are referring to diagnostic and psychodynamic criteria. Although the terms may equally well be applied to homogeneity of age, sex, color, religion, etc., we have used, and are now using, this terminology only in reference to diagnosis and to underlying psychopathology. A homogeneous group, then, is one in which a reasonable similarity in psychodynamics and pathology is known to exist among the members of the group. All other similarities or differences in this discussion are set aside.

Our accent has been placed on research techniques and we have employed the method of parallel and control group to throw further light on certain basic questions. We have, for example, material based on intensive study of two homogeneous and two heterogeneous groups, otherwise similar in make-up and nature. Each group has been carefully selected; detailed observations of each session were recorded by an observer, and cases reasonably well followed after treatment. We use an interview type of therapy, analytically oriented, and our patients are all private patients on a fee basis who have voluntarily applied for treatment.

Only conclusions will be given here.

Observations on homogeneous groups of anxiety neurotics lead to the following conclusions:

1. Group identification takes place quickly and transferences are rapidly formed.
2. Re-education takes place rapidly and insight develops quickly.
3. Psychodynamics are more rapidly laid bare.
4. Duration of treatment is lessened.
5. Attendance is more regular.

*Reprinted by permission of the author and publisher from *International Journal of Group Psychotherapy* (1951), 1, 120–123.

6. Interferences, resistances, and interactions of a destructive nature are lessened.
7. Intramural groups or cliques are uncommon.
8. Recovery from symptoms is more rapid.

On the negative side, in dealing with homogeneous groups, we note:

1. Homogeneous groups are difficult to put together. Careful screening and a large number of patients from which to select are necessary.
2. Because of the absence of interaction factors the level of therapy is relatively superficial.
3. Despite removal of symptoms, character structure is relatively untouched.
4. The opportunity for reality testing is lessened by the absence of interaction with heterogeneous personalities.
5. The opportunity to develop multiple and shifting transferences in accordance to needs is lacking.

Our experience with heterogeneous groups would lead to the following observations. On the negative side we would conclude that:

1. Recovery takes place more slowly. Anxiety neurotics, for example, in a homogeneous group become symptom free faster than in a heterogeneous group.
2. Problems of interaction and resulting tensions within the group become magnified. The problems of the therapist are multiplied.
3. Group identification takes place slowly.
4. Transference to the therapist is delayed.
5. Insight is slow in developing. Common denominators are difficult to work out in the field of psychodynamics.
6. Attendance is likely to be more irregular.

On the positive side there is evidence that:

1. Heterogeneous groups by their very nature tend to take the therapist, whether or not he so desires, into deeper levels of therapy.
2. Character structure as well as symptom formation are influenced by the process of therapy.
3. Reality testing is more adequate and thorough.
4. Intra-group transferences of a diverse and shifting nature can be formed readily in the heterogeneous group in accordance with individual needs.
5. Heterogeneous groups are easy to assembly and screening need not be as thorough.

As a result of our observations, derived from actual comparison of homogeneous and heterogeneous groups, certain broad generalizations are justified. We are firmly convinced that both types of groups can be utilized in group therapy. However, the make-up of the group has an important bearing on the type and nature of therapy, and we submit the following conclusions for consideration:

1. Heterogeneous groups are necessary for activity therapy, for interaction therapy, and for group psychoanalysis. Homogeneous groups are not as suitable for these types of group therapy.
2. Interview therapy, analytically oriented, can be carried out successfully with both homogeneous and heterogeneous groups.

The question of "level of therapy" is closely linked to the make-up of the group. It is difficult to do deep therapy with a homogeneous group. It is difficult not to do deep therapy with a heterogeneous group. Homogeneous groups do not put as much strain on the therapist and do not require the skill and experience on his part that heterogeneous groups require.

Homogeneous groups then should be chosen:

a. When the interview type of therapy is utilized.
b. When less profound and nonintensive therapy is indicated.
c. When the therapist is not prepared or trained to handle deep levels of therapy.
d. When the factors of time and expense are important.

Heterogeneous groups on the other hand are to be chosen:

a. When deep levels of therapy are desired.
b. When modification of character structure is necessary.
c. When the training and experience of the therapist is adequate.
d. When time and expense are less important.

In conclusion, one can make the following generalization: Level of therapy and make-up of the group are factors which are closely correlated. Any discussion of one must involve the other factor. Neither homogeneous nor heterogeneous groups are best. They are to be used in accordance with the goals of the therapist.

37

Effects of Group Size*

Edwin J. Thomas

Clinton F. Fink

This paper reviews 31 empirical studies of small groups in which the major independent variable, group size, was related to several classes of dependent variables: group performance, distribution of participation, the nature of interaction, group organization, member performance, conformity and consensus, and member satisfaction. Many of these variables were found to be significantly affected by group size, but methodological shortcomings characterizing this group of studies preclude the assertion of broad generalizations. Several dependable and nondependable intervening variables are suggested which may help to account for many of the observed effects. Conclusions are: group size is an important variable which should be taken into account in any theory of group behavior, and future research on group size should proceed more systematically than in the past.

This report is an effort to formulate generalizations about the effects of group size from a critical review of past research and an analysis of methods and problems relating to this subject. It is focused mainly on studies of face-to-face groups ranging in size from 2–20 members, in which behavior was studied directly by observations, questionnaires, or interviews. Because of their relevance a few studies are included that depart in some respect from these criteria. While making no claim to comprehensiveness, we have included all studies that we could locate through 1960 meeting the above standards. In earlier reviews of research relating to small groups there were sections on group size [23, 27] , but no thorough review has been written. Studies of the size of families, organizations, cities, and societies are only generally relevant in this context and therefore have been excluded (see Caplow [8] for a review of studies relating to organizational size).

The studies discussed here do not represent an integrated attack upon a single problem or set of problems. Instead, they deal with a wide range of dependent variables and are concerned with establishing empirical relationships rather than with testing the implications of some general theory.

*This article reports portions of a research project financed by a grant from the Horace H. Rackham School of Graduate Studies of the University of Michigan. Reprinted by permission of the author and publisher from *Psychological Bulletin* (1963), 60, 371–384.

To order the findings meaningfully, we have found it convenient to discuss them as specific topics under one of two major categories: (*a*) effects on the group as a whole, which include group performance, the distribution of participation, the nature of interaction, and group organization; and (*b*) effects on member behavior, including individual performance, conformity and consensus, and member satisfaction.

EFFECTS FOR THE GROUP AS A WHOLE

GROUP PERFORMANCE

Ten experimental studies dealt with the effects of group size on group performance in problem solving or judgmental tasks. These findings are summarized according to four main classes of dependent variables: quality of performance, speed, efficiency, and productivity.

The quality of group problem solving was examined in four studies with mixed results. Taylor and Faust [41] found that in playing the game Twenty Questions, four-man groups correctly solved more problems than did two-man groups. Similarly, Fox, Lorge, Weltz, and Herrold [14] found that the quality of solutions to complex human-relations problems was significantly greater for groups of 12 and 13 than for groups of 6, 7, and 8. In contrast, Lorge and Solomon [29, 30] discovered no relationship between group size (2–5 members in the first study and 3, 4, 6, and 7 members in the second) and the proportion of groups which arrived at the correct solution to the Tartaglia problem.

The quality of group judgments based on collective decisions also showed mixed relationships to group size. South [36] found no difference between three-person and six-person groups in their ability to judge emotional expressions from photographs, but he did find that the six-person groups were better (i.e., agreed more with expert opinion) at judging the quality of English compositions. Ziller [46] presented groups of two to six Air Force officers with two types of task: he found a positive relationship between group size and the quality of the group's judgment concerning the importance of certain facts for making military decisions; however, there was a curvilinear relationship between size and the accuracy of the group's judgment of the number of dots on a card with four- and five-man groups doing less well than two-, three-, and six-man groups. Perlmutter's study [34] involved group memory rather than judgment: he found that three-person groups had somewhat better immediate recall for a story (The War of the Ghosts) than did two-person groups, but the difference was not statistically significant.

Speed of group performance was observed in three of the above studies [34, 36, 41] as well as in the Study by Kidd [25]. In each case, speed was measured in terms of the amount of time required for the group to complete the task. Group size did not influence speed in the case of four problem solving tasks or the memory task. However, in the two judgmental tasks used by South, three-person groups were faster than six-person groups. South suggested that the judgmental tasks required the group to reach a compromise; to the extent that more discussion is needed in order to reconcile a wider variety of initial opinions. This would account for the fact that the larger groups took longer to reach a decision.

The efficiency with which the group solves a problem was considered in connection with two tasks we have designated as "concept attainment" tasks. According to Taylor and Faust, two-person groups were more efficient than four-person groups since they expended fewer man minutes of "labor." However, this is not really a new finding, since it is mathematically implied by the fact that there was no difference in speed as a function of size. Another meaning of problem solving efficiency involves the amount of intellectual effort expended, which in this case is measured by the number of questions asked by the group before they reached a solution. This measure of efficiency failed to differentiate between two- and four-person groups in the Taylor and Faust study, but South found that six-person groups were more efficient than three-person groups.

Group productivity, defined as the number of correct units produced in a given time period, was examined in three experiments. Comparing groups of Sizes 3–10 Watson [45] found a correlation of .65 between size and the number of different correct words created in an anagrams task. With a similar task, unscrambling sentences, Kidd found no differences in productivity between groups of two, four, and six. Gibb [16] briefly reported a comparison between individuals and groups of Sizes 2, 3, 6, 12, 24, 48, and 96 and reported that the number of suggested solutions to a complex problem increased as a negatively accelerated function of group size.

Considering the group performance findings as a whole, it appears that both quality of performance and group productivity were positively correlated with group size under some conditions, and under no conditions were smaller groups superior. In contrast, measures of speed showed no difference or else favored the smaller groups. The heterogeneity of tasks and of measurement procedures prevent more precise generalizations.

DISTRIBUTION OF PARTICIPATION

Four studies were focused on the relative degree of participation of each member. In one of the earliest investigations in this area Dawe [10] kept a record of the number of remarks made by each child in kindergarten classes ranging in size from 14 to 46. The total number of remarks decreased with increasing size, but not to a statistically significant degree. While an increase in the size of the group was accompanied by an increase in the total number of children who spoke ($r = .82$), there was a decrease in the proportion of the group who spoke ($r = -.58$). Dawe reported also that the members who were seated toward the front of the room tended to speak more often than those seated further back, indicating that a spatial factor may be one determinant of the relationship between size and participation.

Using Bales' categories, Bales, Strodtbeck, Mills, and Roseborough [3] observed interaction in leaderless discussion groups ranging in size from three to eight members. As size increased there was in increase in the relative discrepancy between the percentage of participation for the person ranked first and that for the person ranked second and a reduction in the difference between the percentage of participation for the person ranked second and for all those with less participation. The authors attempted to fit a harmonic function to these curves, but with no success. Later Stephan [38] was able to fit an exponential curve more successfully to the same data.

Stephan and Mishler [39] conducted an experiment to assess the generality of their exponential model beyond the type of group and method of gathering data used in the study by Bales et al. [3]. The unit of participation was all the verbal behavior exhibited by an individual between the time the previous speaker finished and the next began—a much larger unit than was used in the earlier study. In groups ranging in size from 4 to 12 members, they obtained results essentially the same as those of Bales et al.

The relationship between group size and the distribution of acts was analyzed by Miller [33] for groups of Sizes 3–10, 12, 14, 16, 18, and 20. Although Miller used the same unit of participation as Stephan and Mishler, the task was different: the game Twenty Questions. As in Dawe's study, it was found that the average number of participations per member decreased as size increased ($r = -.80$). This of course is what would be expected when the length of the discussion period and the rate of participation are both held constant: as the group increases in size there is less opportunity for any individual to speak. However, this reduction in opportunity to speak did not seem to be accompanied by decreasing participation of the members not ranked highest, for there was found a small, nonsignificant negative correlation between group size and the number of persons who deviated from their expected percentage of participation based on equal distribution. Thus Miller's study casts doubt on the generality of the findings of Bales et al. and Stephan and Mishler and of the models developed to depict the results.

NATURE OF INTERACTION

Four additional studies provided information about the qualitative characteristics of group interaction. To study the "interaction profile" of the acts in the 12 categories of Bales' scheme, Bales and Borgatta [2] observed discussion groups ranging in size from two to seven. The raw number of acts in each category was made a percentage of the total number of acts in the 12 categories and then converted by an arc-sine transformation. Analysis indicated that as size increased, there was an increase in the categories of showing tension release and giving suggestions; and a decrease in categories of showing tension, showing agreement, and asking for opinion. In addition, two-person groups appeared to have certain unique properties, namely, a high rate in the category of showing tension coupled with low rates in the categories of showing disagreement and showing antagonism. An odd-even effect was also apparent: groups of four and six showed higher rates than did groups of three, five, and seven in the categories of showing disagreement and showing antagonism, but lower rates in the category of asking for suggestions. These findings must be interpreted as representing *relative* increases or decreases in an interaction category. Bales and Borgatta offer intriguing speculations to interpret the trends, but it is difficult to draw conclusions about what the *critical changes* may be as size increases from two to seven because a relative increase in one category may come about due to either an absolute increase for the category or an absolute decrease for all other categories, or both.

Bales and Borgatta also analyzed variabliity over four sessions for individuals and groups. They found increased variability for each individual's performance as size increased. The authors claimed that scores may have been less reliable in the larger groups because of partitioning scores among a greater number of persons. Another interpretation given by these researchers is that there may have been more shifting of roles in larger groups because there were more persons to perform role functions. Trends of variability among individuals, of given groups over successive sessions and among groups, revealed no clear-cut size effects.

Salter [35] used Bales' categories with groups ranging from two to seven and concluded that there were inhibiting forces in the smallest groups which prevented the expression of dissatisfaction and disagreement. Scores on an Inhibition Index (the ratio of the number of acts in four agreement categories to the number of acts in five disagreement categories) were significantly higher in groups of two, three, and four than in groups of five, six, and seven. Slater's explanation was that the consequences of alienating a single member may have been more severe in the smaller than in the larger groups.

A study by Berkowitz [5] of groups of 3, 4, 6, 7, 9, and 10 members revealed that there was more disagreement in solving logical problems in the larger groups than in the smaller groups—a finding consistent with those of Slater and Bales and Borgatta.

Bass and Norton [4] observed leaderless discussion groups of 2, 4, 6, 8, and 12 members in which each member was rated on nine aspects of leadership behavior. As group size increased, the average leadership rating assigned to group members decreased significantly—group size accounting for 83% of the variance. There was also a nonsignificant tendency for the within-group variance of ratings to increase with size. The authors concluded that opportunity to adopt leadership functions decreased directly with an increase in group size.

Tentatively it would appear that smaller groups inhibit expression of disagreements and dissatisfactions more than larger groups and give each individual more opportunity to interact and to exhibit leadership behavior. The possibility that there are unique, odd-even and near-linear size effects on the nature of interaction, as Bales and Borgatta suggest, should be pursued further, possibly using different methods from the ones employed by these researchers.

GROUP ORGANIZATION

The last set of studies related to effects on the group as a whole concerns group organization. In Berkowitz's study of the social organization of problem solving groups, 20 variables were found to be significantly affected by group size and most of these were reduced by a cluster analysis to two relatively independent sets of variables. The first cluster was called group cohesion, consisting mainly of sociometric variables such as the number of friendship choices. The components of this cluster were negatively related to size. The second cluster consisted of variables reflecting organization and division of labor. The variables in this cluster and their relationship to size follow: as size increased, there was decreasing contribution of the least active member, higher member variation of interaction, higher variation in the number of rules for solving the problem suggested by members and subsequently adopted by the group, increasing number of leaders, higher variation of rules suggested by each man, increasing number of votes required to reach decisions, increasing suggestions conveyed by those who did not originally make the suggestion, and higher specialization in the use of rules to solve the problems.

In a study of factors affecting consensus in decision making groups, Hare [19] found a greater tendency for groups of 12 than for groups of 5 to break into factions or cliques. This trend was not significant, however, and was based on the reports of group members. Probably more reliable are the findings of Miller who observed directly the frequency with which two or more members of a group talked or whispered among themselves rather than to the group as a whole. A significant correlation of .77 was found between the number of members (3–10, 12, 14, 16, 18, and 20) and the number of cliques. Also, Miller found that this increase in cliques was associated with a decrease in group cohesiveness; a Cohesiveness Index correlated −.52 with group size and −.60 with the number of cliques.

After familiarizing subjects with the concept of the primary group,

Fisher [13] asked them to describe the primary groups to which they belonged and rank them for intimacy. Within the size range of 2–12 members, smaller groups were ranked as significantly more intimate.

Taken together, these studies indicate that as size increases there will be decreasing group cohesiveness and increasing organization and division of labor in the group, along with the development of cliques and possibly of factions.

EFFECTS ON MEMBER BEHAVIOR

INDIVIDUAL PERFORMANCE

The effect of group size on individual performance has been considered primarily in connection with practical problems. In education, for example, there is a long history of concern with class size as a possible influence on classroom learning. We will not attempt to review this literature here, since it has been covered by Hudelson [20], Von Borgersrode [44], Goodlad [18], and McKeachie [31]. Hudelson reported on 59 controlled experiments of the effects of class size, 46 of which favored large over small classes. In Von Borgersrode's review 73 studies were appraised, 19 of which were classified as semicontrolled and 24 as controlled; his conclusion was that "On the whole the statistical findings definitely favor the large classes at every level of instruction except kindergarten" (p. 199). In his review of the effects of lecture size at the college level, McKeachie noted that more recent studies have not been as complimentary to large lectures as were the earlier studies done during the 1920s. Nevertheless, he concluded that large lectures were not generally inferior. Lorge et al. [27] made reference in their review of together-alone studies to some of the literature on classroom learning and concluded that there was probably an interaction between class size, teaching methods, and study methods as determinants of educational effectiveness. But even so, the consensus of the reviewers was that large classes are either superior to small classes or at least not inferior.

A second area of practical concern is the productivity of individual workers as a function of the size of work groups. Marriot [32] found that the amount produced by male workers in a British factory, as measured by average piece-work earnings per man, declined significantly as the size of the work group increased from 10 to 50 members. In contrast, Gekoski [15] found a nonsignificant positive relation between individual productivity and size of work group (4–19 members) among female clerical workers in an American insurance company. Because these studies differed simultaneously along several dimensions, we have no basis for speculation as to the specific conditions which determine whether group size will be positively or negatively correlated with individual productivity.

Two experiments dealt with the individual's improvement in problem solving as a result of his interacting in groups of varying size. Taylor and Faust [41] found that practice in playing Twenty Questions enhanced the individual's ability to solve such problems, but it did not matter whether the practice was obtained alone, as a member of a two-person group, or as a member of a four-person group. By contrast, positive results were reported by Utterback and Fotheringham [43] in regard to the quality of solutions to human relations problems. Individual answers were recorded both before and after a discussion in groups of 3, 6, 9, or 12 members. Improvement in quality of the individual's solutions was significantly greater for the larger groups. However, there was also a significant interaction between group size and the manner in which the discussion was led: when the moderator intervened a great deal ("full moderation"), individual improvement was greatest for 12-person groups; but when the moderator intervened very little ("partial moderation"), individual improvement was greatest for 3-person groups. Thus group size sometimes is related to individual problem solving, but the direction of the relationship is highly dependent on group conditions other than size.

CONFORMITY AND CONSENSUS

In his famous experiment on yielding to a group of peers who, unknown to the naive subject, had been instructed to report unanimous but incorrect judgments of the length of visually presented lines, Asch [1] manipulated the size of the unanimous opposition. He found that as the number of confederates increased from 1 to 3, the amount of yielding to their unanimous judgment increased significantly; but there was no further increase in conformity as the confederates increased in number to 4, 8, or 16. In two related studies, Goldberg [17] and Kidd [25] failed to find any effect of group size even though their manipulations of group pressure did succeed in producing a significant amount of conformity. Goldberg's subjects, in groups of 2 or 4, made individual judgments of the intelligence of persons from their photographs; while Kidd's subjects, in groups of 2, 4, or 6 made individual judgments of flicker frequency. In both experiments, each individual made a second judgment after being exposed to false feedback concerning the group's average first judgment. Conformity, as measured by shifting toward the bogus group average, occurred in all groups, but the amount of yielding was not related to group size in either experiment. In contrast, Kishida [26] found a significant size effect using groups of 5, 10, and 30 Japanese university students. Subjects responded individually to an opinion questionnaire, then received true feedback as to the majority opinion, and finally responded a second time to the questionnaire. Although there was a shift toward conformity in all groups, magnitude of opinion change showed a curvilinear relationship to group size, being greatest in 10-person groups and least in 5-person groups. The results of these four studies indicate that the magnitude of the group's influence on the individual is a function of group size under some conditions, but differences in task and procedure again preclude specification of the relevant conditions.

A second set of findings involved measurement of the individual's opinion both before and after group discussion of a problem. Half of Kishida's [26] groups discussed the opinion items and arrived at a group decision. Analysis of the individual postdiscussion responses indicated that shift toward the group opinion bore the same curvilinear relationship to group size under discussion conditions as in the condition involving feedback of the majority opinion. A negative effect of group size was found by Hare [19] with groups of 5 and 12 Boy Scouts, with two measures showing that consensus increased more in the smaller groups. Finally, Utterback and Fotheringham [43] reported a significant interaction between group size and the amount of intervention by the discussion moderator. Increase in consensus was greatest in 12-person groups under full moderation, but greatest in 3-person groups under partial moderation. However, there was no main effect of group size in this study. These findings lend further weight to the conclusion that group size is an important factor in determining the amount of yielding to conformity pressures.

MEMBER SATISFACTION

Questionnaire measures of members' subjective reactions to the group were included in four of the studies cited above. Both Hare [19] and Slater [35] found that members of larger groups were significantly less satisfied with the amount of time available for discussion, with their opportunity to participate, and with the group meeting or its decision. In addition, Slater found that his subjects considered five members to be optimum (i.e., neither too large nor too small) for the task of discussing a human relations problem. In contrast to the others, Ziller [46] found no clear relationship between group size and members' satisfaction with their own part in the discussion, and Miller [33] found no relationship between group size and three measures of satisfaction. With this exception, the general trend of the findings indicates that the smaller the group, the more likely it is that the individual will be satisfied with the discussion and with his own part in it. McKeachie's [31] review of studies on discussion groups at the college level also indicated that larger groups were less satisfying to both students and instructors. It must be remembered, however, that the studies referred to here all dealt with discussion groups attempting to solve particular problems, and that the generalization may not apply to other types of groups.

EVALUATION

More converging findings emerged from this review than one might have expected considering that only 31 empirical investigations of group size were found to be relevant. But many more studies will have to be conducted and appraised before general conclusions can be drawn with confidence about the numerous effects of group size. Aside from their relatively small number, this set of studies, when considered collectively, has other limitations as a basis for generalized inferences. These shortcomings and problems are discussed below.

METHODOLOGICAL DIFFICULTIES

The arbitrary and unsystematic selection of sizes for comparison is perhaps one of the most serious methodological shortcomings of this group of studies. The pertinent range of sizes in order to generalize safely about small groups would seem to be 2 through at least 20. Two biases in drawing samples from this range are common. One is to sample a truncated series of the range, such as Sizes 2–4, and the other is to draw samples omitting various adjacent sizes so that there is an overrepresentation of odd or even sizes. Such biases may obscure the true functional relationship between size and the dependent variable. There is no reason to expect only a single type of function, such as a linear relationship, to hold between size and any dependent variable: in the studies reviewed here it was not uncommon to find a curvilinear relationship [1, 16, 26, 46]. From information about a limited portion of the size range, it is of course impossible to extrapolate with confidence to the type of functional relationship characterizing the entire range. As Borgatta and Cottrell [6] have noted, the effects of size may be quantitative or discrete. The apparent linear effects, the odd-even differences, and the uniqueness of Size 2 would not have been noted by Bales and Borgatta had they sampled a more limited series of sizes.

A second limitation of this group of studies is that many independent variables other than group size were involved. The most conspicuous of these were the population characteristics of the subjects. In many cases, the observed groups were composed of either all male or all female members; in other cases, the groups were mixed; and a few investigators failed to report the sex of their subjects. The age and education of subjects were other population characteristics with respect to which the studies differed. The tasks employed were similarly heterogeneous, and like the population characteristics, cound have interacted with group size to produce the obtained results. In general, these studies provide very little information concerning the conditions under which group size is related in some specific way to some particular variable.

Another shortcoming of this group of studies is the failure of the majority of the investigators to seek to determine *why* changes in group size had the observed effects. Rather than focusing on causal analysis, most of the researchers have used what might be called a "correlational" approach, which generally begins and ends with an empirical concern with

the relationship between group size and a given dependent variable. It is
as if many of the studies proceeded on the assumption that size should
somehow have an immediate effect upon some aspect of behavior, and, as
a consequence, relevant intervening variables were almost never measured
or varied experimentally.

A basically different approach to the study of group size follows from
the view that the size variable will have no behavioral effects when stripped
of various social and psychological accompaniments. It is apparent, for
example, that if there is no interdependence or communication between
members, the size of the group is irrelevant to the prediction of behavioral
changes for the members. An analysis and design oriented toward isolating
the critical intervening variables in the relationship between size and the
dependent variables should be the objective of studies which aspire to
understand why size has effects.

Indik's [21] study of the relationship between the size of voluntary organizations and the tendency of members to participate, clearly illustrates
the importance of establishing a procedure to search for, and examine, the
effects of possible intervening variables. Although voluntary organizations
ranging in membership from 15 to 2,983 were studied, the method illustrated is fully applicable to the small group. It was hypothesized that the
negative relationship between size of organization and tendency of members to participate (as indicated by absenteeism in a service company and
attendance in a women's association) is mediated by organizational variables (e.g., amount of communication, job and task specialization, higher
level interpersonal control and coordination) and psychological variables
(e.g., attraction of members to the organization, satisfaction with one's
activities performed in the organization, and perceived bureaucratic inflexibility). Four explanatory schemas were proposed in each of which size
was linked to an organizational and a psychological intervening variable.
The schema which found the strongest support was the one which hypothesized that the size of the organization would be negatively related to the
amount of communication among members, that the amount of communication of each member would be positively associated with the attraction
of members to the organization, and that the attraction of the members to
the organization would be positively associated with tendency to participate.
Analyses were also made of the other schemas and from these it was concluded that various intervening variables mediated the relationship between size and participation. This approach to the problem is distinctly
more sophisticated than that of relating size to a given dependent variable
without considering possible intervening conditions. However, Indik did
not let the problem rest with the results reported above, for he ran higher
order partial correlations, holding constant pairs of intervening variables,
to see what effects this would have on the magnitude of the original cor-

relation of −.53 between size and tendency to participate. When the combined effects of the specialization-satisfaction linkage were removed the correlation between size of organization and tendency to participate dropped from −.53 to −.26; when the effects of lack of coordination and perceived bureaucratic inflexibility were removed, the correlation dropped further to −.17; and finally, when the communication-attraction linkage was removed, the partial correlation was left at −.08.

DEPENDABLE INTERVENING VARIABLES

If group size is phenotypic and really but a correlate of the social and psychological conditions capable of producing changes in member and group behavior, it would be fruitful to stipulate what these intervening variables are. Can we say that some intervening variables will always or most always be influenced by variations in group size? If there are such variables and if these variables also produce relevant outcomes, then hypotheses predicating such outcomes as a function of size should be more or less axiomatically correct. Various classes of such variables are discussed below, along with examples and probable effects.

Input Quantity. Two types of input may be assumed to increase with group size. The first is *resource input*, such as interaction skills, knowledge, capacities, and physical strength. If we designate the amount of any given resource brought to the group by an individual as r, and the total amount of the resources of all group members made use of in the group as R, then $R = f(r, n)$ where n equals group size. For some resources each individual will contribute approximately equal amounts in which case $R = r \times n$; for other resources the amounts will vary widely among individuals and the functional relationship between r and n will be more complex. Whether R is greater than, less than, or equal to the sum of the individual resources $\left(\sum_{i=1} r_i \right)$ depends upon facilitating and hindering group conditions. But in general, R increases with increasing group size, whether or not the relationship is linear.

The relevance of viewing resource input as a dependable intervening variable is clear in the case of group problem solving. If knowledge is needed to solve a problem and each individual brings particular knowledge that others do not have, with increasing size there will be greater likelihood that the total amount of knowledge pertinent for solving the problem will be available in the group. If intelligence is the resource required for solving the problem, then the addition of each individual increases the likelihood that someone will have the capacity to solve the problem. Assuming that problem difficulty is known, the application of elementary probability theory to this problem readily makes possible the writing of formulas to

express the likelihood of intellectual capacities being brought to the group
with the addition of each individual. Thus one may state the likelihood
that there will be at least one member in the group with the correct answer,
that there will be more than half with the correct answer, that everyone
will be correct, that everyone will be incorrect, or that there will be mixed
correct and incorrect answers. If p equals the probability of the success of
the individual working alone on the problem, n is the number of individuals
in the group and q equals $1 - p$, then the probability that there will be at
least one person in the group arriving at the right answer equals $1-$
$(1 - p)^n$. Taylor [40], Ekman [11], and Lorge and Solomon [28] have all applied
this basic idea to group problem solving where it is useful to compare results against theoretical probabilities based on the assumption that if one
member gets the correct answer the group will accept it.

The formula given above applies to problems having one state in their
solution, but may be extended to multistage problems, as Lorge and Solomon have done. Their formula for the probability of a group solving a
multistage problem is the product of the probabilities that the group can
solve the problem for each stage. Steiner and Rajaratnam [37] have further
extended the basic idea by developing formulas, applicable to interval
data, which make it possible to test the null hypothesis that groups function
at the level of the most competent member, of the least competent member, or at any level of competence. In considering group solutions that can
be represented as distributions of individual answers, Thomas and Fink
[42] have elaborated three models (independence, rational, and consensus)
which state varying antecedent group conditions and the associated
theoretical probabilities of having everyone correct, some correct and incorrect, and everyone incorrect for problems involving two-alternative and
multialternative solutions.

A second type of input that increases with size is *demand input*. The
demands each individual brings to the group include the need for recognition, affection, a minimum amount of social interaction, and so on. As
size increases the sum of these individual demands increases. One of the
main implications of an increase in demand input with increasing size is
that larger groups will need more resources than smaller groups in order to
meet the demand. Furthermore, we may assume that to the extent that
larger groups are unable to satisfy demands of the members there will be
decreased attractiveness, lack of reward, resulting in dissatisfaction,
lowered morale, and a tendency to leave the group. If we assume that each
person has some desire to communicate in group discussions, then restrict-
ing the amount of time to discuss a problem, as Hare [19] did, will result in
greater demand on time in the larger groups. Hare's finding that there was
decreased satisfaction with the discussion in the larger groups as compared
with the smaller groups is understandable in terms of the above comments.

Increasing Sample Size. As the size of the group increases, there is obviously an increase in the size of the sample of individuals. One consequence of increasing sample size is that there is more accurate estimation of parameters of the parent population when the sample is taken from a nonhomogeneous universe and the individuals are not added to the group by a biased method. Parameter estimation is illustrated by the results of a study by Eysenck [12] in which the rankings of a sample of 200 subjects concerning their preferences for 12 black and white pictures were compared with the criterion of the average rankings by 700 subjects. It was found that as the number of unbiased judges increased, the correlation of their pooled rankings with a criterion increased. Sampling and test theory abound with other illustrations. In Ziller's study, judgments of the number of dots on a card should have been more accurate with increasing group size in the same way that he found increasing correspondence between the judgment of military experts on human relations problems with the judgments of the group members as size increased. One can only conclude that the errors in judgment were not random in the problem of judging dot numerosity, or that biased samples of judges were drawn, or both.

A second consequence of increasing sample size is that the heterogeneity of the variates sampled increases due to the inclusion of more variates from the extremes of the distribution. Applied to social groups, it follows that with an increase in size there will be more varied talents, more individuals with requisite skills and knowledge for performing specialized tasks, and more individuals who are likely to be liabilities. The foregoing review revealed that as size increased there was increasing variability of individual performance and increasing organization and division of labor in the group; both effects are probably due in part to an increase in the heterogeneity of the sample.

Potential Relational Complexity. Various writers, among them Bossard [7] and Kephart [24], have pointed out that as group size increases arithmetically there is a geometrical increase in the number of relational possibilities among the members. For example, the number of possible diadic relations in any group increases according to the familiar formula: $(n^2n)/2$. Potential relational complexity becomes important in groups because most individuals have a limited capacity to establish relationships with others. For example, Jennings [22] has indicated that the average repertoire of choices for associating closely with others (working, etc.) is about 8 and that this number is increased to about 12 when leisure time activities are included. Individual relational capacities limit the variables of informal and formal organization and the degree of role differentiation that may develop. Thus an upper bound is automatically set on the actual relational complexity of a group by the limited capacity of individuals to establish particular relationships and by the potential relational possibilities.

Several studies reviewed here indicate that as group size increases there is a decrease in cohesiveness, along with the development of cliques and possibly of factions. These findings are understandable generally when the limited choice capacities of individuals are placed against the potential relations that multiply with group size. First consider cohesiveness, for which we may assume that positive attraction among all members at some degree of intensity is generally required. If we acknowledge that individuals have a limited capacity to like others (as the findings of Jennings [22] suggest), and that the sociometric structure of a group must be filled up with a certain relatively high number of liking linkages in order for cohesiveness to exist, then as group size increases the potential relations will exceed the capacity of individuals to fill them, the average member attraction in the group will decrease, and consequently so will group cohesiveness. The development of cliques and factions should eventually occur, for as size increases a smaller proportion of the possible linkages will be made.

Differences between diads and triads can be understood partially in terms of relational possibilities. As Bales and Borgatta [2] have noted, in a two-person group there can be no majority other than by unanimity, whereas in a three-person group there can be a majority of two against a minority of one. In a three person group there are eight possible coalition possibilities [9], whereas in a diad the power relations are much simpler: one member may have power over the other or they may be equal.

NONDEPENDABLE INTERVENING VARIABLES

Nondependable intervening variables are those which are affected by changes in group size only under certain conditions. Almost any social or psychological condition influencing group process or outcome may be a nondependable intervening variable. There are numerous examples: the time allowed for group discussion may be held constant while group size is increased, thereby reducing the opportunity to participate; a group pay-off may be held constant in cooperative groups of different sizes, thus varying the amount of reward that each member may possibly get when the pay-off is divided among them; expectancy of reward may decrease with increasing size of a competitive group; the relative contribution of each member in cooperative groups may decrease with size, thereby decreasing the individual's sense of importance and worth in the group; the interdependence of the members may be high, thus increasing the likelihood that with increasing size there will be at least one individual who will perform poorly and hinder the group's progress; the cost in time and money represented by each additional group member may eventually exceed the possible gain to be derived from having more individuals work on the problem; and the complexity of the cognitive field may become great with increasing size to the extent that members try to attend to impinging social stimuli.

Most of the observed effects of size reviewed here appear to be contingent upon the operation of one or more of these nondependable intervening variables. Where such mediating variables are affecting an outcome, the proper focus for explanation should be on the theoretical framework of which the intervening variable is a part and only secondarily on size.

CONCLUSIONS

On the basis of this review it is apparent that group size has significant effects on aspects of individual and group performance, on the nature of interaction and distribution of participation of group members, on group organization, on conformity and consensus, and on member satisfaction. This appraisal suggests that the variable of group size should be included in theories of group behavior, distinguishing where possible between the effects that result from the interaction of group size with other independent variables and the effects arising from intervening variables that are dependably and nondependably associated with size.

It is concluded furthermore that future research on group size should proceed systematically, making every effort (*a*) to vary size in complete sequence over a suitably large range; (*b*) to conceptualize, identify, and measure relevant intervening variables; (*c*) to determine in advance whether these variables should be expected axiomatically to be correlated with size or would be only contingent variables; and (*d*) to use multivariate designs, where appropriate, in which group size and significant intervening variables are both manipulated experimentally.

REFERENCES

1. Asch, S. E. "Effects of Group Pressure Upon the Modification and Distortion of Judgments." In D. Cartwright & A. Zander (Eds.). *Group Dynamics* (Evanston, Ill.: Row, Peterson, 1953), pp. 151–163.

2. Bales, R. F., & Borgatta, E. F. "Size of Group as a Factor in the Interaction Profile." In A. D. Hare, E. F. Borgatta, & R. F. Bales (Eds.). *Small Groups* (New York: Knopf, 1955), pp. 396–413.

3. Bales, R. F., Strodtbeck, F., Mills, T., & Roseborough, Mary E. "Channels of Communication in Small Groups," *Amer. Sociol. Rev.* (1951), **16**, 461–468.

4. Bass, B. M., & Norton, F. T. "Group Size and Leaderless Discussions," *J. Appl. Psychol.* (1951), **35**, 397–400.

5. Berkowitz, M. I. "An Experimental Study of the Relation Between Group Size and Social Organization." Unpublished doctoral dissertation, Yale University, 1958.

6. Borgatta, E. F., & Cottrell, L. S., Jr. "Directions for Research in Group Behavior," *Amer. J. Social.* (1957), **63**, 42–48.

7. Bossard, J. H. S. "The Law of Family Interaction," *Amer. J. Sociol.* (1944), **50**, 289–293.

8. Caplow, T. "Organizational Size," *Admin. Sci. Quart.* (1957), **1**, 484–506.

9. Caplow, T. "Further Developments of a Theory of Coalitions in the Triad," *Amer. J. Sociol.* (1959), **64**, 488–493.

10. Dawe, Helen C. "The Influence of Size of Kindergarten Group upon Performance," *Child Develpm.* (1934), **5**, 295–303.

11. Ekman, G. "The Four Effects of Cooperation," *J. Soc. Psychol.* (1955), **41**, 149–163.

12. Eysenck, H. J. "The Validity of Judgments as a Function of the Number of Judges," *J. Exp. Psychol.* (1939), **25**, 650–654.

13. Fisher, P. H. "An Analysis of the Primary Group," *Sociometry* (1953), **16**, 272–276.

14. Fox, D., Lorge, I., Weltz, P., & Herrold, K. "Comparison of Decisions Written by Large and Small Groups," *Amer. Psychologist* (1953), **8**, 351 (Abstract).

15. Gekoski, N. "The Relationship of Group Characteristics to Productivity." Unpublished doctoral dissertation, Ohio State University, 1952.

16. Gibb, J. R. "Effects of Group Size and Threat Reduction on Creativity in a Problem-solving Situation," *Amer. Psychologist* (1951), **6**, 324 (Abstract).

17. Goldberg, S. C. "Three Situational Determinants of Conformity to Social Norms," *J. Abnorm. Soc. Psychol.* (1954), **49**, 325–329.

18. Goodlad, I. I. "Classroom Organization." In C. W. Harris (Ed.). *Encyclopedia of Educational Research* (New York: Macmillan, 1960), pp. 221–225.

19. Hare, A. P. "Interaction and Consensus in Different Sized Groups," *Amer. Sociol. Rev.* (1952), **17**, 261–267.

20. Hudelson, E. *Class Size at the College Level* (Minneapolis: Univer. Minnesota Press, 1928).

21. Indik, B. P. "Organization Size and Member Participation." Unpublished doctoral dissertation, University of Michigan, 1961.

22. Jennings, Helen H. "Sociometric Choice Process in Personality and Group Formation," In J. L. Moreno (Ed.). *The Sociometry Reader* (Glencoe, Ill: Free Press, 1960), pp. 87–113.

23. Kelley, H. H., & Thibaut, J. W. "Experimental Studies of Group Problem Solving and Process." In G. Lindzey (Ed.). *Handbook of Social Psychology* (Cambridge, Mass.: Addison-Wesley, 1954), pp. 735–785.

24. Kephart, W. M. "A Quantitative Analysis of Intragroup Relationships." *Amer. J. Sociol.* (1950), **60**, 544–549.

25. Kidd, J. S. "Social Influence Phenomena in a Task-oriented Group Situation," *J. Abnorm. Soc. Psychol.* (1958), **56**, 13–17.

26. Kishida, M. "A Study of the Effects of Group Norm upon the Change of Opinions." *Jap. J. Psychol.* (1956), **27**, 172–173 (Abstract).

27. Lorge, I., Fox, D., Davitz, J., & Brenner, M. "A Survey of Studies Contrasting the Quality of Group Performance and Individual Performance." *Psychol. Bull.* (1958), **55**, 337–370.

28. Lorge, I., & Solomon, H. "Two Models of Group Behavior in the Solution of Eureka-type Problems," *Psychometrika* (1955), **20**, 139–149.

29. Lorge, I., & Solomon, H. "Individual Performance and Group Performance in Problem Solving Related to Group Size and Previous Exposure to the Problem," *J. Psychol.* (1959), **48**, 107–114.

30. Lorge, I., & Solomon, H. "Group and Individual Performance in Problem Solving Related to Previous Exposure to Problem, Level of Aspiration, and Group Size," *Behav. Sci.* (1960), **5**, 28–39.

31. McKeachie, W. J. "Research on Teaching at the College and University Level." In N. Gage (Ed.). *Handbook of Research on Teaching* (Chicago, Ill.: Rand McNally, 1963) pp. 1118–1172.

32. Marriot, R. "Size of Working Group and Output," *Occup. Psychol.* (1949), **26**, 47–57.

33. Miller, N. E., Jr. "The Effect of Group size on Decision-making Discussions." Unpublished doctoral dissertation, University of Michigan, 1951.

34. Perlmutter, H. V. "Group Memory of Meaningful Material," *J. Psychol.* (1953), **35**, 361–370.

35. Slater, P. E. "Contrasting Correlates of Group Size," *Sociometry* (1958), **21**, 129–139.

36. South, E. B. "Some Psychological Aspects of Committee Work," *J. Appl. Psychol.* (1927), **11**, 348–368.

37. Steiner, J. D., & Rajaratnam, N. "A Model for the Comparison of Individual and Group Performance Scores," *Behav. Sci.* (1961), **6**, 142–148.

38. Stephan, F. F. "The Relative Rate of Communication Between Members of Small Groups," *Amer. Sociol. Rev.* (1952), **17**, 482–486.

37. Stephan, F. F., & Mishler, E. G. "The Distribution of Participation in Small Groups: An Exponential Approximation," *Amer Sociol. Rev.* (1952), **17**, 598–608.

40. Taylor, D. W. "Problem Solving by Groups." In *Proceedings of the XIV International Congress of Psychology: 1954* (Amsterdam: North Holland Publishing, 1954).

41. Taylor, D. W., & Faust, W. L. "Twenty Questions: Efficiency in Problemsolving As a Function of Size of Group," *J. Exp. Psychol.* (1952), **44**, 360–368.

42. Thomas, E. J., & Fink, C. F. "Models of Group Problem Solving," *J. Abnorm. Soc. Psychol.* (1961), **63**, 53–63.

43. Utterback, W. E., & Fotheringham, W. C. "Experimental Studies of Motivated Group Discussion," *Speech Monogr.* (1958), **25**, 268–277.

44. Von Borgesrode, F. "Class Size." In W. S. Monroe (Ed.). *Encyclopedia of Educational Research* (New York: Macmillan, 1941), pp. 197–200.

45. Watson, G. B. "Do Groups Think More Efficiently Than Individuals?" *J. Abnorm. Soc. Psychol.* (1928), **23**, 328–336.

46. Ziller, R. C. "Group Size: Determinant of the Quality and Stability of Group Decisions," *Scoiometry* (1957), **20**, 165–173.

38

Some Principles and Procedures for Group Psychotherapy*

Walther Joel

David Shapiro

A. ORIENTATION

It is now generally accepted that group therapy is *not* individual therapy applied to groups, nor is it considered to be merely an economical make-shift. It is rather regarded as something quite different with a rationale and justification of its own. While it is true that some of the principles and procedures known from individual psychotherapy can be applied in modified form to group therapy, group therapy is *not* mass individual therapy, and many of its features are quite unique.

More specifically, it appears that the course of group therapy, the therapeutic process as a whole, is quite different from that of individual psychotherapy. This difference is not merely a difference in degree. It appears that the prognostic indicators, and even the nature of the changes brought about after successful treatment, are different in group therapy. Personality changes, for example, are in group therapy very often unac-companied by intellectual insight; social reality testing, on the other hand, is an integral part of the actual therapeutic session and is an important element of the therapeutic process from the beginning.

As we can see, group therapy is more than merely quantitatively different from individual therapy. Once the evidences for this fact are ac-cepted, the therapist can begin to look for their cause. Once, in other words, we stop looking for the processes of individual therapy in a situation where they don't exist, we can really look for the crucial factors in group therapy, which will also distinguish it clearly from individual therapy.

As group therapy has grown up, more and more workers in the field have come to emphasize what has been called the "Group dynamics," the "intra-group dynamics," or what we may refer to here as simply the re-

*Received in the Editorial Office on September 7, 1949, and published immediately at Provincetown, Massachusetts. Copyright by The Journal Press. Reprinted by permission of the author and publisher from *The Journal of Psychology* (1950), 29, 77–88.

lationships within the group. From individual therapy we have learned to consider the relationships of the various members of the group to the therapist, that is, the traditional one-way patient-therapist transference. It is clear now, however, that although these relationships are certainly a significant part of group dynamics, they are very far from being the whole of it. For relationships and transference exist not only from patient to therapist, but also from patient to patient, and even this addition does not complete the story. The individual relationships, from patient to patient, or from patient to therapist, cannot be considered apart from the group situation as a whole. The particular relationship between two individuals in a group often assumes clear meaning only when at the same time, the relationship of one, or both of these two to a third, and a fourth member of the group is considered, and so on. The basis for the analysis of behavior of each individual and, in the terminology of recent analytic literature, the basis for the corrective emotional experience lies in the analysis and handling of these relationships. If they are overlooked, the results obtained from group therapy will be disappointing, just as the results of individual therapy would be disappointing if the relationship between the patient and the therapist were overlooked.

It is only in terms of these group interrelationships that the group process as a whole becomes meaningful, or that any specific occurrence in the group situation assumes its true meaning. The fact, for example, that a patient suddenly brings up the topic of homosexuality in the group, cannot be explained merely by saying that such and such things have changed in his individual dynamics. These changes in individual dynamics and his bringing up of the particular topic can only really be understood in terms of the group relationships and group dynamics in which they are embedded and out of which they have emerged. An oversimplified but useful illustration might be that such a patient has been involved in an increasingly warm attachment to another group member of the same sex at the time when he raises this issue.

Whether the analysis and interpretations that the therapist offers to the group are made only in terms of the particular verbal content of the sessions or in terms of the group relationships which form the context of this verbal content means the difference between intellectual discussion and real working through of problems.

B. PROCEDURES

This part takes up a number of practical problems of group therapy. It is not meant to be exhaustive, nor should the procedures presented here be considered in any sense final. They are suggestions, which by and large are derivable from the orientation presented in Section A, and which, to some extent, have already proven their usefulness.

1. HOW TO SELECT GROUP MEMBERS

a. How Many?

The optimum number of patients for a group is probably between six and eight. In larger groups, such as have been conducted for reasons of expediency, there is not enough opportunity for interaction. Interpersonal relations can best be brought into focus and seen in all their ramifications if the group is small. A minimum of six patients will make certain that the group can still function effectively in case of the occasional absence of a member or two.

b. What Kind?

(1) Diagnosis. Diagnostic label per se does not appear to be a very useful index of capacity for social interaction. Group psychotherapy has been conducted with patients of all nosological categories. While we have no definite information concerning its relative value for schizophrenics, hysterics, alcoholics, epileptics, etc., it is safe to state that some patients will respond more quickly or profoundly to group therapy than others, and that these differences are less due to differences in diagnosis than to individual differential capacity for establishing relationships with people. Group therapists, therefore, are beginning to lose interest in diagnostic labels.

It follows' that the problem of "homogeneous" vs. "heterogeneous" diagnosis is not a major issue in group composition. While it is deemed helpful to group formation that the members have some problem in common, this does not necessarily mean identical diagnosis; e.g., among hospitalized patients the anxieties and frustrations of the hospital situation itself form something of a bond. In our experience, groups made up of about equal numbers of "neurotics" and "psychotics" made excellent progress.

It should be noted, however, that it would be unwise to put into a group one individual whose problems or dynamics differ widely from those of the rest, thus isolating him. For example, it would not be desirable to have one single delusional patient in an otherwise non-psychotic group.

(2) Sex Composition. Representation of both sexes is desirable because it offers a better opportunity to live through some of the relationships involved in the genesis of the psychological disturbance. Where, for administrative reasons, mixed-sex groups are impossible, it should at least be attempted to have both sexes represented in the persons of the therapist and the co-therapist (recorder, observer).

One often hears that groups of the same sex talk more freely about sexually tinged problems. This may be so, but it should be remembered that intellectual discussion or even discussion with a certain amount of catharsis is no substitute for the working through of problems in interpersonal relations. It is our experience that all sorts of personalities, with a great variety of dynamics will benefit from being in a mixed-sex group.

(3) Age Composition. The problems here are much the same as those discussed in the preceding paragraph. A wide age differential among group members may at first appear to impede free expression and communication of problems. In the last analysis, however, older persons, if not entirely isolated, would offer more significant transference and identification opportunities to the younger members and vice versa than would be possible in a group of relatively similar age. For this reason a mixed age group seems desirable.

(4) Conclusion. Generally, we should select *groups* for group therapy—not individual patients. The prognosis for a specific patient cannot be determined without knowledge of the composition of the group in which he will function.

Even though in the practical situation it may often be necessary to select patients without such knowledge it would be a mistake to be restricted by the ordinary prognostic indicators of individual psychotherapy. Experience has shown that patients whose prognosis from this latter point of view might be poor, may in a particular group make excellent progress.

2. INITIAL INTERVIEW WITH THE PROSPECTIVE MEMBER

Some therapists have found it valuable to precede introduction into the group with at least a few preparatory individual sessions. When this is not done, the following comments apply.

The decision to join the group must be left to the patient. This approach to the patient is particularly important because even a single unwilling member may seriously disrupt or impede the progress of the whole group.

Some general description of the purpose of group therapy should be given. One might say:

> We have found that it helps people to get better if they meet in a small group where they have a chance to talk about any problems they may have, or about anything they wish, for that matter. We are meeting three times a week (indicate days and hour), and if you would like to come, we will be glad to have you.

Some patients, especially if they have already heard about group therapy, will be pleased with the invitation. Some will perhaps decline, and many will ask further questions. They may want to know how many people are in the group, who they are, whether some conflict in their schedule can be straightened out, where the meeting is held, etc. Most of these questions should be answered according to fact. There is, however, another kind of question, namely: "How does group therapy work?" "Will it help me?"

It will not be necessary to go into a very lengthy and abstract discussion about this. It is better to tell the patient that "the best way to find out what it is like, is to come to a group session."

Some encouragement will be needed for depressed, withdrawn, or shy patients who express fear of social contact. They should be told: "It is not as embarrassing as you think, and some of the others were just as reluctant as you before they joined the group."

3. MECHANICS OF GROUP MEETINGS

a. How Often? This is largely a matter of expediency. Groups meeting only once or twice a week exist in many places. Three meetings a week, well spaced, are to be preferred because continuity of personal interaction in the group is facilitated by greater frequency. Meeting more often than three times a week is not recommended because it tends to encourage the continuation of the group into social life and the narrowing of desirable outside social contacts. Opportunity for social reality testing may thus be seriously curtailed.

b. How Long? While one hour is entirely satisfactory if the group meets three times a week, it may be desirable to meet for an hour and a half twice a week, or for two hours if there is only one meeting a week. In the case of a two-hour meeting, a brief intermission might be introduced after the first hour.

c. Where? It is often difficult to find the ideal room for group therapy. A very large room or hall, though not ideal, is generally acceptable because the group can draw together. But crowding in too small a room does not permit a sense of physical freedom and may at times be frustrating. Noise and distractions, such as conspicuous pictures, should, of course, be excluded if possible.

d. Seating. Chairs should be comfortable. They are best arranged in a circle rather than a semi-circle. A simple circle is to be preferred to sitting around a table, because a table can serve as a psychological barrier to free interaction. Semi-circular arrangement would place the therapist in a focal position and thereby structure the group in a way not consistent with our basic principles of group therapy.

In the case of a co-therapist (recorder), the two therapists should be separated from each other by one or more patients in the circle, i.e., they should not sit together. They should also avoid sitting opposite one another since this might give the impression of glance communication between them.

Seating of the patients should be entirely free, governed only by their individual preferences or possibly by the rulings of the group.

4. STRUCTURING THE GROUP

The basic purpose of structuring should be to focus the attention of the group on the free expression of feelings towards each other and towards the therapist, and to avoid intellectual discussion. Not only in words, but by his behavior, the therapist can give evidence of a permissive and accepting attitude.

The group therapist will find it necessary to structure the group not only at the beginning but also at frequent intervals throughout the life of the group. This job of structuring is done both explicitly and implicitly. The initial structuring can be done somewhat as follows.

a. Goals.

We are all here in the hospital largely because we found it hard to get along with some person or with some people, or with people in general. We have been nervous or emotionally upset chiefly about our relations with others, our feelings about others.

Now this group is so to speak a miniature society. But it is different from the usual social situation because here we are free to express our feelings toward people and toward each other. Here we can examine how we feel about people and about ourselves, and we can work out some of our difficulties.

b. Limits.

In this group we can freely express *in words* any idea or any feeling we have. There is no limit here on what we may *say*. We can't actually punch some one in the nose, but we can say that we feel like doing it.

c. Confidential Nature.
Patients' concern over the secrecy of their own statements is a greater problem in group therapy than in individual therapy. It is a very common form of resistance and must be dealt with from the start. Reports on indiscretion should be handled by the group, and nobody should remain in the group who violates persistently the confidence of the group session. The topic might be introduced as follows:

Naturally we can talk freely about anything we please only if we know that nothing that is said here ever gets out of the group. So we expect that every one of us will keep strictly confidential all that is going on in these sessions.

d. Inducing Interaction.
This aspect of structuring, more than any other, will require frequent reemphasis. In order to overcome the initial resistance to interaction a number of techniques can be employed. The most important of these is to encourage a democratic spirit in the group with regard to specific decisions affecting the group as a whole. Problems, such as meeting time and place, physical arrangements, etc., can within limits be referred to the group for discussion and democratic decision. Questions

directed at the therapist can generally be met by asking: "How does the group feel about this?" Finally, by keeping his structuring comments as brief as possible, the therapist will encourage interaction.

5. INTERPRETATION

While many of the generally accepted principles of interpretation apply here, this section will be limited to a few important aspects which are unique to interaction group psychotherapy.

a. Encouraging Group Formation and Interaction. In order to function therapeutically, the patients must cease being isolated individuals wrapped up in their own problems. They must cease focussing all attention either upon themselves or upon the therapist. They need to become aware of the others in the group, of their feelings about the others, and of the others' feelings toward them. In short, they must become a group.

Group formation needs to be encouraged from the earliest moment. It is usually not difficult to detect similarities in the patients' feelings or attitudes. Thus it will be possible to point out even in the first meeting of the group that "All of us felt a little self-conscious today, although not everybody showed it in the same way."

b. Interpreting Resistance. It should be realized that almost all the group discussion which is not of an interaction nature is fundamentally resistance. Groups and group therapists are particularly prone to intellectualizing, such as discussing diagnoses, symptoms, life histories, ancestry. The discussion of personal problems is often an indication of resistance. Even the expression of feelings towards people or objects outside the group must be redirected to the here and now of the group situation.

The therapist must, of course, recognize the patients' difficulties and conflicts around the face-to-face expression of feelings, but he must make the group aware of these conflicts as well as of his acceptance of them. He should also realize, however, that many patients have preconceived notions of group therapy as a discussion situation.

c. Pointing Out Group Interrelations. Group interrelations should form the framework for all interpretation. In contrast to much individual therapy, interpretation of the relationships in the group can be made largely on a here and now basis. This is because much of what is relived in fantasy in individual therapy, is, in group therapy, relived on a level closer to reality.

It must be remembered that the reactions of each member of the group must be interpreted in the context of the dynamics of the group as a whole. For example, Patient *A*'s sudden outburst of hostility toward Patient *B* may be meaningless when interpreted exclusively in terms of the relationship between *A* and *B*. A proper interpretation will take into account also the warmth expressed by *B* to *C*, and the attention previously focussed on *B* by *D*.

The therapist must recognize that the *realistic* rivalry situation in group therapy is very intense. He must, therefore, be extremely careful to avoid any indication of preference or favoritism. At the same time, he must continually encourage the group members to express their feelings of rivalry.

6. RECORDING

a. **Recording.** Recording what goes on in group therapy sessions may serve several purposes, among them supervision and research. While verbatim records taken on machines or by shorthand may prove valuable, group therapists will find with us that these methods have considerable disadvantages. Above all, they are prohibitive in cost and therefore not available under ordinary conditions. Besides, a large portion of the complete content record of a session contributes little to an understanding of the therapeutic process. Those who are interested in inter-personal relations will want to bring group interaction into clear focus. To this end, a method of recording has been devised by the authors [1].

b. **The Recorder.** This guide so far has been written from the assumption that the group therapist alone fulfills the functions described. Experience has shown that it is of considerable advantage to have two therapists; a therapist and a co-therapist or recorder. As the name indicates, one of the co-therapist's functions is to record what goes on in the group session. He is best introduced to the group in the first session, somewhat as follows:

> This is Dr. X. He is taking notes so that he can summarize for us toward the end of the session what went on in the group. Needless to say, that outside the group, nobody besides him and myself will see these notes. Any member of the group who wishes to see them is welcome to it. Incidentally even if an outsider should get hold of them, it would not do him much good, because they are written in a sort of shorthand.

The recorder near the end of the session is called upon by the therapist to give his "summary." "It is about time for Dr. X to sum up from his notes what went on in today's session." This "summary," being the main interpretation of the session, is of the greatest importance. It affords a certain closure to the patients and at the same time stimulates further interaction between the members themselves, as well as between them and the therapists. In order to allow for this interaction before the hour is up, it is wise to begin with the summary after about two thirds of the session.

Interpretation has been discussed in a previous section. Here we want merely to repeat that group interaction should be the center of gravity throughout.

Because of his function, the recorder will draw upon his own person much of the hostility which otherwise might have been directed toward the therapist, leaving the latter very much in the role of the benevolent and non-threatening authority figure.

It might also be mentioned that two therapists, particularly if they are of opposite sex, more immediately revive the family situation.

C. RESEARCH IN GROUP PSYCHOTHERAPY

The statement that there is a great need for research in group therapy hardly needs repetition. The results of research in individual therapy would seem to indicate that experiments designed to give only *yes* or *no* answers about the effectiveness of therapy or even "before and after" pictures, are of very limited value. First of all, the results of such work are not very informative even for the particular situation studied; secondly, it is always very hazardous to generalize from such studies. For group therapy, which presents even greater difficulties in such matters as controls, the need for a reorientation of research would seem even more clear. Here, particularly, the inadequacy of static research methods for the study of dynamics is obvious. What we need to know is not so much the percentage of success in this group or in that group, as the nature of the group therapeutic process. What is the character of the relationships in the group? How do they develop and change? For answering such *dynamic* questions, methods which may have been perfectly appropriate for answering questions of psychophysics, are clearly inappropriate.

Certainly the great contribution which individual projective tests can make to the understanding of personality dynamics is by now clear to everyone. But even such tools fall short of adequacy in research on group dynamics in at least two basic aspects mentioned before. First of all, they present a picture of personality which, no matter how detailed, is essentially a static picture in that it presents the structure and balance of personality forces only at a given time. Secondly, they tell us very little about particular specific relationships. In research in group therapy, merely lipservice to the influence of the social field on the individual will not suffice—here this very thing becomes the specific object of detailed investigation.

Methods of research which are appropriate to the dynamic, social problems of group therapy, are still in a very primitive form. The development and refinement of such methods, including basic theoretical concepts, is certainly one of the most important tasks that confronts us. In the meantime, however, we must use whatever makeshift tools are available, provided only that they meet to some degree, our basic demands.

The most successful and promising of such tools is, in the opinion of the writers, the interaction record method. Although this procedure may in some respects be crude, it is unique in meeting our criteria in that (*a*) it can provide a continuous record, (*b*) it can clarify and be used to examine specific, detailed, inter-relationships of a group situation.

A number of such interaction schemes, of various degrees of value, have been proposed. In considering the value of these schemes, one basic question of both theoretical and practical importance arises: what categories or classes of interaction are used. From a practical standpoint, it is clear that an interaction scheme must provide a kind of shorthand; it is physically impossible to record every aspect of interaction which takes place in a group. But more important, even if it were physically possible to do this, it would be undesirable; an interaction scheme must be not merely a recording, but an analyzing device. We want, in other words, a device which will help us recognize and record those important aspects of interaction through which we can really understand the dynamics of the group therapeutic process.

It is to this second type of interaction scheme that the writers [1] have applied the term "genotypical," in the Lewinian sense, as opposed to the other, phenotypical types. In short, the phenotypical system generally describes its interaction categories in terms of surface verbal content, trying to set up enough classifications to fit every conceivable kind of surface interaction behavior. The genotypical scheme, on the other hand, restricts itself to only a few categories. It tries to choose those categories which are of particular importance for an understanding of dynamics. The categories of such a scheme are not described in terms of surface behavior, but in terms of feelings which underlie the surface behavior. Thus, for example, many kinds of surface behavior may be subsumed under the genotypical category of hostility. One can, of course, also set up a genotypical scheme covering particularly those aspects of interaction in which one is interested for a particular research project.

Another kind of tool which seems very well qualified for research problems in group therapy is the situational test (semi-structured group, leaderless group, etc.). Practically speaking, such procedures offer many of the values of observing interaction in the group therapy process itself, and yet are less time consuming. In addition, the situational test offers a certain advantage over direct therapy observation for the study of group interaction in that it is possible to achieve a greater degree of standardization. Needless to say, the usefulness of situational tests depends largely upon the researcher's capacity to understand the group interaction which goes on in the particular situation. The value of a situational test, therefore, is greatly enhanced when it is used with a good interaction scheme.

We have found that many of the more traditional research methods and techniques are not adequate for the study of the social-dynamic problems of group therapy. Actually, however, it is not only in group therapy that clinicians interested in more dynamic research have found the usual approaches wanting. More and more, we find that research problems in clinical work must be approached dynamically, and that we can no longer postpone a direct research attack on the movement and change processes which are the crux of so many clinical problems. In addition, we find in many clinical research areas the need for a social-field approach for an adequate understanding of the individual. Yet, in the broad clincial areas where these two factors assume great importance, we meet essentially the same difficulty that presented itself in relation to group therapy, viz., the inadequacy of the usual research methods and tools. It may well be that in the social, dynamic kind of observation—observation of how a person behaves in a group situation, how he responds to various kinds of social stimuli, how he changes under the influence of these stimuli, etc.—we have the methods and tools with which we can derive answers to many of the problems of clinical research as well as to problems directly related to the psychotherapeutic process.

This guide[1] to group therapy is intended chiefly as a training instrument. It starts from a definite fundamental hypothesis, viz., that emotional disturbances have their genesis in disturbed interpersonal relations, and that interaction is the basic therapeutic agent in group therapy. Although we are aware that there are many other approaches to group therapy, we believe that the consistent orientation of this brief outline will offer a measure of security to the beginner.

REFERENCE

1. Joel, W., & Shapiro, D. "A Genotypical Approach to the Analysis of Personal Interaction," *J. of Psychol.* (1949), **28**, 9–17.

[1]The statements and conclusions published by the authors are a result of their own study and do not necessarily reflect the opinion or policy of the Veterans Administration.

39

A Beginning Counselor's Experience with Group Counseling*

Wallace K. Harris

Dozens of articles have been written by the experts about group counseling. But I have never come across an article written by a person after his initial experience with group counseling. Most writers wait until they have had more experience and feel more secure about their advice before expounding. It would seem that a beginning experience would be helpful to others who are thinking of taking the plunge, yet are a little wary.

PROCEDURE

Group counseling seemed to offer a solution when I found I was spending most of my time at the beginning of the school year with 15 or 20 of the acting-out, aggressive students while seeing few of the "normal" population. "Group counseling," I remembered from my reading, "is at least as effective as individual counseling."

I began by asking my young friends, as I saw them individually, what they thought of the idea. Their repsonses went from a mild "O.K." to an enthusiastic "I'll try it!" Only one student refused to take part.

After an individual interview, I had each student complete the Rotter Incomplete Sentences Blank and declare on a Differential Aptitude Test "talk sheet" where he felt his abilities lay. This was for the purpose of evaluation. At the end of the school year I planned to have the students repeat each form (providing they were still with us).

I had decided to start with two groups of six, each meeting once a week. This was about all I felt I wanted to attempt at first, because I felt rather insecure about the whole business. In one group I placed mostly underachievers (Group I), while the other group I loaded with the more agressive, troublesome type of student (Group II). At the start of the first session for each group I laid the only ground rules: no smoking, no physical contact or abuse of facilities, and no mention outside of the room of anything said or done. "Outside of this," I stated, "anything goes."

*Reprinted by permission of the author and publisher from *School Counselor* (1965), 13, 47–50.

357

GROUP I

I began with Group I because I felt more secure with them. I asked first why they felt they were in the group. Most felt it was because of trouble with teachers (common problems?). They began by criticizing teachers, first in general, then as individuals; they then started on the principal— but only mildly, always talking to me to catch my reaction. One boy, probably the lone member of this group that could be termed aggressive, began attacking everything at this point, and the others turned on him. This pattern continued for several weeks. I felt pretty good about this group. The boys were orderly, kept within certain moral bounds, and seemed to discuss what appeared to be deep, philosophical subjects as well as common school problems.

As I listened to the tapes of these group sessions, however, I felt something was missing. I finally decided that this group had never really tested me. They were only discussing what they felt I wanted to hear. This is probably why I felt so secure with them.

After about four weeks, one or two boys would be missing, usually different ones each time. Finally only one or two would show up. I decided to disband this group. But in spite of poor handling on my part and the seeming failure of this group, some members felt they would actually miss not meeting.

From this point Group I operated fairly well. The boys were honest in their discussions and carried the ball by themselves. This still was my favorite group, the one I felt most secure in, and it seemed to take on a different atmosphere after the climax, when we had discussed what was wrong with the group.

GROUP II

Group II was completely different, calling themselves the "goof-offs" from the first meeting. These boys started testing me right from the first minute as I attempted to lay the ground rules, and they never really stopped testing. For example, they voted in two more members, their friends who were also "bad." Also, they would come individually to sit in with Group I.

It was almost impossible to carry on any kind of discussion with Group II. There were always at least two or three talking at the same time. With this group I quite often felt uneasy about going into the session, often to the point of dreading it. Nothing seemed to go according to the books.

I sought advice from other counselors at conferences and conventions. I attended special meetings on group counseling, but no one had much to offer. (As usual, my advisers only reflected my queries, as if to counsel me.) At one conference I learned that only about 60 per cent of such groups were considered successful anyway. I was told not to get discouraged just because

I happened to get one of those unsuccessful ones the first try. I grasped this as an effective excuse, but it still didn't help my feelings.

These boys kept showing up religiously for their meetings, though nothing that I could see was being accomplished. Some skipped school on that day, but showed up for the meeting. Some stated they had not been in trouble with the office since the group had started. If this was progress, it certainly was hard on the counselor.

They came to look on me as "one of them." Sometimes they would walk down the halls with me, an arm on my shoulder. Many of the things that went on in the group, obscene comments about teachers and dirty jokes, were leaking out around the school and getting back to me. I began to wonder how far this permissiveness bit went. However, a real group-cohesiveness developed among these boys, something that Group I never achieved.

GROUP EVALUATION

About three weeks prior to the end of the school year, I broke up the groups. I then began calling the members in individually for evaluation of the experience. Once more they filled out the Rotter Incomplete Sentences Blank and the DAT "talk sheet," but the results turned out, as I had suspected they would, to be almost useless. I was at a loss as to how to evaluate any individual progress.

The picture concerning evaluation was pretty bleak. Accompanying the failure of my measuring devices were the facts that, except in one case, marks had not improved; attendance at school had not improved; behavior in class had not changed; and comments by the students themselves within the group situation had not altered in a positive direction. On these bases the groups were a complete failure and waste of time.

As I began calling the students in individually to evaluate their experience, however, a different picture began to unfold. Almost every member stated that he had looked forward to coming to school on the day of his session—a feeling he had never had before in connection with school. Each one stated he had gained something from the experience, but could not explain exactly what it was. All thought it was a lot of fun.

None of the boys felt that the experience had straightened him out or solved any problems. They had all enjoyed getting out of class for an hour. Most of them felt we should have met more often. Some stated that the groups should have been smaller, or that so-and-so should have been kicked out.

Many made the statement that it had given them a chance to blow off steam, or get things off their chest. After sitting there and griping for an hour, there seemed not to be anything to gripe about any more.

One boy said he felt more relaxed around school. He didn't know how this had come about. It just had, and he was sure it was a direct result of his participation in the group.

Another stated he had never gotten along, had always wanted to fight with one boy in his group; but since the experience, each had gained an understanding of the other and listened to the other's ideas and feelings.

One felt he had gained in understanding as a whole. Another felt he had not really gained much—kind of a waste of time, but that maybe later he might realize some benefits.

One boy stated he had changed *for* the group: he had not been called to the office since the group started. He had been doing his work and behaving in class so he wouldn't be given a "three-day pass" and miss "counseling."

One said he was surprised to find that others had the same things bothering them as he had. Another stated he had gained encouragement to do better in school from the experience—didn't know how, though.

A couple of the boys felt the groups would have been more beneficial if I had been more selective in how the groups had been made up. They also thought I should have been more directive, selected some topics; but more important, I should have kept them on the topics instead of letting them get sidetracked. One boy felt I should not have allowed them to cuss as much as I did.

Something happened during the individual evaluation that I had not expected. Every student began talking about himself, his personal problems, or something that had been bothering him. It seems I had really developed rapport with them, and they felt I was someone who had taken an interest in them personally. It was quite surprising that each one of them followed the same pattern. Many things were mentioned that had never been touched upon in the groups. Occasionally I would attempt to pull them back to the discussion about the group experience, but they always went back to themselves again.

DISCUSSION

It might be said then, that, if nothing else, group counseling is an excellent measure to be used for developing rapport and for an introduction to individual counseling (if only there were that much time available for all students).

In listening to tapes of certain sessions, the times when I took a more active part and tried to stimulate discussion were the most productive. This was possible, however, only after considerable rapport had been built. At times I tried to provoke them, told them they were wasting time, used some of their language, swore. These measures seemed to be very effective.

Both groups seemed to want more active participation on the part of the counselor. Possibly, now that they had before them an adult they felt they could trust, he became someone to use as a model; they were dissatisfied with the ones they had had up to this time. They really seemed to be interested in my personal experiences.

Probably what bothered me most all year, especially with Group II, was the disorderly way the students operated. This feeling, however, may have been a facet of my own personality.

My biggest problem, after all, was how to evaluate whether or not my groups were successful and if anything had been accomplished. Questions began to arise in my mind: What makes up a successful group? Does a counselor feel he has experienced a successful group when he feels good about going into each session? Or does he feel good about his group because the members are discussing *what* he feels they should *in a way* that he feels they should? If a counselor feels a little uncomfortable about his group experience, possibly because of certain middle-class values, it could mean the group is operating well. He may be getting some real feeling if he will only listen and observe more carefully.

All but one of my boys was in school at the end of the year. I am not sure they all will be back next year, but some I have seen through the summer have said, "If you will have the group again, I will come back."

I will always wonder about these boys because I came to know them so well. I will always wonder what effect I or the group experience had on them concerning their future. At any rate, I feel that I am a better person and a more effective counselor as a result of the experience.

40

Counseling Within a Group Setting*

Merle M. Ohlsen

Since group counseling is a controversial term, and in my estimation often misused, I should like to begin this paper with my definition, first of counseling, then of group counseling. When one first observes counseling, he may conclude that it involves nothing more than a friendly conversation between a counselor and his client or clients; even a naïve observer soon realizes that it is an intimate, trusting relationship. The counselor struggles to understand exactly what each client is feeling and thinking. The client, on the other hand, gains increased self acceptance and acceptance of others, with new understandings of himself. He learns to assume increasing responsibility for his actions, and to solve future problems more effectively. In other words, counseling focuses attention on the individual, even when provided in groups, and helps the individual learn to do things for himself rather than to rely on others.

THE PROCESS DEFINED

In many ways group counseling is similar to individual counseling. In both, the counselor tries to help the pupil to identify and clarify the problems which disturb him, to improve his understanding of himself and of his situation, to define, examine, and test alternative solutions for his problems, and to select an alternative on which he acts. The relationship which the counselor develops with each pupil enables them to discuss problems which heretofore the pupil was unable to discuss adequately. He learns to examine reasons for his difficulty in talking about certain topics, to challenge and consider the limits within which he is expected to work, and to request information whenever he feels the need for it.

On the other hand, there are some real differences between individual and group counseling. Though the counselor must concentrate his attention on trying to capture the speaker's feelings and to help him tell his story, he also must observe how each speaker's comments affect other members, and help each to participate in the discussion. The counselor's behav-

°Reprinted by permission of the author and publisher from *Journal of National Association of Women Deans and Counselors* (1960), 23, 104–109.

ior gradually conveys to each and everyone in the group his warmth, understanding, and acceptance of them. From the counselor, the members learn to accept one another and to help each talk about his problems.

Group counseling differs from individual counseling in another respect. Each member is given an opportunity to test his tentative solutions in an accepting group of peers and to obtain from them multiple reactions simultaneously, prior to translating his verbalizations into overt behavior. Thus, members learn to help others while they are obtaining assistance from others.

Many have used the term group psychotherapy to label what I have defined as group counseling. I have chosen the term group counseling to indicate thay my clients fall within the normal range of adjustment and that I treat them in a non-medical setting. Group counseling is to group psychotherapy what individual counseling is to individual psychotherapy. In both counseling and psychotherapy, the counselor must try to understand each client, and to help each client to understand and to accept himself, and to help each to face and to increasingly improve his ability to solve his problems. Both require special professional preparation, including supervised practice in counseling.

THE CLIENTS

Group counseling, useful with adults, upper-grade elementary school pupils, and to some extent with primary school children, is particularly appropriate for the adolescent because of his very strong desire to be like his peers. Moreover, he is usually struggling for independence from the important adults in his life; therefore, it is easier for him to accept help from other adolescents than from an adult. In obtaining help from his peers, he solves his problems with the assistance of those individuals who he thinks understand him best. Then, too, the fact that others in his peer group have problems similar to his own reassures him, makes him feel that, after all, he is like the other teen-agers whose company he enjoys. The adolescent also wants to be reassured that his peers understand and accept him. In a counseling group he discovers that they not only come to understand and accept him, but that he also learns to understand them better—that he can empathize with them and help them solve their problems.

In our own research program at Illinois, on group counseling, we have decided to give special attention to the gifted underachiever. We believe that this technique is particularly appropriate for them.

Gowan [6] found that gifted underachievers were self-sufficient, unsociable, hard to reach, hard to interest in social activities, indifferent to their responsibilities, and less identified with their parents than are other gifted youths. Shaw and Grubb [13] and Kirk [8] found underachievers to be hostile. Kirk [8] and Drasgow [4] also found that underachievers' failure was associated with goals which were not their own. Generally these perceptions agreed with our observers' descriptions of our clients. Further, our observers' judgments agreed with Shaw's and Grubb's [13] hypothesis that underachievement is not a surface phenomenon which is easily modified, and with their conclusion that others' demands for more and better quality of work tend to have detrimental results. Our observers also concluded that most of the underachievers included in our sample questioned our judgment that they were gifted. From this picture of underachievers, we concluded that if group counseling could improve relations with others and increase acceptance of self, it should play an important part in motivating these youth to accept and to use their untapped resources.

The youth described in the previous paragraph appear to be similar to Caplan's [3] unruly, antisocial, and incorrigible boys and Gersten's [5] juvenile delinquents. Group counseling did improve the attitudes and classroom behavior of Caplan's clients. The members of Gersten's experimental group became less inhibited and evasive, more productive, more responsive to mature promptings from within, and better able to establish wholesome relationships with others. In an even more unfavorable setting, Paster [12] found that suspicious, hostile, psychoneurotic casualties treated in groups in an Army hospital learned to discuss their problems in groups, to socialize with others, and to cope better with their guilt feelings and feelings of inferiority.

METHOD

Our study was conducted in an outstanding four-year high school which provided considerably better than average counseling services. The group counseling described in this paper was provided in an ordinary classroom which was furnished with movable arm chairs, arranged in a circle.

The sample was composed of ninth-grade students who as eighth-graders ranked in the top ten per cent of their class on the California Test of Mental Maturity and at the ninth decile or below, in grade-point average earned in the eighth grade. Of the 34 pupils identified by this method, 29 actually participated in group counseling. The parents of one child refused to grant permission for their child to participate. Another, at his mother's request, was dropped from the project because his work had improved significantly during the first six weeks grading period. Scheduling problems prevented the other three from participating in counseling.

The 29 who actually participated in the project were divided into four small groups; two experimental and two control groups as follows: E_1—2 girls and 4 boys; E_2—3 girls and 5 boys; C_1—2 girls and 6 boys; and C_2—2 girls and 5 boys.

After the sample had been selected, every prospective client was interviewed for three purposes: (1) To acquaint him with what he might expect from group counseling and to inform him what would be expected from him; (2) To answer his questions about the experience; and (3) To appraise the seriousness of each client's problems. The interviews were followed by a meeting of the parents at which the project was described in detail; their questions were answered; and written permissions for pupil participation were obtained. Though the investigators stressed the point that they wanted only those pupils who themselves recognized the value of group counseling and elected to participate, they learned from the pupils' comments during counseling that every counseling group except one contained some pupils who participated as a consequence of parental pressure.

An effort also was made to control the educational and guidance experiences during the experimental period. During the course of the experiment, none of these pupils was referred either for assistance with study skills or for counseling.

Each counseling group met for one class period twice a week for eight weeks. They were excused from a study hall for these sessions. The director of the project was the counselor for all four groups.

Growth of clients was evaluated with reference to three variables: (1) academic performance as measured by the California Achievement Test Battery and grade-point averages earned in high school; (2) acceptance of self and of others as revealed in responses to a picture story test; and (3) behavior in interpersonal relationships reported on the Behavior Inventory by the pupils themselves and, also, the five members of each observer team,[1] the clients' parents and the counselor.

Before presenting our major findings, I should like to digress a bit to comment on the selection of clients for group counseling. Those who are interested in introducing group counseling should select group members in accord with their own professional competence and the ability of their prospective clients to profit from the experience. Members selected must not only be able to profit from this type of counseling but also to have a therapeutic influence on each other.

"Are there among the prospective members some who are not likely to respond to counseling in a group? Once the pupil knows what the group will expect from him, and what he can expect from others, if allowed to decide without pressure, he will usually be able to determine whether he should join a counseling group.

"How will the group affect each individual? How will each individual affect other individuals in the group and the group process itself? Once the

---

[1] Both observer teams included four of the schools' counselors who observed every counseling session from another classroom by closed-circuit television. The fifth person was the clinical observer who operates the closed-circuit TV.

pupil decides that he would like to join a counseling group, the counselor assigns him to a group in which he can help others as well as receive help for himself. This means, of course, that the pupil will not be assigned to a group until he can be placed in an appropriate group.

"Very aggressive, extremely shy, and seriously disturbed persons tend to be poor risks for group counseling. But before the counselor classifies anyone in any of these three categories, he should study all the information available. It is entirely possible that an individual who is a poor risk for one counseling group may fit into another one where personalities are more nearly compatible with his. It is interesting to note, for example, that the child who is socially ahead of his age group and the aggressive child often fit well into a counseling group with children somewhat older than themselves. Their opposites, the shy child and the child who is socially immature, tend to adjust better to groups with children younger than themselves.

"Having other members of the family in that group may inhibit the pupil's participation and create unnecessary conflicts outside the counseling sessions. The presence of close personal friends has a similar effect. If they are involved in the personal conflicts which the pupil is trying to work out in the group, their presence may block his free examination of the issues.

"Should the counselor try to select a relatively homogeneous group? Even though he may prefer a homogeneous group, the best he can hope to do is to select pupils whose scores on some measurable traits fall within a certain zone. First, however, he should ask whether he wants homogeneity. Different kinds of people, and people with different types of problems, often enrich the counseling experiences for the group. But on the other side, the more heterogeneous group also faces communication problems. Successful untangling of communication problems can in itself contribute to growth, but while adults may be able to overcome such problems, it is usually very difficult for young pupils, even senior high school students, to overcome such problems" [9].

RESULTS OF THE STUDIES

In three of our four groups, clients made significant growth on at least two of the measures, and some of the individuals in even the unproductive group made significant growth [2, 11].

The significant changes in those groups having the special counseling included increased acceptance of themselves and of others and improved behavior at home and at school. Parents' and counselors' descriptions of clients, pre- and post-counseling on the behavior inventory, indicated that these underachievers' behavior became more congruent with ideal adjustment. Those changes were, for the most, maintained over the eighteen-month period following counseling. But they did not improve their grades significantly [2].

AN EXPLANATION

In conclusion, I should like to explain what I believe happened to the clients in the productive groups. These are clinical impressions only, but the eight school counselors who observed the groups by closed-circuit television and the four research associates who observed at least the first and last fourths of the sessions, on kinescopes, agreed with these impressions. With varying degrees of depth, each client discovered: (1) that expressing his own real feelings about people, things, and ideas helped him to understand himself and the forces that worried and disturbed him; (2) that at least one adult could accept him and that this adult, the counselor, wanted to understand him; (3) that his peers had problems too; (4) that, in spite of his faults, which they wanted to help him correct, his peers could accept him; (5) that he was capable of understanding, accepting, and helping others; (6) that he could trust others. When a client discovered that others accepted him he found that he could accept others better, and eventually, that he could accept himself better. After he began to accept himself better, then, and only then, could he accept the fact that he was gifted, and make plans which required him to use his potentialities. All of this takes time—these changes come ever so gradually—yet they must precede substantial improvement in grades. What is more, each client must learn to live with his new self, communicate this new self to others important in his life, and teach them to understand, to accept, and to live with the new self. For example, it is difficult for the average teacher to believe that these hostile and uncooperative students have really changed and for the distressed parent to believe that these youngsters are willing to take responsibility for their work without nagging. The setting in which group counseling takes place offers these unique advantages. It provides an accepting climate in which a client can test new and improved ways of behaving. It assists the client in discovering his new self and in revealing it to others, and at the same time, in learning to help others accept and adapt to this new self.

REFERENCES

1. Ackerman, N. W. "Group Psychotherapy with a Mixed Group of Adolescents," *International Journal of Group Psychotherapy*, V (1955), 249–260.
2. Broedel, J. W., Ohlsen, M. and Proff, F. "The Effect of Group Counseling on Gifted Adolescent Underachievers." A mimeographed paper. College of Education, University of Illinois, 1959.
3. Caplan, S. W. "The Effect of Group Counseling on Junior High School Boys' Concept of Themselves in School," *Journal of Counseling Psychology*, IV (1957), 124–128.

4. Diasgow, James. "Underachievers," *Journal of Counseling Psychology,* IV (1957), 210–211.

5. Gersten, Charles. "An Experimental Evaluation of Group Therapy with Juvenile Delinquents," *International Journal of Group Psychotherapy,* I (1951), 311–318.

6. Gowan, John C. "The Underachieving Gifted Child—A Problem for Everyone," *Journal of Exceptional Children,* XXI (1955), 247–249.

7. Katz, E., Ohlsen, M. M., Proff, F. "An Analysis of the Interpersonal Behavior of Adolescents in Group Counseling." A mimeographed paper, College of Education, University of Illinois, 1959.

8. Kirk, Barbara. "Test Versus Academic Performance in Malfunctioning Students," *Journal of Consulting Psychology,* XVI (1952), 213–216.

9. Ohlsen, M. M. *Guidance: An Introduction.* Chapt. 14. "Counseling Individuals within the Group Setting," pp. 297–298 (New York: Harcourt, Brace and Company, 1955).

10. Ohlsen, M. M., Proff, F. C., and Roeber, E. D. "Counseling and Adjustment." *Review of Educational Research,* XXVI (1956), 292–307.

11. Ohlsen, M. M., Proff, F., and Southard, C. "The Effects of Group Counseling on Two Groups of Gifted Adolescent Underachievers." A mimeographed paper, College of Education, University of Illinois, 1959.

12. Paster, S. "Group Psychotherapy in an Army General Hospital," *Mental Hygiene,* XXVIII (1944), 529–536.

13. Shaw, M. C. and Grubb, J. "Hostility and Able High School Underachievers," *Journal of Counseling Psychology,* V (1958), 263–266.

41

*Group Counseling: Applying the Technique**

Charles F. Combs

Benjamin Cohn

Edward J. Gibian

A. Mead Sniffen

The authors have recently conducted a series of experimental projects designed to demonstrate the values of group counseling as a technique in the public school. They worked in practical situations in regular school buildings and within the limits of the usual school curriculum. From these experiences certain common patterns of procedure relating to the use of group counseling have become apparent.

Group counseling is often the most feasible tool available to the counselor in reaching the difficult or troubled student. It seems to be especially effective when applied to adolescents. Many studies have emphasized the importance of a peer group to the adolescent; the concept of group counseling capitalizes on this peer group identification.

Group counseling is a social process. The persons involved approach problems at their own speed within the safety of a social setting. Here they may explore problems that are important to them within the security of a group of peers who share their problems and with whom they identify. Moreover, they may do this without fear of external direction or the pressure of adult coercion. The adult whom they experience within the group is an adult in a new role—the helpful, non-judgmental, non-threatening adult.

In addition to these advantages, group counseling offers to the school the attractiveness of an efficient use of the counselor's time, energy and influence for dealing with personal problems. Thus the counselor may work with greater numbers of those students who need help most or present the greatest threat to smooth school operations.

The counseling pattern to be used in any particular school must be

*Reprinted by permission of the author and publisher from *The School Counselor* (1963), 11, 12–18.

tailored to the school system in which it is to be applied. A counseling program must always meet the needs of the framework within which it exists. If it does not meet these needs, it will soon cease to exist.

Counseling must be experienced, then, as helpful not only to the students but also to the administrators and, particularly, to the teachers of the students who are being counseled. Involvement of administration and faculty will avoid the hazards of a counseling program that may otherwise be viewed by these people as capricious or threatening. They should be drawn into the formation of the group counseling program, and there should be continual feed-back in order to maintain a high level of involvement.

SELECTION OF STUDENTS

The classroom teachers must be made to feel that they are active participants in the selection of candidates for the group. The opinions and reactions of the faculty and administrators are extremely valuable to the counselor in identifying the disruptive student, the gross underachiever and others who are of deep concern to the school.

Likely candidates for group counseling may also be identified by studying school records. For instance, if the purpose of the proposed group is to deal with the disruptive or disorderly, school records will often have valuable indications of such previous difficulties. If the basic presenting problem is underachievement, candidates may be identified in terms of differences between measured capacity and achievement, or teachers' recorded comments of classroom difficulty.

FORMING A GROUP

It is important in a new or formative program that the groups be carefully balanced. The members of a group should have a common presenting problem, but they should also have different levels or degrees of the problem. The counselor who tries to establish a group composed only of the most severe and recalcitrant persons who present a particular problem is almost assuredly foredoomed to disappointment. Members of the projected group should present mild as well as severe evidence of a particular problem.

The composition of a group will also be determined by the maturity of its members. It must be borne in mind, in this respect, that groups having both boys and girls will present certain special types of problems. For instance, on the junior-high-school level, in the same age range, there may be wide variations in maturity of the two sexes and in their psychosocial readiness to discuss certain issues.

In the final analysis, of course, the composition of the group will, to a larger extent, be predetermined by the period of the day that prospective members will be available.

Since group counseling is, insofar as possible, non-coercive, the composition of the group will depend upon the identification of the members with each other and with the counselor. As groups are instituted and as members experience success and satisfaction, other students will hear of them and will volunteer for these and for future groups.

SIZE OF GROUP

The size of the group will depend on several major factors: the maturity of the students who are being considered for the projected group, the level of adjustment that they present and the topic to be discussed.

Elementary school children seem less capable of deferring their actions and reactions than are older children. The elementary-age child seems to be neither as verbal nor as group-oriented as the junior-high or secondary-school student. Therefore, a small group of four to six seems to afford these younger children a better opportunity to interact with their peers and to gain social experience than they would find in a larger group. The counselor must also be a more active group member with this age child than with older students.

At the junior-high and secondary-school levels, the optimal size seems to be six to eight students, depending upon the students and the topic or purpose for which they will be meeting. The more antisocial or antischool the attitudes of the group members, the lower the number that can be easily handled within the group. In a group of eight, each member seems to have an opportunity to talk and yet also to listen or to be less active when he wishes.

As the group size increases, the number of its interactions seems to increase geometrically. Beyond ten members the number of interactions definitely hampers the progress of the group. In counseling with aggressive students, even a group of eight is often too large. Six seems to be a more practical size.

PHYSICAL SETTING

Group counseling in regular school buildings must, of necessity, use existing facilities. One of the appeals of this technique is that it does not require a glorified setting and can be easily adapted to what is available. The authors have successfully conducted group counseling sessions in regular classrooms, locker rooms, store rooms, cafeterias, stages of auditoriums, conference rooms and small offices.

Ideally, the room where the students meet should be as plain as possible. The optimum room size for a group of six to eight students seems to be about $15^1 \times 15^1$, with a round or square table having a seating capacity of approximately ten people.

There should be enough room between members of the group so that, while they can readily communicate with all of their neighbors, they are not so close to others that they are tempted into diversionary activity. It is also highly desirable to have a soundproof or isolated room, so that any noise of the group will not disturb the rest of the school.

With students having academic difficulties it is also important that there be as little distraction as possible. The room should be small enough that the individual cannot readily back away from the group or walk about the room in a manner that would be distracting. While groups are meeting, the central office should be requested to cut off the public address system and telephone calls to the room.

LENGTH OF SESSION

At the junior-high and secondary-school level, the length of group counseling sessions will usually be determined by the length of the class period. In the elementary school, the class periods will not comprise so great a complication. Group counseling sessions seem most effective when they are of 35 to 45 minutes' duration. Sessions lasting less than 30 to 35 minutes do not seem to allow a group to approach and develop topics. On the other hand, sessions that last longer than 45 minutes may result in boredom.

INITIATING COUNSELING

There are certain techniques that may be of help to the beginning group counselor who is concerned about the important step of initiating the counseling sessions. A sample of an initial structuring might go somewhat as follows:

"I think we all know each other. We are going to meet during this period, in this room, every week for the next＿＿weeks. We're going to be getting together to try to solve problems that we all share. Everyone in this group, for instance, seems to have a lot more ability than is actually being used. Somehow, something is getting in the way and keeping each one of us from being all that we can. We are going to be meeting together to try to find out what some of these reasons are and what we can do to solve them.

"While we are here in this group we are going to talk about anything that is of concern to us. We can say anything we want in any way that we want. Obviously there are going to be some limits. We don't want to disrupt the rest of the school, and of course we can't destroy any of the equipment in this room—or each other, for that matter. But other than these limits, I want you to feel free to express yourselves in any way you like.

"What we say in this group is our business. Nothing we say here is to be told to anyone outside of the group by you or by me. No one else is going to know what goes on here—that's our business. I am here to work with you and perhaps help you to work through the problems, but together we may be able to work something out which will help us all. We must all work together; we must all try to understand each other.

"Okay, who would like to begin?"

Very definite "Rules of the Game" can assist group members in adjusting to the new situation. Certain of the authors, for instance, have found it useful to distribute mimeographed material to the members of the group, somewhat as follows:

RULES OF THE GAME

1. Group counseling is a cooperative job. We must all work together to help each other solve problems.

2. We can't solve problems if we refuse to look at them honestly. Let's try not to let our previous ideas get in our way.

3. Try to really listen to what the person next to you is saying. Don't just try to convince him that you're right. Listen to what he says, just as you expect him to listen to you when you have something to say.

4. Stick with a topic; don't get side-tracked. Wait until the rest of the people seem to be willing to let a topic rest for a while before you try to change it.

5. Speak whenever you have something to say. Don't be afraid to speak up even if what you have to say isn't particularly clear in your own mind. But on the other hand, be careful not to cover up what you mean to say by saying too much.

6. One of the best ways you can help the others is to let them know that they are not alone in what they feel. If you have experienced the same feeling, tell them. You may be surprised to find that you will be able to understand more about the way you feel as you find yourself talking to others about how they feel.

7. Don't feel that you have to come to a group solution or agreement. The purpose of the group is to explore problems together. The decision that you as a person come to must be your own. The only solutions that are good for you must be those that have a personal meaning for you. Someone else's answer may not apply to the way you feel.

8. A group discussion goes along best when everybody trusts each other. Be careful that the others don't feel that you are making fun of them. If you are going to work together and solve problems, you're going to have to trust each other. The more quickly you get to know the others and they get to know you, the more quickly this group is going to "pay off" for you.

ATMOSPHERE

The group counseling situation must be a permissive one. There must be an openness to all of those experiences that can and should be explored within the framework of the educational setting. The counselor must be experienced by the students as an accepting and facilitating adult. However, he must also remember that he is operating within a school framework and that there are certain limits and restrictions by which the group must abide. Permissiveness does not mean anarchy.

The limits observed must be those which are really necessary to the functioning of the group. Children and adolescents find that the security of limits is very important. They are in formative social periods and find security in the periodic restructuring of the group and of its aims. This often enables them to abandon courses of action which they may have already begun to experience as largely unrewarding.

The control of the topics to be explored should be in the hands of the students. It should be their decision to change the subject of discussion and, if necessary, to reorganize the group. The problems presented by the group should be explored where possible in terms of generalized, rather than specific, situations. The boy who presents the group with a specific problem about one certain teacher should find the group discussing behavior of teachers and pupils in general. The counselor must be careful, when clarifying a specifically presented problem, to re-present it in its more general framework.

The counselor must continually attempt to draw out the members of the group, to be aware of the feelings of the counselees and to reflect these feelings to the group. The counselor serves as a catalyst. He clarifies the statements that the group makes and the feelings expressed. He reflects these sentiments in a way that allows each member to examine his own feelings and the group to explore their feelings together. Thus he crystallizes feelings and meanings.

The authors have found that members of the group seem to have built-in controls for the depth of problem they are willing to explore. A topic will be handled only if the group feels it can actually deal with and solve the problem. When the group or particular members feel beyond their depth or not yet prepared to deal with a subject, progress may be effectively blocked by their lack of participation or their changing the subject. Restlessness, resistiveness, aggression or hostility often appear at this point.

If the counselor pushes the group too fast toward a particular solution or even toward a particular problem, the group will usually try to stop him and will give indications that he is losing them. If he responds to these signs and slows down or stops and allows the group once again to assume control and catch their breath, psychologically, the group will usually move ahead rapidly.

The counselor must always seek to respond to the true feelings underlying the statements that the counselees make. He must not fall into the trap of responding to the content of what the students say or, worse yet, to his own needs and attitudes toward these problems.

The members of the group will often test the sincerity of the counselor (who is, after all, a representative of the adult society) and the other members of the group. Before they will reveal themselves or explore problems of deep meaning to them, they must have faith in the integrity of the other members of the group.

As they become able to express their pent-up feelings and needs within the safety of the group, they test and reorganize their perceptions of themselves and of the world around them. Essentially, they are groping toward greater self-adequacy and greater self-acceptability. As they work through group problems, they will be able to see new relationships and will thus become more effective individuals.

DURATION

It is very important to establish at the beginning of a series of counseling sessions a definite duration for the group counseling experience. This seems to give structure to all members of the group so that they can more readily judge the available time remaining. That is, each group member can assess the gains already achieved at any point in the series and the time needed to reach a goal.

Group counseling seems to be most effective on a one-period-per-week basis, running approximately 15 to 20 weeks. Of course, the needs of the particular school will largely dictate the initiation and duration of counseling.

The timing of the start of a series of group counseling sessions is important. Members of the group seem to be more able to tolerate interruptions in counseling after the group has been well established rather than in the formative period, when consistency seems to be very essential. Members often feel rejected if they experience a break in the group pattern in the early periods. It is important that group sessions not be started shortly before Christmas or Easter vacations or semester breaks, for if the formation of a group is thus broken the members may return rather coldly to the group.

The greatest gains from group counseling will take time. The counselor should not be too concerned if there is a lack of observable difference in behavior or attitude early in the counseling process. Counseling often seems more effective if the groups terminate after the designated period and reopen at a future date.

It may be that the group will decide to close prior to the originally decided length of time. The counselor should beware of becoming so personally involved with the group that he feels that an expressed desire for closure is a rejection of himself. If the counselor is unthreatened by the request for closure, the problem of closure will be a rather simple one.

If the counselor is informed by the group that they feel they have discussed all they want to at this time, he should begin structuring for closure. However, he should also leave the door open for them to return. He might say, for instance:

"Okay, some of you seem to feel like stopping. Let's take a vote on it and decide. If as a group we decide to quit at this time, let's begin to taper off over the next few sessions. We'll review what we've discussed and what conclusions we've come to. If in the future we as a group or as individuals want to come back, we can resume this group or start a new one."

It is often in the discussion of closing that many problems not previously discussed will come up. This gives additional material for the tapering-off sessions. Two to five sessions should be used for closing. However, the control should be entirely in the students' hands. If the group decides on four sessions for tapering off, and then later decides to stop after two sessions instead, this is their prerogative.

During the tapering-off sessions, the counselor should assist members of the group to summarize, clarify and restate the problems that have been covered. He should help them discuss the various solutions they have previously explored. It is very important that all members of the group have the opportunity to express themselves on the various problems and their own unique solutions.

The tapering-off sessions are exceedingly important since some students may be deeply threatened by the idea of the closure of the group. They may find it quite difficult to give up the relations formed in the group.

CONCLUSIONS

Group counseling is an exceedingly valuable tool, far too seldom used within the regular school framework. Its advantages are manifold:

1. In dealing with several students simultaneously, it spreads the effect of the counselor and at the same time preserves his effectiveness.

2. It seems to be more readily accepted by students in that, since it occurs within a peer group, it is not as "different" or as threatening to them as individual counseling.

3. It makes effective use of the social setting and peer identification.

4. The adult experienced by students in group counseling is unique in that he is accepting of them and facilitating their experiences, rather than imposing an external judgment. He is a resource, a catalyst and, perhaps, a new kind of adult.

5. Often the establishment of counseling groups within the school may

facilitate individual counseling and other new opportunities to meet the needs of the students.

The authors would like to emphasize that group counseling is not an art known only to a few practitioners who possess unique skills and talents. Group counseling is a technique that is effective and highly efficient of the counselor's time and energy. Most important, it is a technique which lies well within the capabilities of the perceptive school counselor.

42

The Transition Stage in Group Counseling in Terms of Congruence Theory*

Warren C. Bonney

Walter J. Foley

This paper describes the nature of the transition stage and explains a possible solution in terms of a theory of congruence. Theories of group counseling do not provide for the resolution of the conflict associated with the transition stage. This critical point in the therapeutic process is defined as an incongruous situation. The incongruity involves a positive attitude toward the counselor and a negative attitude toward what the counselor expects of the client in the therapeutic relationship of group counseling. To establish congruity, the counselor communicates that personal problems should not be discussed in social groups but that the discussion of personal problems is not only acceptable but also therapeutically necessary in the normatively different context of the counseling situation.

The increased demand for public school counseling services and a shortage of adequately trained personnel have increased interest in group counseling. In the literature, a group process phenomenon termed the transition stage is cited as the first critical incident a counselor must face in group counseling. In this paper the authors will describe the nature of the transition stage and explain its resolution in terms of congruence.

THE SEQUENCE OF GROUP DEVELOPMENT

ESTABLISHMENT STAGE

The first few meetings of a counseling group, the establishment stage, follow the pattern of interaction defined by Sherif and Sherif, who state that "when individuals interact in activities with common goals, they produce a group structure with hierarchical positions and roles" [4]. The common goal in group counseling is the achievement of better personal adjustment. The nature of this common goal creates special problems which would not be characteristic of groups oriented toward the resolution of an external

*Reprinted by permission of the author and publisher from *Journal of Counseling Psychology* (1963), 10, 136–138.

task. Once a counseling group becomes established, it enters its second and unique phase of development.

TRANSITION STAGE

In group counseling, the transition stage is the first crisis situation that the group must face. This transition represents a movement from an essentially social atmosphere to a therapeutic atmosphere. Members realize that the goal for their existence as a group is therapy through the discussion of personal problems. The emotional climate that this realization creates is characterized by peak levels of resistance and anxiety.

The high level of stress and ambivalence encountered at the transition stage is caused by the violation of a perceived social norm. The crisis arises as the client finds himself in a conflict between his hope of relief through psychotherapy and his fear of social sanctions. The resistance that arises out of this conflict can be attributed in part to personality attributes, especially habitual ways of perceiving and dealing with unfamiliar social circumstances. In part the resistance is the result of what is seen as the objective realities of the group situation—the perceived attributes and behavior of other group members and the counselor.

Some writers [1, 2] suggest methods of dealing with the resistance characteristic of the transition stage, but current thinking in group psychotherapy fails to propose any method for averting, within the group, the formation of this phenomenon. According to Bach, "there is in a way no management of the initial resistance. It is a natural phenomenon, a step toward a healthy group therapy culture."

THE TRANSITION STAGE IN TERMS OF CONGRUENCE THEORY

A model of the attitudes that cause the transition stage is shown in Figure 1. The counselor (held in high esteem by the client) asserts that personal problems (not a fitting topic in groups) are proper topics for group discussion. The placement of the attitudes of the client on the grid as to height, or intensity of the attitude, are in this example arbitrary.

In this figure, the counselor is assigned a positive place on the grid. It is assumed that the client will have a positive attitude toward the counselor

Figure 1

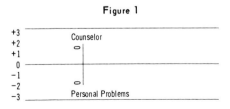

due to the counselor's education, training, and prestige, while in the eyes of the client, personal problems are ascribed a negative position. This attitude is due to the client's past experiences and conditioning. Personal problems are perceived as improper topics for discussion in a group situation. The connecting line, the line of assertion, is positive in that the counselor has communicated, either verbally or nonverbally, the implication that personal problems are a fitting topic for group discussion.

The transition stage is an incongruous situation. The rationale, in terms of congruence theory, is that a positive sign (the counselor) has made a positive assertion (being in favor of the discussion of personal problems) about a negative sign (personal problems). In congruence theory, the outcome of this situation is stated as follows: "Whenever two signs (objects, persons, ideas, beliefs, etc.) are related by an assertion (coupling action), the mediating reaction characteristic of each shifts toward congruence with that characteristic of the other, the magnitude of the shift being inversely proportional to the intensities of the interacting reactions" [3].

KNOWN SOLUTIONS

A client may resolve his dilemma in one of three ways. He can change his attitude about the counselor and assign him to a negative position on the grid of Figure 1. In this manner, the client's perception would be of a negative person making a positive assertion about a negative concept. This situation would be congruous. Second, the client can change his attitude toward the social sanctions encountered in the discussion of personal problems in groups. This would change the position of personal problems in Figure 1 to a positive attitude which would be congruous with the positive assertion made by the counselor. In the third solution, which is not a choice in a positive sense, the client can leave the field, relinquishing group identity and membership. These three solutions would be made with (much or considerable) resistance and anxiety, especially if the client holds strong attitudes about group membership, the counselor, or social norms for personal conduct in a group. Each solution involves a high level of anxiety and resistance because all three solutions to some extent involve an attitude change by the client.

PROPOSED SOLUTION

The authors suggest that structuring by the counselor during group counseling might alleviate the crisis proportions of the transition period. They further suggest that the counselor take an active role in the group during the early stages. The position of the authors, as expressed in terms of the Osgood-Tannenbaum theory of congruity, are presented in the remainder of this paper.

It is important in this solution that the counselor communicate understanding of the group's situation, as well as his agreement with their attitude toward the discussing of personal problems in social groups. By doing so, he communicates a negative assertion toward discussing personal problems in social groups, which makes the situation shown in Figure 1 congruent in the eyes of the client.

Simultaneously aligning with the group attitude, the counselor structures a new context for the concept *personal problems.* His presentation of the discussion of personal problems in a counseling situation is then viewed by the clients as uniquely different from the discussion of personal problems in a social situation. This allows for formation of a new and different attitude toward "personal problems" in the context of the therapy situation. A graphic representation of this concept is presented in Figure 2.

Figure 2

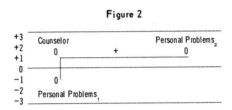

By introducing this new semantic concept, personal problems$_2$, the counselor permits the client to find that his perception of discussing personal problems in social situations is in agreement with the attitude of the counselor. By structuring, the counselor clarifies his use of the concept personal problems as being special, unique, and different from the concept personal problems in the social setting. *In effect, the counselor communicates that personal problems should not be discussed in social groups but that the discussion of personal problems is not only acceptable but also therapeutically necessary in the normatively different context of the counseling situation.*

The authors recognize that there are many forms of resistance that must be dealt with in the group therapy setting. This paper is not meant to be a panacea for the counselor; it is presented as a possible solution to the first crisis situation that a group must face. In the early meetings, the counselor, by clarifying his feelings, identifying with the group and their attitude about the discussion of personal problems in social situations, and by introducing a new context for the concept that does not threaten the held attitudes of the client, can avert the transition stage.

Received August 3, 1962.

REFERENCES

1. Bach. G. R. *Intensive Group Psychotherapy* (New York: Ronald, 1954).

2. Ohlsen, M. M. Illinois Personnel and Guidance Association. *Newsletter* (Fall 1961).

3. Osgood, C. E., Suci, G. J., & Tannenbaum, P. *The Measurement of Meaning* (Urbana, Ill.: Univer. of Illinois Press, 1957).

4. Sherif, M., & Sherif, C. W. *An Outline of Social Psychology* (New York: Harper, 1956).

43

*So You Want To Try Groups?**

David W. Catron

When a counselor returns to his familiar school setting after a summer course or two in group techniques, he may be left wondering how he can apply his newly found knowledge of group counseling. The counselor who has become interested in groups through readings but has not been back to college for further training and supervision may also reach a stage where he would like to apply what he has studied. So, whether through formal courses or personal readings, many counselors reach a point of wanting to get involved, to some degree, with a group. The question is where to start.

Counselor educators and writers in this area generally agree that counseling in groups offers distinct advantages to the participants, advantages of a different kind than those offered in individual counseling. Furthermore, group methods permit services to be offered to a wider range of students, as well as providing more efficient use of counselor time. Because of these advantages, it is not surprising that a general trend has developed in counselor training toward the inclusion of more courses in group process. The trend emphasizes the idea that the use of groups has its place within the repertoire of skills of the broadly educated counselor. However, simply making these declarations does not necessarily mean that counselors will, in fact, practice what they learn in group courses. It seems that relatively few students who take courses in group procedures actually begin groups when they return to their counseling setting. If they do begin a group, they often become frustrated or discouraged and are reluctant to try another group, or they may "lock in" on one type of group experience and find it difficult to initiate other types of group experiences. Either condition would be unfortunate. Consequently, this paper will attempt to encourage counselors to develop group skills by offering practical suggestions for starting a group under conditions where they will have a high probability of success and, hopefully, where they will be encouraged to continue in group work and develop their skills further.

°Printed by permission of the author.

BEGINNING GROUP WORK

As a counselor considers going into group work, two main ideas should be kept in mind. First, there is a wide variation in the degree of complexity of groups in terms of their structure and dynamics. Second, there are varying "levels of aloneness" under which a counselor may work in specific groups in his situation.

DEGREES OF COMPLEXITY AMONG GROUPS

Groups do not equal groups; that is, whenever a change occurs in one of the many dimensions of a group there is a change in the complexity of that group. For example, suppose a group of eight seniors was invited to meet with a counselor for one session of an hour and a half in order to discuss procedures for applying to colleges in the area. Such a group probably would be rather straight-forward. The group would be simple in structure and not too complex in its goals or dynamics. If, however, the subject matter was changed from college application forms to dating behavior and the sessions were extended over several weeks, the result would be a much more complex group situation. One could say that with each change in a dimension or the addition of other dimensions, the complexity of the group would vary. A hierarchy of complexity, then, seems possible. Each person, as a function of his training and experience, would probably vary in his ranking of each group, but, within his own framework, each counselor could develop a hierarchy of groups as he sees them.

Dimensions that would affect the complexity of a group would include such variables as group size, group composition (sex distribution, degree of pathology, volunteer-nonvolunteer status of the members, etc.), the degree of structure imposed by the leader (the process dimension), the subject matter under discussion (content dimension), and the number of contact hours the group experiences each month (density of contact dimension).

Figure 1 combines these last three dimensions into a schema that may facilitate thinking about variations in group complexity. This framework is an extension of Goldman's two dimensional view of counseling which emphasized combinations of content and process in group counseling [2]. The front face of Figure 1 illustrates the three subdivisions which Goldman suggested for both the content and the process dimensions. The *process* dimension was divided into a highly structured category, a semi-structured category, and a relatively unstructured category. The structured end of the process continuum was typified by a lecture-type approach to the content under consideration. The unstructured end was more non-directive in approach and emphasized feelings and group self-direction rather than an imposed orientation.

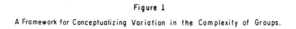

Figure 1

A Framework for Conceptualizing Variation in the Complexity of Groups.

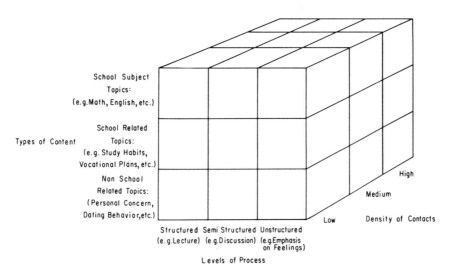

The *content* dimension of Goldman was also divided into three categories: school subjects, school related subjects, and non-school related subjects. With this schema, nine combinations of process and content resulted. Obviously, a group could be formed from any of the nine combinations and, even after forming, a group might sift from one combination to another. For example, a class in history (lecture-type process and school related content) may, on occasion, drift into a student led discussion of non-school conditions such as feelings regarding parental regulations at home.

In addition to the process and content dimensions of Goldman, Figure 1 also includes a *density of contacts* dimension [1]. This dimension refers to the average number of contact hours per unit of time. For example, in Figure 1, the low density category might refer to an average of from one to four contact hours per month; whereas medium and high density categories might refer to five to eight and eight to more hours per month respectively.

LEVELS OF ALONENESS

When a counselor thinks about beginning his first group, he may feel inadequate and apprehensive. However, there are many alternatives to simply venturing out alone. Every community has resource people who may be available to help a counselor with his group. These people can serve as co-counselors, consultants, supervisors, referral sources, and confidants (someone with whom the counselor can talk about the progress of the group). These persons would include experienced group workers, fellow counselors, specialists in the community, and even students. Each counselor can determine the level of help he needs and utilize those resource persons who are able to offer the training, experience, or aid that he desires.

PRACTICAL SUGGESTIONS

The following suggestions are designed to help a new group counselor (1) to recognize the range of possible groups he might consider, (2) to rank order these groups, (3) to assess his own abilities in group skills, (4) to become aware of the resource people available to him in his community, and (5) to select a group that seems to fit best into his situation. This should enable him to initiate a group where he has the highest probability of a positive group experience and then, hopefully, he will gain confidence and move into a more complex group counseling situation.

LISTING POSSIBLE GROUPS

A counselor could begin by listing as many groups as he can think of that might be offered in his setting. These groups ought to run the gamut and include as wide a variety of groups as possible. Figure 1 might be used as a framework for generating ideas and conceptualizing possible groups. By considering variations in group size, group composition, problem area, and degree of adjustment, additional groups can be added. Such a list can be lengthened and reassessed as the counselor becomes aware of new types of groups through his reading and experience.

In making his list, the counselor should not restrict himself to groups that he feels he can adequately handle. There will be ample time later to evaluate and decide on the merits of each group on the list. For the time being, evaluation should be set aside in order that ideas for groups can flow freely.

RANKING GROUPS

By making a list of possible groups, the counselor becomes aware of the wide variety of groups to be considered and also the different levels of complexity which these groups represent. A second suggestion concerns a rank ordering of these groups in terms of their complexity as defined by the counselor himself. He is the person who will be leading the group or at least making the arrangements for the group; consequently, it is *his* evaluation of the complexity of each group that is most important.

Evaluation of whether a particular group is feasible, legitimate, etc., should still be held in abeyance. Simply ranking the groups in terms of complexity is all that is called for at this stage. Fine differentiations between groups are unnecessary.

LISTING PERSONAL QUALIFICATIONS

A third suggestion concerns the counselor's awareness of his own skills and competence in group work. As difficult as it may be, it would be highly desirable for each counselor to assess his qualifications as frankly and openly as possible. A listing of formal courses, readings, and group experiences will help to focus on strengths and weaknesses which might affect his work with various groups.

To this list, the counselor might add informal groups in which he has participated in the past and also those groups in which he is presently involved. These may be school committees, student groups, civic groups, church groups, etc. He should recognize that group counseling skills may be developed outside the classroom setting and that current group involvements offer a kind of group laboratory for observing group dynamics and for practicing group skills. By listing these involvements, the counselor may become aware that he *already* has considerable experience in groups and that these experiences have been and will continue to be learning experiences.

LIST OF RESOURCE PEOPLE

A close scrutiny of the counselor's particular community can usually produce a list of persons who might help with a group. In addition to professional group workers, such as counselor trainers, clinical psychologists, psychiatrists, and experienced group counselors or social workers, persons with little or no group training may be of help (e.g. other counselors or teachers in the school). Novice group counselors may find it more comfortable to team up with another inexperienced counselor for this first group. Having a co-counselor, whether experienced or not, offers several advantages to the new group worker. He would have someone with whom he could discuss the selection and plans for the group, and then, after the group gets underway, he would have someone who, by sharing the same experiences, could discuss the group with him after each session. Furthermore, during each session, it is often helpful to have a co-counselor, because as one counselor follows the interaction very closely, the other counselor has time to reflect on what has been said, for observing individual and group reactions, and for thinking through what is being said. So much happens in some group sessions that it is helpful to have a few moments to think about the dynamics that might otherwise have been by-passed.

In addition to peers as co-counselors, another possibility would be to utilize students who have participated in previous groups experiences. Such students are often quite eager to assist in forming a new group and working with the counselor as a co-worker. These students often have a desire to share with other students an experience that has been meaningful to them.

Selection of such a student would need to be based on the needs of the group being formed and the particular qualifications of the student. For example, a student who had previously been underachieving but who has since broken the academic slump might be very helpful in forming a group for undersachieving students. Such a student might be a role model and, as such, a source of encouragement to the group members. In addition, he might be of significant help in opening communication processes within the group.

SELECTING A GROUP

From these several lists, a counselor should be able to pull together a combination of possible groups, personal skills, and available resource persons and select from the hierarchy of groups the one or two groups which seem to harbor the greatest possibility for success, that is, of being helpful to the students and also facilitating the counselor's learning experience. By sifting through the lists and finding the combination of students, content, process, density of contacts, personal qualifications, and resource persons which comprise the most logical "package," the counselor will be able to pick the combination that makes sense and begin.

CONCLUSION

Individual counseling will remain as an important method in many counseling situations; however, because of the advantages of group procedures in other situations, there is a need to span the gap between academic training in groups and actual practice. It is hoped that procedures, such as those suggested in this paper, will be helpful in encouraging more counselors to become involved in group counseling.

REFERENCES

1. Catron, D. W. "The Effects of Educational-Vocational Group Counseling on the Perception of Self and Others." Doctoral dissertation, George Peabody College for Teachers (Ann Arbor, Mich.: University Microfilms, 1965), No. 65–3561.

2. Goldman, L. "Group Guidance: Content and Process," *Personnel and Guidance Journal* (1962), 40, 518–522.

VII

GROUP COUNSELING: SOME
SPECIAL CONSIDERATIONS

TRAINING FOR GROUP COUNSELING

If group counseling is to achieve a more prominent place in school guidance programs and the helping functions of other agencies, it is necessary
and proper that more deliberate attention be given to the training of personnel for roles as group counselors. As the province of group counseling
is more precisely delimited, training for the activity can become more
direct. Group counseling, it has been suggested, is neither didactic group
instruction nor is it therapy for an assembly of disturbed persons. Rather,
group counseling is a situation which capitalizes upon peer group support
to encourage an individual search for meaning and value in a changing
world.

The group counselor should bring to his work the understandings of
human development and personality dynamics now commonly expected of
the individual counselor. He also needs a broad general education both
formal and experiential in order to be able easily to enter into the life spaces
of group members and to help build bridges of communication and meaning from one to another. He must have heightened sensitivity to the dynamics of group participation and he must demonstrate the discipline of
reflective thinking which can process and derive meaning from both data
and feeling. In sum, he is a model of an integrating person being himself
in a social setting where he need be neither authority, judge, nor clinician.

To prepare for such a role would seem to require more than a course or
two, and indeed it does. On the other hand, it is not required that an entirely new professional program be developed to parallel the training of
the guidance counselor. A proliferation of new courses for group counseling
might, in fact, militate against the development of the integrating person
who is a group counselor.

It is proposed that counselor education continue its emphasis on building competencies in understanding, accepting, and helping the individual.
But in recognition of learning as a *process*, and one which requires integration of diverse experiences, it is proposed that group counseling as a growth
experience for all counselors in training be added to the non-academic
side of counselor education. By participating in small groups with a coun-

selor-leader dedicated to using the group as an aid to help individuals examine and recast the meanings of their current experiences, neophyte counselors should experience both personal growth and some insight into the dynamics of group counseling.

While some didactic study of small group theory and dynamics is desirable for a prospective counselor, the emphasis should continue to be on experiential learning. Even in a didactic course on group procedures in counseling some observation of group counseling should be arranged. Advanced students in counselor education should have the opportunity to become deliberately analytical of the process of group counseling in which they and others have been engaged earlier in their programs. For this purpose, a practicum-type arrangement in group counseling may be needed. The practicum should provide first for a period of several weeks of sensitivity training in a T group setting with other practicum members. This should be followed by an apprenticeship as co-leader in a counseling group carefully critiqued by the co-leaders and non-participating supervisors. Finally, the practicum should place the candidate in a group of his own while still under some degree of external supervision. The supervision of this practicum experience, if optimum resources exist, would utilize video-tape facilities in order that the group counselor may study and restudy the nonverbal as well as verbal dynamics of his group.

Throughout the practicum in group counseling supervisory meetings should continue to emphasize the growth purposes of group counseling in contrast to either instructional or treatment purposes. In this way, the counselor who moves into employment will have not only skills but a sense of identity and mission which should help him develop and fulfill a role which is separate from that of both teacher and therapist.

ETHICS IN GROUP COUNSELING

A code of ethics is simply a standard or prescribed code that is expected of each person who has affiliation with a professional group. Standards of behavior though they are often nebulously defined and enforced are not uncommon in society as a whole. Professional football players for example, follow certain unwritten standards that could be broadly conceived as a code of ethics. Piling on an individual whose forward running motion has already been stopped is frowned upon by many professional football players, and is in this sense unethical. Other groups may have principles or standards of conduct that they follow and such concepts as "behavior among thieves" and the "achievement ethic" of middle class society are well-known examples.

Both the American Personnel and Guidance Association and the American Psychological Association have developed ethical standards to guide the professional behavior of their members [1, 6]. These standards are in essence the principles that these professional groups have formulated from experience, judgment and in the framework of the basic attributes of the profession.

In group counseling the code of ethics as presented by the American Personnel and Guidance Association must and should apply, but the nature of the group counseling relationship presents some special problems that should be considered.

1. CONFIDENTIALITY

The statement on ethics in counseling of the American Personnel and Guidance Association states that the counseling relationship and the information that results from this relationship must be kept confidential but that records, notes, data, correspondence, and recordings can be used in such professional activities as research and teaching. Such use of information, however, must be used in such a manner that the identity of client is protected and no harm may come to him [1]. Since the problem of confidentiality can be a dilemma when *one* counselor works with *one* student, it is not difficult to foresee the problems that could arise when one or several counselors work with a group of students. The counselor may very well abide by the principle of confidentiality and only use group verbalizations and records in a professional manner; however, individuals in the group could not be automatically assumed to abide by this principle. Therefore, it is extremely important that confidentiality be structured into the counseling sessions as soon as possible, preferably during the first meeting. A discussion of confidentiality between counselors and group members is extremely important and may well determine the whole nature of the counseling experience. Students are not likely to discuss personal concerns among peers when they are very much aware that what is said may become the topic of conversation at dinner tables or in the shower room. The counselor and the group will also have to make decisions with regard to what happens if a member of the group breaks a confidence. It would not contribute to rapport in a new group to start a counseling group by announcing that punishment will be applied if a confidence is broken. Rather, counselors may approach the problem by involving group members in role-playing a hypothetical situation in which a confidence has been broken in order to help the group achieve an understanding of the personal impact of such phenomena.

2. COUNSELING RESPONSIBILITIES

Patterson [11] discusses the counselor's responsibilities to the client, to the client's family and relatives, to the employer, referring source, profession, society, and himself. In essence he states that the counselor's *major* responsibility is to the client, and that he will have no professional relationships with the family or the friends of the client without first having the permission of the client to do so. Responsibilities to the school administration have not been clearly resolved, nor are the responsibilities to the referring source of a client or to society.

These issues become even more hazy when the counselor works with a group. For example, the boy who relieves some of his anxiety by verbally attacking another group member may be deriving a measure of benefit through the release of such feelings although the student who is the target of the attack may not be able to handle such communication. The counselor's judgment as well as his counseling skill must be adequate to the task of intervening to direct the group process toward interactions which promise growth for both members.

Other problems arise when we consider the counselor's relationship to the school administration, referral sources, and the family and friends of the student. Even if an individual in a group permits the counselor to consult with parents or the school administration, he may also have to take into consideration that the information involves *other members of the group*. It would seem that if the counselor makes a decision to divulge information that all had agreed was confidential, he should secure the consent of all those involved.

GROUP COUNSELING WITH THE HANDICAPPED

While one of the objectives of American schools is to provide the child with certain skills and knowledges, educators have long recognized the need for specialized services for pupils and such reasoning has hastened the development of school guidance and counseling services. Although increased federal funds and the interest of numerous private organizations have played an increasing role in working with handicapped children, the major responsibility for their education still rests with the public schools. Although exact figures of the number of handicapped children in the public schools would be difficult to estimate because of less than clear definitions of what constitutes a handicapped individual, a conservative study would probably reveal that over eighty percent of the handicapped children would be enrolled in public education.

Since there is abundant evidence that "normal" children are, at some time in their lives, in need of specialized guidance and counseling, it also seems probable that such services are even more appropriate for the handicapped, in that a physical defect has a unique, personal, and often unconscious significance for the disabled person. An individual's physique is one of the ingredients that helps make up his "personality" and in addition, physique is one of the grounds upon which class and caste distinctions are made. In such cases the disabled child may require an unusual amount of help and attention. As early as 1946, Barker, Gonick and Wright [3] indicated that handicapped children exhibit more maladjusted behavior than do nondisabled and that persons with long histories of disability are more likely to exhibit maladjustment than those of a short history of disability.

There is no evidence, of course, to prove that effective group counseling with the handicapped child need be conducted in groups where only children with disabilities are included. In fact there may be some basis for "mixing" the handicapped child with the "normal" since most children with physical disabilities wish to be accepted as equals with their peers. Such acceptance may be gained in effective group counseling sessions. Regardless of the grouping method, however, the group counseling experience can be meaningful for the handicapped in many ways, some of which are explored here.

1. *The group can provide recognition of the handicapped child as an individual.* As previously noted the handicapped child wishes to be treated like all normal children. He has the same drives, wishes, and emotions as other children and wants recognition both from his peers and adults. He should receive the same attention in the counseling group as do other members without being singled out for special praise or support since this is likely to hamper total group functioning and be interpreted by the handicapped child as more adult pity.

2. *Group counseling can aid the handicapped child to appraise his difficulty realistically.* Handicapped children may react in a variety of ways to a physical disability. Some with relatively minor defects may try to overcompensate for them or conceal them entirely. A child who has lost an eye may be convinced that he is ugly and that his peers merely tolerate his presence instead of accepting him as he is. Often he has distorted perceptions of how others see him and tends to be defensive about his appearance. In the permissive atmosphere of the counseling group the child's fears can be brought into the open and examined in ways that are impossible in normal social situations. He may learn that the loss of an eye or arm is not as bad as he had expected and that many of his fears of rejection were largely unfounded.

3. *The group itself is a social learning experience for the handicapped child.* Most handicapped children do not like to be separated from normal group activities. Yet the very nature of our society and the school in particular make it difficult for the exceptional child to gain social approval. The common activities of the high school that lead to popularity are frequently such cocurricular experiences as athletics, drama, cheerleading, dance clubs, and student government. The very nature of such activities prohibits the handicapped child from participation in many of these events,

and he encounters difficulty in finding the key to group approval. He may be lonely, suspicious of others, and self-conscious. Since these feelings may be a result of unpleasant earlier group experiences, the exceptional child may need to discover a social learning experience where he is a part of the group from the very beginning and does not need to possess specialized motor and social skills to be an accepted group member. Since he is not being graded for his participation and his responses are not judged "right" or "wrong" as they may have been in the classroom he does not need to be exceptionally brilliant to earn group recognition. Once he learns to function in the counseling group, he may become a more effective group member in other social situations since the skills learned in the counseling sessions may aid him to become freer and less rigid in the social situations of the school and community.

GROUP COUNSELING IN NONSCHOOL AGENCIES

Graduate school programs in guidance and counseling have traditionally placed major emphasis on the preparation of counselors who will work in public school settings. Beginning courses, often labeled Introduction to Guidance or Introduction to Counseling have been directed primarily toward the guidance and counseling function as it is related to teachers, administrators, and the overall structure of the school. This focus is reflected both in the text books available in the field and the outlines of counselor education courses. While this essentially parochial approach to guidance and counseling has been effective in preparing counselors to work in educational settings, counselor educators now recognize that the counselor is finding employment in a large number of institutions. For example, the May 1966 issue of the *Placement Service Bulletin* published by the American Personnel and Guidance Association had fifty-four listings of available positions in rehabilitation counseling. Some of the job opportunities had openings for ten or more counselors.

Thirty-six additional listings appeared in the same bulletin and a survey of these available positions indicates that counselors are needed to work with the U.S. Department of Labor, United Airlines, Science Research Associates, and United States Army Enlisted Evaluation Center. The American Personnel and Guidance Association published this placement service bulletin seven times during 1965–1966 and similar opportunities in nonschool settings were contained in each issue.

Since there appears to be an ever growing need for counselors to work in non-school agencies, the application of group techniques to these settings should be considered.

1. MARRIAGE AND FAMILY COUNSELING

Marriage counseling has been fairly common in the United States for over thirty years. Much of the work done in this area has been done primarily by priests, ministers, and family relations agencies. At least two organizations, the American Association of Marriage Counselors and the National Council on Family Relations, are actively engaged in professionalizing the field [4]. The problems involved in marriage counseling are complex and the effects of marital troubles on society cannot be easily measured. It is probably safe to assume, however, that disruptions on children, some homicide, and alcoholic and drug addiction can at least be shown to be partially related to homes where serious difficulty has arisen between husband and wife.

Group techniques can be readily adapted as an effective vehicle for marriage counseling since marriages are concerned with group living. All the dynamics that apply to any group setting are at work in a marriage, and such factors as cohesiveness, goals, communication, and interaction contribute to the relative stability or lack of it in family relations.

Married couples brought together in a group setting could learn that the problems that pose such dilemma in their marriage are not unique, but difficulties that other couples face and attempt to resolve. In addition the group provides a reality testing ground in which individual perceptions, perhaps long distorted by the constant use of defenses, are examined. Unresolved arguments can be examined in the light of the perceptions of others who have similar concerns and new insights can be gained. The object of such counseling is not necessarily to solve all the problems of a marriage but to provide the individuals with ways of reaching a higher degree of adjustment, to lessen disruptive effects on children, and to provide a broad and comprehensive understanding of common marital difficulties.

2. ADULT COUNSELING IN THE COMMUNITY

The rapid rise of adult education in many communities presents an interesting possibility for the counselor to extend his special skills to a segment of the population who usually do not have the assistance of a professional counselor. Many schools which offer special interest courses of a non-academic nature have also begun to assume responsibility for helping individuals who have either lost their jobs because of economic factors, or who need retraining or upgrading to assume new responsibilities in their present position.

Some of these schools provide counseling help for adults on an individual basis, but much of this is simply a procedure of administering an

aptitude battery and interpreting a score. The problems involved in working with such adults, however, call for more than testing. Adults who have
lost jobs or who are about to accept new positions have doubts about their
abilities, may be too insecure to attempt to learn new skills, and may need
help in making the adjustments caused by unemployment. The increasing
number of older workers in the community with their declining capacities
pose additional problems that require counseling help. Super [12] indicates that the older members of our society need to modify their self concepts, work roles and way of life.

A group counseling approach which offers peer group support, pools
problem solving skills, and reinforces sound judgments can help adults
to discover new meanings in lives from which the old meanings have been
drained by the march of time.

3. GROUP COUNSELING WITH DISADVANTAGED YOUTH

As of November 10, 1966, 29,126 young people were enrolled in 112
Job Corps Training Centers, including 88 conservation centers, eleven
urban centers for men, eleven urban centers for women, and two special centers. Project Upward Bound has awarded grants to 224 colleges and universities to serve 20,429 students. Project Head Start has enrolled 233,250
children in year round and follow through projects, and there are currently
eighty-four Indian programs financed at a federal cost of $12,565,356. In
addition the government has invested over 15 million dollars in VISTA,
and an additional $148,514,594 dollars in the Neighborhood Youth Corps
[10].

In several of these programs, young men and women from all parts of
the United States have been brought together in residence centers in an
effort to provide them with the necessary skills to earn a living and "break
the poverty cycle." These programs involve the learning of special skills,
academic subjects, and various trades and the development of strengthened
self-concepts through counseling services. Group counseling, again, has a
significant contribution to make to the objectives of these youth projects.

As background for group counseling with disadvantaged youth the
counselor must have some understanding of the child with whom he is
working. Golden and Margolin [8] point out the term disadvantaged means
disadvantaged according to middle classed standards or those individuals
who are not making social, emotional, and vocational adjustments at the
level of their maximum capacity. In their thinking a disadvantaged individual is one who for physical, social, economic, emotional, and educational
reasons cannot satisfactorily meet the stresses and demands of life.

Such students are likely to have low academic motivation which may
manifest itself according to Farquhar [7] in the form of hostility, intolerance

for delayed rewards, negative reflected self-concept, persistent syndrome of underachievement, low job-task involvement, and rejection of unique accomplishment. Ascher [2] in his discussions of the dimensions of poverty with slum children points out that many of these children come from one parent families or are illegitimate, have a poor self image, and have only limited communication skills. Woodruff [13] indicates that the self concepts of minority group youth may develop negatively because of poor family situations, poor education, and the role models available for them to emulate are not the kind that lead to high vocational aspirations.

Counselors faced with counseling disadvantaged children will soon discover they have undertaken a most difficult task. Changes are not likely to be rapid and dramatic, and the counselor who expects a magic change in his clients will probably experience more than one disappointment.

How can group counseling be effectively utilized in such agencies as Job Corps training centers? Several possibilities exist.

1. Orientation to the Center. Youth enrolled in Job Corps and other programs bring with them a complex combination of backgrounds. Recruited from the city slums, the rural shacks, and the small community, the boy or girl who arrives in a Job Corps camp is probably wholly unprepared for the experience. Perhaps he has never ventured over sixty miles from home and has little idea of what is expected of him and what he is to expect from this new situation. The importance of an effective orientation to this new situation cannot be minimized since so many of these youth have experienced failure in the past. They may enter the center with a "failure set" or the preconceived notion that their chances for success are slim. In addition some children from minority groups, particulary Negro and Puerto Rican children may have had little contact with accepting white male adults and suspicion or even fear would not be uncommon. There is also the problem of meeting and making new friends, and the experience in group living that may be completely new to many of them.

A small group counseling approach to orientation to a center can be a meaningful way to introduce a young man or woman to a whole new way of life. Skillful counseling combined with factual information about the center will allow the individual enrollee to ask significant questions about this new experience, discuss his fears, and clarify his misunderstandings. He can learn that many of his peers have similar fears, doubts, and lack of trust. A group counseling approach may also enable him to form his first meaningful relationship with an adult—and for many it may be the first adequate role model he has encountered. Effective emotional orientation ιω the center is vital in that none of the other benefits that can occur in the experience are possible if he leaves. If the center is seen as "just another school" or the counselor as "just another teacher," the enrollee may decide that he is once again in an impersonal, hostile world where eventual failure is imminent.

In addition to the benefits that group counseling could provide for the young men and women who enroll in the Job Corps program, the group counseling approach to orientation may also be beneficial to the total program in that individuals who are in need of intense psychological services could be identified and referred to agencies that are designed to provide such specialized care. Special learning and medical problems which have not been detected during initial screening procedures may also be identified in group counseling sessions. Through this highly personal, group approach to orientation the transition from the world of the disadvantaged into a new and vital learning system can be made smoother.

2. Counseling for Improved Self-Image. Many of the writers and researchers who publish literature related to the disadvantaged child point to the fact that disadvantaged almost automatically means a poor self-image. Although the programs at Job Corps Centers are designed to provide experiences that will improve that image, the group counselor can play a key additional role in this process. If the work of Super [12] and others is accurate, the improvement of the self image of the Job Corps Youth may be the single most important facet of the total program. Teaching a boy to read or a girl to type is not enough. These newly acquired skills and others must become a part of the youth's self-concept. He must see himself in terms of "I can" rather than "I can't"; he must be able to see new learnings as part of himself rather than isolated exercises he has had to learn to "get through the program."

Skillful group counseling can provide an atmosphere of psychological safety where new learnings, attitudes, and feelings can be tried out. Negative views of the self may with time and skillful counseling change in a more positive direction. The youth who has always seen himself as unsuccessful and unskilled, may find that he has a chance for success. Since evidence continues to mount to show that an individual may well behave in the ways that he sees himself, counseling sessions designed to enhance this self-image may be the key to the total Job Corps program.

3. Changing Perceptions of the World of Work. The disadvantaged child is likely to have limited knowledge and a distorted view of the world of work. Poor identification models, sub-standard schooling, and economic conditions that did little to motivate the disadvantaged youth to fulfill his potential have probably taken their toll. Group counseling can help the individual by providing a proper identification model in the person of an effective counselor who has moved up from a disadvantaged background himself. In counseling sessions the youngster may explore occupational roles to which he has been introduced in a parallel instructional program and to discover some of the feelings which he would have were he to step into such roles in later life.

4. Group Counseling in Social Development. Youth enrolled in Job Corps centers are not there for vocational and educational training alone. Most programs provide opportunities for recreation, social development, and cultural education to prepare each young man and woman to become a well-rounded citizen. These programs require the learning of certain social skills that may have been neglected in the early training of many of these youth. Simple social skills such as asking a member of the opposite sex to dance may be formidable roadblocks to boys or girls who have never been exposed to such situations. Group counseling that includes role playing can aid in the development of such skills and provide young men and women with the confidence they need to function effectively in a variety of social situations.

5. Ventilation of Feelings. Karon [9] has shown how the impact of caste sanction and minority group membership is related to tension, hostility, and anxiety in Negroes. Such feelings can cause aggression or withdrawal in groups and one need only to read the newspaper accounts of the minority group riots in numerous American cities and towns to see evidence of such behavior. Deutscher and Chien [5] in a study that included the opinions of over five hundred scientists report that segregation of minority groups produces such harmful effects as reality distortion, sense of inferiority, self depreciation, and confusion and frustration.

These feelings can be examined in group counseling, and ventilated in an atmosphere where fear of reprisal causes neither withdrawal nor aggression. The client can find in the counselor an adult who makes an effort to understand him and accept him as he is. He may learn that not all adults are enemies to be feared and hated and that some of the confusion and frustration can be "worked through" with a group of peers and an understanding counselor.

6. Preparation for the Future. The success of this sector of the War on Poverty will depend to a large extent on what the disadvantaged youth does *after* his program at a Job Corps is terminated. The boy from the urban slum who returns to that environment and does not change his behavior so that he now lives differently than he did prior to the Job Corps experiment would perhaps be classified as a "failure." Although the word change may be harsh to the ear of many counselors, the whole concept of the War on Poverty is, in essence, one of social change. Youth are expected to change; they change their work habits, ways of living, attitudes, and so on. It would seem that a counselor who accepts a position in a Job Corps camp would agree that change is necessary. The code of ethics of the American Personnel and Guidance Association indicates that the individual being helped retains the full freedom of choice and decision and the counselor has no responsibility or authority to approve of change. The job of the group counselor in a Job Corps or elsewhere is not to tell the individual what he should do or attempt to direct him into certain occupations. The counselor's role in working with disadvantaged youth would be one of assisting young men and women to define and set realistic goals in light of a new found meaning in life.

REFERENCES

1. American Personnel and Guidance Association. "Ethical Standards," *Personnel and Guidance Journal*, 40 (1961), pp. 206–207.

2. Ascher, Albert I. "How the City Slum Acts As a Deterrent to the Vocational Rehabilitation of the Emotionally Disabled." Paper read at the American Personnel and Guidance Association Convention, Washington, D. C., April 1966.

3. Barker, Roger; Wright, Beatrice; and Gonick, Mollie. *Adjustment to Physical Handicap and Illness: A Survey of Physique and Disability* (New York: Social Science Research Council, 1946), Bulletin 55.

4. Brammer, Lawrence M. and Shostrom, Everett L. *Therapeutic Psychology: Fundamentals of Counseling and Psychotherapy* (Englewood Cliffs, New Jersey: Prentice-Hall, 1964).

5. Deutsher, Max and Chien, Isidor. "The Psychological Effects of Enforced Segregation: A Survey of Social Science Opinion," *Journal of Psychology*, XXVI (1948), pp. 259–287.

6. Ethical Standards of Psychologists. Washington, D.C.: Committee on Ethical Standards for Psychologists, American Psychological Association, 1953.

7. Farquhar, William W. "Motivational Problems in Counseling The Underprivileged." Paper read at the American Personnel and Guidance Association Convention, Washington, D. C., April 1966.

8. Golden, George J. and Margolin, Reuben J. "Motivation and the Disadvantaged." Paper read at the American Personnel and Guidance Association Convention, Washington, D. C., April 1966.

9. Karon, Bertram. *The Negro Personality* (New York: Springer, 1958).

10. O.E.O Public Affairs Pamphlet, "A Summary of the War on Poverty," 1–36 (Washington, D.C.: United States Government Printing Office, November 10, 1966).

11. Patterson, C. H. *Counseling and Psychotherapy: Theory and Practice* (New York: Harper and Brothers, 1959).

12. Super, Donald S. *The Psychology of Careers* (New York: Harper and Row, 1957).

13. Woodruff, James W. "Minority Youth Perception of the World of Work." Paper read at the American Personnel and Guidance Association Convention, Washington, D. C., April 1966.

INDEX

Academic performance, 163, 167, 178, 183, 213, 223, 233, 280, 298
Ackerman, N. W., 175, 184, 276, 278, 367
Adler, A., 37
Adolescent, 67, 167, 174, 264, 276, 363, 369
Adult counseling, 395; *see also* Parents
Aggression, 26, 364
Ahmann, J. S., 173
Allen, R. D., 5, 11
Allport, G., 38, 56, 57
Almada, A. A., 319, 324
Ansbacker, H. L., 136
Ansbacher, R. R., 136
Antenen, W., 253, 255
Anxiety, 225, 234, 391
APA, 390, 400
APGA, 390, 391, 394, 400
Arbuckle, D. S., 224, 235, 290, 317, 324
Aronson, E., 252, 256
ASCD, 11
Asch, S. E., 252, 255, 335, 343
Ascher, A. I., 397, 400
Attitude, attitudes, 109, 138, 153, 262, 292
Auld, F., 272, 276, 278
Axline, V., 320, 324

Bach, G. R., 108, 111, 251, 255, 295, 310, 316, 323, 324, 379, 382
Bailey, B., 18, 21, 122
Bales, R. F., 272, 278, 305, 310, 331, 337, 342, 343
Barker, R., 393, 400
Barrett, H. B., 297, 302
Barron, F., 295
Basdell, B. J., 264
Bass, B. M., 322, 343
Bates, M., 186, 295
Baymur, F. B., 122, 209, 235
Behavior, 84, 199, 220
Bell, H. M., 264, 265, 270
Benne, K. D., 305, 310
Bennett, M. E., 11, 15, 21, 44, 54, 57
Berdie, R. F., 21, 97, 237, 242
Berelson, B., 272, 278
Berger, I. L., 235
Berger, M. M., 56, 57, 310
Berkowitz, M. I., 332, 333, 343
Berman, L., 310
Berman, S., 175, 184, 276, 278
Bills, R. E., 295
Bilovsky, D., 69, 75, 91, 97, 122

Bion, W. R., 202
Blaine, G. B., 235
Blum, M. L., 21
Bonner, H., 43, 54, 57
Bonney, W. C., 250, 255, 256, 296, 304, 378
Bordin, E. S., 21
Borgatta, E. F., 331, 332, 337, 342, 343
Borow, H., 123
Bossard, J. H. S., 341, 343
Boy, A. V., 98, 107, 111
Bradford, L. P., 12, 68
Bradt, K. W., 217
Brammer, L. M., 22, 123, 296, 319, 323, 324, 400
Brenner, M., 334, 344
Bresse, C. W., 264, 270
Briggs, L. J., 217
Broedel, J. M., 122, 167, 173, 174, 184, 235, 276, 278, 297, 302, 367
Brookover, W. B., 168, 173
Brown, D. J., 218
Brown, O. B., 103, 296
Brown, W. F., 217, 235
Burke, C. J., 76
Buros, O. K., 249

Caldwell, E., 1, 3, 46, 57, 292, 315, 324
Calhoun, S. R., 217
Calia, V. F., 290
Caplan, S. W., 14, 18, 21, 104, 111, 122, 160, 175, 185, 297, 302, 364, 367
Caplow, T., 328, 343, 344
Carlson, M. B., 264, 270
Carter, L. F., 207, 310
Cartwright, D., 23, 34, 43, 54, 57, 122, 272, 278
Case conference, 240
Catron, D. W., 383, 388
Cattell, R. B., 41, 42, 57
Change in people, 23f, 30
Charles, D. C., 290
Chess, S., 297, 302
Chien, I., 399, 400
Citizenship, 164
Clark, D. H., 272, 279
Clarke, M., 236
Coch, L., 34
Coffey, H. S., 258, 263
Cohn, B., 148, 297, 303, 369
College, 86, 90, 113, 219, 223, 237, 280, 293
Colver, R. M., 236

Combs, C. F., 369
Communication, 25, 56, 105, 110
Conformity, 335
Congruence theory, 378, 379
Content analysis, 253, 265, 272
Corsini, R. J., 105, 108, 111, 136
Cottrell, L. S., 337, 343
Counseling, 5, 13, 14, 69, 216, 240
Counselor
    as leader, 10, 15, 20, 44, 49, 77, 78, 85,
        86, 87, 98, 99, 109, 133, 145, 150,
        162, 186, 220, 240, 294, 321, 351,
        357, 374, 380, 387, 391
    training, 304, 389
Covner, B. J., 272, 278
Criterion, 69, 72, 75, 93, 96, 113, 114, 211,
    220, 225, 227, 238, 282
Cronbach, L. J., 75, 114, 122
Crutchfield, R. S., 16, 17, 21, 122
Culbertson, J., 168, 173
Cultural island, 167
Cunningham, B. W., 264, 270
Curran, C. A., 272, 278

Darley, J. G., 292, 296
Davitze, J., 334, 344
Dawe, H. C., 330, 344
Denny, J. P., 223
Deutscher, M., 399, 400
Dinkmeyer, D. C., 36
Disadvantaged youth, 396
Dixon, W. J., 310
Dogmatism scale, 258, 293, 295
Dollard, J., 272, 278
Drasgow, J., 217, 364, 368
Dreikurs, R., 36, 37, 57, 136, 298, 303
Dressel, P. B., 292, 296
Drews, E. H., 217
Driver, H. I., 1, 2, 18, 21, 46, 69, 76, 77, 98,
    101, 102, 122, 165
Drucker, A. J., 270
Duncan, C. P., 217
Dymond, R. F., 166, 254, 256, 272, 279

Edson, K., 265, 270
Edwards, A. L., 249
Ekman, G., 340, 344
Elementary school, 36, 59, 127, 138, 297
Entwistle, D. R., 281, 290
Ethics, 390
Evraiff, W., 136
Eysenck, H. J., 341, 344

Failor, C. W., 122
Farquhar, W. W., 396, 400
Faust, W. L., 329, 330, 335, 345
Feedback, 130
Festinger, L., 30, 34, 121, 122, 252, 256
Feyereisen, K., 217
Fink, C. F., 328, 340, 345
Fisher, P. H., 334, 344
Foley, W. J., 250, 256, 296, 378
Ford, D. H., 84
Fox, D., 329, 334, 344

Frank, J. D., 290
Frankel, E., 264, 270
Frankl, V. E., 6, 12
French, J. R. P., 32, 34, 35
Froehlich, C. P., 14, 15, 18, 21, 69, 76, 98,
    102, 122, 123, 160, 165, 290, 292,
    296
Fromm, E., 56, 57
Fuller, M., 224, 235
Funkenstein, D. H., 235
Furst, W., 325

Garrett, H. E., 249, 306, 310
Garrison, K. C., 264, 270
Gaskill, E. R., 21
Gawrys, J., 103, 296
Gazda, G., 290, 292, 293, 296, 297, 298, 303,
    304, 310, 318, 322
Gekosi, N., 334, 344
Geller, J. J., 310
George, C. E., 310
Gerken, C. D., 217
Gersten, C., 175, 185, 217, 364, 368
Gibb, J. R., 330, 344
Gibian, E. J., 369
Glanz, E. C., 1, 2, 7, 9, 12, 42, 44, 54, 55,
    57, 111, 219, 220, 322, 324
Gleser, G. C., 75, 114, 122
Goals, 5, 6, 7, 37
Golburgh, S. J., 219, 220
Goldberg, S. C., 335, 344
Golden, G. J., 396, 400
Goldman, L., 104, 111, 281, 290, 384, 388
Gonick, M., 393, 400
Goodlad, I. I., 334, 344
Gordon, L. V., 270
Gorlow, L., 111, 272, 274, 278, 305, 310
Gowan, J. C., 175, 185, 363, 368
Group, groups, 7, 8, 17, 41
    attractiveness, 31
    characteristics, 15, 101
    cohesiveness, 54, 342
    developmental stages, 251, 378
    dynamics, 16, 24, 33, 42, 112, 281, 384
    formation of, 99, 239, 315, 348, 370
    goals, 7
    growth-centered, 8
    guidance, 14, 43, 104, 257f
    member, 11, 29, 316, 334, 393
    norms, 55
    procedures in counseling, 14
    process, 52, 251, 330f, 351, 378, 385
    productivity, 28, 329
    size, 316, 328f, 348, 371
    standards, 11, 29, 55, 252
    structure, 53, 316, 325, 328, 333
    target of change, 32
    therapy, 10, 14, 17, 48, 281, 325, 346, 354
    use of, 17, 30, 104, 106
Group counseling, 9, 10, 11, 13, 38, 46, 67,
    86, 101, 112, 257
    content, 151, 157, 170, 186f, 227, 253,
        264, 271, 275, 385
    duration, 319, 372, 375

Group counseling (*continued*)
  initiating, 313, 349, 357, 365, 372, 384
  as learning, 129
  objectives, 104, 148, 198, 238, 292, 298, 317
  planning research in, 243f
  process, 39, 241, 358
  rationale for, 9, 36, 129, 238, 281
  results, 80, 82, 93, 116f, 140, 142, 146, 152f, 157, 162, 171, 177f, 184, 212f, 221, 228, 259f, 284f, 294, 299, 352f, 358, 366
  setting, 318, 350, 371
  short term, 297, 301
  structure, structuring, 133, 149, 220, 351, 373
  vs. individual counseling, 97, 106, 209, 269, 362
Growth, 68, 77, 80, 182, 276
Grubb, J., 175, 182, 185, 276, 279, 363, 364, 368
Grunwald, H., 21
Guidance, 5
Gulley, H. E., 41, 42, 57
Gustad, J. W., 21
Guthrie, C. M., 217

Haas, R. B., 66
Hahn, M. E., 57
Handicapped, 392
Hare, A. P., 333, 336, 340, 344
Harris, P., 144
Harris, W. K., 357
Hays, W. L., 249, 256, 296
Healthy individual, 237
Heintz, R. K., 30, 35
Hermann, L., 57, 242, 305, 311
Hermon, L., 68
Herrold, K. F., 21, 329, 344
Hersko, M., 272, 279
Heterogeneous groups, 326
Hewer, V. H., 237, 238, 242, 281, 290
High school, 78, 175, 198, 203, 209, 364, 371
Hilden, A. H., 217
Hinkley, R. G., 57, 68, 242, 305, 311
Hobbs, N., 102, 106, 111, 316, 324
Hoch, E. L., 272, 274, 278, 305, 310
Hoehn, A. J., 218
Holtzman, W. H., 217, 235
Homans, G. C., 42, 57
Homogeneous groups, 325
Hoppock, R., 76
Hoyt, D. P., 91, 92, 93, 97, 112, 123, 242, 290
Hoyt, K. B., 112, 123
Hudelson, E., 334, 344
Indik, B. P., 338, 344
Individual, 68
  in group, 105, 106, 334f, 380, 393
Insight, 130, 134
Isaksen, H. L., 98, 107
Jacques, M., 111
Jenkins, D. H., 173

Jennings, H. H., 341, 344
Joel, W., 199, 202, 346, 356
Johnson, E. G., 136
Johnson, J. A., 8, 12
Jones, O., 236
Junior high school, 138, 144, 148, 156, 160, 167, 370, 371

Kagan, N., 9, 12
Kallejian, V. J., 21
Karon, B., 399, 400
Katz, E., 16, 21, 123
Katz, E. W., 175, 182, 185, 202, 276, 278, 368
Katz, M. R., 170
Katzenmeyer, W. G., 235
Kaufman, P. E., 272, 278
Kehas, C. D., 297, 303
Kell, B. L., 272, 279
Kelley, E. C., 129, 136
Kelley, H. H., 344
Kelley, T. L., 303
Kemp, C. G., 1, 2, 42, 57, 136, 257
Kennedy, E. C., 111
Kephart, W. M., 341, 344
Kidd, J. S., 329, 330, 335, 344
Kimball, B., 218, 264, 270
Kinnick, B. C., 296
Kirk, B., 175, 185, 218, 363, 364, 368
Kirte, B., 297, 303
Kishida, M., 335, 336
Klems, M. A., 21
Kugelmass, S., 311

Landsman, T., 218
Large, I., 329, 334, 340, 344
Lasswell, H. D., 272, 278
Laughlin, H. P., 21
Lawson, J., 56, 57
Lazarsfield, P. F., 16, 21, 123
Leader, leadership, 27, 30, 49, 77, 78, 106, 108
Learning, 129
Lecky, P., 218
Leites, N., 272, 278
Lerner, A., 21
Lev, J., 249
Levin, H., 173
Lewin, K., 25, 27, 30, 34, 111
Lewis, D., 76
Lifton, W. M., 1, 2, 44, 57, 111, 148, 155, 292, 296
Lindquist, E. F., 235, 249
Lippitt, L., 68
Lippitt, R., 27, 29, 31, 33, 34, 35
Locke, N., 17, 21
Lodato, F. J., 137, 141, 296
Luborsky, L., 290
Luchins, A. S., 43, 48, 56, 57, 319, 324

Maccoby, E. E., 173
MacLean, M. S., 57
Mahler, C. A., 1, 3, 46, 57, 292, 296, 315, 324

Margolin, R. J., 396, 400
Marriage and family counseling, 395
Marriot, R., 334, 345
Marrow, A. J., 32, 35
Maslow, A., 6, 12
Mass procedures, 86
Massey, F. J., 310
McArthur, C. C., 235
McCann, W. H., 319, 324
McCorkle, L. W., 21
McDaniel, H. B., 102
McGowan, B., 288, 290
McKeachie, W. J., 334, 336, 344
McKenzie, J. D., 297, 303
McLean, O. S., 295
McMasters, W., 97
McNeil, H., 272, 279
McNemar, O., 300, 303
Meeks, A., 297, 303
Mental health, 26
Metcalf, H. H., 203
Meyers, J. L., 249
Meyersburg, A. H., 297, 303
Miller, N. E., 331, 333, 336, 345
Mills, T., 331, 343
Mink, O. G., 167
Mishler, E. G., 331, 340, 345
Mooney, R. L., 270
Moore, G. D., 112, 123
Moreno, J. L., 53, 57, 59, 106
Morrow, W. R., 264, 270
Morse, W. C., 173
Mosak, H. H., 298, 303
Mowrer, O. H., 166, 272, 278
Mudd, E. H., 21
Mullin, M. M., 168, 173
Multiple counseling, 13, 14, 15, 16, 17, 18,
    20, 46, 69, 77, 98, 101, 104, 112, 120,
    167
Muro, J., 292, 324
Murphy, G., 6, 12
Murray, E. J., 272, 276, 278

National training laboratories, 8, 52
Neidt, C. O., 173
Neugenboren, B., 290
Newcomb, T. H., 304, 311
Newcomb, T. M., 32, 35
Noble, F., 273, 278
Non-verbal behavior, 199f, 276
Norton, F. T., 332, 343

Ofman, W., 280, 290
Ohlsen, M. M., 1, 3, 9, 12, 67, 101, 102, 122,
    123, 136, 167, 173, 174, 175, 178,
    182, 185, 202, 235, 243, 245, 249,
    271, 273, 276, 278, 290, 296, 298,
    303, 304, 305, 310, 322, 324, 362,
    367, 368, 382
Ohnmacht, F., 292, 324
O'Neil, H. W., 217
Osgood, C. E., 382

Parents, parent group, 135, 170, 172, 175,
    189, 276, 297

Parloff, M. B., 290
Paster, S., 175, 185, 364, 368
Paterson, A., 168, 173
Patterson, C. H., 57, 122, 209, 235, 391,
    400
Patton, J. D., 21
Peers, 10, 175, 369
Penney, J. F., 220
Pepinsky, H. B., 123
Peres, H., 69, 76, 272, 278
Perlmutter, H. V., 329, 345
Perry, J. D., 218
Peters, C. C., 76
Peters, M., 136
Phelps, M. O., 264, 270
Pine, G. J., 98, 107
Polansky, N., 31, 35
Porter, E. H., 272, 278
Preston, B. H., 22, 30, 35
Proff, F. C., 9, 12, 167, 173, 174, 175, 182,
    185, 202, 235, 273, 276, 278, 367, 368
Psychodrama, 53, 59f

Quinn, R. D., 110, 111

Raimy, V. C., 272, 278
Ransom, M. K., 290
Recorder, recording, 353
Redl, F., 31, 35
Relationship, relationships, 106, 108, 109,
    110, 128, 133, 179, 224, 347
Remmers, H. H., 270
Research in group counseling, 18, 33, 69f,
    91f, 113f, 169f, 175f, 199, 210f,225f,
    243, 258f, 273f, 281, 293, 298f, 337f,
    354
Research instruments, 248, 305
Richardson, H., 123
Richardson, L. H., 218
Ricklin, M., 291
Riesman, D., 6, 12
Robinson, F. P., 280, 290
Roe, R. M., 217
Roeber, E. D., 368
Rogers, C. R., 22, 57, 109, 111, 160, 165,
    166, 254, 256, 272, 278, 279
Rokeach, M., 263, 296
Roles, role playing, 60, 305, 307, 391
Roseborough, M. E., 331, 343
Rosenberg, P. P., 224, 235
Rossberg, R., 105, 111
Roth, R. M., 297, 303
Rubenstein, E., 290
Rust, R., 290

Salts, B., 218
Schmidt, L. C., 291
Schoenhard, G. H., 218
Schossberger, J., 311
Schreiber, D., 297, 303
Schultz, M. E., 178, 185
Schulz, J. A., 198
Schwartz, L. J., 137, 296
Sears, R. R., 168, 173
Seeman, J., 272, 279

Self, self-concept, 9, 120, 160, 163, 168, 177, 294, 295, 398
Self-esteem, 26, 37
Self-ratings, 69
Serene, H. F., 218
Shannon, J. T., 296
Shapiro, D., 199, 202, 346, 356
Shaw, J. G., 280, 290
Shaw, M. C., 175, 182, 185, 218, 265, 270, 276, 279, 297, 303, 363, 364, 368
Sheats, P., 305, 310
Sheerer, E., 272, 279
Sheldon, M., 218
Sherif, C. W., 256, 378, 382
Sherif, M., 256, 378, 382
Sherrifs, A. Ca., 218
Shertzer, B., 1, 3, 42, 52, 58, 322, 324
Shimberg, B., 270
Shlien, J. H., 298, 303
Shoben, E. J., 97
Shorr, J. E., 97
Shostrom, E. L., 22, 123, 296, 319, 323, 324, 400
Siegel, S., 249, 296
Singer, S. L., 97
Slater, P. E., 332, 336, 345
Slater, P. H., 305, 311
Slavson, S. R., 22, 56, 58, 98, 102, 320, 324
Slow learners, 137, 141
Sniffen, A. M., 148, 369
Snyder, W. V., 272, 279
Sociodrama, 53, 79
Sokoloff, M. A., 127, 136, 296
Solomon, H., 329, 344
Soltz, V., 136
Sonstegard, M. A., 36, 127, 136, 297, 303
South, E. B., 329, 330, 345
Southard, C., 122, 167, 173, 174, 235, 276, 278, 368
Southworth, R., 297
Speilberger, C. D., 223, 235
Standards, 11, 16
Steiner, J. D., 345
Stephan, F. F., 331, 340, 345
Stephenson, W., 166
Stevenson, C. S., 236
Stewart, C. C., 291
Stock, D., 272, 279
Stone, C. H., 90, 97
Stone, S. C., 1, 3, 42, 52, 58, 322, 324
Stormer, G. E., 136
Strang, R., 52, 58, 77, 207
Strodtbeck, F., 331, 343
Strupp, H., 290
Study group, 11
Study habits seminar, 281
Suci, G. J., 382
Sullenger, T. E., 264, 270
Super, D. E., 13, 22, 97, 101, 102, 123, 396, 398, 400
Sutker, A. R., 235

T Groups, 8, 9, 10, 390
Talland, G. A., 272, 279, 311
Tannenbaum, P., 382
Taylor, D. W., 329, 330, 335, 340, 345
Taylor, J. A., 236
Teahan, J. R., 217
Teigland, J., 264
Telschow, E. F., 272, 274, 278, 305, 310
Test interpretation, 88, 112, 205
Thibaut, J. W., 344
Thomas, E. J., 328, 340, 345
Tincher, W. A., 292, 296
Torrance, E. P., 136
Training, 28, 33
Tresselt, M. E., 291
Trotta, F., 144
Trow, W. C., 167, 173
Tyler, L. E., 215, 218

Underachievers, 144, 167, 174, 209, 216, 223, 264, 271, 297, 364
Utterback, W. E., 335, 336, 345

Values, 24, 29, 129, 132
Vance, E. L., 295
Verbal behavior, 219f, 253f, 276
Vocational counseling, 90, 205, 398
Vocational choice, 121
Volsky, T., 123, 237
Von Borgersrode, F., 334, 345

Walker, H., 249
Warkentin, J., 311
Warters, J., 1, 3, 42, 46, 55, 58, 105, 111, 323, 324
Watson, G. B., 330, 345
Weitz, H., 223, 236
Wells, C. G., 59
Welsh, G. S., 236
Weltz, P., 329, 344
Wert, J. E., 173
White, R. K., 27, 34
Wigell, W. W., 271
Wilkinson, H. J., 236
Wilson, R. C., 264, 270
Winborn, B., 291
Winder, A. E., 272, 279
Wittenborn, J. P., 291
Woal, T., 156
Wolberg, I., 101, 102
Wolf, A., 311
Woodruff, J. M., 397, 400
Woolf, J. A., 242
Woolf, M. D., 242
Wrenn, C. G., 17, 22, 67, 113, 123
Wright, B., 393, 400
Wright, E. W., 9, 12, 13, 22, 104, 111, 112, 123, 291

Zander, A., 43, 54, 57, 122, 173, 272, 278
Ziller, R. C., 329, 336, 341, 345
Zojove, R., 256